Crude Intentions

Crude Intentions

How Oil Corruption Contaminates the World

ALEXANDRA GILLIES

OXFORD
UNIVERSITY PRESS

OXFORD
UNIVERSITY PRESS

Oxford University Press is a department of the University of Oxford.
It furthers the University's objective of excellence in research, scholarship,
and education by publishing worldwide. Oxford is a registered trade mark of
Oxford University Press in the UK and certain other countries.

Published in the United States of America by Oxford University Press
198 Madison Avenue, New York, NY 10016, United States of America.

© Oxford University Press 2020

CIP data is on file at the Library of Congress

ISBN: 978–0–19–094070–6

9 8 7 6 5 4 3 2 1

Printed by Sheridan Books, Inc.
United States of America

CONTENTS

Map   2

CHAPTER 1. The Crisis of Corruption   5

CHAPTER 2. "Being a Friend in a Nest of Vipers"   25

CHAPTER 3. Corruption and the Competition for Power   61

CHAPTER 4. The Kleptocracy Kings   101

CHAPTER 5. "An Octopus That Reaches around the Globe"   139

CHAPTER 6. Corruption's Motley Foes   176

CHAPTER 7. We Know How to Fight Corruption   210

*Appendix: The Scale of the Oil Boom in Selected
Oil-Producing Countries*   222
Notes   223
Acknowledgments   265
Selected Bibliography   267
Index   281

Crude Intentions

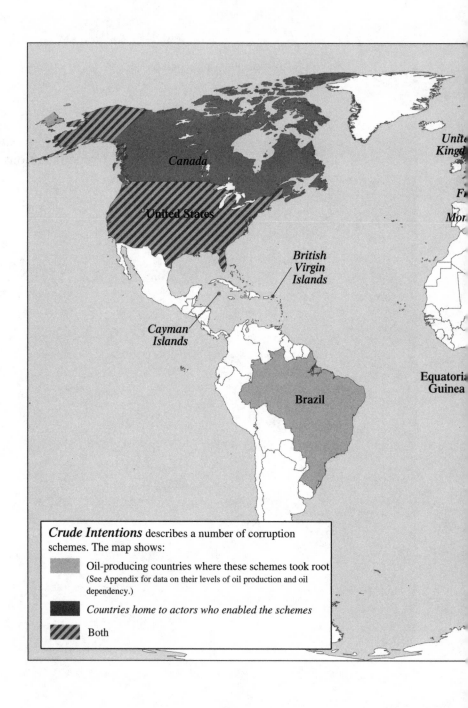

Canada

United States

British
Virgin
Islands

Cayman
Islands

Brazil

Unite
Kingd

F

Mor

Equatoria
Guinea

Crude Intentions describes a number of corruption
schemes. The map shows:

Oil-producing countries where these schemes took root
(See Appendix for data on their levels of oil production and oil
dependency.)

Countries home to actors who enabled the schemes

Both

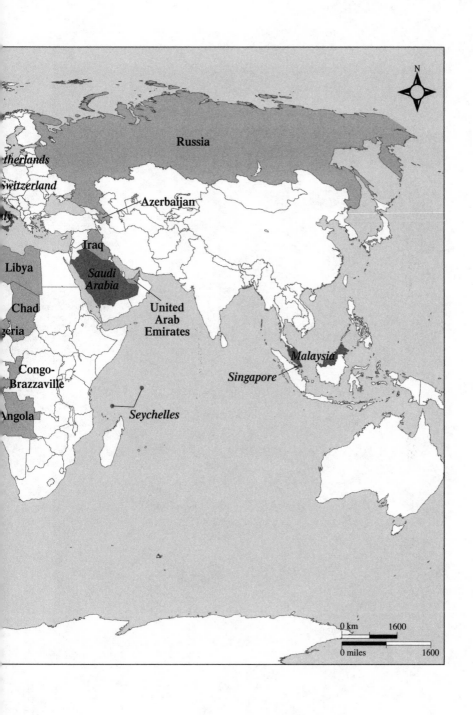

N

Netherlands
Switzerland
ly

Russia

Azerbaijan

Libya

Iraq

Saudi
Arabia

Chad

geria

United
Arab
Emirates

Malaysia

Congo-
Brazzaville

Singapore

Angola

Seychelles

0 km   1600

0 miles   1600

CHAPTER 1 | The Crisis of Corruption

OVER DINNER, WE WONDERED how bulky $400 million would be. The latest rumor making the rounds in Abuja, the capital of Nigeria, was that a servant of a senior government official had wandered into a back room of his boss's house and stumbled upon $400 million in cash. According to the story, the servant packed as much as he could in a suitcase and split town. And so, my friends and I threw out our guesses . . . Is it bigger than a couch? More like a small truck?

During normal times, a rumor like this would have seemed crazy. $400 million is, after all, an enormous amount of money to leave lying around. But these were not normal times. These were the boom years, and anything seemed possible.

Briefly in 2008 and then for a historic four-year stretch beginning in 2010, oil prices averaged above $80 per barrel. For most of that period, prices topped $100. To provide some perspective, during the twenty years prior, prices had languished around $20 or $30 per barrel. The rise in prices created more than $9 trillion in new oil money, and lots of people wanted a share. The governments and companies involved in the industry hadn't seen opportunities to profit like this since the 1970s. Government coffers overflowed, company profits soared, oil men and women took home record-high pay, and hustlers of all types cashed in big.

In oil-rich capitals like Abuja, the deal-making reached a fever pitch. I was living there when prices spiked in 2008, working on my PhD dissertation. I wanted to understand why, during the previous few years, the Nigerian government had embraced some oil sector reforms. It had awarded oil blocks through competitive auctions rather than backroom deals, published detailed data on how much oil money it collected, and created a fund for saving oil revenues for future generations. Steps like these were exciting as well as a real surprise in a country more famous for corruption, environmental disasters, and the other damages oil wealth can bring.

But by the time I arrived in Abuja, not much reform was happening anymore. I spent a year running around the country, passing out my little grad student business cards, and interviewing dozens of officials, executives, and activists about the oil industry. They credited the reform with delivering some short-term gains. But mostly they talked about how much was left to be done. The reform's champion, the former president Olusegun Obasanjo, had left office, and his successor was physically and politically weak. Oil prices had risen, removing the government's need to be efficient. The oil sector was in shambles, especially the national oil company. Vested interests had captured corners of the industry for their own enrichment, and oil companies operated without adequate oversight. Everyone in power fully understood how dysfunctional it all was, yet the reform agenda sat inert.

The absence of reform carried a heavy cost, which could be seen only by leaving the orderly confines of Abuja. An estimated 90 million Nigerians, around half of the country's citizens, live in extreme poverty. The country has 2 percent of the world's population but 14 percent of its maternal deaths, with one Nigerian woman dying every thirteen minutes from preventable problems with pregnancy and childbirth. The challenges do not end at birth. One in ten Nigerian children dies before reaching age five, and one in three is chronically malnourished. With a population projected to double by 2050, the number of people facing hunger, disease, and premature death looks set to increase.[1]

Adding insult to injury, Nigeria's potential is as evident as its challenges. I loved experiencing its world-class arts scene and vibrant intellectual life, and admire its countless entrepreneurs who thrive despite the rough terrain. Most countries struggling with extreme poverty and unmet promise are not major oil producers; Nigeria is the world's twelfth largest. In 2008, Nigeria was churning out oil worth over $200 million a day. The government could have been saving millions of lives if it ran the oil sector properly and channeled the earnings into reducing poverty and creating jobs. The more I learned, the more outrageous the situation seemed.

In fact, the cause for outrage was just getting started. In 2010, Goodluck Jonathan became Nigeria's president, right as oil prices reached historic heights. I had finished graduate school by then and was working for a nongovernmental organization (NGO) that promoted transparency and good governance in the oil sector. Our aim was to help developing countries avoid the kinds of corruption and missed opportunities that too often accompany oil wealth. I was in Nigeria every few months, working on various small projects. We trained local journalists to monitor some of the more technical aspects of the oil industry, pushed state governments in the oil-producing Niger Delta to reveal details about how they spent their money, and offered comments on various versions of an industry reform bill that sat for years gathering dust in the legislature. It was mostly useful stuff, but with each subsequent trip I made, the projects seemed more and more like rearranging deck chairs on the *Titanic*.

In 2012, a scandal broke and revealed that the government had paid fuel importers for billions of dollars' worth of gasoline and diesel that never actually entered the country. But then no senior officials lost their jobs, no one was convicted of wrongdoing in court, and many of the alleged culprits kept doing business with the government. Around the same time, the government began awarding huge and oddly structured contracts to secretive local oil companies with hardly any industry experience. Stories of back-room payoffs, stolen cargo-loads of oil, and other crimes grew more frequent and convincing. The mythology around the oil minister grew too. Friends and acquaintances traded stories about her apparent neglect of important industry functions, the crew of loyal henchmen who gathered in her house at night, and her plans for using the booming oil sector to benefit herself and the president.

During this time, you'd walk into Abuja's Hilton hotel, the country's unofficial deal-making headquarters, and it was just throbbing. Power players and their retinues clustered around the elevators, heading upstairs to the private suites where various bigwigs held court. Businessmen and women from around the world staked out corners of the lobby's piano bar to hold meetings with the previously bit-part players who suddenly commanded serious wealth. Large paintings of the petroleum minister could be purchased at the hotel's tourist shop alongside overpriced traditional clothes and jewelry. Five-figure watches and designer bags became standard attire for the drivers, security guards, and mistresses who crowded the hallways. You could smell the money in the air.

Despite all the bling and all the stories, I struggled to pin down exactly what was going on. The tales of theft and misdeeds, like the one about the servant making off with a suitcase of cash, were difficult to confirm. The government explained away accusations of corruption with indignant statements and dumps of data. Friends of mine who worked in government accused the opposition party of fomenting rumors to vilify the president and his allies. Other top officials spoke the language of reform and commanded international acclaim.

The silence of the international community made it even more confusing. The United States, the United Kingdom, and other Western donors gave large amounts of money to fighting poverty and other causes in Nigeria. The International Monetary Fund, the World Bank, and the UN promoted Nigeria's economic growth. These players enjoy a lot of influence in Nigeria, and they all claim to actively oppose corruption. Surely they would act if billions of dollars in oil money were walking out the door. They had tools at their disposal that they had deployed in other countries, such as issuing critical statements, cutting off aid, tracking down the dirty money flows, or preventing corrupt officials from traveling abroad. But none of this was happening. Western governments and international organizations, several of whom funded my organization's Nigeria programs, continued to collaborate with the government as though things were just fine. A haze of uncertainty obscured the crisis of corruption unfolding around me.

During these same years, similar crises broke out across the oil-producing world, from Moscow to Rio, Houston to Baghdad. Using a dizzying array of tactics, companies and political elites scrambled to capture a share of the growing windfall. Corruption schemes accelerated in both size and creativity, as did elaborate efforts to hide stolen funds offshore. Since then, the boom has ended, political sands have shifted, and investigators and journalists have gotten to work. Slowly, finally, the haze is lifting, and we can see what really happened.

In the case of Nigeria, the real story finally started to become clear when the central bank governor broke ranks and took action. In 2013, he came forward with evidence that $20 billion in oil revenues was "missing." He accused the country's chronically dysfunctional national oil company of transferring far too few revenues to the government during the boom years.

He was promptly fired for his efforts. However, his story did not go away. Over the next few years, various documents, media stories, and investigations confirmed his account. My colleagues and I produced one such report. We described how the former petroleum minister had handed out oil trading contracts to several companies headed by her close allies. The contracts allowed these companies to capture billions of dollars that should have gone to the government. The contracts were so irresponsible and lopsided that just one of them contained provisions that could have cost Nigeria over $300 million in a single year.[2] But by the time we figured that out, the boom had ended.

Law enforcement agencies have shed more light on what likely happened. In 2017, the US Department of Justice (DOJ) announced its case for seizing $144 million in assets bought with funds stolen from Nigeria. The DOJ alleged that the minister's allies moved oil money out of Nigeria through offshore shell companies and foreign banks and then used it to buy a megayacht and luxury real estate in New York and California.[3] Italian prosecutors charged the global oil giants Shell and Eni with bribery in a single dirty deal that allegedly saw political elites, including the former minister, make off with nearly $1 billion.[4] Nigeria's anticorruption commission reports that it identified $600 million worth of cash, jewelry, and real estate that the former petroleum minister allegedly acquired during her time in office.[5] The UK authorities hauled her in for questioning and seized her passport, stranding her in London as they continued their investigations.[6] All these matters were ongoing when this book went to press.

While the roles played by specific companies and individuals remains subject to legal proceedings, these investigations provide a much clearer view of how the boom-time corruption may have worked. While chapter 3 describes the Nigerian experience in greater detail, the bottom line is that corruption kept the Nigerian people from benefiting from one of the largest oil booms in history.

In hindsight, I can see that epic corruption happened all around me. I'd even interacted with a few of the alleged participants around the same time that they were running their deals. A middleman who ended up in an Italian jail once gave me a lift home. I'd chatted at a conference dinner with a Shell executive who is now on trial. A colleague did some work for one of the minister's front companies. And so on. However, despite being so close to the corruption and aware of its possible proportions, I was among the many who did not sound the alarm early or loudly enough. By the time it became clear what was happening, it was too late and the money was gone.

During the boom years in Nigeria, oil industry corruption faced few obstacles in its acceleration. A lack of understanding and a lack of urgency kept all kinds of Nigerian and foreign actors from speaking up and taking action. Nigeria is hardly alone: over and over again, oil deals benefited a few powerful players at the expense of the wider public. This book is my effort to add more understanding and more urgency to addressing this challenge so that corruption is less able to inflict such historic damage again.

The Global Reach of Corruption

Headlines from around the world make it clear: trillions of dollars in illicit money are circling the globe, enriching powerful individuals and keeping crooked leaders in power, all at the expense of everyday citizens. But headlines don't provide much insight into how corruption actually works. Too often, corruption is described in sweeping generalities: it is "pervasive," "systemic," or "endemic." When reports do dig deeper, they often focus on the lurid details. The son of Equatorial Guinea's dictator bought the glove, covered in Swarovski crystals, worn by Michael Jackson on his "Bad" tour. Money stolen from the Malaysian government paid Britney Spears to jump out of a birthday cake. Saudi Arabia's crown prince liked the look of a yacht owned by a Russian vodka tycoon and snapped it up that same day for a cool $550 million. Details like these may show how gross corruption can be, but they reveal relatively little about how it can be reined in.

Examining the recent oil boom provides a fuller picture. Observing oil boom corruption is like placing a drop of dye in the circulatory system of global corruption and watching it reveal the system's channels and pathways as it spreads and spreads. The chapters that follow sum up what I found by reviewing dozens of oil boom corruption cases, many of which speak to trends that extend well beyond the oil industry.

Chapter 2 focuses on companies, banks, and other private sector players and describes how they bent the rules during the boom years. In Angola, Australia, Chad, Congo-Brazzaville, Libya, Nigeria, Norway, and the United States, company executives concocted elaborate plans to capture an outsized share of riches from the boom. Bribery and cozying up to political elites were the most prominent types of company corruption, but I examine instances of collusion and tax avoidance too.

Recent fraud by mammoth companies such as Wells Fargo and Volkswagen indicate that well-respected industry leaders can end up embroiled in corruption scandals, despite having sophisticated corporate governance systems. The oil boom proved no different, and the chance to gain unusually high profits lured Royal Dutch Shell, Goldman Sachs, and other big fish into murky waters. Other cases show how the incentives for corruption run particularly high in two parts of the industry: oilfield services and oil trading. Investigations have also uncovered some common tactics, for example, companies hiring middlemen to do their dirty business for them. These problem areas represent obvious locations where the regulators and investigators who fight corruption could net big wins.

Companies were hardly the only ones conniving to capture oil wealth. Governments of all stripes joined in too. There's an outdated view of corruption as something that happens mostly in places like Nigeria, where large swathes of the population endure poverty while well-connected elites rake in the dough. Recent events make it crystal clear how incomplete a view this is. In the first six months of 2018, corruption scandals brought down the leaders of countries as diverse as Armenia, Malaysia, Peru, Slovakia, South Africa, and Spain. In 2017, South Korea's president was impeached and arrested for back-room conniving with the country's business elites, and Pakistan's courts removed the prime minister for hiding illicit wealth offshore. In total, over the past five years, more than twenty world leaders have lost their positions after their corruption has been exposed, and even more have faced historic protests.[7]

The Panama Papers further exposed corruption's global spread. In 2016, journalists got their hands on a store of documents from a Panamanian law firm that specialized in helping wealthy clients move their money offshore. The leak exposed the offshore financial dealings of 140 politicians from fifty countries.[8] They included officials from the Democratic Republic of the Congo, Iraq, and Sudan—the kind of countries that appear at the bad end of indices that measure levels of corruption. But officials from Argentina, Australia, Iceland, and dozens of other countries were also caught squirreling money away in secretive shell companies. Using shell companies and doing business with Panamanian law firms are not evidence of criminal behavior. But the scandals that followed have revealed wrongdoing across countries north and south, east and west, and rich and poor.

Oil boom corruption assumed different forms depending on the type of political system where it took place. In chapter 3, I discuss how political elites went after oil money in three democratic oil-producing countries: Brazil, Nigeria, and the United States. In all three, politicians sought oil money to help finance their expensive election campaigns. In Brazil and Nigeria, landslides of corruption followed, and billions of dollars in public funds were lost. National oil companies proved particularly susceptible to abuse. In just one part of Brazil's Car Wash scandal, the national oil company paid over $18 billion for a refinery that should have cost around $4 billion.[9] Those cost overruns, a large share of which were skimmed off and shared among top politicians and business elites, could have paid for educating 4 million Brazilian schoolchildren for a year. In the United States, the tactics were more subtle. Recent Supreme Court rulings have expanded the amount of money rich actors can pour into election campaigns and narrowed the legal understanding of what constitutes a bribe. Thanks in part to developments like these, the flow of money from the oil industry to American politicians is mostly legal. It still endangers citizens, though, especially when the agenda of the company donors includes gutting policies meant to lower carbon emissions and otherwise address global warming.

In the democracies, good news was mixed in with the bad. Certain government institutions and oversight bodies succeeded in calling out and containing the graft. Authoritarian kleptocracies lack this kind of balance, as the events of the oil boom years make very clear. In a kleptocracy, corruption and the exercise of power go hand in hand. Political leaders manipulate the entire government and much of the private sector, too, in order to advance their personal goals.

The word "kleptocracy" has become more prominent in the last few years. Actors in North America and Europe are waking up to just how much dirty money from this type of country has infiltrated their economies and institutions. The US government has investigated whether President Donald Trump and his campaign team had inappropriate relations with Vladimir Putin, perhaps the world's most prominent kleptocrat. Trump's former campaign manager Paul Manafort was convicted for laundering money he made working for Ukraine's kleptocratic former leader. Trump's company partnered with a prominent Azerbaijani oligarch on a hotel deal, and a Kazakh billionaire accused of corruption bought three condos in the "Trump SoHo" property.[10] In the United Kingdom, billions of pounds from Russia, Saudi Arabia, Kazakhstan, and elsewhere have flooded British banks, real estate markets, businesses, and universities. Germany's Deutsche Bank has paid huge fines for laundering illicit Russian money. Several African dictators openly use France and Switzerland as their homes away from home. The Council of Europe revealed how Azerbaijan mounted a complex campaign of lobbying, "caviar diplomacy" and "corruptive acts" to convince the body's members to ignore the rougher aspects of its human rights record.[11] Many Portuguese businesses now depend on Angolan investment, including from political insiders and members of the former first family. Kleptocracy is relevant the world round.

Running a stable, successful kleptocracy is much easier if billions of dollars of oil money flow into your treasury every year. Chapter 4 examines the umbilical tie between kleptocrats and their oil, and describes how the industry helps keep them alive. I focus on the rulers of Angola, Azerbaijan, and Russia, and I explain how they used their booming oil industries to strengthen their political positions. Thanks to their long-term horizons and monopolies on power, these leaders fostered the growth of the oil sector while also selectively milking it for corrupt purposes. Above all else, they channeled the oil boom windfall toward their allies, making sure that the riches only fattened the pockets of oligarchs loyal to their regimes.

Like all forms of large-scale corruption these days, kleptocracy functions internationally and inflicts international harm. Chapter 5 describes the roles played by dozens of international actors in the campaign of an ambitious young Malaysian businessman to steal and spend at least $4.5 billion in public money. Reports of the scheme suggest that top officials from an Abu Dhabi sovereign wealth fund, flush with oil boom money, played a central enabling role, as did executives at a Saudi oilfield services company. Other supporting players, either witting or unwitting, included Goldman Sachs, banks in Switzerland and Singapore, American law firms and real estate agents, art dealers, diamond sellers, public relations firms, Hollywood film companies, a top Republican Party operative, a DOJ official, and a former member of the 1990s hip-hop group Fugees.

The different players who enable corruption often use the same playbook. This is especially true when it comes to helping corrupt actors move their loot. In case after case from the oil boom, hired professionals set up shell companies in jurisdictions that deliberately court secret money, from Delaware to the Seychelles. These shell companies then opened accounts in foreign banks, and these accounts received the stolen funds. The funds then entered further accounts opened by further shell companies. Layer after layer, accountants, lawyers and other enablers masked the corrupt money until it could be freely enjoyed by those who stole it. Through these channels, dirty money spread around the world. Eighteen of Europe's twenty largest banks have paid money laundering fines in the past decade. Individuals under investigation by US authorities for corruption, drug trafficking and other crimes, as well as governments opposed by the United States, such as the Nicolas Maduro regime in Venezuela, find it easy to stash their funds in American companies and properties thanks to lenient policies. The Malaysia story and a couple of others told in chapter 5 trace how the tentacles of corruption reach all over the world.

International linkages are a modern corrupt actor's greatest strength. But the oil boom cases reveal another finding that is surprising and full of potential: these linkages also create great vulnerability. In case after case from the oil boom, the cross-border elements of the scheme led to its undoing. This is not the only major lesson the oil boom teaches about how to fight corruption. After all, many of the corruption cases mentioned in the book are success stories, at least to some degree. Misdeeds came to light, and the perpetrators were kept from enjoying their winnings in peace. In chapter 6, I describe the gains made by a motley set of anti-corruption actors.

While some domestic anticorruption campaigns were political power grabs in disguise, such as the one led by Saudi Arabia's crown prince, other domestic actors took on corruption and won, such as the Brazilian police who dared investigate powerful figures, the Nigerian electoral officials who protected the vote, and the journalists in Angola and Azerbaijan who refuse to be intimidated by repression. Other cases show how police, prosecutors, journalists, and other enemies of corruption now operate globally, just like the corruption they are trying to fight. They have successfully exposed oil boom schemes and punished the parties involved, often by latching onto corruption's international tentacles. Foreign governments have stepped up enforcement of their antibribery laws and launched innovative tools for going after dirty money flows. Oil-rich kleptocrats find it harder and harder to relax while visiting their London and Paris mansions. International networks of journalists have recorded huge wins, exposing corruption on an unprecedented scale. Even the professional enablers of corruption—those bankers, lawyers, and accountants who help the dirty money flow—have shown on occasion that they can be anticorruption heroes as well.

As chapter 7 sums up, strategies for building a smarter fight against corruption are there for the taking. Past cases reveal certain areas where corruption risks crop up over and over again. These are the obvious problems to address. Past cases also show which anticorruption tactics are working and need to be scaled up. Taken together, these observations form a practical agenda for tackling corruption in the oil sector and beyond. The difficult question is not what needs to be done but whether those in power will do it with enough consistency and vigor. As in Nigeria during the oil boom, the fight against corruption is frequently sidelined out of uncertainty, apathy, or inconvenience.

Neglecting corruption causes all kinds of harm, some of it deadly. Corruption costs the world economy at least $3.6 trillion a year, which is around 4.5 percent of global GDP, according to some experts.[12] But that's likely on the low side. The International Monetary Fund has estimated the costs of bribery at $1.5 to $2 trillion every year,[13] and bribery is just one form of corruption. Whatever the tally, no headline figure can capture all the channels through which corruption harms citizens and costs lives. It has wreaked havoc on the politics of many countries. As noted, the leaders of more than twenty countries have made early exits due to corruption or allegations of corruption. Elsewhere, leaders have hung onto power, but billions of people have still lost faith in their governments. This disillusionment has fueled the rise of extremist or populist leaders. Betrayed by the dirty deeds of the incumbent political class, fed-up citizens either disengage or seek a radical change.

Corruption weakens the ability of governments to address the world's most pressing challenges, including climate change and poverty. In some places, it also fuels violent conflicts. In South Sudan, a severely poor country mired in civil war, officials at the national oil company misappropriated money to fund militia groups that went on to destroy villages and attack civilians.[14] In Nigeria, government officials stand accused of stealing funds meant for fighting the extremist group Boko Haram, which has killed nearly 40,000 people and displaced 2 million more.[15] In Afghanistan and Iraq, widespread government corruption has weakened the military, disenfranchised citizens, and prompted some of them to take up arms against the state.[16]

Corruption also acts as a brake on economic development. According to the International Monetary Fund, it discourages foreign investment, makes it difficult to start or grow businesses, increases the cost of government borrowing, and comes with high inflation—all drains on job creation and growth. It also reduces a government's ability to collect taxes and citizens' willingness to pay them. Corruption drives up the costs of public projects and drives down the quality of social services, disproportionately impacting women and the poor.[17]

After causing all kinds of political and economic harm within a country, corrupt money then spreads overseas and destabilizes every foreign entity it touches. As mentioned, the affairs and associates of Donald Trump show how widely this contamination can spread. At each point where suspicious money touched Trump's affairs, it created distraction, controversy, and conflicts of interest. While the Trump team appears particularly porous, it is hardly alone in attracting corrupt money flows. A single Brazilian construction company bribed senior officials in at least ten Latin American countries, exporting scandal and instability across the entire continent. Corruption and its destabilizing effects appear unbounded.

We live in a golden age for corruption. Enormous cross-border schemes keep billions of people living in extreme poverty, drive deadly conflict, and undermine political representation. But norms are changing. Behavior that, a decade or two ago, would have been dismissed as "just how things work" has instead prompted outrage and even criminal investigation. Those who fight corruption now enjoy accelerated information flows, new law enforcement tools, and growing cross-border cooperation. This means it's a golden age for fighting corruption too.

The Oil Boom and the Resource Curse

Before diving into the book's specific cases, it's worth spending some time describing the oil sector, its players, and its peculiarities.

In the mid-2000s, many analysts predicted that oil prices would likely rise, driven by growing demand from China and other emerging economies, increased speculation in commodity markets, and unpredictable supply from key oil-producing states such as Iran, Libya, and Nigeria. A couple of bold analysts even predicted that oil would top $120 a barrel before the decade's end. While all this proved true, the oil market's reputation for unpredictability is safe and sound. No one projected that prices would take the erratic path shown in figure 1.1. First came the great climb from just $18 in 2001 to over $140 in 2008. Then the price plunged down again at a pace that caught everyone by surprise. A recovery soon followed, with the price quickly rebounding to above $120 in 2011. It stayed high for a three-year stretch before dropping again in 2014. Thanks to the rise in prices, over $9 trillion in new money flooded into the oil industry during the overall boom period of 2008 to 2014, creating unprecedented opportunities to profit.

Natural gas prices also rose during the period 2008–2014. A few of the corruption cases I describe involve natural gas rather than crude oil. The two products have important differences, especially in how they are extracted, transported, refined, and sold. But when it comes to corruption, the dynamics

FIGURE 1.1 Price of crude oil per barrel, 2000–2018.

SOURCE: Monthly averages of European Brent spot price (a widely used benchmark oil price) in US Energy Information Administration, "Spot Prices for Crude Oil and Petroleum Products," https://www.eia.gov/petroleum/data. php#prices.

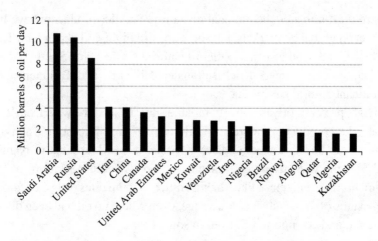

FIGURE 1.2 Top fifteen global oil producers by average daily production, 2008–2014. (This measure includes crude oil, shale oil, oil sands, and natural gas liquids, and excludes natural gas.)
SOURCE: BP, *Annual Statistical Bulletin*, 2018.

are similar enough to discuss the two together, as I do in the chapters that follow.

The mammoths of the global oil industry are Russia, Saudi Arabia, and the United States, as seen in figure 1.2. These three countries produced over one-third of the world's oil during the boom years. From 2008 to 2014, Russia and Saudi Arabia both produced an average of 10 million barrels of oil per day. At the boom's start, the United States was producing fewer than 7 million barrels of oil per day. By its end in 2014, the United States was pumping out more than 11 million. Well beneath these three are a cluster of major producers that include Iran, China, Canada, the United Arab Emirates (UAE), Mexico, Kuwait, Venezuela, Iraq, Nigeria, Brazil, Norway, and Angola. Each of them produced around 2–4 million barrels per day on average during the boom years.

The importance of oil to these top producer countries depends on the size of their economies. Take the United States and China, for example. Both are significant oil producers, but oil forms just a small part of their overall economies. In Saudi Arabia and Iraq on the other hand oil is the only game in town. Those governments rely on oil for over three-quarters of their revenues. In such places, oil has a much stronger impact on the country's politics as well as its economy.

Oil is hugely influential in other producing countries too, and they feature prominently in the stories of corruption that follow. These include midsized producers such as Algeria, Kazakhstan, Libya, and Azerbaijan, where oil dominates the national economy. Smaller producers have little impact on global oil markets, but some are still highly oil dependent. These include Chad, Congo-Brazzaville, Equatorial Guinea, and South Sudan in Africa, as well as the oil-rich sultanate of Brunei, and Turkmenistan, a significant natural gas producer.

High prices motivated oil companies to strike out away from these established producers and look for oil in new places. Exploration activities took off up and down both Africa's coasts, from Mauritania to Namibia and Somalia to Mozambique, raising the hopes and expectations of governments and citizens alike. In the frenzy, companies splashed around large sums of money to access acreage, even where no oil had been discovered yet, and corruption followed in some cases.

In producing countries, the oil boom sent record-high revenues pouring into government accounts. Receipts from the sector often doubled in just a couple of years and then crashed down again alongside the price. The Iraqi government, for example, took in around $40 billion per year in oil revenues before the boom. Then, suddenly, they collected over $90 billion per year. On a smaller scale, the government of Congo-Brazzaville took home $2 billion from its oil sector in 2009 and three times that amount in 2013.[18] It was like winning the lottery.

Oil companies of a few different types also enjoyed record-high returns during the oil boom. National oil companies are entirely or majority owned by governments. According to one leading study, these entities produce between 55 and 75 percent of the world's oil and control as much as 90 percent of its oil reserves.[19] This dominance got its start in the 1970s, when the governments of countries such as Iran, Iraq, Kuwait, Saudi Arabia, and Venezuela grew tired of relying on Western companies to produce their oil and created powerful national oil companies to assert more control over the sector. In some cases, the governments took assets away from foreign companies and gave them to national oil companies to run instead.

Today, national oil companies play major roles in the oil industries of all major producing countries except Canada, the United Kingdom, and the United States. China has three giant national oil companies, Sinopec, the Chinese National Petroleum Company (CNPC), and the China National Offshore Oil Corporation, and they operate in dozens of countries around the world. Many other large national oil companies, such as those from India, Malaysia, and Norway are active overseas as well. Many of these big players are listed on international stock exchanges, meaning that the government shares ownership of the company with private investors. Other governments, such as Iran and Saudi Arabia, have chosen instead to maintain full control over their national oil companies. While these big players often compete with private oil companies, they differ in important ways too. First and foremost, they remain under the firm control of the country's political leadership and are often called on to support political, foreign policy, and other noncommercial goals.[20] The same goes for smaller national oil companies, such as many of those in Africa. While they may lack the capacity to actually produce oil, they collect lots of money and are powerful actors on the national stage.

In the private sector, the best-known oil companies are those giant players that work across the oil industry, from exploring underground for crude to selling gasoline to consumers. ExxonMobil and Chevron are the largest American oil companies. In Europe, BP, Royal Dutch Shell, Total, and Eni top the charts along with Russia's Lukoil. These oil companies operate roughly on the same scale as the largest national oil companies in terms of revenues and production. Many other companies, large and small, publicly listed and privately held, also produce oil alongside these well-known giants.

Companies that produce oil are not the only players who matter in the industry, especially when it comes to corruption risks. Oil traders are the middlemen of the industry, making sure that supplies move from buyers to sellers all around the globe. They make money off of the margins on these sales, buying low and selling high, and playing the ups and downs of the oil price to their advantage. The largest oil traders include the trading divisions of major oil companies, including BP, Shell, Total, Lukoil, and China's Sinopec, and companies that specialize in trading, such as the five large Swiss traders Glencore, Gunvor, Mercuria, Trafigura, and Vitol. Smaller traders then fill the gaps.

Oilfield services is another part of the industry where corruption rears its head. The companies that hold exploration and production licenses, like ExxonMobil or China's CNPC, do not do all the work themselves. They outsource some of the operations by awarding contracts to a set of players called oilfield service companies. These contractors include large multinationals that drill oil wells, build infrastructure, and deliver other expensive and highly technical services all around the world. Some of the biggest names in the oilfield service industry are the French company Schlumberger, the American companies Halliburton, Weatherford, and BakerHughes, Switzerland's Transocean, Italy's Saipem, and Petrofac in the United Kingdom. Contracts also go to smaller, often local players who provide more basic services like logistics, catering, or transport. For every dollar spent on producing oil, more than half goes into a service contract, creating enormous opportunities to profit for the companies that win these contracts.[21]

Along with the traders and the service companies, a whole manner of other players flocked to oil-rich countries during the boom years, looking for a piece of the action. Many governments moved large chunks of their oil revenues into specialized savings accounts called sovereign wealth funds. By the end of the oil boom, over $4 trillion in oil revenues had entered these funds.[22] Financial institutions scrambled to win business managing and investing these funds. Accountants, lawyers, consulting firms, and public relations groups also pitched their services to the wealthy governments. Purveyors of upscale real estate, yachts, private jets, jewelry, and other luxury goods set their sights on the oil-producing world too.

All these actors—the governments, the oil companies, the service providers, the wheeler-dealers, and more—wanted to capture a share of the oil boom. A couple of oil's unusual attributes intensified the scramble.

First, countries only get one shot to benefit from their oil and gas resources. Because they were formed many millennia ago, whatever hydrocarbons a country has, that's all it's going to get. Oil's nonrenewable nature raises the stakes for the industry's profit seekers, as well as for the citizens of countries where oil is found. Oil can either help develop the rest of the economy and benefit both current and future generations, as it has in Norway. Or oil revenues can be wasted, with countries losing their best chance at funding social and economic development.

Second, oil is a high-rent industry. Rent is an economic term to describe the difference between the cost of producing something, including a small profit for the producer and taxes paid to the government, and the market price at which it can be sold. For most products—phones, cars, corn, shirts—these two figures are similar in size. Not so for oil, especially during a boom.

The cost of producing oil varies from place to place, depending mostly on the terrain. Some oil in the Middle East is found not too deep beneath the desert sands and can be produced for less than $20 per barrel. When prices topped $100, the rent from this oil exceeded a whopping $80 per barrel. Other oil is more expensive to produce. Offshore oil can cost anywhere from $30 to $60 per barrel to extract, depending on the depth and location of the waters. When the price is high, the rents on this oil also grow to be quite large.

During the oil boom, trillions of dollars in new rents worked like an enormous load of bloody chum and set off an unprecedented feeding frenzy among the industry's many carnivorous species. Rents are essentially extra money that's up for grabs. Depending on who strikes the best deal, they can go to any of the government or private sector players involved in the industry.

The 2008–2014 price boom was not the first time that oil rents triggered frenzy. In the mid-1970s, oil prices began to climb. Then in 1979 they shot upward and stayed high for seven years. Economists and political scientists studied how this earlier oil boom affected oil-producing countries and invented the term "resource curse" to summarize their dismal findings. In 1995, Jeffrey Sachs and Andrew Warner published one of the first large studies of resource-rich economies across the globe. They found that the economies of resource-rich countries actually performed worse than those of their resource-poor counterparts.[23] Illustrating the trend were the divergent trajectories of South Korea and Taiwan on the one hand and oil-rich Mexico, Nigeria, Saudi Arabia, and Venezuela on the other.

Experts offer a few economic explanations for this poor performance. Large oil or mineral exports can cause the domestic currency to grow stronger, which is tough on a country's other industries. When exchange rates appreciate, a country's exports grow more expensive and become harder to sell on the global market—a phenomenon known as Dutch disease. In addition, oil is a "point industry," meaning that it has few linkages with the rest of the economy. When oil business ramps up during a boom period, it does not create many additional jobs or pull up other sectors along with it. Finally, oil revenues are famously volatile, a challenge that governments find difficult to manage. Lots of oil producers get hooked on spending big when prices are high, for instance, and then end up falling deep into debt when prices drop.

Oil wealth has damaging political effects too. The political scientist Michael Ross found that from 1980 to 2006, oil-rich countries were three times less likely to democratize than non–oil producers.[24] His findings echo many smaller studies that observe how, in oil-rich countries, power often concentrates in the hands of a few individuals. Checks on that power, such as elections or independent legislatures and judiciaries, often weaken. Many oil-rich governments don't bother taxing their citizens or nonoil businesses, so they lack any vested interest in their people's prosperity and don't foster the credibility that broad-based taxation usually requires. Instead of delivering public goods, leaders and officials spend their time engaged in "rent-seeking behaviors," that is, trying to capture oil wealth for themselves, their political allies, or their home regions.

Corruption has traditionally played a big role in these resource curse dynamics. Several of the most corrupt leaders in recent history, such as Sani Abacha in Nigeria and Suharto in Indonesia, fed off oil wealth. The leaders of other oil producers, such as those in the Persian Gulf, are famous for living lives of utmost luxury. Many of recent history's longest-serving dictators, in Angola, Cameroon, Equatorial Guinea, Libya, and elsewhere, spent decades using oil money to buy off their enemies and keep allies loyal. Oil companies have played along. In the 1980s and 1990s, French and African political elites received funds routed through the state-owned French oil company Elf Aquitaine.[25] Hundreds of companies broke the rules of the UN-administered Oil-for-Food program and paid $1.5 billion in kickbacks to the Saddam Hussein government in Iraq.[26] And on and on.

With a history like this, the prevalence of corruption during the recent oil boom hardly comes as a surprise. Its predictability does not undermine its importance. By the time prices made their historic climb, governments and companies had updated old corruption schemes and invented new ones, including many that exploit today's global financial system. Opposition to corruption had evolved too, with anticorruption actors enjoying many more tools at their disposal. The recent oil boom is the perfect petri dish for examining all of their behaviors.

Writing about Oil Boom Corruption

During the oil boom, industry players used all kinds of tactics to tilt the playing field in their favor and capture an unduly large share of the available oil wealth. Some actors engaged in outright corruption while others played a supporting role or inadvertently brushed up against the wrongdoing. They operated in diverse country contexts that impacted the tactics that they chose. To capture this breadth and diversity, I cast a wide net in my research and adopted a broad approach to defining corruption.

Transparency International, a leading anticorruption advocacy group, defines corruption as "the abuse of entrusted power for private gain." Many of the actions I discuss fit squarely under this definition. However, the concept of "entrusted power" often leads to a focus on corruption by government officials. I examine actions taken by private sector actors as well, as citizens pay the price for their efforts to bend the rules too. Oil rents are finite and nonrenewable. So when a company captures more than its fair share, it eats into the returns that should have accrued to the oil-producing country and its people. By this logic, I include in chapter 2 a wide range of damaging private sector behaviors, including bribery, doing business with political elites, collusion, tax evasion, and tax avoidance. I also examine the behavior of corruption's enablers, such as the bankers, accountants, lawyers, and middlemen who help run the deals that reward certain elites at the public's expense. Some of these enablers deliberately engage in wrongdoing while others are unwitting helpers.

Using a broad definition of corruption also means that some of the abuses I describe were legal in the jurisdiction where they took place. This is true even of textbook corruption offenses such as bribery. Most countries have laws that forbid companies from paying bribes to public officials. This seems simple enough. But, in practice, there is much debate about what constitutes a bribe. Take hospitality, for instance: there is no agreement across legal jurisdictions, or even within them, on what amount of "wining and dining" constitutes a bribe. As described in chapter 2, a UK civil court found no problem with Goldman Sachs's extensive wooing of Libyan oil officials, which included providing fancy hotels, elaborate meals, and even a couple of prostitutes. But US authorities dinged the oil and mining company BHP Billiton for providing foreign government officials with trips to the Beijing Olympics.

In other cases, the behavior I describe is clearly legal—and is still corruption. Nigeria's Petroleum Act places few limitations on the ability of the petroleum minister to choose who receives oil contracts. So when the former minister allocated contracts to poorly qualified companies headed by her allies, she did so with the Petroleum Act's blessing. She may have broken other laws, especially when these allies started buying her houses and other treats, as described in chapter 3. But the discretionary award of oil business to her friends did not, in and of itself, break Nigerian law. In other countries, such as Azerbaijan and Russia, savvy political leaders made sure certain oligarchs won big from the oil boom. These leaders influence the entire government and the rules by which it operates, so it is not difficult for them to accomplish this objective within the boundaries of the law. It is still corruption. The possibility of *legal corruption* means that when I describe actors as corrupt, I am not claiming that they have necessarily broken laws or engaged in criminal behavior.[27]

The book focuses only on grand corruption: the large-scale corruption undertaken by those who hold positions of power. It does not address petty corruption: the corruption citizens confront as they try to access everyday services, as when an immigration officer solicits a bribe at a border.

To tell the corruption stories that follow, I rely exclusively on publicly available sources. Most are documents issued by governments as part of legal cases, such as statements of charges, complaints and plea agreements, media reporting, and investigations published by NGOs. I did not conduct my own investigations nor do I expose new evidence of corruption or make accusations that have not been made elsewhere. However, there is significant public value in pulling together this kind of evidence from across cases and across countries and pointing out the patterns that repeat themselves. This exercise reveals what practices can help rein in the systematic forms of corruption described in the book.

Corruption cases often peel apart like onions and take years to reach a final outcome. When investigators get wind of wrongdoing by one actor, they dig into the case and begin to piece together what happened. This initial work reveals more wrongdoing by more actors, who then require their own investigations, and so on. Due to the highly complex and cross-border nature of contemporary corruption, law enforcement authorities find these investigations to be immensely time-consuming. Then, once charges are filed, a whole further set of delays begins, such as lengthy appeals. In many countries, investigations of corruption don't even get started until a new government comes to power and starts digging into what happened under their predecessors.

Due to these dynamics, many of the cases I write about had not reached their ultimate conclusion when this book went to press, even though the alleged corruption took place quite a few years earlier. More information might emerge, and perhaps change how the entire story looks. Further parties might be found guilty. Or guilty verdicts might be appealed and overturned.

This is just one of the many challenges of writing about corruption. Information comes out in unpredictable spurts. Different sources may offer different accounts of events. The complexities of the schemes sometimes defy clear description. The parties involved may resent being named and stand ready to retaliate. Nevertheless, my accounts reflect the serious investigation and reporting by reputable persons and institutions, including, often, official proceedings, and the conclusions here represent my considered judgment based on the evidence I have collected.

These stories matter. Mighty politicians, wealthy companies, and conniving hustlers grabbed more than their fair share of the world's oil wealth during the recent boom. But they are not untouchable. They used common tactics and exhibit common vulnerabilities, and these observations can form the building blocks of a smarter response.

CHAPTER 2 | "Being a Friend in a Nest of Vipers"

LIKE MANY AMBITIOUS ENTREPRENEURS, Brad Griffiths sought to make his fortune off the rising tide of oil prices. A work-hard, play-hard type, Griffiths was a Canadian financier well known in Toronto circles for his cowboy approach to business. One colleague called him a "deal guy extraordinaire." "He had the ability to, as we say, break the back of a deal, and figure it out."[1]

In early 2011, things were looking up for Griffiths. His deal-making prowess had landed another sterling opportunity. His newly created oil company, Griffiths Energy, signed a contract with the government of Chad for the rights to two highly promising oil blocks. On the back of the Chad deal, the company quickly raised $165 million and began preparations for an IPO later in the year. Alongside this big win, Griffiths, at fifty-five, appeared to leading a healthier lifestyle and leaving past demons behind. A colleague remarked: "he was on his best run ever, both professionally and personally." According to one Toronto newspaper, Griffiths had "overcome years of hard partying by settling down and reconnecting with his family, especially at the cottage on Lake Joseph, 200 km north of Toronto."[2]

Out at Lake Joseph, however, events took a tragic turn. Taking a break from preparing for the IPO, Griffiths was enjoying a summer break at his family's vacation home. On a calm July day, he took his boat out to do some fishing. Soon after, a neighbor spotted a man waving his arms from the water far offshore. Griffiths had somehow fallen out of the boat, and he soon drowned. A few days later, police recovered his body from the deep water. While authorities ruled out foul play, the family did not release the autopsy results, leaving much of what happened that day a mystery.[3]

In the months that followed, those who remained at Griffiths Energy sought to pick up the pieces and make the best of their valuable oil assets. New management arrived and began looking through the transactions that had led to the deal with Chad's government. What they found caused concern, and they launched an internal investigation. In 2012, the company's new management reported to the Canadian authorities that Brad Griffiths and several of his colleagues had bribed government officials.[4]

Chad was a proven oil destination by the time Griffiths began pursuing deals there. Back in the 1990s, ExxonMobil discovered oil in the country's southern interior and built a long pipeline to a port in neighboring Cameroon for transporting the oil for export. The $4 billion pipeline project attracted all kinds of critical attention, as Chad seemed a perfect candidate to suffer from the cocktail of corruption and economic turmoil that define the "resource curse." The country's long-standing dictator, Idris Deby, had little tolerance for dissent, the population shouldered some the world's highest poverty rates, and the government lacked the capacity and the motivation to turn oil revenues into benefits for the people. So Exxon reached out to the World Bank to help with the pipeline project and asked for its help in setting up safeguards so that the oil money helped Chad's citizens.

The plan did not work out very well. The World Bank succeeded in pressuring the Chadian government to adopt some reforms, including commitments that oil revenues would go toward development projects and the formation of a new council to oversee the revenue flows. Predictably, however, the government disregarded these constraints once the oil money started flowing. The political rights and economic well-being of most Chadians failed to improve, despite the oil wealth that began filling up their government's coffers. And corruption would end up infecting the next phase of oil sector deals in the country.

On the back of Exxon's discoveries, other companies became interested in acquiring nearby oilfields in southern Chad—especially as oil prices began to climb. Griffiths Energy was among them. In 2009, Brad Griffiths and his business partners held their first meeting with Chad's ambassador to the United States and Canada, Mahamoud Adam Bechir, and his wife, Nouracham Niam. According to a US government investigation, the Griffiths Energy partners offered the ambassador $2 million and the opportunity to buy shares in their company in exchange for his "unlawful assistance" in securing rights to two oil blocks in Chad.[5]

Next, Griffiths Energy signed an agreement with a company set up by Bechir called, not so subtly, Ambassade du Tchad LLC. The agreement stated that Bechir would receive a $2 million fee for so-called consulting services if the government awarded Griffiths the rights to the two oil blocks. It somehow took Griffiths's lawyers a few weeks to realize that it was way too risky for the company to transfer funds to a sitting government official via a company literally named after his position. According to Canadian court filings, the lawyers advised Griffiths to terminate the deal with Ambassade du Tchad LLC because of the ambassador's status as a sitting government official. A week later, Bechir's wife set up a company called Chad Oil Consultants LLC, who signed an agreement with Griffiths instead.[6]

In the months that followed, the bosses of Griffiths Energy chased their Chad deal, making various offers and overtures to top officials, often accessed with the ambassador's help. Finally, in early 2011, the deal came through, and Griffiths won the rights to the two oil blocks. As agreed, the lawyers retained by Griffiths Energy transferred the $2 million from an escrow account to the ambassador's wife's company and transferred to her and two associates 4 million founder shares in the company for a nominal fee of around $2,000. In a few short years, the shares were worth $34 million.[7] In the years after the scandal broke, law enforcement in the United States and United Kingdom went after the bribe money the ambassador and his wife received.[8]

The bribe changed hands just a few months before the death of Brad Griffiths. After the new management reported the bribes to the Canadian authorities in 2012, the company was found guilty under Canada's Corruption of Foreign Public Officials Act and agreed to pay a fine of $10.35 million— the largest ever assessed by Canada for foreign bribery at that time.

Despite this penalty, the deal Brad Griffiths struck in Chad still paid off big. The Chadians took no legal action against the company, so Griffiths Energy kept the rights to the two oil blocks. After the bribery scandal broke, the company changed its name from Griffiths Energy to Caracal Energy in an effort to refresh its identity. The company's leadership remained confident about the value of their Chadian assets, which formed the vast majority of the company's holdings. The company began to develop the oilfields and soon was producing 25,000 barrels per day—oil worth over $900 million in 2013. In its first big step toward cashing in, Caracal sold shares in its Chadian blocks to the large Swiss commodities company Glencore for $331 million in 2013. A year later Glencore bought the entire company for $1.3 billion—a hefty price, amounting to 61 percent more than the value of the company's shares.[9] The family trust of Brad Griffiths remained Caracal's largest shareholder at the time of the sale.

The story of Griffiths Energy's dealings in Chad shows how corruption can pay off, especially during an oil boom. Unlike many instances of corruption, Griffiths Energy was actually prosecuted and fined. Yet the $10 million fine looks awfully small when compared to the $1.3 billion that the company sold for.

Weighing Risks and Rewards

Oil companies and other private sector actors used a number of different tactics to capture an outsized share of the wealth on offer during the oil boom. Some of these tactics, like the bribes paid by Griffiths, fell squarely within standard definitions of corruption. Others were more subtle or more creative but no less damaging. This chapter explores these company maneuvers. Chapters 3 and 4 focus on the corruption orchestrated by the political elites and government officials of oil-producing countries.

Chapter 1 introduced the different types of private sector players who operate in the oil industry. One set of oil companies explores for oil and undertakes its production. These "upstream" companies can be government-owned national oil companies, which feature extensively in chapters 3 and 4. But many others are not owned by governments. These include the well-known giants of the industry, such as Exxon and Chevron in the United States and BP, Eni, Shell, and Total in Europe, as well as smaller players like Griffiths. These producers typically outsource large portions of the work involved in exploration and production, awarding large contracts to the set of players called oilfield service companies. Another big set of companies are the traders, the industry's savvy middlemen. The largest oil traders are a set of five Swiss-based companies (Glencore, Gunvor, Mercuria, Trafigura, and Vitol) and the trading divisions of certain large oil companies like BP, Shell, Total, and Sinopec. Finally, there are the fixers and middlemen oil companies hire to help them land deals in challenging or new environments, and the banks, accountants, and lawyers who help arrange various oil sector deals. A full discussion of oil sector corruption would not be complete without examining their role as well.

The oil boom created ample motivation to take corruption risks, as enormous sums of money were at stake. When oil prices top $100 per barrel, running the right maneuver at the right time can deliver historic returns. The recent financial performance of ExxonMobil, BP, and Shell, three of the world's largest oil companies, shows just how much wealth was on the table and how directly their fortunes hinge on the price of oil. As shown in figure 2.1, the gross earnings that entered Exxon's accounts during the peak boom years of 2008, 2011, and 2012 reached nearly $500 billion per year. Profits rose too. In 2005, Exxon earned the largest profits ever for a US company of any type, around $36 billion.[10] As oil prices continued to rise, Exxon's profits exceeded that record in five of the next seven years.

These giants were far from alone on the hunt for record-breaking profits. During an oil boom, the demand for oil sector construction and engineering

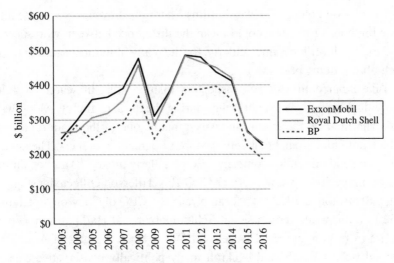

FIGURE 2.1 Oil company revenues, 2003–2016.
SOURCE: Data compiled by author from company annual reports.

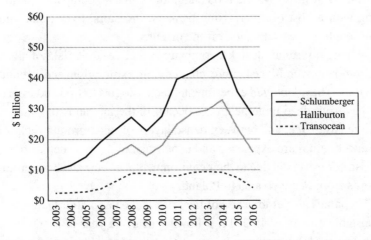

FIGURE 2.2 Oilfield service company revenues, 2003–2016.
SOURCE: Data compiled by author from company annual reports.

work goes up because companies like Exxon and Shell want to do more exploring, more producing, and more refining. They hired oilfield service companies to perform much of the work, such as building oil platforms and pipelines. As the demand for oilfield services rose, so did the rates that companies commanded for providing them. Service companies also took in record high returns during the oil boom. Figure 2.2 shows how the revenues of the two largest service companies, France-based Schlumberger and the US company Halliburton, skyrocketed during this period.

Smaller oil companies like Griffiths Energy had even more on the line. One big boom-time deal could mean the difference between wild success and total failure. The same held true for the many individuals aiming to get rich off the rising prices.

Like nineteenth-century prospectors rushing west in search of gold, individual executives sought riches during this time of frenzy. Along with tech and finance, the energy industry remains one of the main routes via which individuals can break into the top 0.1 percent of earners. The annual pay of oil and oil service company CEOs regularly broke $10 million during the boom period. Exxon's former CEO Rex Tillerson collected a staggering $40 million in 2012.[11] That same year, the CEO of Chevron took home $32 million, while the bosses at Schlumberger and Halliburton received over $15 million apiece. Charles and David Koch are part of America's second richest family and bankroll many politically conservative causes. They owe a large portion of their fortune to oil industry ventures, including major refining and petrochemical operations and US and Canadian oil production.[12] Further down the food chain, the midlevel company employees, along with a host of enterprising bankers, investors, fixers, and middlemen, sought to get rich quick off the oil rush.

With great fortunes at stake, company executives took risks of all kinds. Oil companies embraced more challenging exploration and production activities. They deployed experimental technologies to find and extract oil and gas from deep underneath the ocean, in the tar sands of Canada, far into the Arctic ice, and between dense layers of underground rock. All of these techniques are expensive and experimental. Some, such as fracking, are also controversial due to their environmental effects and have prompted protests from Pennsylvania to Poland.

Companies also embraced political risk and chased after lucrative deals in unstable countries. In 2011, following nearly a year of secret negotiations, ExxonMobil announced a major agreement with the semiautonomous Kurdistan Regional Government in Iraq. Predictably, the government in Baghdad was livid, as it does not recognize the Kurdish regional authority's right to enter into oil deals. The Baghdad government also saw Exxon as *their* partner, following an enormous deal they had signed with the company just two years earlier. Even for a famously conservative company like Exxon, the oil boom warranted such bold maneuvers. In another politically risky move, the Swiss oil-trading company Vitol signed deals with Libyan rebel groups right in the middle of the highly volatile and unpredictable 2011 civil war, providing the combatants with a lifeline of fuel and funds. "We expect to play a role in the future [of Libya's oil industry]," said Vitol CEO Ian Taylor, explaining why such risks were worth taking.[13]

Corruption risks are not that different from the other risks that a company might decide to take. Companies can estimate, albeit with uncertainty, the potential downsides. If a company gets caught breaking anticorruption laws, it might face expensive legal bills, fines, and—much less often—penalties and jail time for individual executives. Companies might also face negative publicity if they are accused of corruption by law enforcement, journalists, or activist groups. This reputational damage can sometimes harm investor confidence, reduce share prices, and generate suspicion from prospective partners.

And so the calculus begins, with executives weighing the potential downsides of corruption against the potential gains. While most large companies have extensive systems to guard against corruption—codes of conduct, specialized teams of lawyers, employee trainings, due diligence systems, and so on—the oil boom period suggests that they do not work often enough. The downsides of corruption simply remained too small to offset the potential gains, especially when historic quantities of wealth were at stake. Corruption scandals very rarely cause the downfall of a company or send executives to jail. Far more often, companies caught for corruption end up doing just fine. Like Griffiths Energy, they pay their penance, say they are sorry, and cash in nonetheless.

When Does Wooing Become Wrongdoing?

Griffiths Energy used bribery to secure face time with top Chadian government officials. The company's bosses took that risk because they understood that in some countries, political elites make discretionary decisions about which companies should receive valuable business opportunities in the oil sector. Instead of running a competitive auction where companies submit their qualifications and price points, many top officials just choose the company that best serves their own interests. As a result, companies go to great lengths to gain favor with these decision-makers, cozying up, making grand overtures, and sometimes paying bribes. The question of when this wooing crosses the line and becomes corruption is the source of extensive debate, especially between companies and the law enforcement agencies that police them.

Wining and dining is one blurry area: when is it corruption and when is it not? The Australian oil and mining company BHP Billiton treated sixty government officials and their family members to generous hospitality packages at the 2008 Beijing Olympics. The packages included tickets to Olympic events, luxury hotel accommodations, and sightseeing excursions and were worth over $12,000 apiece. At the time, BHP Billiton was in active negotiations with some of the officials they hosted, even though the company's own policies prohibited such behavior. For instance, among those enjoying the Olympic fanfare were the then minister of mines of Burundi and his wife. In 2008, BHP Billiton held shares in a company that operated a nickel mine in Burundi. The company was in danger of losing its exploration permit, a matter that fell under the responsibility of the minister.[14] While many industry insiders would see BHP Billiton's hospitality as normal company-government relations, the US Securities and Exchange Commission (SEC) thought otherwise and brought a civil claim against the company under the Foreign Corrupt Practices Act (FCPA). BHP neither admitted nor denied guilt in the case. The company paid a $25 million fine and agreed to restructure its internal anticorruption procedures.[15]

In Turkmenistan, an isolated country with some of the world's largest natural gas reserves, little information escapes about the government's relationships with its investors, which have included China's CNPC. However, the movements of American pop star Jennifer Lopez are difficult to keep secret. In 2013, CNPC paid for Lopez to travel to Turkmenistan and perform as part of a week-long festival that coincided with the president's birthday. At the last minute, Lopez was asked to convey a birthday greeting to the notorious dictator. After changing from her glamorous stage attire into a traditional Turkmen dress, she returned to the stage to convey her good wishes to the president. Human rights groups lambasted her. Doing damage control, Lopez's publicist stressed that it was CNPC who requested the birthday greeting just before Lopez took the stage and that the singer "graciously obliged." She had not known about the country's human rights record and would not have attended if she had.[16] The amount Lopez charged for the performance remains unknown, as do the size of the oil and gas deals CNPC has struck with the president of Turkmenistan.

Internships are another small-scale tactic that occupy the same gray area. During the oil boom, banks scrambled to win business from oil-rich governments that had billions of dollars to invest. In 2010 and 2011, the Bank of New York Mellon agreed to give internships to the son and nephew of "a key decision maker" at an unnamed Middle Eastern sovereign wealth fund. Soon after, the son of another key official received a similar opportunity. One bank executive complained in an email: "its [sic] silly things like this that help influence who ends up with more assets/retaining dominant position." However, eager to please the oil-rich client, his colleague concluded that the bank was "not in a position to reject the request from a commercial point of view.... By not allowing the internships to take place, we potentially jeopardize our mandate with [the Middle Eastern sovereign wealth fund]." Placed at the bank's Boston offices, the three young men proved lackluster additions to the bank's workforce: two recorded frequent absences, and the third was deemed not hard-working.[17]

The interns did manage to attract the attention of the US authorities, who opened an antibribery investigation into the matter. In 2015, Bank of New York Mellon agreed to pay fines of $14.8 million. The bank neither accepted nor disputed the bribery charges. At the time of the offense, it held around $55 billion of the sovereign wealth fund's assets in its servicing arm, with $711 million under active management—lucrative business worth some risks to protect.[18]

Goldman Sachs, among the world's largest investment banks, also employed creative, risky, and controversial methods to woo government officials in Libya. The story illustrates that the boundaries of what is wrong or corrupt are controversial. Ask ten people and you will get ten different views on whether the bank's actions were corrupt, or perhaps inappropriate, or just normal conduct that happened to lead to remarkably bad outcomes.

In 2003, Libya's longtime dictator, Muammar Gaddafi, launched a series of overtures aimed at reopening relations with the West. He publicly renounced terrorism, agreed to pay compensation to the families of the victims of the 1988 Lockerbie bombing, and promised to give up his country's weapons of mass destruction. In response, relations between Libya and the West began to thaw. The United States and the United Kingdom lifted economic sanctions. The UK prime minister, Tony Blair, visited Tripoli in 2004, and the US secretary of state, Condoleezza Rice, followed in 2008. This normalization opened up new opportunities for Western businesses, including in the oil industry.

Around the same time, as oil prices rose, Libya began collecting record high revenues. Libya had produced oil for several decades and by 2008 was the seventeenth largest producer in the world. With a population of just 6 million people, oil utterly dominated the country's economy. Alongside Gaddafi's opening of relations with the West, he also pursued a few half-hearted efforts to modernize the Libyan economy, while maintaining a repressive stranglehold on the country's politics. As part of this economic campaign, he authorized his son Saif Al-Islam to establish a sovereign wealth fund, the Libyan Investment Authority (LIA) in 2006 and allocated a beefy $40 billion in oil money toward its founding capital. The fund's assets soon exceeded $60 billion.

With the LIA's creation, Libya joined many oil-producing governments in setting up special funds to hold their oil wealth. Between 2007 and 2015, the assets held by the world's sovereign wealth funds doubled, reaching $7.2 trillion by the end of the oil boom. To provide some perspective, these stockpiled government funds exceeded the amount managed by all the world's hedge funds and private equity funds at that time. Around 60 percent of the $7.2 trillion was oil and gas related; the oil-rich governments of Norway, the UAE, Saudi Arabia, and Kuwait hold four of the five largest sovereign wealth funds.[19]

Large pots of wealth create opportunities to make money. Wall Street banks and other financial institutions looked with eager delight on these booming funds. Investment banks, hedge funds, and private equity funds all sought to manage some of the ballooning sovereign wealth fund assets or provide related financial services. As early as 2008, the US authorities realized that the booming oil funds carried bribery risks. The DOJ announced that investigations involving sovereign wealth funds were "at the top of the Justice Department's hit list" and made it clear that sovereign wealth fund officials should be treated as government officials—that is, they should not be paid off.

The LIA's creation kicked off just the type of feverish competition that worried antibribery authorities. Soon after its launch, at least twenty-five of the world's leading financial institutions began courting the fund's top officials. Goldman Sachs sent thirty-one-year-old Youssef Kabbaj to Tripoli to lead their charm offensive.

Born in Morocco and trained at MIT, Kabbaj began work at Goldman's London office in 2006 as an equity derivatives salesperson. As the LIA's coffers began to swell, he sniffed out an opportunity to make his big break. The challenge was winning the trust of LIA officials and convincing them to invest some of their billions with Goldman.

The process began in mid-2007, when the LIA's deputy chief executive, Mustafa Zarti, visited Goldman's London offices. The visit helped convince higher level executives at Goldman of what Kabbaj already knew: managing LIA funds could result in major profits for the bank. Kabbaj's boss told him that he should "stay a lot in Tripoli. It's important you stay super close to the client on a daily basis. Teach them, train them, dine them." Another of his superiors wrote: "you need to own this client. This is a once in a career opportunity."[20] Kabbaj eagerly complied. Wining and dining was one obvious approach. Kabbaj charged tens of thousands of dollars to his corporate card, treating LIA officials to five-star hotels, elaborate sushi dinners, West End musicals, and top sporting events on their visits to London and other capitals. On a trip to Dubai, Kabbaj hosted Zarti's younger brother, an aspiring banker himself, at the Ritz-Carlton. According to media reports, upon arrival, Kabbaj texted a prostitute to see if she and a friend could join them for the evening.[21] In addition, in response to a direct request from Zarti, Kabbaj secured a bespoke internship at Goldman for the same brother.[22]

Kabbaj offered more than just pampering to the LIA. The fund's staff had a very weak understanding of financial markets, including the kind of complex derivative trades that Goldman wanted to sell. One Goldman representative said talking to them was like giving "a pitch on structured leveraged loans to someone who lives in the middle of the desert with his camels."[23] A foreign consultant to the LIA called them "a team of clearly naïve and unqualified individuals."[24] So Kabbaj arranged for the LIA's staff to receive classes, books, and consultants aimed at improving their financial literacy.

After all these overtures from Goldman, the LIA decided to invest a great deal of money with the bank in late 2007 and early 2008, including in nine large derivative trades. The accolades for Kabbaj poured in, as did the offer of a $9 million bonus. "Bravo Youssef. Well done. You are a hero," wrote his manager. Another internal message called him "perhaps Goldman's top salesman globally."[25]

In all likelihood, Kabbaj and his questionable sales techniques would have gone unnoticed if it weren't for what happened next. The LIA lost the entire $1.2 billion it invested in the nine derivative trades with Goldman—a complete wipeout. Goldman, meanwhile, earned over $130 million in fees from the deals.[26] The complex trades, described by Goldman at one point as "a cash-settled forward purchase agreement for Citigroup shares with downside protection in the form of a put option at the same price as the forward," basically bet that the stock of certain struggling banks such as Citigroup would improve. Instead, the 2008 financial crisis caused the opposite outcome, and the LIA lost all of its money.

Was Goldman at fault for this catastrophic outcome? The LIA certainly thought so. Just after news of the loss reached the LIA, Kabbaj made the familiar trip to the fund's offices to pitch some new investment products. In a riveting account of the encounter, *Bloomberg* reporters narrate what happened next:

Zarti exploded. Screaming in a mix of English and Arabic, he accused Kabbaj of deceiving the LIA into deals it didn't understand. He called Goldman "a bank of Mafiosi" and said that he could behave like a Mafioso, too. He stormed out of the room, leaving Kabbaj, Pentreath [another Goldman representative], and a clutch of LIA staffers in a Marlboro haze.

Shaken, Kabbaj asked Zarti's aides what had just happened. None had an answer. After a few minutes, Zarti burst back in, angrier than ever. Catherine McDougall, an Australian lawyer who was in the office that day, later recalled Zarti's words as along the lines of "F— your mother, f— you, and get out of my country." Kabbaj and Pentreath packed up their things.

Zarti followed them into the corridor. If Kabbaj didn't make amends, he shouted, "we will go after your own family in Morocco!" The Al-Fateh Tower elevators were agonizingly slow to arrive. "What are you still doing here? Get out of my building!" Zarti screamed. He told Pentreath that if he didn't get in the lift soon, he'd throw him out the window.

Kabbaj was white with shock. Zarti had saved his most chilling remark for him. "You are only a Moroccan here in Libya," he said. "I can make you disappear, and nobody will ever hear back from you."[27]

The LIA's outrage didn't stop there. In 2014, the LIA sued Goldman Sachs in a UK high court, charging that Goldman had employed "undue influence" over the "naïve and unsophisticated" LIA. The LIA also criticized Goldman's fees, the unsuitability of the trades for a sovereign wealth fund, and the improper influence Goldman had gained through the hospitality and the internship the bank had provided.[28] The "undue influence" argument is typically used in marital disputes, where one party is said to have so much power over the other that the contract between them is not valid.[29] It was a new argument in financial litigation and one Goldman needed to defeat to avoid setting a precedent that might benefit other aggrieved clients.

When the trial began in 2016, the details of the fancy hotels, prostitutes, and internships came spilling out, as did accounts of the LIA's weak financial expertise and the high-risk investments that Goldman's team had peddled so aggressively. One advisor to the LIA testified that he had felt "almost under attack" at one meeting with Goldman Sachs representatives, who "acted like a swarm" in pursuit of the fund's business.[30] Goldman contested all parts of the LIA's claim. The bank argued that the trades represented legitimate commercial transactions and the LIA was simply suffering from "buyer's remorse." The bank contended that their relationship "never went beyond the ordinary relationship of a bank selling investment products to a wealthy client."[31]

In the end, the court ruled with the bank. The judge found that the fees earned by Goldman did not seem excessive and that even if the LIA's junior staff were naïve, the fund's top brass understood the deals that they were making. The internship and the hospitality arranged by Kabbaj appeared inappropriate and in violation of the bank's own policies, but they did not cause the LIA to enter into the trades. Overall, the judge found that the "relationship did not go beyond the normal relationship that grows up between a bank and a client."[32] Indeed, she cited how around twenty other banks had feted LIA staff as well. The large fees, the internship, the fancy travel, and the complementary training courses were all just part of doing business, as was the LIA's enormous financial loss.

In contrast to Goldman, another bank more obviously crossed the line in their efforts to lure the LIA into high-fee investments. The LIA also sued the large French bank Société Générale (SocGen), with whom the LIA had invested $2.1 billion. By 2009, the LIA had lost $1.5 billion of this amount too.[33] The lawsuit claimed that SocGen had paid millions of dollars to a Panamanian consulting company, Leinada, and that one of Leinada's owners, a politically connected Libyan businessman, had then channeled some of the funds to the Gaddafi family and other top officials in exchange for directing LIA business to the French bank.

When the accusations first became public in 2014, SocGen denied wrong-doing and called the allegations "unfounded."[34] The bank would slowly walk back this statement. In 2017, SocGen chose to pay $1.1 billion, an enormous sum, to the LIA to settle the lawsuit. The bank accompanied the decision with a statement that placed the blame on a few of its personnel: "Société Générale wishes to place on record its regret about the lack of caution of some of its employees. Société Générale apologises to the LIA and hopes that the challenges faced at this difficult time in Libya's development are soon overcome."[35] In 2018, the bank finally made a fuller admission and pleaded guilty to bribery. In a settlement agreement negotiated with the French and US governments, the bank admitted to paying some $90 million to Libyan middlemen entities and that some of that money had gone to bribe top Libyan officials.[36]

When the LIA entered into its ill-fated trades with Goldman and SocGen, Gaddafi was enjoying the thirty-first year of his repressive rule, unaware that his days were numbered. A couple of years later, the Arab Spring spread across North Africa, and revolution took hold of Libya. After months of fighting, rebels captured and killed their so-called Great Leader. A transitional government took over, attempting the difficult task of building a state on weak and unstable foundations. Due largely to long-standing regional divisions, the state-building effort soon fell apart. As of 2019, Libya has no agreed government, only competing political factions and an array of militant groups. Should a single government ever emerge, the billions of dollars that remain in the LIA will be a critical resource for rebuilding the country, albeit one that could have been larger were it not for the deals the LIA made with SocGen and Goldman Sachs.

The Men in the Middle

While Goldman Sachs saddled its own staff with the task of wooing government officials, SocGen went the popular route of outsourcing this risky function to an intermediary.

Also called middlemen, agents, or fixers, intermediaries can provide legitimate services, often when a company is trying to enter an unfamiliar country. However, they sometimes help their clients engage in corrupt behavior while providing a layer of insulation from the wrongdoing. Some intermediaries are individuals for hire who have good connections with the bigwigs in a given country. Others are companies who specialize in providing their clients with a leg up in new or challenging environments. Either way, working with them carries high corruption risks. Sometimes they are only paid if the oil company succeeds in winning the business opportunity that they seek. The intermediaries' business model depends on providing their clients with a special advantage over the competition, above and beyond whatever technical or financial capacities the client brings to the table.

Intermediaries feature frequently in the oil boom corruption cases, especially those involving companies trying to gain favor with governments. One question permeates them all, and it is often quite difficult to answer: did the middlemen take money from their clients and use it to pay government officials? In other words, were they intermediaries for bribery?

In 2016, police in Monaco raided the offices of a company called Unaoil and held its top executives overnight for questioning. The next day, *The Age* and the *Huffington Post* released a series of stories based on a leak of over 10,000 internal Unaoil files. In the months and years that followed, authorities in Australia, the United Kingdom, and the United States opened investigations of some of Unaoil's most prominent clients, including several of the largest oilfield service companies in the world. By 2018, the United Kingdom had charged four Unaoil executives with conspiracy to make corrupt payments to Iraqi government officials in order to help the company's clients win valuable contracts.[37] One of them, Basil Al Jarah,

Unaoil's lead representative in Iraq, pleaded guilty in 2019.[38] Client companies have admitted to enabling bribery via their Unaoil dealings too.[39] The other executives charged have denied any wrongdoing as have Unaoil's bosses who also claimed they were the victims of extortion.[40]

Companies hired Unaoil to take risks on their behalf. The Monaco-based firm specialized in helping oilfield service companies win business in difficult overseas markets, especially in Central Asia, the Middle East, and North Africa.

Iraq was just the sort of difficult operating environment where an actor like Unaoil came in handy. In the late 2000s, the country's oil sector was booming, with Western companies rushing in to snap up postwar opportunities. Iraq boasts 150 billion barrels in oil reserves, the fourth largest in the world. Much of the oil is located onshore and is relatively cheap to extract, making the potential profits all the more enticing. Production levels more than doubled between 2007 and 2015, creating countless juicy prospects for upstream companies, service companies and, of course, middlemen. As this frenzy unfolded, Nouri al-Maliki was serving as prime minister of this fractious and unstable country. Under his rule, reconstruction and reconciliation stalled, insecurity and sectarian tensions escalated, and public services failed to improve. Corruption thrived, including in the oil sector.

The leaked emails, published by *The Age* and the *Huffington Post*, provide a glimpse of how some of the deals worked. In early 2008, the CEO of Unaoil received an email from Al Jarah, his top employee in Iraq. It concerned how much to pay two government contacts Al Jarah called Jassim and Lighthouse. Al Jarah wrote to his boss: "at the time of award, our sub agents were on: $10 per drum for Jassim and $3 for Lighthouse. Since the involvement this year of new friends in the Ministry, I shifted $5 from Jassim's share and gave it to Ministry people. Total is still $13. Although I'd like to increase Lighthouse's share by $1–2, he has been the most helpful to us."[41]

Two months later, Al Jarah wrote to his boss again, imploring him to squeeze a meeting with the helpful senior official known as Lighthouse onto his schedule. To make his point, Al Jarah listed the ways Lighthouse, a carefully groomed contact, had helped Unaoil over the past three years. While some of the shorthand is difficult to interpret, the list suggests that Lighthouse served as "a friend in a nest of vipers." He lobbied for Unaoil's interests, provided insider information, and perhaps overlooked some shortcomings in the work provided by Unaoil's clients. Al Jarah's list of Lighthouse's contributions is as follows:

(1) Process Al Kassim order,

(2) Keep lid on product quality issues.

(3) Pushed for Unaoil's side on 2891, 3403 3253 (Demulsifier and Corr. Inhb enquiries) even though these didn't materialize or were canceled.

(4) First hand source info, particularly on what is happening on chemicals in SOC [one of Iraq's national oil companies].

(5) Metering comes under him now. His dept. is currently processing the two FMC offers. [FMC Technologies was one of Unaoil's clients.]

(6) Sludge cleaner enquiry comes under him, we have an offer on that being evaluated.

(7) Process letter we require to the field and Ministry, being a friend in a nest of vipers.

(8) Promoted to deputy [director general] late last year. Possibly takes over as [director general] later this year.

(9) Politically well connected. When Prime Minsters visit [*sic*] Basrah, he accompanies them first and holds private sessions with them. While [director general] is kept out.

At first, according to the leaked emails, Unaoil offered just the basics to build their relationship with Lighthouse. Al Jarah took the official clothes shopping ("around $1–2K each time"), arranged English classes for his son, and helped organize his application for a UAE visa. But eventually Unaoil began to provide him with a cut of the business he helped their clients win. For instance, they discussed giving Lighthouse a full 1 percent of the total value of a contract sought after by one of their big US clients, FMC Technologies.[42]

Lighthouse was far from the only entry in Unaoil's Iraqi Rolodex. According to the leaked emails, Kifah Numan was a government official who had influence over the award of a contract sought by the UK-based engineering company Rolls-Royce, a Unaoil client. Al Jarah worked to befriend Kifah, and this task required spending some money. The Unaoil home office questioned some of his expenses. Like most employees, Al Jarah felt annoyed by having his expense report queried and fired off a testy email in response:

Mr. Kifah is our key contact to obtaining the current contract valued at $17m (Job number 730) and I am pursuing him hard for the next set of turbines valued in excess of $23m.... Getting hold of Kifah to just spend any time with him is a bonus other contractor/suppliers would give their right arm for. Hence spending $2,684 on a key decision maker and remain in his good books to process things like name change from RR to Unaoil, is worth 100 times that value without which we would have no contract in our hands now. Plus the fact is I need help now, this month, not in two year's time. When contract is settled.

The occasion for the gift expenditure as explained earlier, comes as and when circumstance dictate, I am never one to spend willy nilly unless en-sure every penny counts. There is no way I am going to go to one side of the shop to call for board member to approve spending $2k on a valued customer, I'd sooner pay it myself and forget about it.[43]

Other government contacts required far more than $2,000 to influence. Emails from 2010 suggest that Unaoil planned to pay $4.5 million to influ-ence two other top officials, nicknamed "M" and "Teacher," regarding a $750 million pipeline contract sought by one of their client companies.[44] That same year, Unaoil offered payouts of $1 million to help their British client Petrofac win a different contract. For that transaction, according to the leaked emails, Al Jarah wanted help sidelining a competitor company, Weatherford, to clear the way for Petrofac. The key to the deal, he ex-plained, was "to remove Wetherford [sic] from the list and clear the way and support for Petrofac to win this order.... We are now agreed the figure 1 [million] for this service. But Petrofac must win so we have to follow it through and you get paid when we get paid."

The leaked Unaoil files detail arrangements in other Middle Eastern coun-tries, including Kuwait, Syria, the UAE, and Yemen. In Algeria, Libya, and Tunisia, the company also ran major operations, including helping Korean companies win $1.8 billion in refinery construction contracts from Algeria's national oil company. Unaoil worked the scene in Azerbaijan and Kazakhstan and sought to expand their reach in African countries, including Angola and Equatorial Guinea. In Congo-Brazzaville, they orchestrated an elabo-rate cross-border deal to help their client bid for a $400 million gas proj-ect. One journalist marveled at that deal's complexity: "people inside an Italian multinational provided illicit information to an Iranian operating in a Dubai-based company, which forwarded it to an Iranian-Englishman liv-ing in Monaco with a British Virgin Islands–registered firm. It was all being done to benefit a Greek company, registered in Lebanon, which wanted to bid on a contract in West Africa."[45]

Sourcing insider information, winning over fickle politicians, predict-ing which way a tender is leaning—this is all hard work in today's oil industry. Moreover, Unaoil often only got paid if its client won the con-tract. Unaoil's staff felt the stress. The company's hard-working Iraq lead,

Al Jarah, wrote: "it's a lot of travel, and I feel like a cockle-shot at the moment, but Iraqis have restriction in travel and I am obliged to go see them where and when I can." In another email, he vented again: "You will not believe the amount of lobbying and chasing we are doing for this job....I am even talking to turban heads to bear influence on the auditors. This is in addition to our people pushing at the ministry plus [a national oil company] getting frantic pressing of the ministry for results....So please don't think nothing is happening because I am keeping quite [sic], only when I receive some solid news I will write in."

Since then, Al Jarah's circumstances have shifted but not eased. In 2017, British authorities charged him with "conspiracy to make corrupt payments to secure the award of contracts in Iraq to Unaoil's client SBM Offshore," a large Dutch oilfield service company. A year later, the British tacked on another charge for making corrupt payments on behalf of different client company that was competing for a $733 million pipeline construction contract, also in Iraq.[46] Al Jarah pleaded guilty in 2019.[47]

A bevy of Unaoil clients have also faced criminal proceedings. SBM Offshore reached a settlement with US authorities in 2017 regarding bribery charges in five countries, including Iraq, and agreed to pay $238 million in fines.[48] Two of its executives received prison sentences. The DOJ also settled with FMC Technologies, a US company that routed corrupt payments via Unaoil, including to the individual nicknamed "Lighthouse."[49] A senior executive at Petrofac pleaded guilty to UK charges of bribery in Iraq, which related to the company's business with Unaoil.[50] As of 2019, investigations into several other Unaoil clients remained open.

One tie binds most of Unaoil's clients: they all sought oilfield service contracts. The record suggests that corruption thrives in the oilfield services sector. Of the oil industry cases pursued by the United States under the FCPA, a majority have targeted oilfield service contractors, including the case against the industry leader Halliburton described below. Along with Iraq, recent investigations by US and UK anti-corruption authorities have targeted possible bribery by service companies in Algeria, Angola, Brazil, Colombia, Ecuador, Equatorial Guinea, Kazakhstan, Nigeria, Saudi Arabia, and Venezuela. Corruption in service contracting will rear its head again later in this book, during my discussions of the corruption scandal that engulfed Brazil's national oil company, Petrobras, and the rent-seeking strategies of political elites in Angola, Azerbaijan, and Russia. The prevalence of corruption risks in the oilfield services sector is one clear takeaway from the oil boom record.

The same can be said for oil trading. One oil-trading company, Gunvor, faced a major corruption investigation related to its activities in Congo-Brazzaville. In chapter 4 I discuss how Gunvor received huge business opportunities in Russia and used them to become one of the largest oil traders in the world. Years later, as the oil boom gathered steam, Gunvor sought to diversify away from Russian oil and set their sights on Africa's trading markets.

Around 2008, Gunvor began targeting opportunities in Congo-Brazzaville, a longtime oil producer in Central Africa.[51] At the time, Congo-Brazzaville produced around 300,000 barrels per day, making it the fourth largest producer in sub-Saharan Africa. The country is highly oil dependent, with over two-thirds of the government's revenues coming from the oil sector during the boom years. The president, Denis Sassou Nguesso, has used oil money to strengthen his hold on power since taking office in 1979. Corruption is one of his favored tactics: the country ranks 159th out of 176 countries on Transparency International's Corruption Perception Index, and major scandals have rocked the oil sector in the past. Oil revenues have been kind to Sassou Nguesso, his high-flying family, and his political inner circle but have done little to benefit most of the country's 4 million people, a third of whom live on less than $2 a day.

Gunvor sought to join the companies who buy oil regularly from Congo-Brazzaville's national oil company. Like most national oil companies, this one receives a significant share of the country's oil production. It then has to sell that oil, and trading companies like Gunvor have perfected the art of making money off of such deals. It can be a messy business: the watchdog group Global Witness alleged that, in the early 2000s, Congo-Brazzaville's national oil company sold oil to two companies owned by top political figures, including the boss of the national oil company himself.[52] But by the time the oil boom was cranking along at full throttle, the national oil company preferred to sell to large international traders who could pay for the oil up front, thereby increasing the government's immediate cash flow.

To break into Congo-Brazzaville's oil trade, Gunvor offered a couple of big sweeteners, according to reports by the Swiss NGO Public Eye as well as journalists at the Organized Crime and Corruption Reporting Project (OCCRP). Gunvor first offered access to the Kremlin.[53] According to Public Eye's report, one of Gunvor's founders flew the son of President Sassou Nguesso to Moscow on his private jet in 2010 and provided introductions to top Russian officials and businesspeople.[54] Months later, Russia and Congo-Brazzaville signed an economic cooperation agreement focused on the energy sector, with Putin's government committing to support Russian companies who invested in Congolese oil. Second, Gunvor offered loans. They were willing to pay for large volumes of oil up front and then receive delivery of that oil over an agreed period of time.

Gunvor's efforts did not stop there. In 2007, they recruited a Belgian man, Pascal Collard, to join their staff. Drawing on his deep experience working in Africa, Collard set about trying to win over top Congolese decision-makers in order to secure oil trading deals for his employer. The deals he struck are described in the indictment and judgment against him filed in a Swiss court: in 2018, he was found guilty of bribing Congolese officials.[55]

The indictment and the judgment lay out how Collard negotiated agreements between Gunvor and several front companies. Gunvor then paid these companies millions of dollars, in some cases for purportedly serving as Gunvor's agents. A large portion of these payments ended up enriching sitting government officials and members of Sassou Nguesso's family, often passing through other offshore intermediaries and bank accounts before reaching their final destination. The Swiss indictment alleges that the officials who received payoffs included the president, the first lady, the president's son, the president's nephew, the minister of finance, and a senior national oil company official, though these individuals have not been charged with any crimes.[56] The judgment against Collard concludes that he fully intended for these payments to reach the officials and set up the partnerships with the intermediary companies for this express purpose.[57]

For example, here's how the indictment describes one of the partnerships Collard arranged with Maxime Gandzion, a presidential advisor and prominent dealmaker:

> In order to obtain the crude oil marketing contract with the SOCIETE NATIONALE DES PETROLES DU CONGO (SNPC) [the national oil company], Pascal COLLARD, working with other GUNVOR employees, made a corrupt agreement with Maxime GANDZION [a presidential aide] according to which remuneration paid by GUNVOR to his company PETROLIA E&P SA under an agency agreement would be used to pay Maxime GANDZION and the family of the President of the Republic of Congo, in particular Denis Christel SASSOU NGUESSO and his father [the president], Denis SASSOU NGUESSO.[58]

Gunvor ended up doing big business in Congo-Brazzaville during the boom years. The charges against Collard indicate that Gunvor won a three-year oil marketing contract and prepayment deals worth at least $625 million.

Public Eye estimates that Gunvor traded over \$2 billion in Congolese oil altogether during the period 2010–2012.[59] Along with their large size, the deals may have brought in higher than usual profits. The Swiss prosecutors suggest that Collard negotiated a favorable approach to pricing the oil that Gunvor traded and Congolese officials received a cut of the extra profits.[60] In its investigation of Gunvor, Public Eye discussed Gunvor's Congolese deals with an executive at a Swiss bank who commented: "when margins are above 1%, I begin to have my doubts. Beyond 1.5% I no longer have doubts. No service can possibly justify such margins. . . . The lack of competitive bidding and the extent of the margins that traders realise explain why we stopped financing operations in Congo."[61]

Gunvor's payments to intermediary companies eventually attracted concern. In 2011, an official at a Swiss bank alerted authorities to suspicious inflows to one of the intermediary companies' accounts. Not long after, Swiss police raided Gunvor's offices. Gunvor quickly fired Collard, filed a criminal complaint of fraud and embezzlement against him, and laid blame for the whole mess at his feet. Gunvor stated: "our systems of internal control were misused by our former employee to get rich at the cost of Gunvor."[62] According to Gunvor, they had been fleeced by Collard, who had a "marked desire to fragment, compartmentalize and falsify information, purposely preventing his colleagues from having a concrete and overall view of the facts that have occurred in Congo-Brazzaville."[63] Gunvor has also responded that it has worked to improve its anticorruption and compliance systems in recent years and has wound down its business in Congo-Brazzaville.

But was just one bad egg to blame? The Swiss indictment emphasized repeatedly that Collard executed the corrupt deals and payments in collaboration with other colleagues at Gunvor. The Swiss prosecutor said that Collard "bathed in a working atmosphere wherein corruption was apparently accepted as a normal business practice."[64] Meanwhile, Gunvor fiercely denies these characterizations.

Swiss courts may help settle the dispute. The government widened their investigation into Gunvor in 2017 to look into whether the company's behavior involved more than just benign neglect of one rogue employee. Pascal Collard will assist this investigation, thanks to the plea bargain he struck with the Swiss authorities.[65] The investigation, which remained open when this book went to press, will likely hinge on the questions that are difficult to answer whenever payments to middlemen are involved: how did money from Gunvor accounts end up in the pocket of Congolese government officials? And who at the company was aware this was happening?

Holding Their Noses

Along with wooing foreign governments, executives have proven willing to snuggle up to some pretty unsavory people and practices in order to maintain their good standing in oil-rich countries. In many cases, the foreign company acts as a host that rent-seeking parasites feed off of. Such behavior is more subtle than bribery and tougher to prosecute under many antibribery laws.

Angola was a hotbed of activities like this, with foreign companies regularly partnering up with political elites in order to hold onto profitable business opportunities. The country produced around 1.8 million barrels per day during the oil boom years, making it the second largest producer in sub-Saharan Africa behind Nigeria. Chapter 5 delves into how former Angolan president José Eduardo dos Santos and his inner circle held tight control over the oil sector during the boom years and used it to enrich themselves. This strategy relied on the willingness of foreign companies to play along.

Quite a few scenarios suggest that they did play along, through various witting and unwitting forms. In 2010, to gain access to a big offshore oil block in Angola, the US company Cobalt agreed to partner with a previously unknown local company partly owned by top government officials.[66] In 2011, Cobalt, along with BP and Norway's Statoil, agreed to pay a whopping $400 million to fund a "research center" run by Angola's powerful national oil company, Sonangol. Unsurprisingly, as of 2017, this research center remained "in the planning stages."[67] The Swiss oil-trading company Trafigura partnered with a number of companies controlled by General Leopoldino Fragoso do Nascimento, a core member of President dos Santos's inner circle who has held several top positions in the regime.[68] The Chinese company Queensway Group also orchestrated a slew of oil sector deals that helped political elites get rich.[69]

Each of these examples, explored more in chapter 5, shows how companies were willing to follow the dos Santos playbook in order to participate in the lucrative Angolan oil sector. But the story of Halliburton in Angola is perhaps the most fascinating, as it reveals how oil boom temptations can run roughshod over the carefully designed corporate rules and procedures meant to safeguard against corruption. Legal documents filed by the SEC detail what went wrong.[70]

The Frenchman Jeannot Lorenz knew that lucrative business would flow his way if he could just please the right people.[71] He lived in Angola and worked as a vice-president of Halliburton, the US oilfield services giant. In

Angola, as in most of the countries where it operates, Halliburton lives off of large contracts awarded by the upstream companies that operate the country's oilfields. In Angola, Halliburton cannot receive these contracts without the approval of Sonangol. For several years, Sonangol had complained that Halliburton was not subcontracting enough of its business to local Angolan companies and threatened to cut it off from receiving future contracts. Halliburton tasked Lorenz with handling this problem.

According to the SEC filing, in 2010, Lorenz arranged for Halliburton to sign contracts with a local company owned by an individual who was a friend and neighbor of the very Sonangol official who would approve the contracts Halliburton sought to win. Halliburton made payments worth a total of $3.7 million to the local company and received negligible services in return. During the months that followed, thanks to Sonangol's approvals, Halliburton went on to win seven contracts that added $14 million to their profits.[72]

What's fascinating about this case is that Halliburton's own internal systems *almost* stopped the corruption from moving ahead. According again to the SEC filing, Lorenz first proposed to hire the local company as a commercial agent and pay it a fee worth 2 percent of Halliburton's Angolan revenues. But Lorenz's managers rejected the deal, as Halliburton has rules against hiring agents for existing contracts. The managers also wanted to avoid the extensive due diligence requirements for new agents, measures adopted by the company after its run-in with the FCPA over corruption in Nigeria several years earlier.

Not one to be deterred, Lorenz tried another tack. Maybe Halliburton could outsource some easy functions to the local company. Once again, he ran into pesky procedures: Halliburton policy requires that subcontractors are chosen through competitive bidding, so he had to run a tender. After several tense months of waiting, the tender took place, and the local company performed poorly. Its bids for providing real estate maintenance and ground transportation services were astronomically higher than those from the other bidding companies.

Again foiled by Halliburton's own safeguards, Lorenz cobbled together a third attempt. The SEC's vividly drafted statement explains what happened next: "desperate for a solution, and feeling intense pressure to get the deal with the local Angolan company done, Lorenz and others pivoted from the outsourced services contemplated under the bidding process to a new proposal where the local Angolan company would lease commercial and residential real estate and then sublease the properties to Halliburton at a substantial markup, and also provide real estate transactions management consulting services. The preferred local Angolan company had minimal experience in these areas and the services could have been provided more cheaply if done internally by Halliburton personnel."[73] Working along these lines, Lorenz signed a letter of intent with the local company in early 2010. The local company then informed Sonangol officials that the deal had gone through so that Halliburton could regain its good standing. The deal would pay the local company $275,000 per month over four years to provide certain real estate services. A month later, personnel in Halliburton's Finance and Accounting department raised concerns about the contract, especially the high cost, the absence of a tender, and the decision to backdate the agreement by a number of months. The concerns ran up the chain, but senior executives allowed the deal to go forward. According to the SEC, they "believed that by this time only this agreement with the local Angolan company would satisfy Sonangol as to Halliburton's local content commitments."[74]

Unsurprisingly, Halliburton did not receive great service from its latest subcontractor. For example, they failed to produce the analysis required by the agreement, "except for one unfinished report that was found in Lorenz's house in Angola in 2011 that appeared to be plagiarized wholly from internet sources."[75] Eventually, in 2011, Halliburton ended the deal, concerned that the misconduct had gone too far. They proactively reported the incident to the SEC, a common practice for companies seeking to negotiate a more lenient deal in the face of wrongdoing. In 2017, they settled with the SEC and paid a modest fine of $29 million. Lorenz, who left Halliburton in 2013, agreed to pay $75,000.[76]

Halliburton may pin blame for the scenario on Lorenz, the same way Gunvor blames Collard for its misadventures in Congo-Brazzaville. In both cases, the midlevel executives may well have been the chief architects of the deals. But these individuals operated within sophisticated company systems and navigated the various hierarchies, procedures, and approvals to undertake their dirty business. These systems and the corporate leaders atop them should shoulder some of the blame.

Not So "Safe Sex" After All

Two of the world's largest oil companies ignored major corruption risks in order to secure control over one of Africa's most promising oil blocks. This decision has come back to bite them. In one of the most dramatic stories of the oil boom and its aftermath, the companies and a number of their top executives now face trial in Italy on criminal charges of bribery.

In 2011, Royal Dutch Shell and Eni bought the rights to Nigeria's Oil Prospecting License (OPL) number 245 for $1.3 billion. The block, which holds large reserves of oil, had quite the checkered past. In 1998, the famously repressive and corrupt military dictator Sani Abacha still ruled Nigeria. In a blatant case of self-dealing, Abacha's minister of petroleum, Dan Etete, awarded OPL 245 to Malabu Oil and Gas, a company that he himself owned along with Abacha's son.[77] Etete established Malabu just five days before the award. Needless to say, the company did not have much relevant experience or financial resources, and it paid just $2 million for the world-class asset. Soon after, Abacha died under suspicious circumstances in the company of several prostitutes, the country held elections in 1999, and a period of civilian rule began. Etete lost his position during the transition, and in the years that followed his reputation worsened still further, with a money laundering conviction in France that involved the purchase of a speedboat, a chateau, and a club membership at the Ritz.[78]

The ownership of OPL 245 remained contested for years to follow. The Nigerian government transferred ownership from Malabu to Shell for a few years, but then reversed their decision and agreed to restore Malabu's claim if Malabu paid the government a $210 million signature bonus. Legal wrangling ensued as Shell sought to reinstate their rights. By 2011, Malabu still held claim to OPL 245 but had not paid the $210 million. With oil prices soaring, the government of Goodluck Jonathan wanted to transfer the block into the hands of a company better placed to ramp up production. They also wanted to make some money in the process.

Chapter 3 tells the broader story of how oil sector corruption escalated under the Jonathan government in 2010–2015. By 2011, Shell and Eni would have been well aware of this emerging trend, as they had run large operations in Nigeria for several decades. As a tide of oil sector corruption rose around them, executives from the two companies undertook a hugely risky deal.

If Nigeria's government had wanted to maximize its long-term returns from OPL 245, they would have dismissed Malabu's claim, settled the dispute with Shell, and run an open and competitive tender for the rights to the asset. Instead, the government entered into private negotiations with Shell, Eni, and Malabu over a period of months. After countless back-and-forths, Shell and Eni agreed to pay the $210 million signature bonus Malabu owed, along with an additional $1.1 billion, in order to secure control over OPL 245. The $210 million signature bonus appears to have entered the government's budget. The companies paid the remaining $1.1 billion—a figure nearly equal to the country's entire health budget that year—into a special Nigerian government bank account set up for this very transaction, and the funds then quickly escaped into private hands.

According to the Italian indictment and other sources, the Nigerian government transferred $800 million to two Malabu accounts controlled by Etete.[79] As shown in figure 2.3, Etete got to keep around $250 million of this transfer, which he enjoyed by purchasing such trinkets as a $57 million jet and an armored car.[80]

Abubakar Aliyu, an alleged associate of President Jonathan who has earned the nickname "Mr. Corruption" in Nigeria, received $520 million in cash.[81] If the Italian and Nigerian charges against Aliyu are proven true, he managed to receive, move, and distribute nearly 6 tons of cash (assuming US$100 was the bill of choice)—a stunning logistical feat that would make excellent content for Nigeria's thriving film industry. According to the Italian indictment, Aliyu parceled out the money to government officials, including the president, petroleum minister, attorney general, and national security advisor, and delivered $50 million in cash to the house of Eni's Africa manager.[82] After Jonathan lost the 2015 elections to an opposition party challenger, the Nigerian government confirmed this account of events in a document filed in a UK court in 2019, providing its own detailed accusations about how these individuals received large bribes via Malabu's accounts.[83] A number of the alleged recipients, including former president Jonathan and the former attorney general, deny any involvement, and none has been convicted of wrongdoing.[84]

Disputes over the remaining $290 million were what turned the OPL 245 deal into a full-blown public scandal. A number of middlemen helped facilitate the negotiations between the government, Shell, Eni, and Malabu. After the deal closed, two of the middlemen felt that they had not received adequate payment from Malabu for their services and argued that some of the $290 million was theirs.[85] So they brought civil cases to court in London, and the court proceedings dragged details of the deal out into the public domain.

Prompted by the new revelations, media coverage picked up in 2013. Global Witness and other public interest groups kept the heat on, pushing for the companies to face consequences. Law enforcement in the United States, the United Kingdom, Italy, Switzerland, and the Netherlands took note and opened investigations, as did the Nigerian authorities after Jonathan

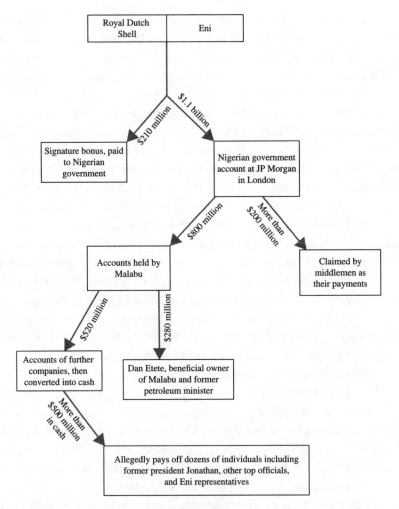

FIGURE 2.3 The alleged OPL 245 money flows.

SOURCE: Sarah Kent and Eric Sylvers, "Inside the Bribery Scandal Sweeping through the Oil Industry," *Wall Street Journal*, February 13, 2018; Global Witness, *Shell Knew*, April 10, 2017; Milan Court, Preliminary Investigations Magistrate Section, Indictment, December 2, 2017, https://shellandenitrial.org/wp-content/uploads/2018/06/decision-to-open-trial-20.12.2017_English.pdf; Federal High Court of Nigeria, Charges against Aliyu Abubakar et al., Charge No. CR/39/201, December 16, 2016, https://shellandenitrial.org/wp-content/uploads/2018/08/2-Adoke-etc-Nigeria-charges-scanned-2.pdf.

left office. In 2016, Dutch and Italian police raided Shell's offices. The next year, Nigerian authorities charged a number of players in the scheme, including Etete, Aliyu, and the former attorney general who helped arrange the deal, though no trial has followed.[86] Then Italian prosecutors filed bribery charges against Eni, Shell, and several of their top executives. In 2018, an Italian court convicted two of the middlemen in the deal and sentenced them each to four years in prison. Later that year, the historic trial against Shell, Eni, and their executives began. Two of the largest oil companies in the world, the current and former CEOs of Eni, and prominent top figures at Shell all face the prospect of criminal conviction. The trial was ongoing when this book went to press.

Throughout this saga, Shell, Eni, and the accused individuals have maintained their innocence. In various statements, both companies have consistently argued that they paid the Nigerian government and have no responsibility for what the government then did with the funds. According to a Shell spokesperson, speaking in 2018, "if the evidence ultimately proves that improper payments were made...it is Shell's position that none of those payments were made with its knowledge, authorization or on its behalf." Representatives of Eni echoed this sentiment in 2018: "it was the prerogative, right and at the discretion of the Nigerian government to decide...how to use the price received from Eni and Shell."[87] Commenting on this defense, one Global Witness investigator explained that Shell and Eni tried to structure the OPL 245 acquisition as a "safe-sex transaction," with the government acting as a "condom" between Shell and Eni on one hand and Malabu, Etete, and other recipients on the other.[88]

It may not be so safe after all.

After the 2016 office raid, Shell's CEO, Ben Van Beurden, called his CFO to gripe. "Apparently there are some really unhelpful emails in there.... The people we hired from MI6 who must have said things like 'I wonder who gets a payoff here and whatever.'"[89] Indeed, some very unhelpful emails appear to undermine Shell's and Eni's "safe sex" defense. Some of these emails were published by Global Witness and several media outlets, and they indicate that senior Shell executives suspected all along that the money they paid for OPL 245 would not remain with the Nigerian government for long.

Some of the emails date back to 2009, when a round of negotiations over OPL 245 was just getting under way. Already Shell knew that Etete had to profit from the deal for it to work and that he might not be the only one seeking to cash in. Shell's strategic investment advisor, John Copleston, indeed a former member of the British intelligence service MI6, wrote to Shell's vice-president for Africa, Peter Robinson, and other top executives, relaying a conversation with one of his contacts: "he spoke to Mrs. E [Etete's wife] this morning. She says E claims he will only get 300m we offering [sic]—rest goes in paying people off." Despite this warning of the planned payoffs, the negotiations continued. Copleston and Robinson met with Etete regularly, often at Paris hotels. "We are getting along very well personally—lunch and lots of iced champagne," wrote Copleston.[90]

In 2010, the negotiations picked up pace amid a highly politicized context, as President Jonathan sought resources to finance his 2011 election campaign. Eni commissioned an external risk report on Etete that raised substantial red flags about his background and his claim on OPL 245.[91] Guy Colegate, another Shell hand in Nigeria who came from MI6, provided an entirely astute briefing to Shell executives on the political climate, saying: "in Abuja it is still a case of all politics and no government. Jockeying for ministerial positions remains intense, with many aspirants offering substantial sums to purchase their way into office....With an election only 10 months away the need to build war chests for campaigning is strong."[92]

The political context worked in Etete's favor. He was friendly with President Jonathan and knew that Jonathan needed cash for political purposes, as electioneering in Nigeria is exorbitantly expensive. In 2010, Etete informed Colegate that Jonathan had written a letter confirming Malabu's rights to OPL 245. Colegate then reported the situation to Shell's Robinson, categorizing the letter as "clearly an attempt to deliver significant revenues to GLJ [Goodluck Jonathan] as part of any transaction." He added, "This is about personal gain and politics." Another email from Colegate, forwarded to Shell's CEO, reported: "Etete can smell the money. If at nearly 70 years old he does turn his nose up at nearly $1.2 bill he is completely certifiable. But I think he knows it's his for the taking."

Robinson echoed this analysis in another email, again obtained and published by Global Witness. He explained that "the President is motivated to see 245 closed quickly—driven by expectations about the proceeds the Malabu will receive and political contributions that will flow as a consequence."

By then, Eni was closely involved, and Attorney General Mohammed Bello Adoke had taken over brokering the negotiations for the Nigerian government. The contours of the deal began to firm up. In January 2011, Shell's head of exploration Malcolm Brinded told then CEO Peter Voser that the $1.1 billion payment "will be used by the FGN [Federal Government of Nigeria] to settle all claims from Malabu." Revealing Shell's fervent desire to be done with Malabu and Etete, he also wrote: "An absolute condition of this is that M [Malabu] are 100% out of the block!!"[93]

By April, the deal was done. Robinson emailed his Shell colleagues about the accomplishment: "Malabu initialed all agreements. Compliments to our legal team who have done a brilliant job." Shell and Eni had OPL 245, and Malabu and friends had $1.1 billion.

All these emails are important because they weaken Shell and Eni's "safe sex" defense. Rather than paying for the oil block with a good faith expectation that the revenues would benefit Nigeria, leaders at Shell and Eni appear to have strongly suspected that the payments would end up funding election campaigns and enriching government officials. Etete and his colleagues received the rights to OPL 245 via a highly corrupt allocation process back in 1998. In 2011, thanks to the deal agreed with Shell and Eni, they received hundreds of millions of dollars as a reward for this behavior. According to the accusations laid out in the Italian prosecutor's case and Nigerian government court filings, top officials also secured large pay-outs, and company executives received a cut as well.[94] Nigeria received a paltry $210 million for one of its richest oil blocks, while the remaining $1.1 billion rewarded those who abused their positions of power. While the payoffs were structured differently than a typical bribe, the tactic employed by the oil companies did no less damage.

Collusion and Evasion

Many corruption cases from the oil boom took the form of those described above. Companies took inappropriate steps to influence government officials or took part in sketchy deals with sketchy partners. But these are not the only options available to companies. Collusion and tax avoidance are two other tactics that have reared their heads. Some definitions of corruption would leave out behaviors like these, even though they are prominent and problematic methods by which companies can trample the public interest.

One day before his death, US federal authorities indicted Aubrey McClendon for conspiring to rig bids for oil leases in Oklahoma. McClendon ran Chesapeake Energy from 1989 to 2013, a period when the company became one of the largest natural gas producers in the United States. An early champion of fracking, he aggressively sought opportunities to profit from the surge in shale gas production that swept the United States during the oil boom. Over ten years, Chesapeake acquired the exploration and production rights for more than 15 million acres of land in the United States, territory about the size of West Virginia, and McClendon became a billionaire.[95] He became famous in his home town, Oklahoma City, hobnobbing with its political leaders, helping revitalize the downtown, donating to scores of charities, and bringing a talented NBA team to town.

The federal collusion charges came in 2016. By that time, McClendon had been removed as CEO from Chesapeake, his net worth had dropped precipitously, and he owed large debts. The indictment alleged that McClendon had conspired with another company to rig the bid prices for several oil and gas leases in Oklahoma over the years 2007–2012. Leases of this kind give companies the right to explore for and produce oil and gas on the land for a period of time. In the United States, it's the landowner rather than the government who typically auctions off the rights, awarding them to the highest qualified bidder.

The DOJ accused Chesapeake and another company of agreeing not to compete with each other in order to keep lease prices down.[96] The two companies allegedly agreed in advance who would bid for various leases, and then the winner would offer the other company a share in the lease in exchange for their cooperation. The DOJ charged McClendon under the Sherman Act, an antitrust statute, and the violations carried a maximum penalty of ten years in prison. According to the attorney leading the case for the DOJ, McClendon "put company profits ahead of the interests of leaseholders entitled to competitive bids for oil and gas rights on their land. Executives who abuse their positions as leaders of major corporations to organize criminal activity must be held accountable for their actions."[97]

McClendon denied the charges immediately. "The charge that has been filed against me today is wrong and unprecedented," he stated. "All my life I have worked to create jobs in Oklahoma, grow its economy, and to provide abundant and affordable energy to all Americans. I am proud of my track record in this industry, and I will fight to prove my innocence and to clear my name."[98]

In 2015, Chesapeake had paid $25 million to the state of Michigan to settle a similar case.[99] The state government had charged Chesapeake with antitrust, fraud, and racketeering violations, all related to the company's quest to snap up natural gas leases at low prices. Unlike the federal charges of bid-rigging in Oklahoma, the Michigan case targeted the company rather than McClendon as an individual. Specifically, the state of Michigan accused Chesapeake of colluding with a competitor company, Encana Corp., to lower the bid prices for leases in 2010, just as the shale boom was gaining steam.

According to leaked emails, executives at Chesapeake and Encana collaborated to carve up the desirable Michigan territory so as to cool off lease prices. One top Chesapeake executive wrote to his counterpart: "also, when you are back in the saddle, I'd like to visit with you about the implications of the impact of our competition on acreage prices and whether or not the sooner we do this the better shot we have of keeping acreage prices from continuing to push up." Later, McClendon himself wrote to Encana about a third company, Northstar, which was offering leases on more than 30,000 Michigan acres. It "looks like Northstar wants us to bid against each other next week, let's discuss who should handle that one—thanks."[100]

Michigan prosecutors argue that the collusion contributed to the lease price falling from $1,510 per acre to just $40 per acre between auctions held just five months apart.[101] They also allege that Chesapeake canceled hundreds of leases on false pretenses. Around 700 landowners suffered losses due to these incidents, according to state authorities.

As part of a negotiated settlement, Chesapeake pleaded no contest to the misdemeanor charges of antitrust violations and false pretenses but did not admit to any criminal wrongdoing. The settlement saw the state drop the criminal charges, and Chesapeake paid $25 million into a compensation fund for the landowners. For its part, Encana also negotiated a deal, paid $5 million in fines and pleaded no-contest to a misdemeanor bid-rigging charge.[102] At the time of the agreement, Michigan's attorney general commented: "these hardworking Michigan residents took a big financial hit due to the actions of this company. I am pleased to see this settlement process moving forward and hope those who were negatively affected by this scam can continue their financial recovery."[103]

Unlike the case in Michigan, the Oklahoma case will never reach its conclusion. The day after the federal indictment, McClendon left his offices around 9 a.m. Driving seventy-eight miles per hour, his car crashed into the bottom of a bridge, and he died. Speculation swirled around the timing of the fifty-six-year-old's accident. Following an extensive investigation into the demise of one of their city's most prominent citizens, the Oklahoma City Police Department found no signs of suicide. One police captain added: "we may never know one-hundred percent what happened."[104]

Along with bid-rigging and collusion, tax avoidance and tax evasion are other risky strategies companies use to capture an outsized share of profits. The issue of tax fairness is a highly complex field unto itself, and one with enormous consequences for global economic affairs. Others tackle these issues much more fully and capably than I can here.[105] But tax avoidance still warrants mention if one is to appreciate the full range of controversial and potentially damaging tactics available to oil companies seeking to maximize their earnings.

Companies who want to lower their tax bills have a wide array of strategies at their disposal. Some are legal. For instance, by setting up subsidiaries in tax havens and assigning certain functions to them, multinational companies can reduce the taxes they owe in the countries where oil is actually produced and sold. Other strategies break the law, such as falsely inflating various costs in order to reduce a company's reported profits. As with the other kinds of corruption risks, some companies flirt with the edge of what's legal in order to make more money.

The government of Norway, with its ample expertise and resources, fought in court for years to prove that Transocean, the world's largest offshore drilling company, skirted an estimated $1.8 billion in tax payments. In 2005, Norwegian authorities opened an investigation into a number of suspicious transactions that had taken place since 1997. After spending years untangling the masterwork of Transocean's lawyers and accountants, prosecutors indicted the company and several of its Ernst & Young tax advisors in 2011.[106]

The indictment centered on the sale of oil rigs by Transocean's Norwegian subsidiary to various other subsidiaries in the company's global constellation.[107] For instance, prosecutors claimed that the sale of the Polar Pioneer, an oil rig, should have been subject to Norwegian capital gains tax, while Transocean claimed that the sale had taken place outside Norway. According to the indictment, the rig had worked in Norway since 1985 and was owned by Transocean's Norwegian division. In 1999, the rig was towed between two locations in Norway in order to receive routine maintenance. On its return journey, the company sent the rig on a sixteen-hour detour that included an eight-hour stint in international waters. During the eight-hour foreign foray, the rig was sold three times among different Transocean subsidiaries, the last of which was based in the tax haven of the Cayman Islands. Inventing these kinds of elaborate machinations—and making them legal—is the bread and butter of global tax advice these days. Transocean's team had done its job well. In 2014, the court ruled in their favor.

Chevron did not get off so easily in Australia. To help finance a major natural gas project, a Delaware-based subsidiary of Chevron lent $2.5 billion to Chevron's Australia division in 2003. The intercompany loan had an interest rate of 9 percent. The subsidiary had borrowed the funds from the commercial markets at a rate of 1–2 percent, resulting in profits for the subsidiary of nearly $1 billion between 2004 and 2008. These profits were not taxed in Australia or in Chevron's home country, the United States.[108] In 2015, the Australian Tax Office charged that the loan had enabled Chevron's Australia division to claim excessive interest deductions, resulting in an inappropriate reduction in its Australian tax bill. Specifically, the loan did not follow "arm's-length pricing," meaning basically that Chevron Australia could have secured the financing at a lower price from an external source. Instead, Chevron Australia had chosen to pay the higher interest rate to their internal partner so that they could then pay lower taxes. In 2017, Australian courts denied Chevron's appeal. To settle the affair, Chevron agreed to pay around $1 billion, including $340 million in back taxes, according to media reports, though the official figure was not released.[109]

One Australian senator spoke out in frustration. "This is a rort!" he exclaimed. "This has always been a rort and it continues to be a rort! In Chevron, we have the godfather of Australian tax minimization and, dare I say it, tax avoidance."[110] "Rort," it turns out, is a word Australians use to describe a fraudulent scheme. Indeed, Chevron is set up to minimize what it pays in taxes. Over half of the company's subsidiaries are based in tax havens, including Bermuda, the Bahamas, and Delaware, even though Chevron has no significant operations in those locations.[111]

While Chevron and other multinational oil companies have extensive architecture for minimizing their tax bills, cases like the one in Australia are rare. According to the accounting firm Deloitte, "the case was extremely complex involving multiple facets of tax law and was heard over some 21 court days making it one of the lengthiest tax cases heard in Australia."[112] Indeed, the settlement occurred in 2017, nearly a decade after the term of the loan had expired. The government prioritized pursuing the case because of the precedent it would set: the Australian Tax Office estimates that 2,600 companies claimed $11 billion in interest deductions on loans in 2014–2015.[113] With the win against Chevron, the Tax Office may be able to go after this money as well. Oxfam Australia estimates that Australia missed out on $4–5 billion in revenue in 2014 due to tax avoidance behaviors by multinational corporations.[114]

Australia is a rich country, and its government enjoys high levels of technical capacity. Given what it took to collect back taxes from Chevron, it is difficult to imagine oil-producing countries in the developing world achieving similar outcomes. Often disputes of this kind end in arbitration or more informal settlements, assuming that they are pursued at all. After all, hundreds of highly capable accountants and tax lawyers make a living from reducing tax burdens for large oil companies. Under the current global tax system, most of their maneuvers are legal. Even when they are not, the mind-blowing complexity of the system typically protects them from facing consequences.

Steep Costs and the Road Ahead

The oil boom shows the medley of ways that companies have bent the rules to access lucrative opportunities. They have paid bribes and otherwise buttered up foreign officials. They have looked the other way as local political elites skimmed off funds. They have cheated in tenders and avoided their taxes. Many of these moves have resulted in big paydays for the companies and individual executives, whether they got caught or not.

Does any of this really matter though? Of course it's unsightly, but isn't corruption just the reality of how things work in the global oil industry, especially in certain poorly governed countries? As the Unaoil executive said, it's difficult to find "a friend in a nest of vipers."

In fact, company corruption inflicts layers of harm. The first layer is the lost public revenues. Especially for many poor countries, the oil in the ground represents a rare source of funds to pay for social services and drive economic development. Because oil is a nonrenewable resource, countries only get one shot at accomplishing these aims. When companies take part in corruption, they keep this dynamic from succeeding. The government of Chad could have received a higher price for the oil blocks it awarded to Griffiths if it had awarded them through a competitive tender instead of back-room negotiations. The same goes for OPL 245 in Nigeria. The block was not awarded through a tender, and most of the money Shell and Eni paid ended up enriching a few lucky Nigerians. The companies received a sweet deal whose overly favorable terms may cost the country as much as $6 billion over the oil block's lifetime—an amount equal to twice Nigeria's annual health and education budgets.[115]

Public officials on Unaoil's payroll may have allowed a more expensive bid to win oil sector contracts, thereby reducing Iraq's oil revenues. The money Halliburton wasted on its politically connected local subcontractor in Angola raised its operating expenses, which eventually lowered the returns the state would receive from the project. Landowners in Michigan lost out big when Chesapeake Energy collaborated with its peers to lower lease prices, and Chevron's tax moves kept hundreds of millions of dollars out of Australia's government budget.

But the harm caused by company corruption goes much deeper than lost revenues. When an oil company perpetrates, facilitates, or even ignores corruption, it reinforces a system where those in power no longer serve their people. When oil companies cooperate with Chad's dictator, they help strengthen his grip on power. When they bribe Iraqi officials, they create more reasons for citizens to become disenfranchised. Payments from foreign oil companies are used by Nigerian political elites to undermine the country's democratic processes. Angola's elite get rich off partnering with oil companies, even when they add no value to the enterprise. Through behavior of this kind, oil companies become complicit in maintaining the undemocratic and unequal systems of governance in many oil-producing countries.

The oil boom demonstrates that many companies are still engaging in corruption despite the damage it causes. However, stories from this chapter also offer some kind of silver lining. Corruption and other troubling behaviors were exposed, and the companies involved faced at least some negative ramification—be they legal or reputational. Chapter 6 explores these corruption remedies in more detail.

Company wrongdoing needs to be reined in. Anticorruption strategies can become more targeted and effective if they address proven problem areas. The use of middlemen, such as Unaoil or the fixers hired by Gunvor, is one practice that warrants greater transparency, oversight, and regulation. Another is the way companies choose their partners and subcontractors, such as the various Angolan entities foreign companies embraced despite their blatant political connections. The stories also indicate that oilfield service companies and oil traders require special attention It is entirely possible to devise safeguards that target specific challenges of this kind, and chapter 7 discusses this endeavor in more detail.

Identifying a concrete agenda to reduce company corruption seems feasible. However, as most of the stories here have made clear: it takes two to tango. What about the roles played by government officials and political leaders? The next two chapters delve into that terrain.

CHAPTER 3 | Corruption and the Competition
for Power

IN JANUARY 2011, a company from the Seychelles bought a five-bedroom mansion in Buckinghamshire, just outside London, for 3.2 million pounds. Called "the Falls" for its elaborate backyard water feature, the house sat on what one real estate agency called the area's "finest road." According to US court filings, the intended occupant of the home was Diezani Alison-Madueke, Nigeria's petroleum minister from 2010 to 2015.[1]

Two months later, a company from the British Virgin Islands bought a house just one block away from Regent's Park in London for 1.7 million pounds. Again, the house was intended for Alison-Madueke and her family.[2] Renovations kicked off soon after the sale, and the former minister helped choose the new stone floors and countertops for the bathrooms.

The man behind the Seychelles company and the man behind the British Virgin Islands company collaborated on more than just real estate deals. They are also the two bosses of Atlantic Energy, a Nigerian oil company. During the same months that they bought houses for the minister, the two landed a big contract with Nigeria's national oil company, the Nigerian National Petroleum Corporation (NNPC). Another large contract followed in 2012. Over the next few years, again according to US court filings, Atlantic Energy received more than $1.5 billion worth of oil from NNPC and provided very few services in return.[3] The company's bosses and the former minister deny wrongdoing.

After the profits started rolling in, one of the Atlantic bosses bought himself much more luxurious digs that he had provided for the minister. He paid $50 million for the penthouse of a Manhattan tower that soars ninety stories above Central Park, and $82 million for a yacht that he later rented to Beyoncé and Jay-Z for $900,000 a week. His enthusiastic spending soon attracted the attention of US law enforcement. Their investigation, along with other sources, sheds light on the torrent of corruption that swept through Nigeria's oil sector during the boom years.

This chapter examines how politicians and government officials abused their power to pursue oil boom riches in Nigeria and in another oil-rich democracy, Brazil. It also looks at how oil money influences policymaking in the United States. These are three countries with competitive politics— far cries from the types of dictatorships often associated with oil-sector corruption. Many oil-rich strongmen have used their country's natural resources to enrich themselves and strengthen their positions. Such political systems are often called *kleptocracies*, a term derived from Greek that means literally "rule by thieves." In a kleptocracy, the ruling regime usually faces very little political competition. They control the entire government apparatus and often significant portions of the economy as well, and do so over long stretches of time. Corruption takes on a systematic form that is highly challenging to combat. With stories from Angola, Azerbaijan, and Russia, the next chapter shows how kleptocrats used the oil boom to cement their hold on power.

What's perhaps more surprising is that political elites in democratic countries also embraced oil boom corruption. Corruption exploded in Brazil and Nigeria during the boom. In the United States, it assumed more subtle forms that some would instead call business as usual. The stories from these three countries reveal a maddening paradox: democracy drives the corruption, and then it comes to the rescue. Political competition motivated the corruption, as politicians sought oil money to secure allies and fund their election campaigns. All three of these countries have fiercely competitive and fragmented political elites, and candidates need deep pockets in order to stay in the game. But then, even when the corruption implicated the most powerful people in the land, democratic institutions kept the perpetrators from enjoying complete impunity and brought about some measure of justice. This struggle between the lure of oil money and the checks and balances provided by democratic institutions, holds relevance for other oil producers with competitive politics, such as Canada, Colombia, Ecuador, Ghana, Indonesia, Mexico, and Norway.

There is no question that what happened in Nigeria and Brazil during the oil boom qualifies as corruption. These two countries provided some of the period's largest and most dramatic examples of graft. Most of this chapter focuses on these two sagas. In contrast, many of the money flows between oil companies and US government officials occupy that expansive gray area surrounding the definition of corruption. Like all the wining and dining by companies described in the previous chapter, they are both legal and problematic.

Whether in democracies or kleptocracies, the oil boom corruption schemes orchestrated by political elites share a few cross-cutting trends. First, the lines separating the public and private sectors are dangerously blurred. Government officials hold business interests in the oil sector, or they depend on oil money to keep their jobs, or both. Oil sector business-people depend on government officials for their profits, or they use their wealth to buy influence with government officials, or both. Playing a key role are the oligarchs: a select set of business moguls who maintain loyal and mutually beneficial relations with the political leaders. The result is a single set of elites who embrace the oil sector from two sides.

Second, national oil companies often serve as venues for corruption because they are easy institutions for political leaders to capture. In the 1970s, during the last major oil boom, most oil-producing governments created national oil companies to assert greater control over the industry and lessen the influence of foreign companies. Apart from the United States, the United Kingdom, and Canada, all major oil-producing countries have national oil companies, and together these state-run giants controlled 90 percent of global oil reserves and between 55 and 75 percent of production.[4] Some are wholly government owned, as in Nigeria, and others are just majority government owned, as in Brazil.

During the oil boom, unprecedented quantities of wealth coursed through national oil company accounts. These companies exist in a gray area between the public and private sectors, well within reach of political influence but outside the control of many formal government oversight systems. Within national oil companies, oil trading and subcontracting appear to be functions that are particularly susceptible to manipulation.

Third, the favorite tactic of government officials is to award overly profitable deals to companies headed by loyal individuals. These individuals then become wealthy, and political leaders can call on them as needed. Officials like this tactic because it often can be executed without breaking any laws, and they do not have to personally touch illicit funds. This kind of corruption is also difficult to prosecute. Unlike simpler instances of bribery, the quid pro quo is less apparent: the company may do a favor for the government official many months before or after receiving a juicy deal.

Fourth and finally, while the corruption may originate in presidential palaces and national oil company headquarters, it ends up being a highly global affair. Many of the bank accounts, shell companies, lawyers, accountants, consultants, and business partners who execute the schemes come from outside the country where the scheme began. The money captured by corrupt officials also flows overseas, infecting foreign businesses, property markets, universities, media outlets, and governments. Chapter 5 discusses these international dimensions.

Oil boom corruption in Nigeria and Brazil has exhibited all these trends, as well as plenty of ingenuity and gall.

The Rise of Goodluck and Madame

Goodluck Jonathan did not set out to become president of Nigeria. But once he ended up in office, he certainly wanted to stay there. Never a particularly talented or ambitious politician, he began his ascent as an unremarkable deputy governor of one of Nigeria's oil-rich states. In 2005, his boss, the governor, was convicted on corruption charges and stepped down.[5] Jonathan took his place. He did little to distinguish himself in this position and stood by as the state's patronage politics ran their typical course.

Two years after Jonathan became governor, Nigeria's domineering president, Olusegun Obasanjo, begrudgingly prepared to leave office. He had tried unsuccessfully to change the country's constitution in order to allow himself a third term as president. With that route blocked, his best chance at retaining influence was to choose loyal and unthreatening candidates to succeed him on the ruling party's election ticket. The highest political offices in Nigeria tend to alternate among the country's largest ethnic groups, and it was time for a Muslim northerner to run for president. Obasanjo tapped the mild-mannered and physically weak Umaru Yar'Adua to be the candidate. He then needed a Christian southerner to serve as vice-president, preferably one from the country's oil-producing Niger Delta region. No one from that region had held top national office in many years, and unrest in the Delta was running high. So Obasanjo tapped Jonathan to join Yar'Adua on the ballot, and the odd pair went on to win the 2007 elections.

Fast-forward through a few years of tepid governance and little change. In early 2010, the whereabouts of President Yar'Adua and the status of his health became the subject of intense speculation. Rumors that he had died in Germany or Saudi Arabia or in an ambulance outside his home spread off and on through the country. Finally, after months of uncertainty, his death was confirmed. Goodluck Jonathan, continuing an unlikely political rise that lived up to his name, assumed the role of president. The 2011 elections were less than a year away, so the ruling party backed Jonathan as its presidential candidate. Thanks to a fractured opposition and prolific spending by the ruling party, he coasted to an easy victory.

With that, Jonathan found himself ruling a country of 170 million that was the world's twelfth largest oil producer. In the 2011 electoral campaign, he indicated that he would only serve one term—essentially serving out what would have been Yar'Adua's second term—and would not stand in the 2015 elections. This was important to many political groups in the North, who saw Jonathan's term as cutting short the eight years in office they had expected. It was also important to the many Nigerians who viewed Jonathan as weak and ineffectual.

Jonathan, however, changed his mind. He and those close to him grew attached to the benefits of power, and winning the 2015 elections became a priority. Jonathan and his team set out to improve their odds by using the country's oil wealth.

The team around Jonathan knew that his chances of winning the 2015 elections were decidedly mixed. He had delivered negligible economic or social change and failed to contain the violent extremist group Boko Haram. The many armchair analysts of Nigerian politics, both in the country and abroad, often defined him as corrupt, consumed by the project of appropriating wealth to his Niger Delta home region, and entirely "out of his depth" when it came to running a large and complex country. He also did not have the kind of broad-based political machine enjoyed by many top Nigerian politicians that could turn out votes across the country.

Perhaps most important, Jonathan was unable to assert control over the factionalized ruling party, which he needed to organize his campaign and deliver votes. Nigerian politics is ruled by those who can craft grand bargains among the country's large and diverse elite, and Jonathan lacked this skill.[6] By 2013, three large opposition parties had merged into one powerful coalition, and several high-profile governors had quit the ruling party to join the new outfit. These were not good signs for the president.

But other factors worked in Jonathan's favor. In Nigeria, as in many democracies, the incumbent enjoys enormous advantages in elections, especially during an oil boom. Sitting presidents can spend on popular social programs. They can allocate revenues to various regions so as to build support with specific groups. They can ensure that powerful business leaders enjoy banner years, for example by awarding large contracts or requiring international oil companies to take on local partners. They can fund the pet projects of key power brokers or increase the funds available to the legislators who can bring in votes from their home regions. They can exert influence over the electoral system and the media.

Corruption is another tool in an incumbent's toolkit. Jonathan and those close to him seized this implement and launched corruption schemes across the public sector. Such practices have plagued Nigeria for decades. However, the booming oil prices of 2011–2015 presented an incomparable opportunity. After surveying their odds and options, Jonathan and his inner circle proceeded to engage in oil sector corruption on a scale Nigeria had never seen before—a staggering achievement, given the massive looting by former leaders. Essentially they used what they had—a booming oil sector and weak government institutions—to get what they wanted, which was another term in office.

Enter Alison-Madueke. Often referred to as Madame or Madam D (or even Aunt Daisy and Lady Macbeth by more creative observers), Alison-Madueke became Jonathan's petroleum minister in 2010 and remained in that role for six years. She was the most prominent of his ministers, the closest to him, and the most infamous. A kind of mythology characterized her tenure, and Abuja swirled with speculation around how she acquired such great power. The story of who captured oil wealth during Nigeria's oil boom is her story.

A woman in her fifties who cultivated a distinguished air, Alison-Madueke became petroleum minister after brief turns as the minister of transportation and the minister of mines. Born into a prominent Niger Delta family, she received her undergraduate degree from Howard University in Washington, DC, and an MBA from Cambridge University. She married a powerful former admiral who had five children from a previous marriage, and the couple went on to have one son. She learned the oil sector ropes during a long career working in Shell's Nigeria division, where her father had also worked. She stayed with Shell from 1992 through 2006, when the company appointed her its first female executive director in Nigeria. When she became oil minister, she joined a long line of Shell executives who have gone on to hold top government positions, creating a revolving door of influence between the company and the Nigerian state. While she was certainly privileged and successful, nothing in her background revealed the magnitude of what was to come.

As in many oil-producing nations, presidents in Nigeria do not like to delegate control over the oil industry. The sector is too lucrative and politically important to outsource its management. Former president Obasanjo, for instance, had served as his own petroleum minister and kept his top oil officials on a short leash. He rotated them often to head off any efforts at empire-building. No one expects petroleum ministers in Nigeria to last more than a couple years.

President Jonathan bucked that trend and handed over near total control of the oil sector to Alison-Madueke. Over time, she became so influential that Nigeria's many business moguls and political bosses stood no chance acting against her. Rather than the president rotating personnel to preserve control, it was Alison-Madueke who used the same trick: she named five different men to run the national oil company during her six-year tenure. It was a phenomenon, how this one person—a woman no less!—acquired and maintained unilateral control over an enormous oil sector. This is particularly impressive in Nigeria. Whereas many African oil producers have dominant "presidents for life," Nigeria's large and competitive political elite usually keeps any single individual from capturing a lucrative position for very long.

Given the timing of her tenure, Alison-Madueke ruled over an all-you-can-eat buffet of oil riches. During the decade before she took office, Nigeria produced oil worth an average of $42 billion a year. This figure climbed to over $100 billion in both 2011 and 2012.[7] By 2011, her first year in office, the oil revenues collected by the government had risen by 54 percent in a single year, reaching a historic $68 billion—most of which flowed through the highly dysfunctional national oil company.

The oil boom would have been the optimal time to reform Nigeria's beleaguered oil sector institutions. Their poor performance loses billions of dollars a year for the Nigerian government, yet consecutive administrations have failed to fix them. As described in the next chapter, the leaders of Russia, Azerbaijan, and Angola ran their oil sectors with skill and care, working hard to ensure that the relevant government agencies and national oil companies performed adequately. If the oil sector is the goose that lays golden eggs, the geese in these countries were well tended to and produced eggs at a healthy clip. By comparison, Nigeria's golden goose was fed scraps once a week and lived in a shed that leaked rain.

The reasons for this neglect are twofold. First, leaders in Nigeria have short horizons, again due to the large and factionalized nature of its political elite. Since independence in 1960, Nigeria has had twelve heads of state, with an average time in office of four years. Compare that with Africa's other long-standing oil producers (Angola, Cameroon, Chad, Equatorial Guinea, Gabon, Congo-Brazzaville, and Sudan), which have had an average of four leaders since independence. The tenures of their leaders have averaged seventeen years, with several strongmen staying put for more than three decades.[8] For leaders with long horizons, it makes sense to maximize the long-term returns from the oil sector, because they will likely still be in power to enjoy the eventual profits. Not so in Nigeria, where leaders only have a few years to get things done.

The second reason is that political leaders can easily manipulate institutions when they are chaotic and poorly run. For decades, Nigerian politicians have used the oil sector to share wealth among the country's factions. Reform would create rules and reduce discretion, making it more difficult to spread the money around. President Obasanjo implemented a wide range of economic and financial reforms during his eight years in office, but his oil sector reform agenda never got off the ground. Even for a powerful, reform-minded leader like him, the political realities of Nigeria required keeping the sector in disarray.

Jonathan and Alison-Madueke also neglected the reform agenda, even though high oil prices would have made many of its elements much easier to accomplish. They did not try to reform the national oil company, the Nigerian National Petroleum Corporation (NNPC), which is both the dominant player in the sector and its dominant problem. Financially, NNPC's structure dooms it to fail. The more oil money NNPC spends, the more money it can justify keeping from the rest of the government. With incentives like this, costs skyrocket, inefficiency spreads, and officials set up all kinds of rackets and shakedowns to extract money for themselves and their friends. This problem is hardly a secret. A 2008 report from the government itself labeled NNPC "the most problematic" of Nigeria's oil sector institutions and said that it "operates as a huge amorphous cost center with little or no sensitivity to the bottom line."[9]

Along with its profligate spending, NNPC has failed to develop much capacity to actually explore for and produce oil, unlike many of its national oil company peers. Its four refineries have absorbed billions of dollars in maintenance costs yet regularly produce at around 10 percent of their capacity. The company also remains perpetually in debt, mostly to the large foreign companies that produce the country's oil and the companies that import gasoline and diesel. With high prices, Alison-Madueke could have invested in NNPC's capacity, paid down its debts, and sold its low-performing subunits or otherwise addressed its chronic performance failures. Instead the dysfunction escalated.

Alison-Madueke and her team also wasted the opportunity to renegotiate important deals and attract new investment into the oil sector. Much of the country's offshore production is governed by several production-sharing contracts signed with foreign companies, including Shell, Chevron, and Exxon. Nigeria entered into these contracts during the low price years of the 1990s and offered the companies highly favorable terms to lure them into the costly business of deepwater exploration. The oil boom provided the government with considerable new leverage, and it could have renegotiated these deals to receive higher returns. Moreover, Alison-Madueke allowed a key piece of oil sector legislation to languish in parliament for years, creating uncertainty among investors at a time when they otherwise would have keenly plowed funds into new oil sector operations.

Along with stymieing reform, she also neglected the day-to-day operations of the sector. During a twenty-month period in 2012–2014, she failed to call formal meetings of NNPC's board, despite a legal requirement that it meet four times a year.[10] Her management style featured a confounding combination of micromanagement and neglect: "while the Minister wants to see every memo, she is always never there to see it," groused one NNPC official.[11] Company executives complained that they struggled to get meetings with her, and the timelines of major investment decisions suffered as a result. Exxon, Shell, and Chevron waited for years to renew their production leases, causing major delays in the maintenance and improvement of their operations. A leading Nigerian oil company reportedly waited more than eighteen months for the minister to sign off on a basic acquisition deal.[12]

Placing both reform and basic management on the back burner allowed Alison-Madueke to focus on her priorities. Working mostly from her mansion in an upscale neighborhood of the capital city, surrounded by a retinue of security men and personal assistants, she worked to exploit the oil boom, executing deals that served the political needs of her administration and enriched her and a small group of cronies.

The Minister and the Missing $20 Billion

Eventually, Lamido Sanusi had enough. After months of observing suspiciously low levels of oil revenue making their way into the government treasury, the widely respected governor of Nigeria's central bank sounded the alarm. In late 2013, he wrote to the president and submitted a statement to Nigeria's Senate alleging that $20 billion had gone "missing" from NNPC. According to the statement, when NNPC sold oil on behalf of the government, it kept a large portion of the sale proceeds rather than sending them to the government treasury. In his estimation, the existing explanations for the withholdings fell short.

A slew of documentation has emerged since Sanusi wrote his submission, and it indicates that he hit the nail on the head. The Nigerian National Petroleum Corporation was a weak institution with shoddy systems and no incentives for financial propriety—the ideal attributes of a honey pot.

Alison-Madueke and her colleagues exploited this scenario. From 2011 to 2013, while NNPC collected record-breaking amounts of money, the oil revenues it actually transferred to the government treasury *dropped* by $10 billion.[13]

Sanusi's accusations made national and international headlines and triggered several responses. President Jonathan fired him as a start. Then various parts of government ordered inquiries and leveled accusations and counter-accusations. These produced a dizzying array of contradictory figures, as NNPC, the Ministry of Finance, and other actors attempted to explain away the situation. The Auditor General's office commissioned an inquiry by the accounting firm PriceWaterhouseCooper that confirmed many of Sanusi's suspicions and documented NNPC's unwillingness to open up its books. The report concluded that NNPC currently was operating with "a 'blank' cheque to spend money without limit or control" and that "this is untenable and unsustainable and must be addressed immediately."[14]

Despite all the accusations and damning evidence, Alison-Madueke kept her position, and the corruption picked up in pace. After all, the 2015 election was fast approaching.

Like many power brokers profiled in this book, her favorite strategy was to award overly profitable deals to companies headed by loyal individuals. Aiteo Energy Resources was one of her favored oil companies. Under her reign, Aiteo received a string of plum business opportunities including, in 2011, an oil "swap" contract. The deal specified that the company would receive around 30,000 barrels per day in oil from the government and would return gasoline, diesel, and other refined petroleum products of equal value. The contract ran for four years and saw Aiteo move as much as $4.7 billion worth of oil. The dysfunction of NNPC, specifically its constantly underperforming refineries, created the need for this kind of makeshift fix.

Aiteo was not an obvious choice to receive this contract. They had never exported crude oil before 2011, though they had some background in the fuel import business.[15] They suddenly faced the task of selling oil worth around $1 billion a year. To tackle this challenge, they outsourced the actual oil trading to more experienced companies, primarily Shell and the Swiss oil trader Vitol, and then collected the proceeds.[16] In 2015, Alison-Madueke rewarded Aiteo with an even larger share of the Nigerian oil trading market. Muscling out other favored firms, the company signed two new swap agreements with NNPC for a total of 120,000 barrels per day— over 10 percent of the country's entire oil production.

Colleagues and I at the Natural Resource Governance Institute, an independent nonprofit group, analyzed the swap contracts, trying to understand how Alison-Madueke's patronage machine worked. We had some of the contracts, leaked to us by various Nigerian contacts. We also wrote to NNPC, Aiteo, and several other companies with questions about the deals. Our research was met with a lot of suspicion. In the scrappy and competitive world of Nigerian oil trading, most of the companies assumed that we were working for one of their opponents—after all, why would people invest in learning the details of these highly technical deals unless they were making millions from them?

Others sought to use our research to damage their competitors' standing. One morning, I arrived in the office to find an anonymous package sent from London. Inside were copies of two swap contracts, both of which we had already viewed. The mysterious sender had helpfully flagged selected provisions in each contract, adding an arrow to make sure that we did not miss that Aiteo had received a much more favorable deal than its peers.

We had already spotted the imbalance. Our analysis found that Aiteo's 2015 swap deal contained terms highly favorable to them. Specifically, the equivalencies used in the contract allowed Aiteo to import fuel that was worth less than the crude they received.[17] Thanks to contract terms like this, the company received hundreds of millions of dollars in profits that should have been collected by the government, and did so without actually breaking any laws. To add insult to injury, during the months before the 2015 election, Aiteo received crude oil from the government and then failed to return with the corresponding volume of fuel, routinely owing the government billions of dollars' worth of refined products.[18] The company then corrected some of the imbalances in later months.

As if the trading contracts weren't enough, the minister also helped Aiteo receive one of Nigeria's juiciest oil blocks. Tired of endless militant attacks and disputes with local communities over environmental damages, Shell decided to sell some of its onshore Nigerian oil blocks and pipeline infrastructure. According to interviews with industry participants and experts, the minister weighed in heavily on which companies Shell should select as the buyers. In 2014, Aiteo was selected as the main buyer of the most valuable block Shell had on offer, estimated to hold around 6 percent of Nigeria's total oil reserves, as well as an important pipeline. Aiteo came out on top even though they had limited relevant experience.[19] On the back of these deals, Benedict Peters, Aiteo's CEO, debuted on the list of Africa's richest individuals in 2014 with a reported fortune of $2.7 billion.[20]

Several investigations provide glimpses of how Alison-Madueke may have benefited from Aiteo's good fortune, although at the time this book went to press they remained subject to contending accounts and legal disputes. In 2019, Nigerian courts convicted multiple former election officials of accepting bribes during the run-up to the 2015 elections.[21] Nigeria's Economic and Financial Crimes Commission alleges that the bribes were "part of the $115 million largesse doled out by a former minister of petroleum resources, Diezani Alison-Madueke, to influence the outcome of the election."[22] Back in 2016, when information about the alleged bribery first began to emerge, the Commission announced that three oil companies had deposited the $115 million into a bank account controlled by the minister and named Peters as being behind one of the companies. The Commission declared Peters a wanted man on the basis of suspicions that he paid $60 million into this account.[23] At the time, the Nigerian authorities complained that "all attempts to get [Peters] have proved abortive. We currently do not know where he is and he is hardly ever in one place because he has a private jet."[24] However, since then, Peters has not been charged. In 2018, following complaints filed by Peters, a Nigerian judge ordered the Commission to remove his name from their list of wanted persons because there were no pending legal proceedings against him.[25]

Peters is suspected of subsidizing the minister's comfortable lifestyle as well as her political agendas. In 2017, the US DOJ accused "Co-conspirator #2" of purchasing a luxury London home worth more than $3 million for Alison-Madueke via a Seychelles-based shell company that he controlled.[26] The friendly conspirator also purchased $100,000 in furniture for the property in just two days of shopping, according to the charges.[27] "Co-conspirator #2" is widely believed to be Benny Peters.[28] The year prior, British authorities moved to freeze the same London house under the UK Proceeds of Crime Act and named both Alison-Madueke and Peters in the court order.[29] However, when Peters began to fight the various accusations, he obtained a ruling from a Nigerian court that the London house was not associated with the minister and therefore could not be frozen by Nigerian authorities.[30]

Peters denies wrongdoing and has not been charged with any crime. He is quoted in a 2017 Aiteo press release as saying: "I maintain my position that all the allegations are baseless and without any truth whatsoever. . . . There is a toxic culture of politically motivated witch-hunts that stains reputations, stifles enterprise and keeps foreign investors away from our country. For two years, I have suffered malicious, unfounded and false allegations hanging over my head."[31]

Along with Aiteo, Atlantic Energy was another company that profited enormously during the Minister's tenure. Many of Nigeria's most prolific oilfields are run by joint ventures between several companies and NNPC. For decades, NNPC has played a nonoperating role, since the company has lacked both the financial and technical wherewithal to actually run the oilfields. In 2011, Alison-Madueke decided to change this arrangement. She called for the Nigeria Petroleum Development Company (NPDC), a secretive subsidiary of NNPC, to take over the operations of several large oilfields.[32]

However, NPDC still lacked the finances or skills needed to produce oil itself. To address this carefully manufactured dilemma, Alison-Madueke arranged for NPDC to enter into several "Strategic Alliance Agreements" with Atlantic Energy, in 2011 and 2012.[33] The agreements said that Atlantic would pay the government's share of expenses for operating a total of eight oil blocks and provide some associated "technical services." In return for these services, left largely undefined, Atlantic would receive a portion of the oil and gas produced from the fields. Atlantic was a brand new company, created less than a year before signing its first Strategic Alliance Agreement, and lacked the expertise needed to meet its obligations in these large and complicated deals.[34]

And so the obligations went unmet. Between 2011 and 2015, NPDC's share of the expenses from the eight oil blocks topped $3 billion, and Atlantic should have covered this amount. Instead, as explained in the charges brought by the US DOJ, the company allegedly paid only around 10 percent of this total and also failed to pay the government many of the fees required by the contract.[35] These debts did not stop Atlantic from collecting large quantities of crude oil as payment. During the same four years, Atlantic received oil and gas from the blocks worth $1.5 billion.[36] Put simply, Atlantic allegedly received payment for services it did not provide.

According to US and Nigerian court filings, the deal worked just as planned.[37] The DOJ asserts that neither of Atlantic's two bosses "ever intended to fulfill their or their companies' obligations under the Brass SAA [one of the two Agreements] but, nevertheless, with the assistance of Alison-Madueke, induced NPDC to enter into the agreement under the false and fraudulent pretense that they intended to and would fulfill their obligations."[38] According to the charges, it was a scam to divert funds from the booming oil sector into selected private pockets.

In 2017, the DOJ moved to seize assets it alleges were bought with the proceeds of this scheme.[39] A colorful jet-setter often photographed with the likes of Naomi Campbell and Jamie Foxx, one of Atlantic's top executives,

Kola Aluko, stands at the center of this investigation. According to the DOJ charges, he moved money out of Nigeria and around the world through webs of foreign companies and accounts. His big US purchases included the $50 million Manhattan penthouse, a few houses in Montecito, California, and an enormous yacht.[40]

According to the DOJ's account, Aluko and his business partner also spent a lot of money on the upkeep of Alison-Madueke herself. As noted at the chapter's outset, they allegedly bought and renovated several London homes for her and threw in a couple $14,000 exercise machines from Harrods for good measure. They footed a $500,000 bill from a chauffeur company that drove the minister and her family while they were in London, and bought vehicles for both the minister and ruling party officials. Leaving a well-marked trail behind them, the two men paid for some expenses on their personal credit cards and emailed directly with the minister about the latest architectural renderings for the renovation of her house and other matters rather distant from oil sector affairs.[41]

While Aluko presided over billions of dollars in oil business, furniture shopping may prove to be his undoing. As part of the US investigation, FBI field agents interviewed several employees of two Houston furniture stores Alison-Madueke would visit while in town for various oil industry meetings. The employees attested that the minister browsed their high-end offerings but never actually made any purchases. Instead Aluko and his business partner footed the bill of over a million dollars for furniture, including items such as a "Luigi XVI Sideboard" for $10,000. One furniture store employee even had Aluko's phone number saved under the name "Kola Aluko Madame D." Nigerian authorities then provided US investigators with proof that the furniture purchased by Atlantic's bosses ended up in the minister's Abuja home.[42]

The US case hinged on the timing of the purchases. Crucially, they were made right around when the minister and Atlantic negotiated the Strategic Alliance Agreements. Therefore, the US authorities could argue that Aluko and his partners conspired to illegally influence the award with their gifts. According to the DOJ, they engaged in the "corrupt purpose of inducing her to use her influence within the Ministry of Petroleum Resources, the NNPC and the NPDC to direct the award of business opportunities to entities under their control and beneficial ownership."[43] It is difficult to legally establish bribery without this type of direct, quid pro quo arrangement.

The US authorities also recovered some recorded conversations Alison-Madueke had with Aluko in 2014.[44] They suggest her discomfort with his approach to wealth management. "You and Jide [the other Atlantic boss] had some of the most support that we could possibly give," the minister reminded Aluko. "At a time when we're not doing anything else, we stuck our necks out regarding the SAA [Strategic Alliance Agreement] and we supported it. [Inaudible sounds] How the two of you have ruined it is incredulous and incredible to all of us."

The minister lectured her crony on his splashy spending:

> I spoke to you several times about your general behavior, acquisition of assets, etc., asking you to be a bit more careful because [inaudible] will start following you. I remember we had this open discussion more than once. You kept telling me that there was no issue because you did it in a certain way, you did it in a certain—and I kept telling you that it doesn't matter how you do it. Once you start acquiring, acquiring, acquiring at a certain level, then you'll be—whether you like it or not, whether it was done in the most transparent—you understand?—manner or not, because they will want to trace where it came from.

Her admonition continued, centering on *Galactica Star*: "if you want to hire a yacht, you lease it for two weeks or whatever. You don't go and sink funds into it at this time when Nigerian oil and gas sector is under all kinds of watch, as we have been for some time, and where Atlantic itself has been the subject of all kinds of speculation."[45]

While Alison-Madueke reprimanded Aluko for his ostentatious spending, it is unclear whether she was taking her own advice. The Nigerian Economic and Financial Crimes Commission raided her main residence in Abuja after she left office, finding boxes of gold, silver, and diamond jewelry along with cash and expensive furniture, including the pieces from Texas.[46] The Commission's inventory of her $40 million accessories collection featured enough wrist wear for an army, with 419 "expensive bangles" and 189 "expensive watches" listed, as well as a customized gold-plated iPhone.[47] A Nigerian court ordered that she also forfeit a whopping 56 houses that she acquired while in office "with suspected proceeds of crime."[48]

Aluko and Jide Omokore, Aluko's business partner at Atlantic Energy, have both denied the imputations of wrongdoing against them, as has Alison-Madueke.[49] None has been found guilty of a crime.

While Aiteo, Atlantic, and their respective bosses were among the most prominent members of the Alison-Madueke network, the oil boom bene-fited many others as well. An earlier scheme involved fuel import deals. Corruption in the fuel import business had long existed in Nigeria, reflect-ing the susceptibility of oil trading to corruption. This problem reached unimaginable heights under Alison-Madueke. Gasoline and kerosene are subsidized in Nigeria, meaning that they are sold to consumers at a price lower than the international market price. Because its government-run oil refineries exist in a constant state of disrepair, Nigeria has to import fuel to meet its domestic needs. Due to the subsidy, Nigerian government and NNPC reimburse the companies that import fuel the difference between the international market and domestic prices—a steep cost even when the system is run properly.

Between 2009 and 2011, Nigeria made subsidy payments to fuel importers for 59 million liters of fuel a day. But the country consumed only 35 million. In other words, the government was paying companies for fuel that was never delivered. The scheme reached its apex in 2011, when Nigeria spent $16.5 billion on the fuel subsidy, a figure equal to over half the federal budget for that year. The number of fuel importing companies rose from 19 in 2008 to 140 in 2011, showing just how many hands had reached into this open till. As reported by *Reuters*, "many firms only existed on paper and collected subsidies on fuel that never existed."[50] By the end of the frenzy, an estimated $6.8 billion in public funds were stolen by politically well-connected individuals.[51]

In early 2012, after the 2011 elections and the associated need to spread around cash, the government removed the fuel subsidy without notice, eliminating what many Nigerians perceived as one of the few benefits they got from their country's oil wealth. People took to the streets in protest. Alongside calls for gasoline prices to lower again, an "Occupy Nigeria" movement erupted and focused its ire on fuel subsidy corruption. In response, the government reinstated the subsidy. They also organized inquiries into fuel subsidy corruption and a few half-hearted cases against companies that received illegal payments. But the punishments were few, and many of the offending companies went on to do business with the Jonathan government again. No government officials were fired. Alison-Madueke remained firmly in place and shifted her schemes to other sets of transactions where scrutiny had not yet reached.

The foregoing examples—Aiteo with its oil trading contract that contained lopsided terms, Atlantic collecting oil without providing services, and the fuel importers receiving subsidy payments for products they never delivered—all involved companies receiving oversized profits thanks to the deals they struck during Alison-Madueke's tenure. The dysfunction of NNPC created the opportunities to sign such makeshift deals. Because its refineries barely worked, it had to import huge quantities of fuel. Because it lacked operational capacities, it had to hire third parties to do the work.

Because it lacked independence and strong corporate governance, it could be easily controlled by the minister and conscripted into political service. Moreover, Nigerian law affords the minister of petroleum tremendous discretion when choosing companies to contract with.

Since the end of the oil boom, investigations have revealed other schemes too. One of the biggest deviates from the trends already noted of enriching local companies, siphoning funds from oil trading deals, and exploiting the dysfunction of NNPC. Instead a couple of the world's largest oil companies played starring roles in a drama that, when this book went to press, was still playing out in Italian courts. In 2011, Shell and Eni paid the Nigerian government $1.3 billion for rights to an enormous oil block. Of this amount, $1.1 billion quickly left the government's possession and landed in private hands. A large chunk of the funds paid off the block's previous owner—a petroleum minister from the 1990s who, while in office, had awarded the block to his own oil company. According to court filings from Italian prosecutors and the Nigerian government, a further $500 million was shared among other political big wigs, sitting government officials, including Jonathan and Alison-Madueke, as well as oil company staff.[52] The two companies, their executives, and the former Nigerian officials named have denied wrongdoing. (See chapter 2 for my examination of this enormous case including more on the alleged roles played by Shell and Eni.)

The physical theft of crude oil, referred to locally as "bunkering," also rose to new heights during the Jonathan and Alison-Madueke years. Some of the theft was small in scale, with individuals in the Niger Delta region hacking into the pipelines that crisscross their homeland, siphoning off crude and transforming it into makeshift types of fuel. Much more oil was lost to sophisticated cross-border operations run by networks with contacts at the highest reaches of government and the military. Like money launderers, bunkerers found many ingenious ways to bring their stolen oil to market. Some tapped into pipelines and then transferred the oil onto small vessels, which then offloaded the stolen crude onto larger tankers parked offshore. Others fiddled with the measurements and paperwork involved in exporting crude, loading more crude onto vessels than they reported or diverting shiploads of oil from their stated destinations. When oil was selling for $80 or $100 a barrel, the individuals running the schemes could cover the costs of bunkering, pay off the necessary officials, sell the oil at a deflated price, and still profit handsomely. Theft levels reached 100,000 barrels per day at various points during Alison-Madueke's tenure, oil worth as much as $3.6 billion a year.[53]

Investigations of foreign companies for bribing Nigerian officials sounded further alarms. Rolls-Royce, the large British engineering firm, hired a local Nigerian company that then made payments to NNPC officials in 2009 to 2013. As part of the arrangement, Rolls-Royce received in exchange confidential information about multiple tenders that the company sought to win, introductions to top NNPC staff, and other advantages. The scheme is detailed in the agreement reached between Rolls-Royce and the UK government to settle charges of failing to prevent bribery in Nigeria and several other countries.[54] In another case, Swiss authorities investigated Addax, a Swiss-based company wholly owned by China's Sinopec, for making suspicious payments in 2015 in excess of $100 million to Nigerian lawyers and a construction company.[55] In 2017, Addax paid a fine of 29 million Swiss francs to settle the Swiss charges of suspected bribery that ensued.[56] It did not admit any wrongdoing.

Through these types of channels, government officials and their businessmen friends captured billions of dollars in oil boom revenues that should have entered government accounts. But the costs didn't stop there. The Jonathan government could have used the oil boom to deliver Nigeria into a stronger economic place. In an alternate reality, the government would have saved some of the record-high revenues to prepare for when the oil price eventually fell. They would have spent another portion to pave roads, subsidize the construction of power stations, strengthen the failing education system, and otherwise address the constraints that hold back the nonoil economy.

Instead, the quest to stay in power captured the attention of Jonathan, Alison-Madueke, and many of their colleagues. In Nigeria's money-driven, highly competitive political environment, winning an election is incredibly expensive. Midlevel managers at the election commission collected millions of dollars in bribes. Just imagine what the real power brokers demanded in exchange for their support. Some analysts estimate that the ruling party alone spent over $10 billion on the contest and much more exchanged hands and enriched insiders.[57] Nigeria's competitive and highly monetized democratic system likely increased the scale of oil sector corruption perpetrated under Alison-Madueke. However, democratic institutions also came to the rescue because some, unlike NNPC, still served the public interest.

Amid the Stench, a Silver Lining

On March 31, 2015, electoral officials, political party representatives, and members of the press gathered to hear Nigeria's esteemed election commissioner Attahiru Jega read out the presidential results. The commissioner, a widely respected former professor with a strong reputation for integrity, proceeded slowly and steadily, reading the results from one state at a time. Across the country and beyond, millions of Nigerians sat glued to their TVs and computers watching the proceedings live. It was looking bad for the ruling party and its candidate, President Jonathan. The opposition candidate, Muhammadu Buhari, appeared to be surging ahead.

Suddenly the orderly reading of results was interrupted. Godsday Orubebe, a well-known ruling party politician and outspoken Jonathan ally, leapt up and convinced some unsuspecting assistant to hand him a microphone.

When Jonathan had become president, he had appointed Orubebe to head the Ministry of the Niger Delta. Under his leadership, the ministry served as a way station for patronage flows to Jonathan's home region. The ministry awarded hundreds of large contracts for infrastructure and social services, but only around 12 percent of the projects ever achieved their intended purpose.[58] This included a whopping $4.5 billion for an infamous road construction project in the region, far exceeding its actual cost.[59] Few individuals in government were more closely associated with the money-sharing approach to governance that thrived under Jonathan's half-hearted watch. So when Orubebe took the mic, all those watching drew in their breath.

For fifteen minutes that felt like hours, the chance for a peaceful election hung in the balance. Orubebe yelled and accused and protested. "You cannot continue!" he implored. Insulting the commissioner, he shouted: "you are compromised! Jega is biased! Jega is partisan! Jega is tribalist!" "We are not going to take it from you!" he yelled in the microphone and paced about the room on live TV. He argued that the commissioner had refused to hear a petition of complaint from the ruling party about the election results in a particular state. Rather than letting the commissioner respond to him in the open forum, Orubebe repeatedly urged the commissioner to stop the proceedings, return to his office, and receive their complaint in private.[60]

All kinds of rumors later swirled around what fate awaited the commissioner had he accepted this invitation, including one view that he would have been kidnapped.[61] But we will never know. The commissioner waited, quietly and calmly, as the yelling continued. In a performance now preserved on YouTube for perpetuity, Orubebe sat himself on the steps in front of the high table, repeating "No please! No please, we won't take it!" and "Let him go to his office!"

Finally, Orubebe's energy subsided, and he passed off the mic. Instructing everyone to take their seats, the commissioner regained control of the room. He explained the formal process by which party representatives could issue petitions—which did not include yelling about them during the formal proceedings. Then he resumed reading the results. Eighteen states later, he announced that President Jonathan had lost his bid for reelection.

I, for one, was shocked. Jonathan had billions of dollars in oil boom revenues at his disposal, and all the advantages that go with incumbency. Yet at the end of the day, all the deals and all of the payoffs could not undo Jonathan's dismal record. With a shallow base of support, an unremarkable record of accomplishments, and a reputation for corruption, he was rejected by the voters of Nigeria.

The country's fledgling democratic institutions proved just strong enough for the voters to dictate the results and ended the impunity that Jonathan and his colleagues enjoyed while in office. The elections were far from perfect. Election officials received bribes.[62] Some states yielded results that indicate extensive amounts of manipulation. Yet the election commission's leadership remained untainted, a new electronic voter ID system prevented the padding of vote tallies, and enough of the votes were counted fairly to unseat the ruling party for the first time in the country's history. In what most agree was his greatest act, Jonathan placed a call to his rival Buhari as the final votes were tallied and conceded defeat, enabling a peaceful transition to begin.

Brazil, too, saw democracy both motivate and constrict corruption. Corruption skyrocketed during the oil boom thanks to elaborate schemes orchestrated by many members of the country's political class. The perpetrators did not, however, get off scot-free.

Politicians, Tycoons, and Petrobras

In 2015, federal police arrested Marcelo Odebrecht, the heir to one of Brazil's most powerful family legacies and CEO of Odebrecht, Latin America's largest construction company. Newspapers across Brazil and beyond showed the tycoon's stunned expression as he was cuffed and led away from his mansion early in the morning, headed to a jail cell rather than to deliver a lecture in Switzerland as he had planned. From the country's first nuclear power plants and megadams in the Amazon forest to World Cup stadiums and the Olympic Village, Odebrecht built the landscape that defines contemporary Brazil. In 2014, its business empire recorded revenues of $46 billion and employed 170,000 people. A year later, Marcelo was sentenced to nineteen years in prison.

A cartel of corporations such as Odebrecht formed one part of a three-sided corruption machine that, when exposed, changed the course of Brazilian history. The other two? The national oil company, Petrobras, and the country's political parties. Together these three groups orchestrated an oil boom corruption scheme that is remarkable for several reasons. The corruption was enormous. The bribes exchanged topped $3 billion; one single Petrobras executive turned over $97 million in stolen funds. The corruption was systematic. As the following account will show, it ran through surprisingly formalized systems, embedded in the companies' day-to-day operations. Finally, as in Nigeria, the corruption did not go unpunished. Hundreds of people have faced investigations already, and the courts have convicted some of Brazil's most powerful political and economic figures.

In 2014, Brazil's federal police launched an investigation into some suspicious financial transfers. They suspected that a former criminal was laundering money through a car wash, along with several other businesses. They arrested the money launderer, who then began to spill the beans. Little did the police know that they'd uncovered a case that would alter the course of the country's economic and political future. From these initial inquiries, the scandal acquired a nickname that would stick: Lava-Jato, or the "Car Wash."

Among the first Petrobras executives ensnared by the investigation was Paulo Oberto Costa. He served as the chief downstream officer and director of supply at Petrobras from 2004 to 2012, a position that oversaw lots of large-scale contracting. During the boom years, Costa's star rose alongside oil prices. A journalist covering the saga painted this portrait: "down to earth, loquacious and accessible, [Costa] curried favor with the press, politicians and the wealthy. He presided over long schmooze sessions with the reporters, dishing scoops and opinions on company inner workings. . . . Costa projected candor and reveled in his perceived role as a straight shooter. He had his own publicists and the Petrobras press office would often wake to Costa interviews in the newspapers that they had no idea were coming. He was often photographed with high-ranking politicians, President Rousseff among them."[63]

Costa's ability to grab headlines only accelerated with his arrest. In exchange for a more lenient sentence, Costa provided the government with one of the first insider accounts of how the Car Wash worked. In his court testimony, now readily viewable on YouTube, Costa methodically explained the mechanics of the scam. The devastating consequences of his testimony, which named dozens of complicit officials, led him to be dubbed "the Human Bomb." Lawyers working on the case commented to journalists: "it was kind of like, in Brazil, we know that corruption is a monster. But we never really see the monster. This was like seeing the monster."[64]

According to Costa's account, which has been backed up by subsequent investigations, each division of Petrobras was assigned a *padrinho*, or godfather, from a political party. The ruling Workers' Party controlled five of the company's divisions, with three other parties in the ruling coalition sharing control of the remaining two.[65] The godfather and other party heavyweights would choose who got to be the director of that division and sit on the Petrobras board. In exchange, these directors then had to keep party leaders happy.

To channel funds into political party coffers, Petrobras would allocate valuable construction and supply contracts to a predetermined group of Brazil's largest construction and engineering companies. The cartel of companies would meet regularly and decide which of them would win a particular tender. Petrobras would help out by providing them with draft tender documents and insider information on what type of bid would be accepted. Winning bids were often inflated by 15–20 percent during this period. The winning company would then transfer around 3 percent of the contract's value to the political party associated with the division of Petrobras that had issued the contract.[66] The companies made the payments through facilitators who moved the money through shell companies, secret accounts, or suitcases of cash and who also received a cut. Along with political party representatives, Petrobras officials and a range of other politicians received kickbacks as well.

The day police arrested Costa, security cameras spotted his daughters and their husbands stuffing their luggage with cash, documents, and a laptop. The cops found about $500,000 in cash in the house and went on to uncover around $28.5 million stashed in Swiss bank accounts belonging to Costa and his family members. Along with his detailed testimony, Costa agreed with the government that he would turn over all the Swiss cash and other assets, including a yacht, a Land Rover, and a piece of land in Rio state.[67]

The kickback scheme unveiled by Costa is not that unusual, as far as corruption goes. Governments often use public sector contracting to misappropriate funds, especially contracting done by national oil companies. As in the Nigeria case, many national oil companies receive and allocate a huge portion of public revenues and do so outside of the standard budgetary and oversight systems. National oil companies in Algeria, Iraq, Nigeria, Venezuela, and beyond have all faced corruption controversies around their contracting processes. But none features the scale and systematic approach seen in Brazil.

How and why did the corruption grow to this scale? The competition among political parties in Brazil and the relations between the country's politicians and its business elites provide some explanation, as does the scale of the oil boom itself.

Around 30 political parties are represented in the National Congress of Brazil. With no group holding anything close to a majority, the party that holds the presidency faces the chronic challenge of building and maintaining a coalition large enough to move things through the Congress. To add to the chaos, until a recent reform, individual politicians frequently shifted from party to party. The political elite is, therefore, very fragmented and competitive, and its members scramble constantly to gain an edge on their rivals.[68]

In 2003, Luiz Inácio Lula da Silva won the presidential elections and ushered in a period of rule by the left-leaning Workers' Party. During his two terms in office, Lula oversaw a historic period of economic growth and poverty reduction. Widely popular and respected, Lula at the time appeared to strike a balance between achieving economic stability and growth while attending to social issues and the needs of lower income citizens. He tapped Dilma Rousseff as his successor, and she went on to win the presidential race in 2010.

Dilma, as she is usually known, formed a coalition of ten parties. While this gave her a majority in congress, she still struggled to get legislation through on occasion. Alliances between parties were based more on pork barrel politics and hard-nosed negotiations than ideological affinity. In particular, the Workers' Party had plenty of disagreements with a major member of its coalition, the Brazilian Democratic Movement Party.

This type of competitive political landscape can create incentives for corruption, as getting anything done requires convincing a range of politicians to come on board, all of whom themselves face challenging and expensive campaigning demands. In 2005, during Lula's first term, the Mensalão, or "big monthly," scandal broke open. The office of the president was making monthly payments to legislators to buy support for the president's agenda and help pay off their campaign debts. Twenty-five officials were convicted, but Lula himself was not charged. The scandal proved, however, that even the popular and powerful Lula had to spread some money around.

The political leaders of Brazil had always maintained close, symbiotic relations with the country's business elites. This practice continued unabated under the Workers' Party despite the more populist content of their platform. Many of Brazil's largest companies owe their success to decades of support from the government. The oligarchs made their money in all corners of the economy, including the media, agriculture, finance, food and beverage, energy, and mining sectors. But those with the thickest ties to government are the construction companies. These large conglomerates are "omnipresent" in the Brazilian economy, which is one reason why their corrupt acts ended up being so far-reaching.[69]

The construction giants—including the "four sisters": Odebrecht, OAS, Camargo Corrêa, and Andrade Gutierrez—have long relied on the government for infrastructure contracts, low-interest financing, and favorable tax and regulatory policies. They have used their close relations with political elites to crowd out foreign and domestic competition. In the 1950s, the government relied on these companies to build the country's new capital city. As some commentators have noted, the companies built Brasília and then never left.[70]

Since then, successive governments showered benefits on Odebrecht and its peers. During Brazil's resource boom, its government-owned development bank quadrupled in size By 2015, over 60 percent of the bank's preferential lending went to "national champions"—the large, industry-leading companies who could probably raise funds on commercial markets without help from the state.[71] Between 2007 and 2015, the bank lent $8 billion to Odebrecht alone, including funds for construction projects not even located in Brazil. This amount represented 70 percent of the bank's entire lending for construction projects.[72] Taxpayers essentially subsidized loans to the country's richest economic players. Odebrecht also won portions of eight of the ten biggest construction projects associated with the 2014 World Cup and 2016 Olympic Games.[73] In the street protests that erupted before the World Cup, one sign summed up the situation: "The $ for healthcare went to Odebrecht/The $ for education went to OAS."[74]

In return, the oligarchs who headed up the companies paid the politicians handsomely. The four biggest contributors to electoral campaigns between 2002 and 2012 were construction companies.[75] This practice may lessen following a 2015 Supreme Court ruling to limit company contributions to electoral campaigns. However, it was in full swing during the oil boom. Along with formal donations, the companies found other channels via which to support politicians. Analysts estimate that as much as 50–90 percent of campaign spending comes from the *caixa dois*, the "second cash register," which receives under-the-table donations.[76] Odebrecht's CEO eventually confessed to making large illegal donations to Rousseff's reelection in 2014, though she denied receiving any illegal funds.[77]

Along with the competition among political parties, these tight-knit relations between government and business created a conducive context for the Car Wash scandal. The journalist Alex Cuadros covered Brazil's billionaires for *Bloomberg* and wrote a book about the experience. Observing this symbiosis as the economy began to heat up, he wrote: "believing it was the only way to govern, Lula and Dilma had allied themselves with Brazil's entrenched interests, and somewhere along the way that old compromise, *rouba mas faz*—'he steals, but he gets things done'—spun out of control."[78]

The politicians and the companies formed two sides of the Car Wash scheme, but they needed a third, and the cash-flush national oil company worked perfectly. Petrobras was the ideal vehicle for channeling money from the country's booming oil sector to its political and business heavyweights.

Petrobras was the showpiece of Brazil's economic boom, which got started around the time Lula took office in 2003. As shown in figure 3.1, from 2003 to 2011, the Brazilian economy grew at historic rates. Many of these riches accrued at the top: the number of Brazilians on the *Forbes* list

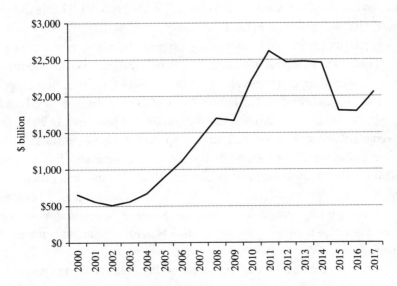

FIGURE 3.1 GDP of Brazil, 2000–2017.

SOURCE: World Bank, *World Development Indicators*, 2018.

of billionaires rose from six in 2002 to thirty-six in 2012. Brazilian wealth spread well beyond its borders: in 2007, Brazilians bought one of every seven houses sold in Miami.[79] However, thanks in part to government policies, other classes benefited as well: poverty rates and income inequality fell, and millions of Brazilians entered the middle class.[80] A heady optimism took hold: Brazil was becoming one of the most important economies in the world.

Petrobras grew in step with the economy. Beginning a period of good news, Petrobras announced in 2007 the discovery of oil deep below the ocean, in a layer of seabed called the "pre-salt." The find doubled the country's known oil and gas reserves. Enthused by this good luck, President Lula declared "God is Brazilian!" and likened Brazil's oil sector to the "prettiest girl at a jamboree—everyone wants a dance." Backing up his zeal, Petrobras grew to be the fifth largest company in the world by 2009, with a market capitalization of $310 billion.

The Brazilian government owns just over 50 percent of Petrobras, with the remaining shares traded on US and Brazilian exchanges. As a publicly listed company, Petrobras certainly performs in a far more commercially sound manner than an entity like NNPC, which is more like a misshapen government agency than a company. In fact, in 2013, the Natural Resource Governance Institute, awarded Petrobras a stunning score of 92 out of 100 points for its transparency and governance practices, placing it in the top three of the forty-five state-owned companies we assessed.[81] Little did we know what was going on behind the scenes.

Despite its growth and world-class exterior, Petrobras remained very much under the government's control, with political leaders exerting influence over board appointments and other key decisions. In 2003, Lula tapped his close ally and chief of staff Dilma Rousseff to chair the Petrobras board, a position she held until 2010, when she was elected president. In 2010, the government adopted a set of reforms to expand the role of Petrobras in the sector and close off opportunities for other oil companies. The reforms called for Petrobras to exclusively conduct all exploration and production activities in the pre-salt fields. Petrobras also had to hold at least 30 percent of the shares in any foreign-led consortium active in the sector. A new local content law also boosted opportunities that benefited Brazilian companies, especially in the provision of various goods and services.

To keep pace with all these opportunities, Petrobras needed to construct onshore and offshore facilities quickly and at a massive scale. And that's where the corruption really took flight.

A Car Wash Runneth Over

From 2001 to 2016, Odebrecht paid at least $788 million in bribes to win valuable contracts, in Brazil but also abroad.[82] Secretly moving hundreds of millions of dollars requires sophisticated systems. So Odebrecht built them, and various court documents now available give a look inside at how they worked.

The Division of Structured Operations, created in 2006, formed the hub of Odebrecht's bribery operations. The division used a special communications system it called Drousys complete with code names and specialized email and instant messenger functionality. They also created a shadow accounting system to keep the Division's transactions off the company's formal balance sheets.

When Odebrecht received an inflated contract from Petrobras or another client, the extra money would be handled by the Division of Structured Operations. In order to move the money off Odebrecht's books, the Division created a number of shell companies, and those companies would issue Odebrecht with fake invoices. The US charges against Odebrecht explained how the bribe money flowed through "multiple levels of off-shore entities and bank accounts throughout the world, often transferring the illicit funds through up to four levels of offshore bank accounts before reaching the final recipient."[83] As is often the case with corruption, Odebrecht favored channeling the funds through secrecy havens like the British Virgin Islands and other countries whose laws protect banking secrecy and prevent the sharing of information about account holders with other governments. Odebrecht paid their favorite banks exorbitant fees to secure their cooperation.

The bribery architecture required constant maintenance. At one point, one of Odebrecht's favorite banks, located in the tropical tax haven of Antigua, began to underperform. So parties to the various conspiracies decided they needed their own Antiguan outfit. They bought the Antiguan branch of an Austrian bank around 2010 and instructed several politicians and other bribe recipients to open accounts there instead.[84]

Odebrecht employed this system inside Brazil and well beyond. The company executes major construction projects across Latin America, including some of the region's largest bridges, dams, and stadiums. Of the known bribes, $439 million went to officials in twelve countries outside Brazil.[85] In several cases, as in Brazil, Odebrecht was angling to receive contracts from oil-rich governments that had lots of money to spend during the boom period. For example, the company paid $50 million to government officials in Angola in order to receive infrastructure contracts. In Venezuela, the bribes topped $98 million, as Odebrecht enjoyed a strong relationship with the country's former president, Hugo Chavez.

Back in Brazil, one 2010 deal typifies the scam. Petrobras announced a tender for a contract to provide environmental and security certification services. Just as Petrobras bigwig Paulo Costa had exposed in his testimony to police, the cartel of Brazilian construction companies met and agreed that Odebrecht should receive the contract from Petrobras and determined the price it should bid. Three companies eventually bid for the contract, but two of the bids were just for show. Petrobras executives, complicit in the scam, made sure that Odebrecht "won."

The Division of Structured Operations then arranged for several of its shell companies, including ones headquartered in the British Virgin Islands and Panama, to submit invoices for $40 million for services that never took place. The Division used its off-budget systems to pay the invoices.[86] Individuals at the companies then transferred the funds through another layer of shell companies and secret accounts, until the money eventually found its way to Petrobras executives, politicians, and other government officials.

Through transactions like this one, Odebrecht paid $349 million in bribes to win $1.9 billion worth of business from the Brazilian government between 2003 and 2016.[87] Most of this flowed through the Petrobras Car Wash.

Those numbers tell us a lot about the boom-time mentality that existed within Petrobras during those years. In order for Odebrecht to afford all those bribes, the contracts had to be significantly overvalued. Petrobras proved again and again willing to pay inflated prices, so as to pay everyone off and still get the work done. Political priorities and greed trumped cost control time after time.

In another example, Petrobras set out to construct the Abreu e Lima Refinery for $4 billion. The project became one of the costliest sinkholes of the entire Car Wash era. According to accusations against Petrobras made in a class action lawsuit, several large construction companies met at Petrobras and received instructions on how high they could bid for the various contracts and add-on contracts associated with the refinery.[88] By the time the refinery opened in 2013, the project had involved 300 contracts with 950 amendments.[89] Thanks to this feeding frenzy, its overall cost came in at over $18 billion.[90]

Petrobras spent a further $21 billion on the Comperj Refinery in Rio, with contracts as large as $3 billion awarded with no tender at all.[91]

Millions of dollars from the project helped fund the election campaign of a politician who controlled the region where the refinery was located; millions more went to several Petrobras executives.[92] Thanks to spending like this, Petrobras's debts increased fivefold between 2009 and 2015, and the company became the largest corporate debtor in the world.[93] Petrobras has admitted that bribery infiltrated both projects.[94]

While most of the corruption involved tenders for construction services, the Petrobras officials and their coconspirators were not one-trick ponies. Braskem is one of the largest petrochemical companies in the Americas. Odebrecht owns just over 50 percent of its voting shares, and Petrobras owns a further 36 percent. Around 2006, Braskem executives decided that the company needed a better system for paying off public officials and decided to make use of Odebrecht's existing Division of Structured Operations. To extract the funds for the bribes, Braskem entered into "fabricated contracts" with "fictitious" counterparts and then paid these shell companies for services that never took place, according to US court filings.[95] From there, the money entered Odebrecht's sprawling bribery operations. Through this channel, Braskem made $250 million in improper payments via Odebrecht's off-book accounts, with at least $75 million in bribes going to Petrobras executives, members of the Congress, and political party officials.[96]

In exchange for the payoffs, Petrobras officials helped Braskem make more money. In 2009, Braskem signed an agreement with Petrobras to purchase naphtha, a byproduct from oil production used to manufacture various petrochemicals. In exchange for $12 million in bribes, Petrobras officials granted Braskem particularly favorable naptha prices.[97] United States authorities estimated that these soft prices helped Braskem make an additional $94 million over the next five years. They also found that Braskem received tax credits and regulatory breaks worth over $187 million, among other juicy favors.[98]

Brazilian companies were not alone in bribing Petrobras. SBM Offshore, a Dutch oilfield services company, is among the foreign players who have admitted to having paid bribes to Petrobras officials. SBM paid a number of large "commissions" to shell companies controlled by an intermediary, and the money then went to Swiss bank accounts controlled by Petrobras personnel.[99]

Some of the corrupt deals involving SBM Offshore may have sprung from Brazil's ruthlessly competitive politics. According to the class action suit filed against Petrobras, around 2009 the Workers' Party sought to quickly commission an oil rig so that they could celebrate the rig's "baptism" around the time of the next elections and take credit for the oil sector's next phase of growth. SBM Offshore agreed to meet their rushed timeline but charged a very high price in return.[100] According to the complaint, "these unnecessary costs were incurred solely to benefit the government's political campaign and cost Petrobras millions of dollars."[101]

By 2014, after years of this system growing and growing, the individuals running Odebrecht's Division of Structured Operations began getting nervous that authorities might discover the rot. Executives began to conceal and destroy evidence of their activities, including the physical encryption keys used to access the off-book budgetary system. In 2015, one executive flew to Miami in order to meet with a government official from Antigua, a favored thruway for the company's laundered funds. The executive offered to pay the official and his colleagues $4 million if they refused to provide foreign law enforcement authorities with certain bank books.[102]

But the cover-up efforts proved too little, too late. Or, perhaps, the corruption had grown too big to hide.

Consequences from Curitiba

A few prosecutors, based in the southern city of Curitiba, filed the initial charges against the money launderer who had run cash through the infamous car wash, and charged Petrobras executive Paulo Costa, whose testimony unveiled the scheme for the first time. They decided to pursue the case wherever else it might lead. They invited other prosecutors believed to be independent to join them in Curitiba, forming a tight-knit team that worked around the clock to develop the case. Many were young and had studied at elite law schools abroad, and they operated outside the political patronage system that enwrapped much of the Brazilian judicial system. It was a stroke of luck that the initial case broke in Curitiba, as its police and prosecutors were less infiltrated by political money and influence than their counterparts in Brazil's largest cities.

Once the investigation got off the ground, the prosecutors and the presiding federal judge fended off efforts from the defense lawyers to move the proceedings to other jurisdictions or to the more ineffectual Supreme Court.[103] The team used techniques not often seen in Brazil to break open the investigation. They would, for instance, immediately throw high-profile suspects in jail so as to pressure them to sign plea bargains, whose contents would implicate others involved in the schemes.

The key protagonists in bringing down the Car Wash became national heroes for a time. In the protests that followed the scandal's discovery, marchers wore masks and carried posters that heralded the policeman who led off the billionaires in handcuffs and the judge who presided over many of the cases. One of the prosecutors, Paulo Roberto Galvão de Carvalho, explained the team's cause: "fear of the law was something that did not exist in Brazil for white-collar criminals and politicians. This needs to change, and is changing."[104]

While corruption in Brazil had infiltrated the national oil company and other government institutions, it had not reached all corners of the judicial system. Some of the police, prosecutors, and courts enjoyed enough power and independence to bring down the country's most powerful individuals. The rule of law, that fragile hallmark of democracy, remained intact, even when the defendants held high office or sat atop business empires. As with the electoral system in Nigeria, the success of these endeavors proves corruption was not the only game in town.

Few in Curitiba suspected how far the investigations would go. With each confession, the number of implicated elites grew and grew. Top politicians began to fall, as did business moguls, including Marcelo Odebrecht, who soon found himself in a Curitiba jail cell.

Soon the case spread far beyond the oil sector as investigators scrambled to manage the snowballing leads. Police and prosecutors began to examine other parts of the construction industry, including the enormous projects commissioned by the government for the 2014 World Cup and 2016 Rio Olympics. In the time since, Sergio Cabral, the mayor of Rio during these showcase events, has been sentenced to fourteen years in prison for soliciting $66 million in bribes, including for the contract to renovate the world-famous Maracanã soccer stadium. Business mogul Eike Batista, once the world's eighth richest man, has been found guilty of bribing Mayor Cabral and sentenced to thirty years in prison.[105] Many others among Brazil's elites joined them behind bars.

Companies also felt the consequences. Petrobras agreed to pay an $850 million fine in response to criminal charges by US and Brazilian authorities and $2.9 billion to settle a civil action lawsuit brought by its shareholders.[106] The value of Petrobras fell to a fraction of its boom-time heights, as the corruption scandal broke just as oil prices crashed. Odebrecht and Braskem negotiated a $3.5 billion combined settlement with the governments of Brazil, Switzerland, and the United States, though parts of the fine have been negotiated downward given the companies' limited ability to pay.[107]

A number of Petrobras's foreign partners, including Rolls-Royce in the United Kingdom, SBM Offshore in the Netherlands, and Singapore-based Keppel Offshore, all paid fines of several hundred million dollars to settle bribery charges.[108]

The large overseas operations of Odebrecht carried the Car Wash scandal across Latin America. Scandals have erupted in Peru, Mexico, Venezuela, Colombia, and Honduras, often exposing how top politicians received funds from the Brazilian construction giant.

Perhaps the most dramatic fallout reverberated across Brazil's political class. Literally hundreds of sitting politicians from all the major parties were implicated in the various confessions. Over eighty members of the Congress have faced legal proceedings.

The public, faced with the scale of the corruption along with a painful economic recession, reacted with outrage. In 2015, Brazilians poured into the streets in protest, with 200,000 marching in São Paolo alone. President Rousseff found herself at the center of the storm. While she had not been directly implicated in the Car Wash corruption at that time, she had served as the chair of the Petrobras board and then as president of the country while all the billions were stolen.

Calls for her impeachment reverberated from the streets and from politicians across the political spectrum. Vice-President Michel Temer, the head of the powerful Brazilian Democratic Movement Party, orchestrated a successful impeachment campaign, finding Rousseff guilty of manipulating federal budget figures in order to misrepresent the size of the public deficit. The offense was not a new practice, and many disputed whether it was sufficient cause for impeachment. But the political climate had turned against Rousseff, and the votes for her departure made that clear. Following his successful power move, Temer soon became president.

But the Car Wash was not done soaking political ambitions. Less than a year into Temer's unpopular presidency, audio recordings surfaced via one of the many Car Wash plea bargains. The tapes appear to reveal Temer approving "hush payments" to keep a prominent politician imprisoned through the Car Wash investigation from naming further names.[109] Prosecutors then discovered evidence that Temer had accepted millions of dollars in bribes, from a large meatpacking company that was also caught up in the Car Wash web, and charged him with bribery. Temer denies the charges and calls them politicized attacks.[110]

More than the impeachment of Rousseff or the charges against Temer, the conviction of former president Lula unleashed the greatest shockwaves. Lula has a legendary status. A former factory worker and union leader, he became president and oversaw historic growth: 30 million Brazilians exited extreme poverty, and the country became one of the world's most powerful economies. He wanted to run for president again in 2018 to help mend his traumatized nation. But the wide net of the Car Wash investigation nabbed him as well. In 2017, he was sentenced to prison for receiving a beachfront apartment and other benefits worth around $1 million from OAS, one of the construction companies deeply embroiled in the Petrobras bribery ring.[111] While serious questions would follow about whether Lula's prosecution was politically motivated,[112] the outcome of the Car Wash was clear: power and wealth no longer offered protection from the law.

Super PACs and Lobbyists in an Oil Boom Democracy

The Brazil story suggests that no one, no matter how rich or influential, should be above the law. But what if the laws are too lenient?

While certainly less dramatic than what happened in Brazil and Nigeria, the US oil boom experience also offers important lessons about how oil money impacts policymaking in democracies. In the late 2000s, a double-barreled oil boom took off in the United States. As prices soared, so too did the scale of the industry: US oil production rose from 6.8 million barrels a day in 2008 to 13 million in 2017. Thanks to this meteoric rise, in 2014 the United States edged out both Russia and Saudi Arabia for the title of world's largest oil producer for the first time since 1975.[113] In a rough illustration of the wealth that followed, in 2009 the value of US oil production totaled around $165 billion; by 2011 it was $400 billion. The oil boom altered US foreign policy, especially as the country now imports much less oil from the Middle East, and transformed regions of the country. North Dakota's oil production increased tenfold in just ten years, and Colorado, West Virginia, and Wyoming debuted as oil hot spots. After decades of decline, production in Texas began to rise in 2009 and then tripled over the next five years.[114]

In 2011, amid all this growth, a lawyer for Devon Energy, one of the largest US oil and gas companies, wrote an email to a staffer in the office of Oklahoma's attorney general. "Crystal: good to see you last week. I wondered if the letter Attorney General Pruitt plans to send the EPA [Environmental Protection Agency] on methane emissions has changed much from the draft we proposed? Thanks, AJF." Crystal replied: "Hi AJ, we are circulating the letter to other AGs [Attorney Generals] for sign on right now. Once we finish we will send it on. Will keep you posted!"[115]

A few days later, the Environmental Protection Agency, a federal regulatory body, received an official letter from Attorney General Scott Pruitt of Oklahoma, a top-five oil-producing state. The letter, published in a *New York Times* investigation, complained that the agency was overestimating the pollution caused by drilling natural gas wells. Pruitt changed only 37 of the 1,016 words contained in Devon's draft.

Drafting correspondence was just part of the thick cooperation between Pruitt's office and a number of oil companies, as the two parties worked to thwart environmental regulations established under President Barack Obama. In another novel form of collaboration, the state of Oklahoma joined with an oil industry lobby group, the Domestic Energy Producers Alliance, to sue the federal Department of the Interior over wildlife regulations that threatened oil production on potentially lucrative territory. Devon Energy is a member of the Alliance, along with dozens of other companies that stood to profit from the lawsuit if it was successful.

In the United States and elsewhere, it is entirely typical for the actions of individual politicians and policy-makers to align with the agendas of some interest groups more than others. Some public officials collaborate closely with environmental groups, for instance, while others lean more toward industry. The tricky question is what motivates this closeness. Is it shared beliefs? Or is it the money provided by rich companies and individuals to help the officials compete in expensive elections?

At the time of the joint lawsuit, the Energy Producers Alliance was headed by Harold Hamm, the richest man in Oklahoma. A self-made billionaire, Hamm was the thirteenth child of sharecroppers and first encountered the oil industry while pumping gas at the age of sixteen. He went on to found Continental Resources, which grew into one of the country's biggest independent oil and gas companies. Known as a pioneer in the world of fracking, Hamm's fortune topped $20 billion at the peak of the oil boom.

Hamm donated money to Pruitt's 2010 and 2014 election campaigns, contributing some of the $250,000 Pruitt received from the oil industry. So enthusiastic was the support of oilmen like Hamm that donations poured in even when Pruitt ran uncontested in 2014, a campaign Hamm chaired himself. Energy companies also donated generously to several political action committees (PACs) that Pruitt helped create.[116] Super PACs, as the committees are widely known, are US entities that allow corporations and individuals to finance election campaigns with amounts over and above what they can legally donate directly to individual candidates.

Pruitt's battles against the Environmental Protection Agency, heralded by his company allies, garnered him wide recognition. When President Trump needed a director for the Agency, he appointed Pruitt, much to the delight of oil and gas magnates, several of whom actively advised Trump before and after his election. "He couldn't have picked a better guy to head the EPA," Hamm told journalists in 2016, while also criticizing the agency for its past "regulatory overreach."[117]

Unsurprisingly, as head of the Agency, Pruitt set about undoing the regulations he had fought against from Oklahoma. Within a year, he had proposed repealing or delaying more than thirty environmental rules, and he offered no opposition to the White House proposal that the Agency's budget drop by 25 percent.[118]

Pruitt's open hostility to the Agency's mission did not bother his new boss. But he also got carried away by the stature of his new post. To boost security and secrecy, he ordered the agency to buy a soundproof phone booth for $43,000. He rented a Washington DC apartment from energy industry lobbyists at an unusually affordable price, and he tried to get a job for his wife using his company connections. He traveled lavishly and proposed leasing a plane for $100,000 per month. He deleted sensitive information about his public schedule.[119] For these transgressions and others, Pruitt became the subject of daily media headlines and over a dozen federal ethics investigations. The scandals began to erode Republican backing for Pruitt, but the president stood fast. Eventually, though, Pruitt's ambitions proved his undoing. According to media reports, Trump finally dropped his support when Pruitt pushed to be named attorney general of the United States. In 2018, he resigned.

While Pruitt flamed out rather dramatically, there is nothing unusual about how he used oil money to rise to power and looked after oil industry interests while in office. Drew Darby also followed this well-worn path. A Republican state representative in Texas, Darby chaired the Texas House Energy Resource Committee for several years. He received $174,000 in donations from the industry between 2013 and 2016, despite running unopposed in at least four of his elections.[120] Along with chairing the Energy Resource Committee, Darby also sits on the US Department of the Interior's Royalty Policy Committee, which weighs in on how much companies should pay the federal government for producing oil on federal lands and in the Gulf of Mexico. A number of the companies that pay these royalties, including Exxon, Chevron, and Anadarko, also donate to Darby.[121] In the American system, none of this is illegal or even kept hush-hush. Instead, partnerships of this kind are celebrated: in 2013, the Texas Oil and Gas Association awarded Darby their Legislative Champion Award.

Campaign contributions from the oil and gas industry rose markedly during the boom years. Comparing years in which there was a presidential race, donations from the industry rose from $27 million in 2004 to $40 million in 2008 and then to $82 million in 2012 before reaching $102 million in 2016.[122] Over three-quarters of the giving went to Republicans. Around half of the money went directly to candidates, especially those from oil-producing states. The rest supported super PACs or other outside groups. The name of the industry's largest donor comes as little surprise to those who follow US politics. Koch Industries, the company run by renowned conservative fundraisers Charles and David Koch, topped the list in 2014, 2016, and 2018, followed by Chevron. Not only did the Kochs open their own pockets but also they spearheaded a "stealthy state-of-the-art counteroffensive" to the growing climate change agenda, as described by Jane Mayer in her study of the family's political influence.[123]

Along with the double-barreled oil boom, another change helps explain the rise in oil industry campaign contributions. In 2010, the Supreme Court ruled in the *Citizens United* decision that there is no limit on what corporations and individuals can spend on convincing voters to support or reject a given candidate. While companies cannot give directly to candidates, they can fund other entities. The decision led to the birth of the super PAC and provided wealthy individuals and companies with new routes for influencing electoral outcomes.

All this campaign money raises difficult questions about what defines corruption. Let's say an oil company provides a large campaign donation to a politician, and that politician later makes a decision that helps that oil company make more money. How large can the donation be before it causes inappropriate levels of influence? How directly must the decision benefit the company before the donation becomes a bribe? Under what circumstances does this transaction constitute corruption?

United States courts have handed down some very conservative answers to this type of question in recent years. A former Virginia governor received $175,000 worth of gifts from a businessman and then did favors for him while in office. He was convicted on corruption charges. But then, in 2016, the Supreme Court overturned the conviction, arguing that the favors did not constitute formal and concrete government actions and rather were the kind of general support that a public official might show a constituent. With legal precedents like that, the symbiotic relationships between oil companies and officials like Pruitt and Darby are safe to proceed.

Campaign donations aren't the only way oil companies use their money to impact public policy. The amount spent by oil and gas companies on lobbying topped $130 million each year from 2008 to 2015, up from around $60 million per year in the decade prior.[124] The list of leading spenders again holds few surprises, with Koch Industries, Occidental, Exxon, Chevron, BP, and Shell topping the tables. Many of the oil industry lobbyists paid for with all this money have passed through the "revolving door." The portion of oil industry lobbyists who previously worked for members of Congress or other parts of government is notably higher than in other industries.[125]

While oil companies used lobbyists to reach policy-makers, they found ways to directly influence the public too. Over eight years, industry players, led by foundations affiliated with the Koch brothers and other prominent oil barons, plowed half a billion dollars into over ninety nonprofit organizations that spread denials of the science behind global warming. They bankrolled research as well. According to Mayer's account, the Kochs along with ExxonMobil and the leading oil industry association funded a non-peer-reviewed study that claimed that the prospects of the world's polar bear populations looked just fine, for instance. One of the academics behind the "revisionist polar bear study" had himself received $1.2 million in industry donations.[126]

After years of fighting the Obama administration, the industry has now shifted to exploiting the opportunities made available by the more sympathetic Donald Trump. Oil-funded groups have enthusiastically funded advertising and social media campaigns that support the Trump administration's efforts to weaken fuel efficiency standards for automobiles. The more gasoline cars consume, after all, the more gasoline is bought. These campaigns adopted the language of personal liberty, with Facebook ads saying "Support Our President's Car Freedom Agenda." Industry money, routed through several associations, funded a petition on the same issue that succeeded in getting 3,300 public comments lodged with the US Treasury Department. As with the other methods, this influencing tactic is both legal and commonplace.[127]

Oil money has influenced government regulators too. Until its recent disbanding, the Minerals Management Service (MMS) was the office within the Department of the Interior charged with managing the offshore oil industry and collecting more than $10 billion a year in royalties. According to a congressional investigation, MMS staff received oil company gifts that violated their ethics rules, including golf, ski, and paintball trips and tickets to a Toby Keith concert and several pro sports games. Officials got drunk, used drugs, and had sex with oil company personnel. At a golf event sponsored by Shell, two MMS officials got so wasted they could not drive to their hotel and instead stayed at lodging provided by the company. The inspector general of the Department of the Interior said that the MMS suffered from a "culture of ethical failure."[128]

Further investigations found that shortcomings in MMS systems led to billions of dollars in lost revenue each year.[129] The 2010 explosion of the Deepwater Horizon rig in the Gulf of Mexico, which killed eleven people and caused tremendous environmental damage, drove the final nail into the MMS coffin. Some reports indicate that MMS had failed to conduct adequate inspections of the rig over its lifetime.[130] In 2010, the MMS was dissolved.

Despite all the campaign spending and lobbying, oil companies do not unilaterally set the agenda in the United States. As in Brazil and Nigeria, democratic institutions and citizen groups often push back using methods large and small. The Government Accountability Office, a congressional research body, reported Pruitt's spending violations when he bought his soundproof phone booth.[131] Campaign donations and even many super PAC contributions are transparent, and the Federal Election Commission and advocacy groups like OpenSecrets.org and the National Institute on Money in Politics make the data available online so that citizens and journalists can see who is funding particular candidates. The same goes for lobbying data.

Despite its deep pockets, the oil industry is just one interest group competing to influence public policy in the United States. In 2017, to the frustration of the oil lobby, Maryland joined New York in banning fracking. Maryland's Republican governor supported the ban, which had been voted through by the Democrat-controlled state legislature. Florida has banned offshore drilling. Outside formal government systems, public protests succeeded in delaying, at least temporarily, the construction of the Keystone XL and Dakota Access pipelines. Media reports expose the industry's more distasteful efforts, and pundits loudly complain. Thanks to the country's pluralism and its democratic institutions, the oil lobby cannot count on carrying the day.

Will the Remedies Be Strong Enough?

In Brazil, Nigeria, and the United States, public officials made decisions that benefited certain companies, and those companies then helped support their political and personal agendas. Using Nigeria's dysfunctional NNPC as a vehicle, the minister Alison-Madueke channeled billions of dollars in oil funds to companies headed by her allies. Tankers filled with cut-price oil streamed out of the country, and oil revenues meant for public spending ended up supporting her luxury lifestyle. In Brazil, politicians, national oil company executives, and construction magnates developed a cynical and sophisticated system to siphon off public funds using inflated contracts. Hundreds of public officials took part, and companies had entire divisions devoted to running the scheme. In the United States, oil money flowed into election campaigns and lobbyist fees, and influenced policy results.

Democratic and oversight institutions can provide some remedy to these ills. There are all kinds of accountability mechanisms that can help curtail large-scale corruption. Inside the government, you have the courts, as seen in Brazil, as well as oversight bodies like the ombudsmen and auditor general. Legislatures can sound the alarm about corruption and initiate investigations, if they do their job properly. Elections too can cause corrupt leaders to face consequences. Institutions outside government matter also, like a free press, academic institutions where independent research can thrive, and activists who can operate without intimidation. In both Nigeria and Brazil, the media and civil society groups picked up the cause of corruption and pressed for it to be addressed. In the United States, these groups work to expose and reduce the oil lobby's influence over government.

In many political contexts, strengthening these agents of accountability can help to fight corruption. Most of these efforts will need to be domestic in nature, in order for them to result in lasting gains. However, international parties can help. As part of their foreign aid, many countries have programs that aim to strengthen these actors in developing countries where corruption risks run high. However, these aid programs constitute a very small portion of overall development assistance. USAID spent less than 10 percent of its 2016 budget on supporting democracy and governance reforms abroad.[132] Ramping up support for democratic institutions seems a clear takeaway from the stories outlined here.

But one should not underestimate the challenges ahead for countries like Brazil, Nigeria, and the United States. The structural factors that explain the corruption remain in place: money-driven politics, the need for ruling elites to secure support from other powerful factions, blurred lines between the public and private sector, and the oil itself. While some of the politicians who masterminded the scams were punished, there is no ready-built alternative political elite who can step in and take over. Those who rise to power will still be a part of the system to one degree or another or at least indebted to those who are.

As Brazil's political and business leaders continued to fall, some asked if the punishments should abate. If the country's economy and political stability depends on the current elite, are they perhaps "too big to fail?"[133] Analysts likened the situation to the "Clean Hands" anticorruption operation in Italy in the 1990s, which took down some powerful figures but also led to a prolonged political crisis. Should the business leaders be spared so they can go on playing their key role in the troubled economy? Should politicians be allowed to stay in office but face tighter rules and greater scrutiny?

Jair Bolsonaro will answer some of these questions. This conservative politician won Brazil's 2018 presidential elections with a mix of anticorruption promises and aggressive right-wing populist positions. Following the Car Wash scandal, an economic recession, and other disappointments of the Workers' Party years, Brazilian voters certainly went looking for a change. Bolsonaro promised that he would not appoint anyone who had been convicted of corruption. But it may not be possible to govern without brushing up against corruption in Brazil. He appointed as his justice minister the judge who sent many of the Car Wash conspirators to prison. Some observers cried foul, questioning whether the judge had been rewarded with the position after sending Lula to prison and keeping him from competing against Bolsonaro in the elections. Others praised the move, saying that it might lead to the passage of stronger anticorruption laws.

In Nigeria, low oil prices and a less corrupt president have cooled off oil sector graft. But in the run-up to the 2019 elections, the various factions of political elites began to jostle again, and candidates sought to raise the hundreds of millions of dollars needed to win. Nigeria's institutions, including its dysfunctional national oil company, remain highly susceptible to abuse. This should come as no surprise: a politician who truly reformed NNPC would lose an important source of the funds and patronage needed to stay in power. And so the system perpetuates itself.

The exposure of corruption in Brazil and Nigeria did not deliver them into a clean and tidy future. Corruption will continue to do battle with democratic institutions and fed-up populations. But at least it's a battle. The next chapter tells the boom-time stories of several countries where kleptocracy stretches seamlessly across the government and the private sector. Paths to progress in these contexts are even harder to see.

CHAPTER 4 | The Kleptocracy Kings

BY EARLY 2018, siblings Isabel and José Filomeno dos Santos both found themselves out of a job. Their father, José Eduardo dos Santos, had ruled Angola for thirty-eight years before stepping down in 2017. He oversaw a decades-long civil war that killed many thousands of civilians and left the Angolan countryside littered with landmines. After ending up on the victorious side of the conflict, he captained the emergence of Africa's most sophisticated kleptocracy.

Since the end of the war in 2002, the country's oil production has more than doubled. During the oil boom, two Angolas grew further apart. Members of the dos Santos family and an inner circle of allies acquired billions of dollars in wealth. Shiny skyscrapers and leafy luxury housing complexes cropped up across the capital city of Luanda, and designer shops, luxury cars, and exclusive nightclubs multiplied. The government declared the city "the new Dubai." Expatriates and foreign currency poured into town, rents rose to among the highest in the world, and stories circulated of $15 Cokes and $150 melons. Not enjoying these pleasures were the majority of Angola's 29 million citizens whose standards of living remained among the lowest in the world. Even in the booming capital city, access to health, education, sanitation, and power supplies remained woefully poor.

In 2017, after overseeing this bifurcation, dos Santos, at seventy-four, decided to orchestrate his retirement. Rather than hanging onto power indefinitely like some oil-rich dictators elsewhere in Africa, he selected a successor. Ahead of national elections, he tapped his political ally João Lourenço to take over leadership of the ruling party. The party then coasted to an easy election victory, dos Santos stepped down, and Lourenço took charge.

Along with hand-picking his successor, dos Santos took other steps to secure his legacy. In 2016, he installed his daughter Isabel as the head of

Sonangol, the country's powerful national oil company. This prominent position, certainly among the top five most influential posts in the nation, added to Isabel's already wide-ranging portfolio. As Africa's richest woman, she led a glamorous life—visiting Cannes, sporting 400-carat diamonds, throwing elaborate parties for her friends. She also controlled a business empire that stretched across the banking, diamond, energy, media, and telecom industries, in Angola and abroad. Her assets included 25 percent of Angola's largest mobile phone network and nearly half of the country's largest bank. In Portugal, she owned shares in the oil company Galp Energia, a large engineering company, and the cable and telecom giant Nos SGPS.[1]

Investments from Isabel and other wealthy Angolans provided a welcome injection of cash to the Portuguese economy, which was suffering from a recession just as Angola was welcoming the oil boom. Portuguese investments provided the Angolans with international legitimacy and a safe place to stash both licit and illicit funds. As one Portuguese anticorruption activist commented, "if Angola was the front office of corruption, Portugal was the back office."[2] But identifying and stopping the stolen funds was not so easy. When the billionaire daughter of an oil-rich dictator is a large shareholder of a major European telecom and media company with millions of subscribers, where do you draw the line between legitimate and illegitimate business?[3]

A 2013 *Forbes* investigation traced the origins Isabel's fortune back to her father's position. "As best as we can trace," the journalists found, "every major Angolan investment held by dos Santos stems either from taking a chunk of a company that wants to do business in the country or from a stroke of the president's pen that cut her into the action."[4] Isabel denies the accusation that she benefited from her father's position, with a spokesperson stating that she is "an independent business woman and a private investor representing solely her own interests."[5] Her father's departure did, however, spell the end of her tenure at Sonangol: she was let go not long after Lourenço came to power, a major blow to the family's effort to retain influence. Adding insult to injury, the company launched investigations into the possible misappropriation of funds while she was in charge.[6]

If Isabel illustrates how kleptocrats acquire wealth and spread it around the world, her brother, José Filomeno, shows how kleptocrats use state institutions to pursue their personal aims. In 2011, Angola followed the lead of many oil-rich countries and set up a sovereign wealth fund with an initial $5 billion investment. The president tapped his son to run the new operation. The son in turn named one of his friends, the Swiss-Angolan businessman Jean-Claude Bastos de Morais, to serve as the fund's asset manager.

The Paradise Papers exposed how the two handled these responsibilities. In 2017, a group of media organizations received a large leak of documents from Appleby, a self-described "leading offshore law firm." Nicknamed the Paradise Papers because of Appleby's large offices in places like Bermuda and the Cayman Islands, the leaked files shed light on how wealthy individuals use tax havens, shell companies, and other tools to obscure financial transactions and avoid taxes.

The Paradise Papers leak revealed how the operations of Angola's sovereign wealth fund benefited allies of the regime like Bastos. While Bastos managed the fund's assets, the fund invested in at least four projects in which Bastos himself was a major shareholder. For instance, the sovereign wealth fund chose to invest in a new deepwater port being built by Bastos's company on Angola's northern coast. The same thing happened with the construction of a luxury hotel and shopping complex in the capital city.[7] This kind of self-dealing creates a glaring conflict of interest. Also, Bastos's firm received fees exceeding $90 million in 2014 and 2015 in exchange for their asset management services. The funds were then dispersed into a chain of offshore companies he controlled.[8] Bastos and his company have denied any wrongdoing, noting that he disclosed his interest in the companies and that the deals benefit all parties: "all shareholders' interests are aligned for the growth and ultimate success of every investment."[9]

After the Paradise Papers revelations, Lourenço fired José Filomeno dos Santos from his position at the sovereign wealth fund. A few months later, Angolan prosecutors charged him with allegedly attempting to steal $500 million in public funds. The finance ministry later put the amount at $1.5 billion.[10] In 2018, the government arrested the former first son along his friend Bastos.

The accusations alleged that, in 2017, as his father was headed out the door, José Filomeno dos Santos and several collaborators concocted an elaborate ruse involving the creation of a fake $35 billion investment fund.[11] Under the guise of the fake fund, they attempted to transfer $500 million from a government account to a private bank account held at HSBC in London by a UK-registered shell company that one of the collaborators controlled. According to the *Wall Street Journal*, "investigators unraveling the transaction for Angola have identified a cache of forged bank documents and an 'Ocean's Eleven'–style cast of characters, including a smooth-alking Brazilian based in Tokyo and a Dutch agricultural engineer."[12] The paperwork accompanying the transfer included a forged letter of guarantee purportedly from the bank Credit Suisse. The group succeeded in making the transfer, but eventually a London bank teller smelled something fishy and filed a suspicious activity report. The Angolan authorities, under Lourenço's leadership, picked up the case from there and filed charges against the former president's son.[13]

The scandals prompted a long dispute among the parties. In particular, the sovereign wealth fund sought to recoup its funds from the possession of Bastos's companies. British and Swiss authorities became involved, raiding offices, freezing accounts, and opening investigations of their own. In 2019, following extensive negotiations, the sovereign wealth fund and Bastos's firm reached a confidential settlement. Angolan authorities reported that they recovered over $3 billion from Bastos, the Swiss and the British closed their investigations, the Angolans dropped charges against dos Santos, and the two friends were set free.[14]

Many Angolans greeted the investigation of the dos Santos heir with both pleasure and surprise. However, it remains unclear whether the new leadership seeks to reform the political system or simply replace old insiders with new ones. Either way, the legacy of the dos Santos regime will be tough to reverse. During the oil boom, it helped political elites to rake in billions of dollars. These individuals now have a huge stake in the system's perpetuation.

The Authoritarian, Oil-Rich Kleptocracy

The kleptocrat kings described in this chapter sit atop sophisticated machines that transform oil into political power. Kleptocracy works best when power is held centrally by a strong authoritarian leader. Unfettered by opposition or oversight, this individual can deploy government institutions and revenues in ways that cement his or her hold on power. In oil-rich countries, the oil sector and its management become central to these pursuits.

Scholars began using the term "kleptocracy" in the 1960s and 1970s to describe the politics of certain African, Asian, and Latin American countries. While their exact definitions vary, the main concepts remain consistent. As noted earlier, a kleptocracy is a country where corruption is widespread, large in scale, and perpetrated by those who hold political power. These ruling elites manipulate the functions of entire government institutions to advance their own personal or political agendas and do so at the expense of the general public. As a result, the corruption becomes integral to the way the government functions, and, according to several leading scholars, "formal institutions [such as the courts or electoral rules] neither place significant restrictions on politicians' actions nor make them accountable to citizens."[15]

Kleptocracies like Angola, Azerbaijan, and Russia, the focus of this chapter, share several traits that make them stable, successful, and very difficult to dismantle. Just as the oil boom corruption in the democratic countries of Brazil, Nigeria, and the United States looked a certain way, so too does corruption in oil-rich kleptocracies. In these contexts, one individual or a small group enjoys a monopoly on power. While there might be pockets of dissent, there is no question about who is in charge. Members of the elite may own oil companies and get very rich, but the oil and the oil revenues really belong to the leader, as he decides who gets what. As a result, the kleptocracy runs in a top-down, hierarchical manner, and loyalty is rewarded.

Because the leader has a solid grip on power, he typically anticipates staying in office for a long period of time. Contrast this with Nigeria and Brazil, where politicians know that their tenure is unlikely to exceed eight years and planning for the next election begins months after the last one ends. With respect to the oil sector, longer horizons make the leader more likely to care about its long-term performance.

Kleptocratic leaders control and dictate the behavior of state institutions. The stories that follow show how leaders used national oil companies, tax administrators, customs services, and many other state organs to serve their personal agendas. In a strong top-down kleptocracy, the leader also controls the formal checks and balances, such as courts or legislatures, and so has little to fear from their oversight.

Finally, as a result of this comprehensive control, corruption becomes systematic and normalized. The various power plays described in this chapter certainly qualify as corruption, in that government officials manipulated state functions in order to advance narrow personal or political agendas rather than the public interest. However, many of them are perfectly legal. When you control the entire government, it is often not necessary to break laws in order to assert your agenda. There's a sense of inevitability to the corruption. It's just the way things are.

This sketch of how a kleptocracy works applies, in varying degrees, to many oil-rich countries. Much of the research on the political effects of oil concludes that oil wealth tends to weaken democratic systems and centralize power in the hands of a few individuals.[16] In a leading study on this question, the political scientist Michael Ross found that oil-producing states are about 40 percent less likely to transition to democracy than their non-oil-rich peers.[17]

Russia, Azerbaijan, and Angola certainly exemplify oil-rich countries where democracy has struggled to take hold. Their authoritarian leaders manipulated the oil sector to acquire more power, primarily by enriching a small group of loyal oligarchs at the expense of most citizens. A few other countries fit this model as well. Oil sector affairs in Kazakhstan and Algeria, for example, followed a similar pattern during the boom years.

While subject to debate, a separate set of very oil-rich countries, mostly in the Persian Gulf, qualify more as "distributional states," though they certainly have some kleptocratic traits. Bahrain, Brunei, Kuwait, Oman, Qatar, Saudi Arabia, and the UAE enjoy some of the highest oil revenues per capita in the world. In these countries, the leaders certainly push economic opportunity toward their allies who have become phenomenally rich. However, the trade-off between their well-being and that of their citizens is less striking. These governments have invested heavily in the welfare of their populations. Fuel subsidies and government jobs are two of the largest forms of distribution, although the governments also provide subsidized access to transportation, education, health, and other services. In several Gulf oil producers, around two citizens are employed by the government for every one employed in the private sector—a rate ten times higher than the global average.[18] Because government spending is high and the population is low, every citizen benefits from the country's oil, and social welfare indicators have improved rapidly in recent decades. One scholar of Saudi Arabia commented "at no point in history has the Saudi state penetrated people's lives as deeply as it did at the peak of the boom in the early 2010s—a factor that likely has contributed to the muted local reaction to the Arab uprisings in 2011."[19] Corruption in these settings can be difficult to spot and to define: very little information emerges about how oil money ends up enriching the political elites. (However, Saudi and Emirati actors play pivotal roles in the scandal described in chapter 5.)

Another category of countries could be called the low-capacity kleptocracies. The governments of several African oil producers have used the oil sector to enrich themselves and their inner circles and failed to deliver many benefits to their citizens. They have also demonstrated the ability to stay in power for decades. Yet they have not built the kind of economically sophisticated kleptocratic machines found in Angola, Azerbaijan, and Russia. They have done little to translate oil revenues into state capacity or international influence, for instance. Cameroon, Chad, Congo-Brazzaville,

Equatorial Guinea, Gabon, Libya under Gaddafi, South Sudan, and Sudan could fall into this category, as could the large natural gas producer Turkmenistan. Corruption in these countries often assumes time-honored forms. For example, French authorities convicted the son of Equatorial Guinea's president for embezzling public funds and using them to buy mansions, sports cars, and other luxury goods.[20] The methods of corruption in these countries did evolve during the oil boom, particularly the growing use of the global financial system to siphon off illicit funds. But the political system underlying the corruption is unfortunately highly familiar and long-standing and has been well explored by others.[21]

The stories told in this chapter are relevant to all the countries listed above, to varying degrees. They illustrate just how many options a kleptocratic leader has at his disposal when it comes to manipulating the oil sector. But before launching into the stories, I first need to talk about geese.

The Goose That Lays the Golden Eggs

The oil sector dominates the economies of countries such as Angola, Azerbaijan, and Russia: it is the goose that lays the golden eggs. The leaders of stable kleptocracies have three motives when it comes to their geese. First, they must control the goose so that no one else can claim the bird or her valuable eggs. Second, they must care for her so that she thrives and lays many eggs, both today and in the future. Finally, the leader must distribute the eggs to other powerful figures so that they become both loyal and dependent on his rule.

All three of these agendas played out during the oil boom. They are not, of course, the whole story of how politics works in Angola, Azerbaijan, and Russia. Along with oil sector machinations, the leaders also used military action, foreign policy, propaganda, constitutional reforms, election manipulations, repression, and other tools to strengthen their rule, but these tactics are not the main focus here. International actors also played supporting roles, and their complicity is tackled in the next chapter.

Controlling the Goose

In oil dependent countries, whoever controls the oil sector wields outsized power. During the boom years, oil and gas accounted for over 90 percent of exports and over 75 percent of the government's revenues in both Angola and Azerbaijan. In Russia, where the economy is more diversified, oil and gas still generated around 70 percent of exports and 50 percent of the federal government's revenues during the same period. When prices dropped, oil still dominated all three country's exports and contributed closer to half of the government's budget in Angola and Azerbaijan and one-third in Russia.[22]

In Azerbaijan and Angola, the presidents who presided over the boom years took power before major periods of oil sector growth. Dos Santos became Angola's second president in 1979, when Angola produced just 146,000 barrels of oil per day. By the time the oil boom kicked off in 2008, production had risen to 1.9 million barrels per day. In Azerbaijan, Heydar Aliyev took power in 1993 and then transferred power to his son in 2003. Between 1993 and 2008, Azerbaijan saw a fourfold increase in oil production, rising to 900,000 barrels per day.

Because they presided over the sector's growth, these leaders had a relatively easy time asserting control over their geese. Their national oil companies, Socar and Sonangol, got in on the ground floor and have infiltrated the sector's operations ever since. The leaders of both companies report directly to the president and serve as loyal henchmen in his kleptocratic projects. Because they controlled the booming sector from the start, Aliyev and dos Santos were able to use the oil industry to extend their influence over the rest of the economy, as I will describe later.

Vladimir Putin, however, faced a greater challenge. In 1999, he arrived in office to find a number of private Russian oil companies already doing big business. Through the epic wave of privatizations that followed the breakup of the Soviet Union, these companies had acquired world-class oil assets at rock-bottom prices. During the tumultuous years that followed, the bosses of these companies became some of the richest men in the world. This first generation of oligarchs did not owe their fortunes to Putin, and therefore their loyalty to him was limited.

Russia's vast oil industry sits at the center of the country's economy. During the boom years, Russia produced around 10 million barrels of oil a day, around 12 percent of the world's total. Much of this production came from Siberia and the Volga-Urals region, but Russia enjoys ample untapped reserves in the Arctic, the Caspian, and other corners of its far-flung territory. This resource wealth bolsters Russia's geopolitical leverage, especially since Europe depends on Russia for more than one-third of its oil imports and more than two-thirds of its gas supplies.[23] Russian oil wealth also helped mint a number of billionaires during the wild early days of capitalism following the Soviet Union's demise.

For Putin, the first generation of oligarchs had too much influence over the golden goose, and he had too little. In response to this scenario, he mounted a campaign to bring the oil sector more firmly under his control.[24] He tapped his ally Igor Sechin to spearhead this effort and used the national oil company Rosneft as one of his primary weapons. In 2004, Rosneft produced 5 percent of Russia's oil. Ten years later, at the height of the oil boom, it produced 39 percent. It also had become the largest publicly traded oil company in the world in both reserves and production.[25]

Igor Sechin got to know Putin when they worked together at the mayor's office in St. Petersburg during the early 1990s and has remained deeply loyal ever since. He served as the deputy head of Putin's office from 2000 to 2008 and deputy prime minister in the four years that followed. Putin named him chair of Rosneft in 2004, and he became the company's president in 2012. Nicknamed "Darth Vader," the intimidating and dour-faced Sechin was described in a US Embassy cable as "so shadowy that it was joked he may not actually exist but rather was a sort of urban myth, a bogeyman, invented by the Kremlin to instill fear."[26] A British oil executive active in Russia observed: "he displays no emotion or expression. You can't read him. He doesn't even nod. He's like a statue."[27]

Since the oil boom, observers have also called Sechin the second most powerful man in Russia. He appeared on the list of individuals subject to the US sanctions that followed Russia's 2014 invasion of Crimea. The US government justified Sechin's inclusion by explaining that he "has shown utter loyalty to Vladimir Putin—a key component to his current standing."

Three episodes illustrate how Putin and Sechin successfully fenced in the goose that lays the golden eggs.

In the early 2000s, Mikhail Khodorkovsky was chief among the oil-rich oligarchs who threatened Putin's control of the goose. Khodorkovsky's entrepreneurial credentials extend back to the Gorbachev years, when he and his friends leveraged their Communist Youth League connections to open a private café and begin small trading ventures like importing French brandy and foreign computers. As the years passed, he entered the banking sector and expanded his trading operations. In 1995, during the first years of post-Soviet Russia, Khodorkovsky at the age of thirty-two acquired, with a few associates, the oil company Yukos at one of many auctions that transferred state-owned economic assets into private hands. He paid a paltry $320 million through a process marred by conflicts of interest. For instance, his own bank lent funds to Yukos before the sale, Yukos defaulted on the loans, and the bank then ran the auction that its boss eventually won.

Yukos held some of Russia's largest Siberian oilfields but was underperforming due to chaotic market dynamics and low operational standards. Following a few rough years at the start, Khodorkovsky began to build a world-class oil company, in part by bringing in Western engineers to improve antiquated production techniques. By 2000, Yukos's production levels began climbing steeply. Khodorkovsky invested in corporate governance and attracted large foreign investments; he listed the company in Moscow and London; and, in 2003, he acquired another major oil company, OAO Sibneft. By 2004, the merged company had a market capitalization of $36 billion— the largest among Russian oil companies—and produced 1.7 million barrels of oil per day or around 20 percent of Russia's total volumes.[28]

Khodorkovsky's stock ascended alongside that of Yukos. He grew incredibly rich, with *Forbes* ranking him as the sixteenth richest man in the world in 2004. He assumed a visible role on the international stage, lunching with US president George W. Bush, donating funds to the US Library of Congress, and recruiting Henry Kissinger and other luminaries to serve on the board of his Open Russia Foundation.[29] As his business empire grew, he also began speaking out on the need for neoliberal economic reforms in Russia and announced plans to support two liberal political parties that had criticized Kremlin policies. His philanthropy grew in size and influence, financing internet cafes in far-flung towns and modernizing schools. With these moves, he tested an unspoken rule of the Putin era: oligarchs will be allowed to make their billions if they stay clear of politics.

In 2003, the tensions came to a head. Putin summoned Khodorkovsky for a meeting that was open to the media. The billionaire delivered a PowerPoint presentation that included data on the high costs of corruption to the Russian economy. He used a recent deal by Rosneft as an example and called out Igor Sechin, who was in attendance, asking him if he wanted to comment. While Sechin demurred, Putin fired back: "some companies, including Yukos, have extraordinary reserves. The question is: How did the company get them? And your company had its own issues with taxes. To give the Yukos leadership its due, it found a way to settle everything and take care of all its problems with the state," implying that Yukos had also manipulated the system in order to reach its current heights.[30]

In the months that followed, Khodorkovsky and Yukos began to feel the repercussions of crossing Putin. Authorities raided the company's offices and arrested a major shareholder in the company on charges of tax evasion and defrauding the state. Yukos employees began to flee the country, but Khodorkovsky remained: "hiding, weaving conspiracies, sitting in the bushes, perhaps that was the right course of action," he wrote in his memoir, "but I don't know how to live like that and I don't want to."[31]

Early one morning in 2003, secret police boarded Khodorkovsky's private jet at a refueling stop in Siberia and arrested him on charges of fraud and tax evasion. At his trial, sitting at times in a cage and at others in a Plexiglas box, he was sentenced to nine years in prison. Serving his time at a remote labor camp near the Chinese border and a Moscow prison with punishing living conditions, the oligarch-turned-prisoner worked "gulag" jobs loading freight and sewing garments and was stabbed in the face by a cellmate. He also maintained a public voice through his writings and inter- actions with allies abroad, inspired tribute events, filed legal cases in inter- national courts, and became Russia's most famous political prisoner.

Writing from prison, Khodorkovsky criticized the kleptocratic system: "I regret profoundly that my personal political position and public activity have served as an excuse for the illegal expropriation of property from all Yukos shareholders, organized by a group of corrupt officials and busi- nessmen working in their own interest. I have never belonged to any party. However, I always believed and continue to believe that it is my right as an individual and citizen to support various political forces financially no matter what the current government may feel about them."[32]

Along with deploying the Russian legal system to jail Khodorkovsky and his associates, Putin used state tax authorities to cause Yukos financial duress. Between 2000 and 2003, the government presented a series of unpaid tax bills, claiming that Yukos owed over $24 billion in back taxes.[33] Court orders froze the company's assets, which impeded its ability to settle the alleged liabilities. The authorities then used the unpaid taxes as an excuse to force the auction of the company's prime assets.

The government announced in 2004 that they would auction off Yuganskneftegaz, the most prolific part of the Yukos group thanks to its vast Siberian oilfields. The minimum bidding price was less than half of the entity's estimated market value, and bidders only had a month to conduct due diligence and prepare their offerings. The surprising winner was an unknown company created two weeks before the auction and reg- istered to an address shared with a grocery story in the small city of Tver.[34] Rosneft lent $9 billion to the mysterious new company so that it could buy Yuganskneftegaz at the auction. Two days later, Rosneft bought the new company and took control of the prime Yukos oilfields.[35]

Speaking about the auction, the then Yukos CEO remarked with regret: "today's announcement is both stunning and expected. Stunning because it is such a bold demonstration of the contempt that the government has for the rule of law.... The sale is made possible by the government's creation of a completely artificial cash crisis brought on by the freeze of assets and bank accounts, and through preposterous and absurd tax claims in excess of the company's revenues."[36] Years later, the European Court of Human

Rights came to agree and ruled on behalf of Yukos's shareholders. The court commented that the auction "was not driven by motives of tax collection but by the desire of the State to acquire Yukos' most valuable asset and bankrupt Yukos. In short, it was in effect a devious and calculated expropriation."[37] Putin defended the transaction, arguing that "the state—using absolutely legal market mechanisms—is ensuring its interests. I consider this perfectly normal."[38]

In the years that followed, Rosneft captured additional parts of the embattled company, including several other upstream companies, six refineries, and the Rosneft shares Yukos held. In 2006, on the back of the Yukos acquisitions, Rosneft held its first IPO on the London Stock Exchange for the amount of $10 billion—the largest public offering ever by a Russian company. In contrast, Yukos finally declared bankruptcy in 2007, having lost the kleptocracy game.

Thanks largely to the Yukos acquisitions, Rosneft production levels increased fourfold between 2004 and 2007, and the value of Rosneft

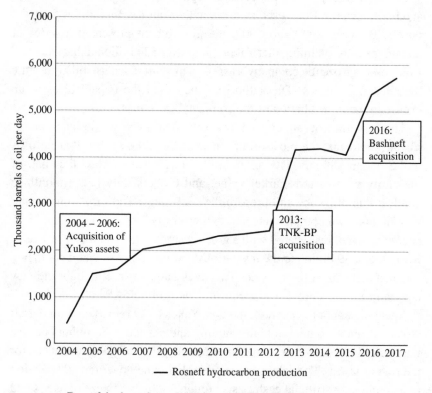

FIGURE 4.1 Rosneft hydrocarbon production and key acquisitions.

SOURCE: Rosneft annual reports, 2004–2017, available at: https://www.rosneft.com/Investors/Reports_and_presentations/Consolidated_financial_statements/.

increased at a similar rate. Figure 4.1 shows how this episode contributed to an overall trajectory of growth. As oil prices began to climb, Putin had successfully sidelined a rival and expanded the portion of the oil sector over which he exercised control. He also sent a powerful message about how he would treat oligarchs who crossed him.

With the Yukos takeover, Putin, Sechin, and the kleptocracy machine were just getting started. As the oil boom gathered steam, new gambits further built Rosneft's might and expanded Putin's control over the oil sector.

In 2003, the large British oil company BP entered into TNK-BP, a joint venture with several Russian oligarchs. The venture grew into Russia's third largest oil and gas company and earned sizeable returns for both sets of partners. However, around 2008 tensions arose between BP and its Russian partners, who wanted more control over the joint venture's operations. The events that followed suggest that Putin wanted more control too.

Sensing an opportunity to gain influence over the powerful British company, the Kremlin began applying pressure, inflicting what Bob Dudley, then CEO of TNK-BP, would call "sustained harassment."[39] Police raided the company's offices. A court revoked permissions for BP's foreign staff to work on certain projects. Foreign employees, including Dudley himself, struggled to secure visas. The CEO faced several legal actions, including a discrimination suit from some TNK-BP employees and sanctions for alleged labor code violations. In a conversation at the US Embassy, Dudley said he believed that the government, including Igor Sechin, was cooperating with BP's Russian partners to push BP into a more subservient role. At that time, according to the embassy cable summarizing the meeting, Dudley predicted that Russia's state-owned oil companies would eventually prey on the business, "with the [Government of Russia] ultimately taking control of TNK-BP through either acquisition by Gazprom, Rosneft, or a rumored merger of TNK-BP with Gazprom Neft and Surgutneftgaz."[40]

Dudley's premonition proved to be correct. Soon after relaying his fears to the Americans, he left Russia, reportedly vowing never to return.[41] He was replaced by a CEO chosen by TNK-BP's Russian shareholders. The shareholder agreement was also revised to lessen BP's influence. Along with all this trouble, oil prices were low at that moment, and TNK-BP was losing money. BP prepared to cut its losses and walk away from the venture.

But then oil prices began to climb, and BP could not afford to turn its back on the booming Russian oil sector. Dudley unexpectedly became BP's CEO during the upheaval in the company's leadership following the disastrous Deepwater Horizon oil spill in the Gulf of Mexico. So, in 2011, Dudley ended up back in Moscow, meeting with Sechin again and trying to find a way out of the ugly impasse. This round of talks went poorly for BP. Dudley and Sechin negotiated a $16 billion deal with Rosneft that would allow BP to increase its exploration activities in Russia's Arctic oilfields. But the deal fell through in spectacular fashion. The Russian partners from TNK-BP raised their opposition, complaining that they had been left out in the cold by their British partner. The government took their side and signed the Arctic deal with ExxonMobil instead.

Left with little leverage, BP accepted the next option Sechin placed on the table. Rosneft would absorb TNK-BP entirely, acquiring all its beefy assets. Figure 4.1 shows how this move further boosted Rosneft's control over Russian oil production. To execute the takeover, Rosneft bought BP's half of the company with $16.7 billion in cash and 12.8 percent of Rosneft shares in early 2013. BP acquired an additional 5.7 percent of Rosneft shares for $4.9 billion, bringing BP's total shares to nearly 20 percent.[42] BP would retain a large stake in the booming oil sector but only through a vehicle controlled firmly by Sechin and Putin.

To the Russian oligarchs who owned the other half of TNK-BP, Rosneft paid $28 billion for their portions of the company. The oligarchs had wanted to be paid in shares of BP instead, but they likely accepted the pay-off with some relief given the high-stakes brinkmanship that had surrounded the deal. One of the oligarchs, Mikhail Fridman, was Russia's second richest man. He, like Khodorkovsky, had acquired much of his wealth prior to Putin's arrival. He had locked horns with Sechin on occasion, one of many clashes between first-generation oligarchs and the Putin regime.[43]

While not what they wanted, the $28 billion payout allowed Fridman and his partners to exit the contentious TNK-BP chapter solvent and intact. Upon the closure of the mammoth buy-out, Fridman and another TNK-BP investor rode off into the sunset, so to speak, embarking immediately on a trek in the Israeli desert with several camels and a Russian TV crew. Singing Ukrainian folk songs around the fire and learning to make local flatbread, Fridman seemed happy enough with the outcome.[44]

Following the $55 billion takeover of TNK-BP, Rosneft became the largest publicly traded oil company in the world—just as oil prices neared their peak. It was a tremendous victory for the Putin team. As one analyst said, "Putin has been crystal clear that the state needs to control strategic industries such as oil. Removing a Western-dominated company like TNK-BP in a strategic sector—and still keeping BP as a minority partner—was part of that strategy."[45] The deal proved a winner for BP too, even if Sechin had dictated the terms. In 2014, BP relied on Rosneft for almost 20 percent of its profits.[46]

Bashneft was Rosneft's third great acquisition. In 2014, out of the blue, Russian police arrested Vladimir Yevtushenkov, the chairman of the major business conglomerate Sistema and Russia's fifteenth richest man.[47] The Kremlin denied that political motives lay behind the money laundering charges filed against the oligarch. Indeed, Yevtushenkov was not known to be politically active. He did, however, own an oil company that the state wanted: Bashneft. Operating in the region just north of Kazakhstan, Bashneft produced around 400,000 barrels per day, nearly 4 percent of Russia's total output.[48] Upon the arrest of Yevtushenkov, Sistema's shares dropped 37 percent. Rumors swirled that the arrest could be a move by Sechin to lower the value of Bashneft so Rosneft could acquire it more easily. A Rosneft spokesperson dismissed that idea as "nonsense" and said Rosneft had no intention of taking over Bashneft.[49]

Later that year, the government seized 72 percent of Bashneft, moving further oil assets from private hands into state control. In 2016, Sechin received a green light for Rosneft to buy Bashneft from the government for $5.3 billion. The government needed money following the downturn in oil prices and wanted to raise the value of Rosneft ahead of a planned issuance of shares.

Certain Kremlin insiders opposed allowing Rosneft to buy the government's equity in Bashneft, arguing that assets should not be shuffled from one part of the government to another. Reports suggest that the economy minister, Alexei Ulyukayev, a relative economic liberal, was among these dissenting voices.[50] Soon after the Bashneft deal went ahead, Ulukayev was arrested for attempting to extort a $2 million bribe from Rosneft in exchange for his approval of the deal. According to *Reuters*, "the role of Rosneft in helping to prosecute the case has led some in Russia's ruling elite to view it as part of a battle between powerful clans within the ruling elite."[51] Ulyukayev denied the charges but was found guilty and sentenced to eight years in prison. He found himself on the wrong side of Sechin, and lost.

Once Rosneft had finished acquiring Bashneft, authorities released the oligarch Yevtushenkov from house arrest and dropped the charges against him. But further punishment awaited. In 2017, Rosneft sued Sistema for $4.5 billion, alleging that Sistema had stripped assets from Bashneft prior to its sale. Sistema denied the charges but lost several court cases on the matter. Cutting their losses, Sistema negotiated a payment of $1.7 billion to Rosneft to settle the matter in late 2017.[52] The case served as an unmistakable reminder that while Yevtushenkov and other oligarchs may run oil businesses, Putin wields the ultimate control.

Through all three power moves—the dismantling of Yukos, the absorption of TNK-BP, and the acquisition of Bashneft—Putin and Sechin used multiple instruments of state power to achieve their agenda. Rosneft played the lead role, but it had some valuable supporting players. Law enforcement agencies raided offices, charged companies with tax violations, and arrested billionaires as needed. Courts ruled in favor of the Kremlin's agenda. State-controlled banks provided funding, such as when Rosneft borrowed to acquire the Yukos assets. Rosneft also received a generous bailout from the central bank in 2014 when it ran into financial troubles following the drop in oil prices. Unlike the scenarios in Brazil or Nigeria, where schemes failed to ensnare all the courts or the electoral commission, Putin's influence blanketed the entire public sector.

Raising a Healthy Goose

The kleptocratic kings have long horizons. They do not need to hurriedly loot the oil sector as the Goodluck Jonathan administration did in Nigeria. Nor do they need to fill up election war chests every few years, as the politicians in Brazil do. As long as the kleptocratic leaders can maintain unilateral control, they benefit from the golden eggs laid by the goose now and in the future. Therefore, along with controlling the goose, they want to maximize the bird's short-term and long-term productivity.

To grow the productivity of the oil sector over time, the kleptocratic leader needs to accomplish a couple things. Oil sector institutions, including national oil companies, must develop adequate levels of technical and financial capabilities. The leaders must also make foreign companies feel comfortable enough to invest billions of dollars. If foreign companies believe that their contract with the government is unstable, or worry about facing reputational or legal crises, or routinely tangle with bureaucratic inefficiency, they may well still invest in the country. After all, oil companies are famously willing to work in difficult environments. But they will demand a larger share of the available revenues to compensate for all those downsides. Some capable kleptocratic leaders avoid this dynamic by running the oil sector in a relatively professional and effective manner.

In Russia, the national oil and gas companies certainly lack the efficiency of their private sector counterparts, but they can pull their act together when the goose's health is on the line. They have invested heavily in the technical approaches needed to coax oil out of aging oilfields, which helped slow the decline in production from some of the older production zones in West Siberia and the Volga-Urals region and boosted government revenues as a result.[53] To acquire the expertise needed to explore for oil in the Arctic, the Russian state has prioritized bringing in Western companies like ExxonMobil rather than becoming specialists themselves. Exxon felt secure enough to sign deals with Rosneft in 2012 and 2014 that projected a whopping $500 billion in possible investment in Arctic and Dead Sea activities. Courting investment on this scale was another capable move by the Russian authorities, though they failed to anticipate the US and EU sanctions that would eventually cause Exxon to pull out of the arrangement.

In Angola, President dos Santos and his allies faced a greater challenge: building a high-performing oil sector in a war-torn country where not much else worked. They seized on the national oil company, Sonangol, to accomplish this aim. Even during the civil war, Sonangol existed as an island of functionality amid an otherwise failed state. Recognizing that his survival depended on a functioning oil sector, dos Santos isolated Sonangol from the vagaries of war and the regime's socialist ideology. He recruited foreign talent and demanded high performance. Throughout the war, Sonangol struck deals with international companies—even US ones, even though the United States supported the rebels fighting against the dos Santos regime. Pragmatism trumped ideology, and the company stayed safe and isolated from its chaotic surroundings. As one long-serving Sonangol executive summed it up, "you see through colonialism, foreign invasion, Marxist-Leninism and capitalism, I have not left the same building."[54]

The war ended in 2002 with an outright victory by dos Santos and his cohort. Oil production levels then doubled between 2003 and 2008, thanks to a number of large offshore discoveries made in the 1990s finally producing returns. By the time the oil boom arrived, dos Santos sat atop a high-performing oil sector operated by top international companies that generated ample revenues to fund his regime's agenda.

The well-run Sonangol attracted foreign investors into an otherwise risky environment. In 2006, for example, the company ran an auction for the rights to several large and promising offshore oil blocks. Despite the country's reputation for instability and corruption, the process was professional and transparent and attracted enormous offers from the world's top oil companies. Sonangol signed contracts with BP, Chevron, and Sinopec. Signature bonuses from the eager investors topped $1 billion in some cases, reflecting a willingness to bet big on Angola. The national oil company also negotiated billions of dollars in loans from China, which would be repaid in oil, and the loans financed a large share of Angola's postwar reconstruction.

Foreign oil executives praised Sonangol's efficiency and professionalism, and oil sector revenues poured into state coffers. By 2013, the company had expanded its operations in all aspects of the Angolan oil sector and held investments in Algeria, Brazil, Cuba, Iraq, Portugal, South Sudan, and Venezuela.[55]

Ricardo Soares de Oliveira, an Oxford University scholar who has written extensively about Sonangol, calls the company the "Angolan miracle." "There is no doubt," he explains, "from a purely technical perspective that Sonangol has been wisely managed. This atypical African corporation mostly runs according to operational principles of technical competence, stability and reliability that are entirely at odds with those of the Angolan public administration. However, it has done so for the sake of the presidency's interests, which has honed Sonangol into the central political tool of its stranglehold over Angola."[56]

Like Angola, Azerbaijan needed professionalism and external expertise to grow its oil industry. These attributes did not emerge right away. Azerbaijani politics took a tumultuous turn following the collapse of the Soviet Union. This country of 9 million people, located on the shores of the Caspian Sea, faces an amalgam of influences from the three giants nearby: Iran, Russia, and Turkey. Unlike its Caucasus neighbors, Georgia and Armenia, Azerbaijan has produced oil since way back in the 1840s.

In the 1990s, as former Soviet countries opened up for investment, Western oil companies enthusiastically chased after access to the large untapped oil and gas fields in Azerbaijan's share of the Caspian Sea. BP, Chevron, Amoco, and Pennzoil in particular courted the government in Baku, dealing with wild characters and rampant uncertainty along the way. They repeatedly got close to signing deals with the new Azerbaijani government, only to have the government then yank them away. During one round of high-stakes negotiations, a government official even pulled a pistol on several Western oil executives.[57] Meanwhile, the rich oil and gas deposits under the Caspian went undeveloped.

This costly chaos did not last long. In 1993, Heydar Aliyev took control of Azerbaijan and held on tight. His regime soon gained strength and stability. With this stability came the inclination to run the oil industry in a more professional and profitable fashion. His son Ilham Aliyev inherited this objective when he took up the dictatorial reins in 2003, just as the country's oil sector began a period of sustained growth. The younger Aliyev, who remains firmly in power today, developed Socar, the country's national oil company, into a loyal and powerful entity. The top staff of Socar reflects these dual goals: Rovnag Abdullayev has served as the CEO since 2005 and maintains this job thanks to his unwavering loyalty to the ruling family. He also serves as a member of Parliament for the president's political party.[58] The executives under him include some of the country's best and brightest minds, and they have orchestrated the company's growth over the years.

Political stability and a professionally run oil sector helped convince foreign companies to bet big on Azerbaijan. BP took on the construction of the Baku-Tbilisi-Ceyhan pipeline, an enormous infrastructure project that cost $3.9 billion. By 2005, the pipeline was transporting Azerbaijani oil from the Caspian Sea across Georgia to the Turkish port Ceyhan.

Thanks to the pipeline and rising oil prices, Azerbaijan had the fastest growing economy in the world for a time. Socar's revenues followed suit, soaring from $6 billion in 2008 to $49 billion by 2014.[59] Like Sonangol, Socar also expanded its operations overseas: it works in Turkey, Ukraine, and Moldova, has divisions in Dubai and Switzerland, and is the largest taxpayer in Georgia.

As Angola's and Azerbaijan's national oil companies grew, they became integral to the way the two regimes functioned. These companies had access to billions of dollars in funds, worked more effectively than other government agencies, and reported directly to the president. As a result, their job descriptions grew and grew. During the oil boom, Sonangol executed many showpiece projects that had nothing to do with oil, such as a flashy, high-end housing development and a poorly conceived manufacturing zone, and the company sprouted subsidiaries dedicated to telecoms, real estate, medical services, and air travel.

A disclosure from the International Monetary Fund provides some sense of the scale of the spending dos Santos routed through Sonangol. In a 2011 report, the Fund raised muted concern about an "unexplained residual in the budget" that totaled $32 billion over the years 2007–2010.[60] Put more plainly, and with a more appropriate level of alarm, $32 billion in public funds had disappeared out the door without explanation. The figure equaled around 25 percent of Angola's GDP at the time. The government scrambled to account for the funds and eventually revealed that Sonangol had spent the money itself on all manner of public projects, from housing to railroads, rather than transferring it to government accounts. By bypassing the government's budget, the government likely avoided some bureaucratic inefficiencies but also blatantly disregarded their own rules and the need for even basic levels of public accountability.

Insider Oil Dealings, to an Extent

By the time oil prices began to climb in 2008, presidents Aliyev, dos Santos, and Putin had secured control over their oil sectors and were running them in a capable manner. The enormous size of the boom posed a dilemma: how much corruption could take place in the oil sector without threatening its overall health? An oil industry riddled with corruption becomes inefficient, scares off foreign investment, and produces much lower returns. This is apparent in Nigeria, where the grab-and-go corruption of successive regimes has left an inefficient and dysfunctional oil sector in its wake.

While the kleptocrats wanted to keep their geese healthy, they were hardly going to sit by and watch billions of dollars in new wealth pour into their oil sectors without plundering anything. With this tension in mind, what did oil boom corruption look like in the well-organized kleptocracies, where the leaders have long horizons and want to maximize oil sector returns?

While it is impossible to assess the full scale of corruption present in an oil sector, it appears that these leaders have kept corruption from running rampant and carefully allocated opportunities to profit to trusted members of their inner circles. They have also steered rent-seeking activities toward certain corners of the industry where profits can be siphoned off without threatening the country's overall earnings. Always the caretakers, the leaders have protected their geese from any truly reckless endangerment.

The most typical mechanism for corruption is the same in the oil sector as it is elsewhere in the economy: insert trusted oligarchs into lucrative deals. In Russia, some of the oligarchs have leveraged these opportunities and now sit atop world-class business empires that include major oil companies. Other elites, especially in poorer countries, such as Angola, have latched onto oil sector deals like silent parasites. The leaders have allowed them to feed off the oil largesse as long as they do not undermine the industry's well-being. Across both types of arrangements, the business activities of many international companies have enabled this behavior.

Some savvy leaders have chosen to steer corruption away from exploration and production deals. An oil sector's profitability depends on these upstream functions running smoothly and big-spending foreign investors feeling happy and safe. Exploration and production deals also attract lots of scrutiny from the media and other audiences. In Angola, dos Santos allowed suspicious behavior to infiltrate several high-value exploration and production deals, and the results show why this tactic is best avoided.

In 2008, as the oil boom gained momentum, the US-based oil company Cobalt International Energy negotiated with the Angolan government for the rights to explore two promising offshore oil blocks. The government insisted that Cobalt partner up with two little known companies, Nazaki Oil & Gas and Alper Oil. Suspicious of these newcomer companies, journalists began poking around. The watchdog group Global Witness asked some tough questions about the partners, and the Angolan activist Rafael Marques de Morais reported that three powerful figures within the government owned large shares in Nazaki.[61] Tom Burgis of the *Financial Times*, whose 2015 book *The Looting Machine* provides a masterful account of the natural resource corruption he observed while reporting from Africa, dug deeper. He looked through Nazaki's registration documents and found evidence to bolster Marques's findings. He also contacted the three officials, and they admitted to owning the company that in turn held shares in Nazaki.[62] Among them was Manuel Vicente—the head of Sonangol at the time the Cobalt deal was signed. This discovery triggered an onslaught of problems for Cobalt. While it was never found guilty of a crime, the company endured an investigation for bribery by US authorities, a civil suit brought by its investors, drops in its share price, and eventually bankruptcy.[63]

By inserting government officials into a prominent exploration deal, the government ended up tainting an important agreement and endangering their future earnings. The parasitic activities of the oligarchs threatened the health of the goose. The three officials quickly sold off their interests for an unknown profit, and abandoned such obvious forms of rent-seeking.

Despite the lessons from the Cobalt experience, Angolan power brokers were not content to abandon their claim on exploration and production deals altogether. Vicente, the boss of Sonangol, and others devised a more sophisticated mechanism. China Sonangol is a joint venture between Sonangol and the Queensway Group—a Hong Kong–based conglomerate headed by Sam Pa, a Chinese businessman who has specialized in making arms deals and natural resource plays across Africa. Tom Burgis and a few other investigators dug into the exploits of Sam Pa and have written detailed accounts of his dealings—which perhaps came to a close with his 2015 arrest by Chinese authorities.[64]

Burgis explained how China Sonangol helped siphon money out of Angola's exploration and production deals: "Manuel Vicente and Sam Pa had constructed an enclave within Angola's oil industry, a corporate bunker within the already opaque walls of Sonangol. Through a network of obscure companies registered in Hong Kong, the Futungo [a nickname for Angola's ruling elites] had plugged itself into an offshore mechanism that channeled the political power of Angola's authoritarian rulers into the private corporate empire that Pa and his fellow founders of the Queensway

Group had begun to assemble." With its creation of China Sonangol, "the Futungo was swapping a Cessna for a Concorde, a trawler for a submarine."[65]

This Concorde of rent-seeking worked its way into some of the country's largest oil deals. China Sonangol, with its hidden owners and secretive financial flows, acquired a significant share in thirteen oil blocks, including Block 18, a major producing asset operated by BP. The joint venture also played an intermediary role in billions of dollars in oil-backed loans taken out by Sonangol.[66] The government often insisted that foreign oil companies, including the Chinese state-owned companies, partner with China Sonangol, even though some companies objected. "Sam Pa had become the gatekeeper to Angolan crude," writes Burgis. From this position, Pa helped to multiply the ways the regime could insert their fingers into high-stakes deals.

As is common in kleptocratic settings, Burgis and other investigators have not uncovered a clear paper trail that demonstrates how China Sonangol enriched members of the regime. He did however come across Hong Kong court documents from a commercial dispute involving the company. In them, an associate of Pa is asked where all the profits went from its Angolan production deals. The company representative explains that yes, China Sonangol did make money from its Angola deals but the money "went to fund projects in Angola undertaken to build goodwill."[67]

It is entirely possible that dos Santos himself never got rich off the China Sonangol deals. In a trend that repeats itself in Azerbaijan and Russia, leaders often allocate lucrative opportunities to their trusted allies without receiving a cut. Instead, these allies act as loyal proxies for the leader: they can be called on to spend their wealth in ways that help out the regime.

Outside the high-stakes exploration and production deals, oil sector corruption could flourish more freely without threatening the goose's health. Observations of Angola, Azerbaijan, and Russia solidify the observation made in chapters 2 and 3: oil sector subcontracting and oil trading were two popular venues for political elites looking to get rich off the oil boom.

Both private and national oil companies spend lots of money to procure various goods and services—pipelines, rigs, construction, welding, housing for workers, and so on. These subcontracts, also called service contracts, offer perfect opportunities to run low-risk corruption scams, especially during a time of high prices. Contracts can be inflated, payoffs can be made, and enough money is still left over for the actual work to get done. The story of Petrobras and its massively overvalued construction contracts and the bribes paid by Unaoil's clients in Iraq illustrate how this works. Examples from Angola, Azerbaijan, and Russia add further evidence.

Like many oil producers, Angola upped its local content requirements during the oil boom years, requiring foreign companies to hire more Angolan suppliers and contractors. As the Angola expert Soares de Oliveira explains, a political process determined which oligarchs got to benefit from these opportunities. Some of the winning local companies lacked employees or an office, and very few had oil sector credentials. When they received a subcontract, rarely did they do much actual work, as in the case of Halliburton's politically connected subcontractor described in chapter 2. "The most frequent outcome," Soares de Oliveira observes, "is that a letterbox Angolan company, many connected with Sonangol officials, would appropriate local content contracts and simply subcontract activities to foreign firms."[68]

Bribery also infiltrated Sonangol's service contracting systems. In order to boost their shot at winning Angolan contracts, the Dutch oilfield service company SBM Offshore paid bribes worth over $14 million to offshore shell companies controlled by at least nine Angolan officials and handed out gifts, travel, entertainment and jobs for good measure, as disclosed in a US court filing.[69] United Kingdom courts convicted several staff of another service company, F.H. Bertling, for bribing an agent of Sonangol as part of an effort to win a shipping contract worth $20 million. In a reminder of the universality of behaviors like these, British authorities launched their investigation into Bertling because they suspected the company of paying bribes to secure a contract from the American oil giant ConocoPhillips for work servicing its operations in the United Kingdom's North Sea.[70]

In Azerbaijan, oil sector subcontracting is also an environment with the potential for corruption. Reporting by the *Wall Street Journal* described one high-risk scenario. BP is Azerbaijan's largest foreign investor. To run just one large gas sector project, the world-class Shah Deniz gas field, BP awarded as much as $2.5 billion in subcontracts per year during the oil boom. A Swiss company, Panalpina, worked as one of BP's largest subcontractors on Shah Deniz, providing various equipment and services needed to operate the field. The *Journal* reported that in 2013, a Panalpina employee allegedly approved hundreds of invoices, worth around $16 million, to pay a shell company for transportation services it never provided.[71] The owners of the shell company were unknown, and the payments went into a Dubai bank account. BP acknowledged that it had investigated the issue but had not found any evidence of misconduct. Panalpina said that they were a victim of fraud by a former subcontractor, and they fired the manager of their Azerbaijan office, who also denied wrongdoing.

In another possible instance, according to the same investigation, BP paid inflated prices for construction services provided by a consortium of contractors that included international and Azerbaijani companies. As the *Journal* reports, "the consortium routinely charged BP well over the market rate for basic services and key construction work, according to documents and people familiar with the matter." The media report quoted a former BP contractor on the project who called out "blatant attempts at profiteering" and observed that "costs went through the roof" when local companies joined a project.[72]

Mixed consortiums like those contracted by BP can serve the dual agendas of the kleptocratic leader: the capable main partner built the infrastructure to a high standard, so that the gas kept flowing, and the smaller partners fulfilled political agendas. High oil prices made it easy to execute both agendas in tandem. BP and the contractor indicated that the project's costs were fully approved and on budget. None of the companies named have been charged with a crime related to this project, though Panalpina admitted in a previous episode to bribing officials from Azerbaijan as well as Angola, Brazil, Kazakhstan, Nigeria, Russia, and Turkmenistan in 2002–2007.[73]

Russia's national oil companies also spent handsomely on various goods and services during the oil boom. As Putin consolidated his control over Rosneft and Gazprom, the two state-owned giants of the oil and gas sector, he could more easily control which oligarch received lucrative subcontracting opportunities. In doing so, Putin decided who got rich—one of the great political tools available to kleptocrats.

Gazprom spent billions of dollars on pipeline construction during the oil boom. Some observers conclude that Gazprom built more pipelines than it needed, forgoing shorter and easier options in favor of longer and more complicated ones. Gazprom also paid well above market price for the pipelines, with one 1,500-mile line costing $44 billion, or three times the industry standard cost.[74]

The brothers Arkady and Boris Rotenberg handled a chunk of this pipeline business. Old friends of Putin from their days sparring at a St. Petersburg judo club, the Rotenbergs sit atop the new class of oligarchs who rose under Putin's rule. Mammoth deals with Gazprom fueled their ascendance and their unshakable loyalty to Putin. Much of the business they received involved purchasing gas pipes from one company and selling them to Gazprom, a middleman function ripe for rent-seeking.[75] As one sector analyst observed, Gazprom "switched from a principle of maximizing shareholder profits to one of maximizing contractor profits," as its projects created a "way of minting new billionaires in Russia: overpay for services and make them rich."[76] Other experts estimate that corruption and inefficiency, including inflated contracts, cost Gazprom $40 billion a year during the oil boom.[77] But for Putin, these were not losses at all. The spending created loyal billionaires dedicated to strengthening his rule.

Gazprom helped Putin enrich allies outside Russia as well. In a string of "sweetheart deals," the Ukrainian businessman Dmitry Firtash bought gas at cut-rate prices from Gazprom and sold it inside his home country. One *Reuters* investigation estimates that the prices given to Firtash helped him make an extra $3 billion.[78] These deals and others steered to him, such as favorable loans from Russian banks, helped him become a billionaire. He also emerged as a rich and powerful supporter of Victor Yanukovych, who became the president of Ukraine in 2010 and remained a solid ally of Putin throughout his time in office. As the reporters concluded in their investigation of Firtash, the deals show "how Putin uses Russian state assets to create streams of cash for political allies, and how he exported this model to Ukraine in an attempt to dominate his neighbour, which he sees as vital to Russia's strategic interests."[79]

Along with subcontracting, oil trading is another area where political elites can access rents without endangering the overall health of the goose. Most national oil companies receive a large share of the oil produced in their countries. They then have to sell that oil to refineries or oil traders. The proceeds of these sales are often among the largest revenue streams in the country.[80] For instance, proceeds of the sale of oil by Azerbaijan and Angola's national oil companies equaled 58 and 67 percent of total government revenues, respectively, in 2011–2013.[81] For national oil companies to get the best prices for their oil, they must master the complex shifts of prices and demand across the global oil market. The stronger their trading skills, the better the returns.

In these two countries, as well as in Russia, a few businessmen won big from the oil trading deals that were steered in their direction. A common thread across the three is that they did not receive these opportunities through a competitive tender but were selected by those in charge.

In Azerbaijan, one of the winners was a young man named Anar Aliyev (no relation to President Aliyev). Unlike the big-time Azerbaijani oligarchs introduced below, few had heard of this businessman before Global Witness published their report *Azerbaijan Anonymous* in 2013. The report questioned why Anar Aliyev had received dozens of lucrative deals from Socar over a six-year period despite having no obvious record in the oil industry. One such deal involved Socar's creation of a trading subsidiary, Socar Trading, in 2007. Global Witness revealed that one of Anar Aliyev's companies, Heritage, which had no known oil trading experience, received a 25 percent share in Socar Trading for just $5 million. Then, five years later, Heritage sold its shares in Socar Trading back to its parent company, Socar, for $103 million.[82] The report called on Socar to be more transparent in its affairs and for Azerbaijan to require oil companies to disclose their ultimate or "beneficial" owners, i.e., the person or people who truly control the company and stand to benefit from its affairs.

The Global Witness report provoked a vigorous response from Socar, who wrote letters of protest, called the report "erroneous and unsubstantiated," and hired a UK public relations firm to set up a website in response, titled rather literally: www.azerbaijananonymousexplained.com.[83] The report also flushed Anar Aliyev out into the public eye. The businessman released a statement, set up a website, and gave a few media interviews, all of which emphasize the legality of his business affairs and insist that he has no links to any political figures. He also changed his name from Aliyev to Alizade because, as he explains, "I was always facing many questions about my family relations to powerful people in Azerbaijan."[84]

The responses from Socar and Alizade (formerly Aliyev) to the Global Witness report shed light on the good fortune of this one businessman. Socar confirmed that Alizade made a 2,000 percent return on his initial investment in Socar Trading and argued that he deserved these profits because he assisted in getting the fledgling Socar Trading off the ground, including helping it secure financing during the difficult years following the global financial crisis.[85] Socar went on to detail other occasions when it created a new entity in partnership with a company owned by Alizade and then Alizade's company sold its shares back to Socar a short time later. In all, Alizade reported that ten of his companies were in various kinds of partnership with Socar.[86]

While Socar and Alizade vigorously deny any malfeasance or the involvement of political figures in the deals, they cannot deny that this one businessman's companies repeatedly received unique oil trading opportunities without any kind of tender or competition. While defending its record, Socar itself emphasized that "under Azerbaijani laws and Socar internal procurement procedures there is no requirement for public offerings or tendering for setting up joint ventures or cooperation with private investors and corporations."[87] The freedom Socar enjoys in choosing its partners is hardly unusual in the oil industry but leaves open lots of room in Azerbaijan and elsewhere for asking: "but why them?"

Socar Trading grew into a large international oil trading company during the boom years, whether thanks to or despite the involvement of Alizade's company. The subsidiary was well run and was known in the industry for snatching up top talent from other big trading firms. By 2017, ten years into its life, Socar Trading reported collecting $45 billion in revenues and trading an impressive 2 million barrels of oil a day, most of which came from outside Azerbaijan.[88] While well-placed businessmen made serious money off its evolution, none of these efforts was allowed to swallow the entity whole. Compare that to the oil trading subsidiaries of Nigeria's national oil company. They have existed for decades but never acquired any kind of commercial viability.

Angola's regime followed a similar playbook, though some of the businessmen who scored big oil trading deals there also held top political positions. General Leopoldino Fragoso do Nascimento, nicknamed "Dino," was one of the leading figures in Angolan political and business affairs under dos Santos. He held several influential government posts while also playing a leading role at a company called Cochan.[89] From 2009 until at least 2012, Cochan partnered with the Swiss company Trafigura, one of the largest oil traders in the world, to create a fifty-fifty joint venture, DTS Refining. Sonangol then awarded DTS Refining several large "swap" contracts. Under these contracts, DTS Refining received a portion of the country's crude oil production and then imported refined petroleum products like gasoline and jet fuel in return.[90] One media report estimates that the imported products were worth $3.3 billion in 2011, and for a time DTS Holdings held a full monopoly on Angola's fuel imports.[91] During several boom years, thanks to deals struck by Sonangol, General Dino profited from every drop of fuel that entered the country.

Putin allies also got rich off oil trading. Like the Rotenbergs, who received juicy pipeline contracts from Gazprom, Gennady Timchenko is also prominent among the new set of oligarchs who became dominant under Putin's leadership. Much of Timchenko's enormous fortune, which had topped $13 billion by 2016, stems from oil sector businesses. He cofounded Gunvor, a Swiss-based company that grew into one of the world's largest traders of oil. Timchenko also holds a major stake in the large gas company Novatek.

When Putin and Sechin dismantled Yukos and transferred its oil blocks to Rosneft, they tapped Gunvor to trade the oil produced from many of the former Yukos fields. Thanks largely to the trading deals with Rosneft, Gunvor's revenues grew from $5 billion in 2004 to $80 billion in 2011, and the company came to handle a full 30 percent of Russia's seaborne exports.[92] In the years since, Gunvor has built on this foundation to expand its operations worldwide (including its controversial entry into Congo-Brazzaville, explored in chapter 2).

Throughout Gunvor's rise, rumors swirled that the company was secretly owned by Putin, with Timchenko acting as his proxy. Why else would Gunvor receive so many valuable deals? In the late 2000s, a Russian academic claimed that Putin was Gunvor's beneficial owner and controlled 75 percent of Gunvor. The *Economist* then reported that Gunvor enjoyed links to Putin, explaining its rapid rise.[93] A number of years later, in 2014, the United States reupped these claims when it announced sanctions against Putin and his cronies following the Russian invasion of Ukraine. The United States included Timchenko on the list of sanctioned individuals, stating that he held "inner circle" status and was "controlled by, has acted for or on behalf of, or has provided material or other support to a senior government official." The accusations continued that Timchenko was "one of the founders of Gunvor, one of the world's largest independent commodity trading companies involved in the oil and energy markets. Timchenko's activities in the energy sector have been directly linked to Putin. Putin has investments in Gunvor and may have access to Gunvor funds."[94]

In response, Gunvor and Timchenko have vigorously denied these claims. In 2009 Timchenko slapped a libel lawsuit on the *Economist*, following its article, which later ended in a settlement.[95] In a 2014 missive responding to the US sanctions, Gunvor said that it "categorically denies that Vladimir Putin has or has ever had any ownership or that he is a beneficiary of our business directly or indirectly. That understanding is fundamentally misinformed and outrageous."[96] Putin's spokesman echoed the point. Timchenko sold his shares in Gunvor when the US sanctions were announced, so as not to impede the company's operations. He called his inclusion on the sanctions list "a little surprising, but it was an honor for me," presumably because Putin's inner circle is not a terrible place for a Russian businessman to be.

This scenario again points to the fact that kleptocratic leaders do not need to profit directly from every deal, as long as they steer the profits toward loyal allies. Providing another glimpse at this kleptocratic architecture, the Panama Papers revealed several oligarchs and allies of Putin who have moved money in and out of shell companies for no discernable business purpose. For example, Rotenberg lent $230 million to a company based in the British Virgin Islands in 2013, with no known repayment schedule.[97] His spokesman said it was for commercial transactions. A reporter for the *New Yorker*, writing about Rotenberg, summed up well the political rationale for the oligarchic economy: "Putin's thinking seems to be that there is no need to own anything himself, at least on paper, when trusted allies can do it for him."[98]

Allocate Eggs to Boost Your Power

Because the leaders took good care of their geese and protected them from the vagaries of unconstrained corruption, they had plenty of eggs on their hands.

Around 2010, the sons of a powerful government minister in Azerbaijan sought to buy two Gulfstream jets. The US airplane manufacturer, as part of its due diligence process into the deal, required the buyers to disclose information about their financial assets. According to a leaked US diplomatic cable, "the family provided Gulfstream an overview of their family holdings, and it appears they own more businesses than any other Azerbaijani family, including companies in food canning, construction materials, concrete, asphalt, chemicals, bricks, textiles, CD and DVD production, milk processing, tourism, gypsum materials, leather, agriculture, pianos, alcohol and spirits, juices, banking, insurance, and construction."[99] The investments of the two sons stretched abroad: they had bought up real estate in Spain, Dubai, and Georgia and several factories in France.[100] This remarkable array of businesses belonged to the family of Kamaladdin Heydarov, Azerbaijan's minister of emergency services—or the "Ministry of Everything Significant," according to the same juicy US Embassy cable.

The rise of Heydarov and other top oligarchs reveals how President Aliyev achieved pervasive control over the Azerbaijani economy. During the price boom, Azerbaijan's annual oil revenues rose from $5.5 billion in 2007 to $23 billion in 2011.[101] Fueled by these riches, Aliyev used government contracts, loans, and other channels to enrich his allies and build a robust and pervasive kleptocracy. These money flows did relatively little to develop the country's nonoil economy, and after the boom the country faced a major recession as a result.

Years before his sons began shopping for jets, Heydarov worked as the head of Azerbaijan's customs agency, where—according to US diplomats—he built his influence and benefited President Aliyev through such means as creating import monopolies for certain products and allocating them to businesspeople loyal to the regime.[102] Aliyev then rewarded Heydarov with larger roles in both the public and the private sectors, which were both bursting with oil funds. In 2006, Heydarov was appointed the country's first minister of emergency services—a flexible portfolio that subsumed a slew of important agencies, including several paramilitary and security units. Given his competence and loyalty to the president, this ministry came to control a wide swathe of profitable functions. For example, the ministry began issuing real estate permits in the booming Baku property market. The government was spending oil revenues on costly construction projects and was lending money to finance further projects spearheaded by its oligarchs. As he did at customs, Heydarov used his new-found regulatory powers to direct these real estate opportunities into the right hands.

A 2007 US Embassy cable provides one account of how Heydarov deployed his government authority to favor his own business interests. "In the first six months of 2007, MES [the Ministry of Emergency Services] reportedly found more than 200 buildings in violation of local building and or safety codes and ordered all activities to stop. In late 2006, the MES shut down the construction of a new large office building for several months on the grounds of building code and safety violations costing millions of dollars. The building's developer later said that representatives reportedly speaking on behalf of senior [government] officials, including Heydarov, demanded a controlling stake of more than 50 percent ownership in the new building."[103] This cable also describes how the ministry used its zoning authority to shut down the offices of two newspapers that had published stories critical of the government. It forced several companies to purchase "MES-approved" fire extinguishers at inflated prices. "According to the businessmen, the MES fire extinguishers were of low quality and would also need to be replaced every six months. Most business officials with whom we spoke believed that the Heydarov had a personal financial stake in the 'MES-approved' fire extinguishers."[104]

When necessary, the Heydarov family would go on the offensive, as part of the regime's efforts to lock down every corner of the country's economy. The operator of a growing chain of bookstores reported how, in 2014, she received an invitation to a meeting at Heydarov's holding company. There, a company official threatened to close down her business. "We are an elephant, and you are an ant—we will crush you," she reported being told. Following the meeting, she said, she faced longer delays at customs when importing her books, the police harassed her staff, and she was the victim of theft. Around the same time, Heydarov's son started a rival chain of bookstores. The new chain denied that it had any connections with the government and said it had not engaged in intimidation.[105]

Along with Heydarov, Ziya Mammadov and his family ranked among Azerbaijan's top oligarchs. Mammadov served as the country's minister of transport for fifteen years. He and his family also grew an enormous business empire off of two common advantages provided by the regime to its allies: unique business opportunities and bloated government contracts. For instance, a company partially controlled by the Mammadovs received the government contract to import 1,000 London-style "black cabs" to serve the capital city's transport needs. To give the new taxi business a boost, the Ministry of Transport then revised the city's parking rules in a manner that disadvantaged competitor taxi companies and required taxi drivers to pay their taxes and licensing fees via a bank owned in part by Mammadov's son.[106]

Companies associated with the Mammadov family played a similarly dominant role in bus transport, road construction, and cargo transportation—no coincidence given Ziya's control over the Ministry of Transport. These companies received lucrative road construction contracts. An Azerbaijani contact remarked to me: "I swear I've seen the same stretch of perfectly good road rebuilt three or four times." Other observers suggest that Azerbaijan has the most expensive roads in the world.[107] According to a US Embassy cable, "with so much of the nation's oil wealth being poured into road construction, the Mammadovs also control a significant source of rent-seeking."[108]

As seen in Angola and Russia, Mammadov and the other oligarchs used this initial injection of government business to grow their empires. The Mammadov family's businesses spread across the construction, sports, hotel, insurance, and oil industries, as well as the banking sector. Mammadov became a billionaire, despite his official salary of $12,000 a year, and his son did as well.[109]

When asked about this network of businesses and their ties to the state, a spokesperson for the Transport Ministry commented: "only the interests of Azerbaijan are important to the minister. Maybe these businesses belong to someone close to the minister. If these people propose efficient and strong projects, why shouldn't they be preferred?"[110] Indeed, in recent years, the business empires of the oligarchs have become so dominant and widespread that it would be difficult to do business in Azerbaijan and avoid them.

Despite this success, Mammadov and his network may have grown less efficient in serving President Aliyev. In 2017, Mammadov was fired as transport minister, providing a reminder that oligarchs may get rich and hold top positions but do so only at the pleasure of the president.

During the oil boom years, Heydarov and Mammadov ranked among the most influential oligarchs. But no one topped the efforts of Aliyev and his own family. Aliyev and his wife have two daughters and a son, and all indulge deeply in the pleasures of wealth. The two daughters, like their mother, are committed fashionistas. When they modeled for a local fashion magazine, Azerbaijani broadcasters were rapturous. The two daughters provided "clear proof that not only physical appearance, but also wisdom, the inner world, charm and individuality are inherited genetically.... Every public appearance of these eastern beauties offers a chance to feast your eyes on their beautiful manners, their skills at socializing with friends, family and the people around them."[111]

The Aliyev children will inherit far more than beauty and charm, thanks to the holdings of the first family. While the total value of their empire remains unknown, hidden behind countless shell companies, tenacious media investigations have uncovered pieces here and there. The first lady and her children reportedly own houses worth over $140 million, including a $25 million London mansion and nine waterfront houses in Dubai worth a total of $44 million.[112] To host the 2012 Eurovision Song Contest in glittering style, the Azerbaijani government funded the construction of Baku Chrystal Hall, a stadium that features 9,500 LED lights that blink along to music. The first lady and her two daughters were among the beneficiaries of a company that received a portion of the stadium construction work, according to media reports, though their ownership was hidden by a string of offshore shell companies.[113] The daughters are also linked to seven five-star hotels that popped up in Baku during the oil boom and two exclusive mountain resorts.[114]

Further media investigations report that companies controlled by the first lady and her daughters also hold shares in several of the large holding companies that dominate Azerbaijan's business landscape.[115] Through these vehicles, among others, the Aliyevs profit off of nearly every segment of the economy. The Aliyev family and their close advisors are also significant shareholders in at least eight major Azerbaijani banks.[116] As in Angola and Russia, political elites in Azerbaijan use their control over certain banks to help support the business interests of the top oligarchs. Pasha Bank, which has ties to the first daughters, provided financing for the Four Seasons hotel in Baku and a mountaintop resort that opened during the oil boom—two of the high-end hotels partially owned by members of the first family.[117] This circuit of self-dealing is closed to all but Aliyev's closest allies.

In 2012 an Azerbaijani journalist, Khadija Ismayilova, broke the story of how the government had allocated a valuable gold mining license to a consortium of companies, one of which was owned by the president's daughters.[118] As is typical across the first family's operations, the deal involved shell companies registered in multiple jurisdictions, the United Kingdom and Panama in this case. In 2015, another of Ismayilova's investigations exposed the first family as the true of owners of some of Azerbaijan's most luxurious new hotels.[119]

However, by the time the story came out, Ismayilova found herself in a prison cell. Arrested on trumped-up charges, she spent eighteen months in prison for revealing the inner workings of the kleptocratic economy. She has been released, but dozens of other journalists, activists, and opposition politicians remain locked in Azerbaijani jails. Aliyev doesn't just use oil money and oligarchs to stay in power: fear and repression are important tools too.

In addition to enriching the first family and its allies, the Aliyev government also used oil money to bolster its reputation and prestige. On a work trip to Baku, I wandered through the intensely tidy park that runs along the shores of the Caspian Sea and over to the base of an enormous Azerbaijani flag. Staring up its 162-meter pole, I struggled to find an angle for a photo that would capture its unusual height. Erected in 2010 for a price of $38 million, the flag was briefly the tallest in the world.[120] Rather rudely, Tajikistan built a taller one just a few months later.

The giant flag was just the beginning. With the help of his oligarch henchmen, Ilham Aliyev invested heavily in marketing the regime as successful, powerful, and inevitable. Baku emerged from the oil boom with a host of elaborate new buildings, many of which could have been inspired by the glittering skyscrapers of Dubai.[121] Images of the Flame Towers, a cultural center designed by a British architectural star, are now ubiquitous across the country's promotional materials. Older buildings received makeovers so that proliferating five-star hotels and designer boutiques looked more at home. The government slapped new facades on many Soviet-era buildings, modeling them after European capitals like Vienna and Paris. As a savvy politician, Aliyev did not confine the upgrades to the swank Baku downtown. New parks, playgrounds, and school buildings cropped up around the country, as did improved roads and other infrastructure. The intended message was clear: Azerbaijan is thriving.

Along with construction, the regime in Baku spent handsomely on politically motivated philanthropy. One motto found on the Heydar Aliyev Foundation's website is a quote from its namesake, the father of the current president and founder of the family regime: "it is easier to prevent danger than remove its aftermath." Indeed, through its widespread programs, the Foundation has worked to prevent dangers for the regime. Domestically, it doles out support for art exhibits, medical clinics, and sporting events and pays particular attention to preserving the memory of the conflict with neighboring Armenia—a long-standing source of national unity.

Abroad, the Foundation raises the profile of Azerbaijan. Erecting statues of Heydar Aliyev in countries around the world is a favorite activity. The Foundation has also supported the renovation of the stained-glass windows in Strasbourg's cathedral, repairs to the Vatican's catacombs, construction of a new hospital in Bosnia, and countless showcases of Azerbaijani culture.[122] If running Azerbaijan is a family business, the Foundation is its well-resourced public relations arm.

Unsurprisingly, investigations have raised questions about the governance of the Foundation. Funds slip easily between government, foundation, and oligarch accounts.[123] The Foundation does not publish its annual budget. The president of the Foundation is the first lady, and the vice-president is her daughter. Individuals and businesses who seek favor with the regime make frequent donations. One opposition politician described donations to the foundation as a "get out of jail free card" for local officials.[124]

The government also spent oil money on elaborate international gatherings, lavishing $75 million on hosting the Eurovision Song Contest in 2012.[125] A few years later, they hosted the first ever European Games. That extravagant affair revealed some of the challenges faced by dictators trying to airbrush their reputations. No leaders of major European Union countries accepted Aliyev's invitation to attend. Instead, he was joined by those heads of state who were more comfortable with his authoritarian style and worsening human rights record, such as those of Russia, Turkey, and Belarus.[126]

The oligarchs helped out with these public relations gambits and benefited from them as well. One of the largest oligarch-controlled holding companies bought the rights to have "Azerbaijan: Land of Fire" emblazoned on the jerseys of the prominent European soccer team Atletico Madrid. The same three families already mentioned—the Aliyevs, the Heydarovs, and the Mammadovs—ran much of the government's Western lobbying apparatus during the oil boom, according to a *Foreign Policy* investigation provocatively titled "The Corleones of the Caspian." The Azerbaijan American Alliance, for example, was founded by Mammadov's son and was chaired by a former US congressman from Indiana. Heydarov's son has handled reputation management in the United Kingdom, wining and dining members of parliament and other top figures via events organized by the European Azerbaijan Society, a lobby group headquartered in the tony Mayfair neighborhood of London.[127]

The tentacles of Aliyev's kleptocracy stretch around the world. They wind through offshore shell companies, bank accounts, and real estate. They have ensnared investors, business partners, and politicians in Europe, the United States, and the Middle East. Even the family business of US president Donald Trump ended up collaborating with the Mammadov family during the oil boom years.[128] The regime has also benefited from the laissez-faire approach taken by European governments who value Azerbaijan as a strategic supplier of natural gas. These actors, among others, have turned a blind eye to the regime's kleptocratic traits (as is discussed further in chapter 6).

The leaders of Russia and Angola followed some similar patterns in the ways they spent their golden eggs. There's no question that Putin topped Aliyev in spending on high-profile sporting events. The 2012 Sochi Olympics took place smack in the middle of the oil boom and could have won gold for the transfer of oil wealth into private pockets. The total price tag for the games topped $50 billion—a figure only exceeded by the Beijing 2008 Summer Olympics and many times greater than the $7 billion spent by Vancouver on the 2010 Winter Games.

As in the case of the Gazprom pipeline construction contracts, the Rotenberg brothers sat atop the list of beneficiaries. The US authorities, in their justification for including the Rotenbergs on the 2014 sanctions list, stated that the two "have provided support to Putin's pet projects by receiving and executing high price contracts for the Sochi Olympic Games and state-controlled Gazprom. They have made billions of dollars in contracts for Gazprom and the Sochi Winter Olympics awarded to them by Putin. Both brothers have amassed enormous amounts of wealth during the years of Putin's rule in Russia. The Rotenberg brothers received approximately $7 billion in contracts for the Sochi Olympic Games and their personal wealth has increased by $2.5 billion in the last two years alone."[129]

Russia no longer enjoys the high oil prices that helped foot the Sochi bill, and the US sanctions have dampened Russia's economy as well. However, Rotenberg and company seem to be doing just fine. The Russian version of *Forbes* published a story in 2015 on the top beneficiaries of government contracts under the Putin regime. Arkady Rotenberg and his son Igor featured among the top five, as did Gennady Timchenko. Together the three received contracts worth $11.3 billion in 2015—despite government austerity policies following the drop in oil prices. One opposition politician called them among "the five kings of government contracts" and concluded: "basically, that's all you need to know about the Russian economy."[130] But here's one more fact anyway: the top 10 percent of Russians own 87 percent of the country's wealth—a higher proportion than in any other major country.[131]

In Angola, the dos Santos regime channeled its oil money into capital projects, many of which were ill-conceived status projects rather than efforts to lift ordinary Angolans out of poverty. From roads and railroads to stadiums and shopping malls, showpiece projects with large padded budgets created ample opportunities for the elites to profit. The recipients of state largesse were very few. Soares de Oliveira has suggested the top flight of beneficiaries number in the hundreds, with perhaps a few thousand more receiving a decent sized cut.[132] The latter category includes certain groups who have to be "fed" as part of the political machine, such as party officials, regional elites, and the military and security services. As for the lucky chosen oligarchs, they would often discover their names listed as the boss of a new economic venture, typically funded by the state or a loyal bank, even if they had no previous experience in that given industry. It didn't matter. The bosses would simply hire foreigners to run the operation and keep a cut of the profits for themselves.[133]

Kleptocracy's Durability

During the oil boom, the Aliyev regime benefited a great deal from its golden goose. The oil sector was relatively well run, causing unprecedented oil revenues to flow into the government's accounts. The first family and several oligarchs received a lion's share of these rents. They made sure that unaffiliated businesses failed to grow, and they channeled money back into the president's patronage campaigns. Prestige projects and public relations campaigns boosted the regime's prominence at home and abroad. Oil money also let Aliyev supercharge the country's military. Spending on the military rose to $4 billion a year during the oil boom, while the country's neighbors, Georgia and Armenia, spent around $750 million a year combined.[134]

Riding high, the Aliyev government also pursued political strategies to consolidate their control. A 2009 referendum vote did away with presidential term limits; the state media have all but taken over what information citizens can consume; independent media outlets are shut down, and access to international websites is restricted; civil society groups are kept from receiving foreign funds; and many journalists, activists, and opposition politicians sit in jail or face regular intimidation.

Ordinary Azerbaijanis saw their standards of living improve during the oil boom. The country of 9 million people is small enough that some of the wealth did trickle down. The construction boom provided well-paying jobs to laborers, many of whom came from the poorer rural areas of the country. Some of the construction dollars were spent on upgrading school buildings, though teachers remained profoundly underpaid. Hospitals boasted fancy new equipment, even if the staff had no idea how to run it. Police received salary hikes, in part to ensure that they remained loyal to the regime. New parks, sports facilities, and cultural centers cropped up thanks to the Heydar Aliyev Foundation, and the children of well-connected families received stipends to study abroad.

Meanwhile Aliyev and his peers groomed the next generation. Aliyev's children now feature prominently among the owners of the country's top corporations, as do the children of several top oligarchs. Dos Santos named his daughter CEO of Sonangol and appointed his son chair of the sovereign wealth fund. Putin's daughter and her husband have a reported net worth of over $2 billion, and the sons of Arkady Rotenberg hold top positions at state-controlled oil companies and banks.[135]

All three kleptocrat kings grew stronger during the oil boom, but their strength was tested when prices fell. Faced with the 2014 plummet in prices, the Azerbaijani government had to cut back its spending and took on large debts. The cost of living rose sharply and jobs funded by government contracting dried up. The government issued two steep currency devaluations that devastated many citizens who had taken out dollar-denominated loans during the oil boom.[136] Frustration rose, and talk swirled of individuals who, unable to cope with mounting financial pressures, committed suicide. Several small protests erupted in 2015 and 2016. Slogans at one rally included "No to monarchy, end to robbery!" and "Where is the $140 billion oil money?"[137]

In Russia, the government lent billions of dollars to bail out Rosneft, in order to protect that crucial engine of its kleptocratic machine. On the political front, challenges also cropped up. The opposition politician and anticorruption activist Alexei Navalny published a video in 2017 that suggests that Prime Minister Dmitri Medvedev used an elaborate network of shell companies and charitable foundations to buy high-end properties in Russia and abroad. Prompted in part by Navalny's work, thousands of Russians across over 100 cities, including many in their teens and early twenties, took to the streets in protest; riot police arrested 700 in Moscow alone. However, as in Azerbaijan, the opposition did not pose an existential threat to the regime.

In Angola, the poor were hit hard by the drop in oil prices and ensuing recession. As one commentator explained, "the most heart-breaking of all recent developments is the collapse of public health services. Not that it was ever good—Angola maintains one of the world's worst child mortality rates—but in 2016 the rainy season, litter and generalised poverty and unhygienic conditions, triggered a mass outbreak of malaria, yellow fever, dengue, chikungunya and acute respiratory and diarrheic diseases."[138] Before dos Santos retired, a few small protests also reared their heads and were met with harsh crackdowns by authorities. However, in Angola, unlike Russia and Azerbaijan, dynamics at the top have shifted. The dos Santos children found themselves without jobs and facing tough scrutiny following surprising moves by Lourenço, the new president. Whether he will take further steps to dismantle the kleptocracy built by dos Santos remains to be seen.

Despite controlling nearly all the levers of power, it is not unheard-of for oil-rich kleptocrats to tumble. Libya's Gaddafi lost power, and his life, at the hands of rebels and revolutionaries during the 2011 Arab Spring. Historic protests rocked oil-rich Algeria in 2019, with citizens successfully demanding that the long-standing president, Abdelaziz Bouteflika, step down. Sudan's long-standing dictator also lost his position to the military in 2019, following widespread activism and unrest. Powerful kleptocratic leaders can fall from their thrones if dissent escalates enough.

However, domestic dissent faces a steep and arduous climb in well-run kleptocracies. The leaders in these countries enjoy pervasive control. They can buy people off with wealth and opportunity or threaten them with legal action, deny them the right to do business or move around freely, and inflict a variety of other harms. The institutions meant to facilitate opposition and protect the public interest, including elections, opposition parties, courts, and legislatures, frequently fall under the influence of the leader. State spending enriches allies who then move to encircle the rest of the economy in their grasp. There is no politically independent wealth as a result.

Because domestic opposition faces such steep odds, it is doubly important to reduce the ways the international system enables kleptocracy. Oil-rich kleptocracies unleash tentacles that reach around the world, creating complicities and interdependencies with many international players. These international ties enable kleptocrats to produce their oil, stash their money abroad, and retain geopolitical legitimacy. But global ties also represent vulnerabilities. The next chapters address how targeting these enablers may offer the best option for curtailing kleptocracy of the kind observed in Angola, Azerbaijan, and Russia.

CHAPTER 5 | "An Octopus That Reaches around
the Globe"

SOMETIMES THE TENTACLES OF corruption reach out and drop off lovely gifts.

In 2014, Hollywood megastar Leonardo DiCaprio received one such gift for his birthday—a painting of a toothy bull skull sat next to a blue vase on a table. The painting, a Picasso, came from a Malaysian business- man who had invested in the actor's recent film about greed and deception, *The Wolf of Wall Street.* The same Malaysian businessman spoiled his girlfriend at the time, Miranda Kerr, an Australian supermodel famous from Victoria's Secret runway shows, with a 9-carat pink diamond pendant worth $4 million.

The tentacles attached to these gifts stretched around the world and unwittingly connected these celebrities to one of the largest corruption schemes in history. The money used to buy the gifts originated in Malaysia, as did most of the scheme's architects. But the story of the funds is a global one.

The diamond and the painting represent just a tiny part of the staggering story of 1MDB, a Malaysian government investment fund. International players helped a few corrupt individuals to steal around $4.5 billion in public funds from Malaysia and hide the money around the world. Countless ten- tacles spread in every direction and crisscrossed dozens of international borders. Nevertheless, journalists and investigators picked up the trail. After months spent tracing the various threads, the DOJ exposed the case's international cast of characters and ordered DiCaprio and Kerr to relinquish their lovely gifts.

Four Kinds of International Enablers

It might seem impossible to counteract the kind of corruption described in the previous chapter. Dictators construct political and economic systems that reinforce their power and bestow benefits on their families and their allies. They write the rules of the game and therefore can reinforce this system and eliminate threats. Even in countries like Brazil and Nigeria, where political competition and some level of democracy ended up curtailing kleptocratic schemes, political elites managed to steal billions of dollars in public funds. How can this kind of systematic theft be combated when its perpetrators hold so much power?

The answer may lie in the intense reliance of kleptocracy on international enablers. As an Azerbaijani activist reminded me, while corruption may begin with political elites in one country, it then becomes "an octopus that reaches around the world." Transparency International's Corruption Perception Index, a commonly used measure of corruption, publishes a world map where most of the world appears in various shades of red, indicating high corruption risks, and the richest countries in North America and Western Europe are a much cheerier yellow. As the 1MDB story and many others make clear, this image of corruption is outdated and overlooks how complicity reaches across borders. For example, Denmark was the least corrupt country in the world according to Transparency International's 2018 rankings. But Denmark's largest bank sits at the center of one of the largest money laundering scandals in history. In 2018, Danske Bank admitted that foreigners routed $230 billion in funds, mostly from Russia, through its tiny Estonian branch with minimal checks, even though most of the transactions were suspicious.[1]

The journalist Oliver Bullough wrote a book on all these international enablers who have combined to create a new realm he calls "Moneyland." "Maltese passports, English libel, American privacy, Panamanian shell companies, Jersey trusts, Lichtenstein foundations, all add together to create a virtual space that is far greater than the sum of their parts," he writes. "The laws of Moneyland are whichever laws anywhere are most suited to those wealthy enough to afford them at any moment in time.... It is as if the very wealthiest people in countries like China, Nigeria, Ukraine, and Russia have tunneled into this new land that lies beneath all our nation states, where borders have vanished. They move their money, their children, their assets and themselves wherever they wish, picking and choosing which countries' laws they wish to live by."[2]

While the international system offers countless advantages to today's kleptocrats, it also creates opportunities to fight back. International linkages can become locations where kleptocrats are frustrated, shamed, punished, or deterred. The intense internationalization of oil sector corruption represents both its greatest strength and its greatest vulnerability.

Many top political analysts assumed that the end of the Cold War and trends of globalization would isolate and ultimately eliminate authoritarian and kleptocratic regimes, with liberal democracy sweeping unencumbered across the globe. Instead, some countries have simultaneously become more globalized and more kleptocratic.[3] Bullough argues that contemporary kleptocracy was born of the marriage of dictatorship with the new system of global finance. He writes: "kleptocracy...is the dark side of globalization. Offshore finance is what made it possible."[4] Rather than curtailing kleptocracy, globalization has actually helped corrupt regimes to secure greater power and wealth.

The author Ben Judah explains further:

> Rather than retreat, democratize and reform towards the rule of law, the autocratic ruling classes of Russia, China, Central Asia, the Arabian Gulf and beyond have globalized with great success. The openness of the new century, the US and the EU are now finding, is in fact rather well suited to the kleptocratic dictator—with a coterie of American lawyers, French bankers, German accountants, and British public relations teams in tow....It has never been simpler or safer to be a kleptocrat....Not only can capital now mask itself and disappear without any trace, but gigantic sums of money are now traveling the world in a concealed manner.[5]

The international tentacles of kleptocracy now make headlines with some regularity. The affairs of Donald Trump have driven some of this attention. For instance, one of Trump's 2016 campaign managers, Paul Manafort, previously served on the payroll of the former kleptocratic president of Ukraine, Viktor Yanukovych. United States authorities indicted Manafort for laundering his Ukrainian income through various offshore financial instruments. In another instance, the Trump family business partnered with a Panamanian bank accused of harboring illicit funds.[6] Several characters associated with kleptocratic corruption have bought apartments in Trump properties, from an exiled former minister from Kazakhstan accused of embezzlement to the daughter of the president of Congo-Brazzaville.[7]

Alongside Trump's election, the Panama Papers also burst onto the scene in 2016, making it even more difficult to ignore the global reach of kleptocracy. Over 100 media outlets collaborated to sift through thousands of leaked documents from a Panamanian law firm, Mossack Fonseca. The resulting stories brought to light how 140 politicians from 50 countries used offshore financial vehicles to move, and sometimes hide, their money. In a number of cases, the money turned out to be stolen. In 2017, another leak surfaced, this time from a financial services company in Bermuda. Dubbed the Paradise Papers, this leak exposed further how lawyers, accountants, and tax havens help the world's superrich stash their money safely away from tax obligations and prying eyes.

Given this rising wave of attention, the time is right to look carefully at how kleptocracy and other forms of grand corruption rely on the international system. Dozens of oil sector corruption cases, when examined, suggest that international actors help kleptocrats in four ways.[8]

First, international actors help political elites to get their hands on wealth. Various kinds of oil companies often feature in this stage, as the oil sector is a popular site for trying to get rich. Second, international actors help move the illicit funds out of their countries of origin and into the global financial system. Third, foreign entities help corrupt actors to spend their money, often in stable countries where both they and their money can feel protected and comfortable. Fourth, a further set of international players helps corrupt actors to polish their reputations and avoid critique.

To illustrate how all four of these dynamics work in practice, this chapter tells the story of the Malaysian investment fund 1MDB. Chapter 6 then presents the flip side of this phenomenon, by showing how international actors help to thwart corruption as well.

First, some background on the 1MDB saga. Najib Razak became Malaysia's prime minister in 2009 via elections, but not very competitive ones. In Malaysia, one party has held firmly onto power since the country's independence from Britain in 1957. Malaysia is a diverse country of 31 million people who represent Malay, Chinese, and Indian backgrounds. The country's economy has grown rapidly and diversified since the 1990s, with gains in manufacturing, tourism, and agriculture. While extreme poverty is quite rare, the benefits of all this economic growth have remained unevenly distributed. Powerful elites control a large share of the country's wealth, and corruption is considered to be widespread. Najib's father ruled the country for a stretch in the 1970s and groomed his son to follow suit. While serving as deputy prime minister, the heir apparent became deeply entrenched in the patterns of trading favors across the political and economic elites. His wife, Rosmah Mansor, became famous and unpopular for her luxury tastes in handbags and jewelry in particular. By the time the 2009 election came around, they were both eager to further enjoy the fruits of power.

Soon after becoming prime minister, Najib called for the federal government to assume control over a provincial sovereign wealth fund and renamed it 1Malaysia Development Berhad, or 1MDB. The fund is wholly owned by the government, and Najib appointed himself chair of its advisory board. The stated purpose of 1MDB was to raise funds, foster foreign partnerships, and invest in key sectors of the Malaysian economy, including energy, real estate, tourism, and agribusiness.

Since then, 1MDB has become home to the largest corruption scandal in Malaysian history and one of the biggest and most brazen schemes ever seen anywhere in the world. Investigations by law enforcement, NGOs, and journalists all suggest that more than $4.5 billion of the fund's assets found their way into the pockets of a few enterprising individuals. After capturing the funds, these individuals stashed that wealth in bank accounts, shell companies, and investments across the globe. Prime Minister Najib himself allegedly received deposits of over $681 million in stolen 1MDB funds in his personal bank account.[9] Najib's attorney general, speaking in 2016, claimed that the payment was a personal donation from the Saudi royal family and that Najib actually returned most of the funds—just one of the story's many ties to the oil-rich Persian Gulf.[10]

The oil boom created ripe conditions for the 1MDB scheme. Malaysia is a medium-sized player in the oil sector, producing around 700,000 barrels per day. But the Malaysian oil industry played only a bit part in this drama. Instead, tentacles stretched from Malaysia to the truly oil-rich Persian Gulf, where a "money to spare" attitude pervaded the oil boom years.

An oil company in Saudi Arabia and an oil fund in Abu Dhabi played essential enabling roles in the scheme, helping the Malaysian fund to raise billions of the dollars that ended up stolen. Enterprising individuals from these countries played more devious parts, making the theft possible and benefiting from it as well. The scheme would not have unfolded without the sheer volume of oil wealth available to Persian Gulf countries during this time or their lax controls over its use.

To tell the story of the 1MDB saga, I have drawn on a range of media investigations and court filings that detail the scheme and the ways the stolen money flowed overseas. In particular, I relied on a 250-page complaint released by the DOJ in 2017 that lays out the US civil case to seize over $1 billion in assets associated with 1MDB corruption, and the reporting of Bradley Hope and Tom Wright, two *Wall Street Journal* reporters who published a captivating book about the 1MDB scheme, *Billion Dollar Whale* in 2018.[11] Since the release of the complaint, US authorities have filed criminal charges against Jho Low, the scheme's chief architect, and several of his colleagues. Malaysian authorities have charged Jho Low as well as Najib. At the time this book went to press, the criminal trials against the main players were ongoing or yet to begin. Many of the parties named in the various complaints and charges have denied wrongdoing and dispute the DOJ's account, including Najib and Jho Low, who maintain their innocence. Jho Low disputes all the charges against him and has refused to cooperate, stating that he "will not submit to any jurisdiction where guilt has been predetermined by politics and there is no independent legal process."[12]

Part 1: Get the Money

First things first: corrupt political elites want to get their hands on big money. Earlier chapters have explained in some detail how powerful individuals use the oil sector to enrich themselves and their inner circles. Some, such as the Petrobras officials in Brazil, receive bribes. Elsewhere as in Nigeria, Angola, and Russia, government officials award lucrative oil sector opportunities to companies headed by their allies. Then the officials can access or influence the profits these allies collect.

International actors often end up assisting with this capture of wealth. Sometimes oil companies are direct parties to the corruption, for example, when they pay bribes or allocate inflated or fraudulent contracts to companies linked to politicians. Chapter 2 described many examples of this behavior. The Canadian company Griffiths bribed a Chadian official to set up meetings with the president. American, Australian, and European oilfield service companies hired the "fixer" company Unaoil to help them win contracts in Iraq, Algeria, and elsewhere, and Unaoil paid off government officials as part of their services. American, British, Chinese, and Swiss companies partnered up with companies closely tied to Angolan officials, thereby helping that country's elites to get rich. Shell and Eni paid the Nigerian government over a billion dollars for an oil block, and most of those funds ended up in private pockets.

In other scenarios, oil companies serve as indirect enablers of corruption. They operate right alongside corrupt deals in ways that help the deals to go through. The discussion of Nigeria in chapter 3 featured the Nigerian company Atlantic, which received highly lucrative deals from the former minister of petroleum. Thanks to those deals, Atlantic ended up with large quantities of crude oil they needed to sell to international buyers. According to the DOJ investigation of Atlantic's business, Glencore, the large Swiss commodity trader, purchased around $800 million worth of oil from Atlantic in 2013 and 2014, despite widespread concerns of corruption around Atlantic and its bosses.[13] Atlantic then allegedly spent portions of the money they earned from selling their oil to buy houses and other lavish gifts for the minister.[14] Glencore was not a direct party to the corruption, nor has it been accused of any crime in this matter. But the company played an enabling role and helped Atlantic fill their bank accounts.

Cases like this raise challenging questions about liability. Should international actors be blamed for playing this kind of indirect, enabling role? Nigeria is far from the only place where this question has arisen. Activist groups published reports in 2018 revealing that South Sudan's national oil company was bankrolling some of the militia groups driving the county's punishing civil war.[15] The national oil company only has money to begin with thanks to its partnerships with foreign oil companies, oil traders, and lenders, including the Asian oil giants ONGC-Videsh, Petronas, and CNPC and the Swiss oil traders Trafigura, Vitol, and Glencore.

International banks, lawyers, accountants, fixers, agents, and other professionals also play an enabling role by helping design or execute corrupt deals or helping corrupt actors move their money, activities that are in many cases legal. Some of these enablers are colorful and notorious wheeler-dealer types who patrol oil-rich capitals looking for juicy deals. Farid Bedjaoui, a handsome and savvy operator with Algerian, Swiss, and Canadian citizenships, was one such figure. He helped mediate one of the largest instances of bribery from the oil boom—the more than $200 million the Italian oil drilling company Saipem paid to Algerian officials in order to win over $8 billion in service contracts. Working from a luxury hotel in Milan, Bedjaoui set up numerous shell companies and bank accounts to help Algerian officials hide the bribes they received.[16] He was convicted by Italian courts for his activities.[17]

Other enabling professionals are among the largest and most respected law, financial, and accounting firms in the world. The class action suit against Brazil's Petrobras criticized another "big four" accounting firm, PricewaterhouseCoopers, for turning a blind eye to the massive Petrobras fraud while they audited the company's books between 2012 and 2014.[18] United States authorities filed criminal charges against several bankers at Credit Suisse for their role in arranging $2 billion in secretive loans to the government of Mozambique, transactions that triggered a massive corruption scandal in that country.[19]

The 1MDB drama was an international production from the start. The motley cast hailed from across the world but were united in a shared desire for wealth. To capture their wealth, the 1MDB conspirators relied in particular on a Saudi oil company, an Emirate sovereign wealth fund, and the world's most famous investment bank.

Soon after Prime Minister Najib set up 1MDB, the fund entered into a joint venture with a private Saudi Arabian services company, PetroSaudi International. The stated purpose of the partnership was to develop oil assets purportedly controlled by PetroSaudi in Turkmenistan and Argentina, though no evidence suggests that the joint venture ever undertook these activities.[20] In 2009, 1MDB issued a press release to announce the partnership, heralding the deal as a "vehicle for investments from the Middle East into the region, thereby giving Malaysia the edge in drawing investments from the cash- and resource-rich region."[21]

When the deal went through, an unusually ambitious twenty-eight-year-old Malaysian businessman, Low Taek Jho (Jho Low), wrote to his family and bragged: "just closed the deal with petrosaudi. Looks like we may have hit a goldmin[e]."[22]

Despite his boyish appearance and soft-spoken demeanor, Jho Low showed an unusual knack for convincing people that he was a big-time dealmaker. A real "fake it until you make it" practitioner, Jho Low launched his ascent during his college years at the University of Pennsylvania's prestigious Wharton Business School. In *Billion Dollar Whale*, Wright and Hope reconstruct Jho Low's early efforts at living the high life.[23] According to their reporting, he was in college when he started throwing elaborate parties he could barely afford, including a $40,000 blowout for his twentieth birthday at a Philadelphia nightclub, where revelers ate sushi off models and drank copious champagne. Always infatuated with beautiful women, seemingly for status reasons, he ensured that sororities received special invitations to his parties, lavished gifts on an exotic dancer girlfriend, and obsessed over celebrities such as Britney Spears and Paris Hilton. He loved to take his fellow students from the Middle East and Asia on gambling jaunts to Atlantic City, and he used outings like those to befriend the ones from wealthy backgrounds. Rumors spread on campus that he was some sort of Malaysian prince.

Along with his tastes for the high life, Jho Low launched other favorite pursuits while in college. At age twenty-two, he convinced some of his Wharton buddies to arrange a networking tour of the Persian Gulf. During the meetings, he identified fellow strivers and pulled them into his network. In the coming years, he gathered more of these contacts and played them off each other, leveraging their shared desire to make it big.

During one hobnobbing adventure around the Gulf, described in *Billion Dollar Whale*, Jho Low met a well-connected and ambitious but inexperienced young man in Abu Dhabi and, in a characteristic move, used him to gain access to officials at the government's giant new sovereign wealth fund. He then used these Gulf contacts to cozy up to Najib, then deputy prime minister. A couple of years later Najib's wife was thanking Jho Low by name at a party to celebrate the finalization of a major investment of Abu Dhabi funds in a Malaysian real estate project. Further thickening the ties, Jho Low attended to the younger generation as well, befriending Najib's stepson, helping the family pay for their daughter's college tuition, and attending her graduation party.[24]

In his final semester at Wharton, Jho Low set up his first offshore company, the Wynton Group, based in the British Virgin Islands. Despite his young age, he sensed that the global financial system could help obscure inconvenient truths. At this early stage in his deal-making career, the offshore trappings could help hide his inexperience and limited finances as he pushed the Wynton Group as a vehicle for Middle Eastern investment in Malaysia.[25]

By 2009, Jho Low had achieved inner circle status in the Najib government, and set his sights on 1MDB for his biggest gambit yet. He never held an official position at 1MDB, but he ran most of its affairs and was the chief puppeteer of the entire 1MDB scam. That year, 1MDB agreed to make an initial investment of $1 billion into the PetroSaudi joint venture. Around the same time, Jho Low set up Good Star, a shell company in the Seychelles, and installed himself as its sole shareholder. According to the US charges, he then directed 1MDB to transfer $700 million of the initial investment into a bank account controlled by Good Star.[26] His top political connections and the complicity of key 1MDB officials led them to comply.

Deutsche Bank, the bank handling the transfer for 1MDB, and RBS Coutts, a division of the Royal Bank of Scotland that held Good Star's accounts, both raised some very pertinent questions about the transfer. They wanted to know why 1MDB, a state-owned entity, was transferring money to a third party rather than to accounts controlled by PetroSaudi or the new joint venture. 1MDB officials falsely assured Deutsche Bank that the money was in fact going to an account controlled by PetroSaudi.[27] 1MDB and Jho Low showed RBS Coutts an agreement establishing that Good Star was an investment manager for 1MDB, which was also untrue. However, their assurances were enough for the banks to approve the transfer.[28]

Just a year after creating the PetroSaudi joint venture, 1MDB moved to exit the partnership. In order to make their balance sheet look less dire, 1MDB converted some of their PetroSaudi investments into loans. In 2011, the joint venture sought to draw down the loan from 1MDB by $330 million. Again the money went into Good Star's account rather than to PetroSaudi. One of PetroSaudi's bosses signed off on the transfer, and 1MDB officials again misrepresented the transaction by indicating that PetroSaudi was the recipient. Jho Low provided the banks with more misleading documents that outlined various business relations between Good Star and 1MDB, including Good Star's intention to sell a New York hotel to 1MDB that neither the company nor Jho Low had ever even owned.[29]

Through a couple of fudged transactions, Jho Low had effectively captured over $1 billion from public accounts.

Rather than satisfying the appetites of Jho Low and his colleagues, the PetroSaudi transactions instead encouraged them to escalate their scheme. As 1MDB began to raise billions of dollars through bond sales, Low and his team found ways to channel more money into their own accounts. Again, they received an assist from players from the oil-rich Persian Gulf, this time from Abu Dhabi.

In 2012 and 2013, 1MDB raised over $6 billion through bond sales. Most of the bonds were guaranteed by the International Petroleum Investment Company (IPIC), a sovereign wealth fund owned by the government of Abu Dhabi.[30] In 2013, IPIC was among the largest sovereign wealth funds in the world. It held assets worth around $67 billion, a threefold increase over just five years. Most of the growth came from the booming oil industry.

One of IPIC's subsidiaries was Aabar Investments PJS Limited, Aabar for short. Aabar's boss at the time was Mohamed Ahmed Badawy Al Husseiny, an American with Kenyan origins. He fell into Jho Low's orbit via a mutual friend and stayed there in part because he enjoyed the celebrity-filled megaparties Jho Low began organizing after the PetroSaudi payday. Al Husseiny also stayed to make money.

Al Husseiny received his position at Aabar because he frequently worked as the right-hand man of Khadem Al Qubaisi, a powerful Abu Dhabi businessman. From 2007 to 2015, Al Qubaisi served as managing director of IPIC. This position brought with it enormous power as IPIC began buying up shares in major companies around the world. He also enjoyed close ties with powerful members of the Abu Dhabi royal family. Like many characters in the 1MDB drama, Al Qubaisi loved luxury with a dangerous passion. As Wright and Hope describe it,

> Even in the brash and showy UAE, Al Qubaisi struck bankers as an unparalleled egoist, traveling with a retinue of Egyptian security guards and embossing his initials—KAQ—on cigars, drink coasters, boxes of tissues, and even his collection of high-end cars worth tens of millions of euros.... In Abu Dhabi, Al Qubaisi wore the traditional emirati cloak and head covering, and had a family home, a sprawling villa, where his wife and four children lived. But like many rich emiratis, he conducted a different life overseas. At his villa on the Côte d'Azur, with Bugattis and Ferraris parked outside, he partied with models, and had a younger Moroccan wife in Paris.[31]

Al Qubaisi and Al Husseiny were both the kind of strivers Jho Low attracted and manipulated. In early 2012, as is detailed in the DOJ charges, the two created a company in the British Virgin Islands, Aabar Investments PJS Limited, or Aabar-BVI. They set up a Swiss bank account for this entity and named themselves its directors. The company's name bore deliberate resemblance to the name of the IPIC subsidiary headed by Husseiny, but it would turn out to be a very different type of company.[32]

Around the same time, 1MDB hired Goldman Sachs to help execute two large bond sales, one for $1.5 billion and another for $1.75 billion.[33] 1MDB stated that it needed the funds for investments in the energy sector, including the acquisition of a large Malaysian power company. IPIC played a role in guaranteeing both the issuances. Within one day of receiving the proceeds from the first bond sale, 1MDB transferred $577 million of the amount to the newly created offshore entity Aabar-BVI. From the second sale, Aabar-BVI received a further $790 million.

The documentation that accompanied the two bond sales said nothing about payments to Aabar-BVI. As in the PetroSaudi deal, Jho Low and his colleagues generated fake paperwork to explain the transfers to the banks and other parties. The Abu Dhabi officials, Al Qubaisi and Al Husseiny, helped with the cover-up including by falsely stating to Swiss and Singaporean bankers that the actual Aabar subsidiary was the ultimate owner of Aabar-BVI's bank account.[34]

In 2013, as Najib faced a tough reelection, 1MDB raised a further $3 billion from a third bond sale, again arranged by Goldman Sachs. The stated purpose of this sale was to raise funds for a new joint venture between 1MDB and Aabar (the actual IPIC subsidiary): the Abu Dhabi Malaysia Investment Company. Al Qubaisi, as chair of Aabar, signed the agreement and was also appointed chair of the joint venture. The agreement was witnessed by Al Husseiny. Each party was to contribute an initial $3 billion, hence justifying the need for another huge bond sale by 1MDB in less than two years.[35]

However, after the bond sale took place, more than $1.2 billion of the proceeds landed in the bank accounts of shell companies unaffiliated with Aabar or the new joint venture. The US government charges explain how, after routing through several intermediary companies, the funds landed in the accounts of two companies, Tanore and Granton. Two close associates and proxies for Jho Low were the signatories on the Tanore and Granton bank accounts, and emails reveal that Jho Low was frequently in touch with them regarding the transfers. Al Husseiny was listed as the "referrer" for one of the accounts and again helped convince bank officials that the transactions were legitimate.[36]

The final money grab took place in 2014. That year, 1MDB took out two loans from Deutsche Bank totaling $1.2 billion. From the borrowed amount, the same team of Al Qubaisi, Al Husseiny, Jho Low, and certain 1MDB officials instructed Deutsche Bank to transfer $175 million to the account of Aabar-BVI and provided Deutsche Bank with the necessary assurances and justifications.[37] Al Husseiny then opened an account for a new entity, Aabar-Seychelles, which he also falsely represented as an affiliate of IPIC's subsidiary Aabar. On instruction from 1MDB and its partners, Deutsche Bank wired a further $681 million of the borrowed funds to an Aabar-Seychelles account.[38]

With these transactions, Jho Low and Al Husseiny seemed to be operating on an "if it ain't broke, don't fix it" basis. United States authorities alleged that "the Aabar-Seychelles, like the Aabar-BVI Account, was a dummy account used to facilitate fraudulent funds transfers."[39]

To summarize this extraordinary string of events: the DOJ filings accuse a small team of conspirators from Malaysia, Saudi Arabia, and Abu Dhabi of diverting more than $3.25 billion in public funds in just over five years. The first billion came from the PetroSaudi scam, with the funds landing in the Good Star account. Next, they diverted $1.37 billion from the first two bond sales into the accounts of Aabar-BVI. Then, they captured $1.26 billion from the third bond sale in the accounts of the companies Tanore and Granton. Finally, again according to DOJ allegations, they grabbed $856 million from the Deutsche Bank loans, moving the funds into the accounts of Aabar-BVI and Aabar-Seychelles. The DOJ and other sources estimate that more than $1 billion more went missing through other channels not detailed in the complaint, for an epic total of $4.5 billion stolen.

At each step, international collaborators made the corruption possible. Jho Low could never have captured so much money without the help of his Saudi and Emirati colleagues. He found willing partners in PetroSaudi's two founders. Tarek Obaid, a thirty-three-year-old Saudi businessman, shared Jho Low's penchant for the jet-setting, hard-partying lifestyle. Prince Turki bin Abdullah was a son of the late King Abdullah who ruled Saudi Arabia from 2005 to 2015, but he lacked much in the way of economic resources and so relied on "trading off his name."[40] The two set up PetroSaudi to leverage their connections in Saudi Arabia and capture a share of the oil boom. As the *Guardian* described it, "PetroSaudi's business was access capitalism: opening doors with the help of friends in high places. The basic idea was to capture a piece of the huge oil revenues being generated by state-owned firms in developing countries—treasure chests waiting to be unlocked by a firm that was a 'vehicle of the Saudi royal family,' which could count on the 'full support from the kingdom's diplomatic corps.' PetroSaudi told potential partners that it controlled oil fields in central Asia, which it would put up as collateral to secure cash from state investors."[41]

In 2009, Prince Turki chartered a 300-foot yacht and parked it off the coast of Monaco for a meeting. Joined by Obaid, the two PetroSaudi bosses met with Prime Minister Najib, Jho Low, and others to hammer out the joint venture agreement. In the months that followed, the two Saudis helped Good Star receive its loot. According to the US charges, Obaid signed the papers authorizing the $330 million transfer to Good Star in 2011. As late as 2015, in response to further bank inquiries, he wrote another letter falsely confirming that Good Star was part of the PetroSaudi group.[42]

The scheme proved lucrative for Obaid and Prince Turki bin Abdullah. Good Star transferred around $153 million to Obaid, who later sent $77 million along to Prince Turki.[43] The prince also received $24 million directly from Good Star. So that all parties from the initial yacht meeting saw a share, Prince Turki later sent $20 million to Prime Minister Najib.[44]

PetroSaudi's bosses were less generous with some of their own employees. One executive, Xavier Justo, a banker from Switzerland and longtime friend of Obaid, grew angry with the company after years of unmet promises. The conflict escalated when Justo resigned in 2011 and Obaid offered him a lower than anticipated severance payment. In frustration, Justo copied data from PetroSaudi's servers, including 227,000 internal emails, and took this material with him when he left.

In 2013, he handed over the files to a journalist who runs an online investigative news site focused on Malaysia, *Sarawak Report*. The journalist then published a story under the title "The Heist of the Century: How

Jho Low Used PetroSaudi as 'a Front' to Siphon Billions out of 1MDB!"[45] The leak thrust the issue of 1MDB corruption into the public eye, unleashing a series of events that eventually included massive street protests, a change of government in Malaysia, and legal actions against many of the players. Having angered many powerful people with his leak, Justo was later arrested in Thailand, where he lived, and sentenced to three years in prison on blackmail charges.[46]

Since the scandal broke, the Saudi collaborators have also faced travails. Prince Turki divested from PetroSaudi in 2013 and was named governor of Riyadh province the next year. In 2017, he was among the eleven princes arrested in an anticorruption sweep orchestrated by Crown Prince Mohammad bin Salman (a move described further in chapter 6). *Reuters* reported that the charges against him involved corruption in the Riyadh Metro project and using his position as governor to award contracts to his own companies.[47] As for Obaid, some of his assets were among those seized by the DOJ in 2017 as part of its 1MDB case, and he has faced investigation by Swiss authorities. He has denied any wrongdoing, including at a US court appearance in 2017.[48] PetroSaudi itself has not been charged with a crime by any jurisdiction and denies any wrongdoing.[49] It did, however, face investigation in Venezuela for a separate matter. The company allegedly used some of its 1MDB funds to buy an oil rig that it then contracted out to the Venezuelan national oil company. Venezuelan authorities suspect that national oil company officials overpaid PetroSaudi for the oil rig and then received a cut of the excess funds; Petrosaudi denies wrongdoing and dismisses the accusations as politically motivated.[50]

In the later parts of the 1MDB scheme, Al Qubaisi and Al Husseiny, the two Abu Dhabi officials, played indispensable roles. On multiple occasions, they provided false assurances to several banks. They also helped set up the necessary corporate entities and bank accounts, such as Aabar-BVI, which received the lion's share of the diverted funds. The DOJ complaint also reports that the two men received large payments themselves. In 2012, Aabar-BVI transferred funds to the two men's bank accounts via intermediary companies. Al Qubaisi received $472 million, and accounts controlled by Al Husseiny received $66 million.[51]

In 2015, both Abu Dhabi officials were fired from their positions following accusations of corruption, and IPIC confirmed that it has no association with Aabar-BVI. The two were arrested several months later, just after Al Qubaisi saw his latest project open: the largest nightclub in Las Vegas. Several governments have seized assets belonging to the Emirati mogul, including tens of millions of dollars held in Luxembourg bank accounts, while he argues from prison that the government is using him as a "scapegoat."[52] Investigators are also looking at whether 1MDB money helped finance the purchase of a 482-foot yacht, complete with its own swimming pool, movie theater, and helicopter pads, for a prominent Abu Dhabi royal.[53]

As is common with international enablers, Al Qubaisi and Al Husseiny may have stayed away from the scheme if not for the lax rules of their own institutions. In this case, the loose governance of IPIC helped make the 1MDB scheme possible. Members of the ruling elite enjoyed discretionary control over IPIC's investment decisions, and Al Qubaisi, as their proxy, could approve investments without seeking board approval. IPIC also failed to create strong walls between its resources and those of its chair. According to Wright and Hope, "Aabar's books contained a tangle of transactions with companies tied to Sheikh Mansour [a top UAE official and Abu Dhabi royal].... In addition to his day job, Al Qubaisi oversaw these private businesses, and his privileged position, close to the Al Nahyans [Mansour's family], gave him free rein to feather his own nest."[54]

The enabling role played by Goldman Sachs worked much the same way: a few enterprising executives knowingly worked with Jho Low to run the schemes and were not stopped by the bank's anticorruption checks. The bank ran the three bond sales for IMDB in 2012 and 2013. Its motive for doing so is easy enough to understand. Goldman received around $600 million in fees and revenues from the three sales—as much as 200 times the typical fees for such services.[55]

Tim Leissner, one of Goldman's top dealmakers in Asia at the time, was another of the strivers drawn in by Jho Low. A "relationship banker," Leissner displayed a great ability to ingratiate himself to key decision-makers across several Asian countries, particularly in Malaysia. He also had a penchant for nightlife and a reputation for bending the rules to make a deal work.[56] He was assisted in his 1MDB business by Andrea Vella, a banker who had played a major role in the deal described in chapter 2 that saw the Libyan sovereign wealth fund lose billions of dollars in risky derivative trades with Goldman Sachs.

Through his links with Jho Low, Leissner locked down the 1MDB business for Goldman. It was then up to the bank to decide whether to go through with the transactions. At the time, courting sovereign wealth fund business was at the top of Goldman's priorities. This may help explain why five committees reviewed the deal and its risks, according to Wright and Hope's account, and ignored a number of very worrying peculiarities and red flags.[57] Large portions of the bond sale proceeds went to a small private Swiss bank, BSI, rather than a large institution, an unusual practice for transactions of this size. It was very unusual for one government, Abu Dhabi acting through IPIC in this case, to guarantee the bonds of another government. The role of Jho Low in the deal also looked suspicious, and Goldman had even recently denied him the privilege of opening a private account at the bank.[58]

The 2013 sale in particular should never have made it past the bank's anti-money-laundering controls or other compliance checks. Along with the red flags already mentioned, the rushed timeline for the 2013 bond sales, which occurred just two months before the prime minister faced a tough reelection, should have provoked suspicions.[59] In advance of the 2013 sale, internal Goldman documents identified the "maintenance of confidentiality" and "speed of execution" as among 1MDB's top objectives in the execution of the sales.[60] For each the sales, the bond circulars prepared by 1MDB wildly misrepresented how the funds would actually be used. While it might have been difficult for Goldman to spot these warning signs on the first sale, it is surprising that they raised no concern by the third one.

The DOJ found that Leissner and another Goldman banker directly conspired with Jho Low to embezzle funds from 1MDB, including arranging to pay bribes to a number of Malaysian and Abu Dhabi government officials so that Goldman would receive the bond sale business. Leissner and his colleague knew about Low's plans to steal the bond sale proceeds, and they also received kickbacks from the scheme. In 2018, Leissner pleaded guilty to the charges and agreed to forfeit $43 million to appease for his 1MDB adventure.[61]

But his institution denies any wrongdoing. As a Goldman spokesperson told the *Guardian,* "we helped raise money for a sovereign wealth fund that was designed to invest in Malaysia. We had no visibility into whether some of those funds may have been subsequently diverted to other purposes."[62] When faced with evidence of how they facilitated corruption, international enablers frequently argue that they are just doing their jobs and aren't responsible for whatever corruption their clients may have pursued. However, as argued in chapter 7, holding these enabling actors more accountable for the consequences of their work will be an essential part of strengthening the fight against corruption.

Part 2: Move the Money

Once the money is captured, corrupt actors turn to the task of getting it out of their home country and into the global financial system. The typical strategy, remarkably ubiquitous across corruption cases these days, is to set up shell companies in a jurisdiction with robust secrecy protections and low barriers to entry. The shell companies then open foreign bank accounts that can receive the funds. Perpetrators often use many layers of shell companies and bank accounts, spread across multiple jurisdictions, to obscure their transactions and frustrate efforts at detection. To manage this complexity, armies of highly qualified lawyers and accountants specialize in orchestrating cross-border financial flows.

The global system of tax havens and offshore finance primarily exists to serve wealthy corporations and superrich individuals. These needs have grown in recent years as the richest households acquire more and more wealth relative to the rest of us. In the United States, for instance, the top 0.1 percent richest adults hold around 20 percent of total household wealth, up from around 10 percent in the 1970s and 1980s.[63] The total amount of money stashed offshore is equal to around 10 percent of the world's GDP. The movement of money offshore inflicts significant costs, especially as these funds escape normal taxation. The EU, for instance, loses around 20 percent of its corporate tax revenues in tax havens, with global losses estimated at 12 percent.[64]

Some oil-rich countries fare even worse. One team of economists investigated where offshore funds came from. They looked at the world's thirty-eight largest economies and found that on average, the amount of their money that sits offshore is equal to around 10 percent of their GDP.[65] A few oil-rich countries buck this trend. For the UAE, Venezuela, and Saudi Arabia, the wealth held offshore is equal to more than half of their GDPs. Russia's numbers are also very high. Russian elites held as much as $403 billion in tax havens in 2012. And they're not alone. Setting up companies in the British Virgin Islands is so popular among Kazakh elites that the tiny island nation ranks among the top five destinations of investment from Kazakhstan, despite the absence of any real business ties between the two nations.[66]

Certain countries court offshore financial flows, and the economies of the Cayman Islands, the British Virgin Islands, the Seychelles, and other countries depend heavily on the financial services industry. The Financial Secrecy Index defines a secrecy jurisdiction as a country that "provides facilities that enable people or entities escape or undermine the laws, rules and regulations of other jurisdictions elsewhere, using secrecy as a prime tool." The Index's rankings feature the usual tropical island suspects but other countries too. Switzerland, the United States (and in particular Delaware, Nevada, and Wyoming), Luxembourg, and Germany also perform badly, for instance, thanks to their subpar policies and important roles in the global financial system.[67]

American and British service providers have proven more than willing to facilitate shady business. To test how often financial service providers follow the rules, a team of Australian researchers sent 7,400 requests on behalf of fake clients, asking various outfits to set up shell companies. In fulfilling these requests, the service providers in the United States and the United Kingdom proved less likely than those from the more notorious offshore jurisdictions to take steps to comply with the prevailing international guidelines, such as asking for proper identification of their clients before setting up the company.[68] Likewise, the banks that receive stolen funds include some of the world's largest financial institutions headquartered in countries with strong anti-money-laundering regulations.

While the superrich motivated the creation of this system of global finance, corrupt actors take full advantage of its existence. Examples abound from the oil boom. The political elites of Azerbaijan ran an expansive offshore finance operation that was dubbed the "Azerbaijani Laundromat" by the investigative journalists who exposed some of its workings. These journalists estimate that over $2.9 billion flowed through the Laundromat in 2012 to 2014. Some of the money went to influence European politicians— a key plank in Azerbaijan's so-called caviar diplomacy. The German parliament has reprimanded one of its members for failing to disclose the funds she received from a lobbyist for Azerbaijan. She had always been soft on Azerbaijan, and even had a picture of herself with President Aliyev on her website.[69] A member of Italy's parliament allegedly received more than $2.5 million in secret payments via UK shell companies and carried out activities that favored Azerbaijan at the Council of Europe, a multilateral organization meant to foster democracy and human rights on the continent.[70] In its own investigation, the Council of Europe found that Azerbaijan had paid several current and former parliamentarians to lobby on their behalf.[71]

The Azerbaijani Laundromat was an international machine. The United Kingdom hosted several shell companies that were central to its operations. The Estonian branch of Denmark's largest bank, Danske Bank, handled key transactions while also laundering billions of dollars in illicit funds from Russia, as already mentioned.[72] The Maltese bank Pilatus was another key node; politically exposed persons from Azerbaijan formed the majority of Pilatus's clients.[73] A British law firm set up a shell company in the British Virgin Islands to help manage the real estate holdings of President Aliyev's daughters. When filling out the requisite forms, the lawyers, remarkably, answered "no" to the question whether the company's owners had any noteworthy political connections.[74] Another British lawyer set up a secretive Panamanian trust for the family. When he was accused of failing to comply with prevailing regulations, he defended himself in part by stating that he "suffered from a phobia of opening any kind of official correspondence."[75]

Another example of how corrupt actors use banks to reach around the globe comes from Venezuela. In 2015, the US Treasury Department issued a finding against a bank in Andorra, declaring it a "primary money laundering concern." Along with banking for Russian organized crime, the US authorities accused the bank of laundering more than $2 billion in funds from Venezuela's national oil company, PDVSA. An Andorran lawyer and a Panamanian agent allegedly worked with senior Venezuelan officials to set up shell companies in Panama, Belize, and the British Virgin Islands, which then opened accounts with the Andorran bank.[76] The team used fake and overvalued PDVSA contracts and currency-trading schemes to generate funds that were then laundered through these vehicles. Oil companies, including a number in China, also paid bribes into the accounts. Through globalized rackets like this one, an estimated $3 billion of the $15 billion spent by PDVSA annually on service contracts went to overcharges and kickbacks.[77]

It would take tomes to detail all the available examples of this trend, including how all the Nigerian, Brazilian, Russian, and Angolan actors introduced in earlier chapters whisked their illicit wealth offshore using shell companies, secrecy havens, and foreign bank accounts. It is difficult to overstate the consistency with which corrupt actors avail themselves of these tools.

The masters of the 1MDB scheme followed this trend to the tee. Jho Low chose to set up his shell company Good Star in the Seychelles, a well-known secrecy haven that requires negligible information about the individuals who set up companies there.[78] The sole director of Good Star was a company called Smart Power, and the sole director of Smart Power was Jho Low himself.[79] Adding to the cross-border tangle, Good Star's address was the Singapore office of a banker employed by the Swiss bank RBS Coutts.

It was Good Star's RBS Coutts account that received the transfers of $700 million and $330 million in 1MDB funds. But Singapore was just the first stop on these funds' trot around the world: $24 million went from Singapore to a Saudi bank account controlled by two Saudi associates of Jho Low; $20 million of that amount then went to a Malaysian account held by Prime Minister Najib; $30 million voyaged off to an account at the United Kingdom's Standard Chartered Bank that was controlled by a well-known associate of Jho Low. Some of those funds then found their way into the Swiss bank account of a shell company controlled by a 1MDB official.

Jho Low sent around $368 million to an account held by the law firm Shearman & Sterling LLP, which is headquartered in New York City,[80] likely fully aware that law firms are subject to much weaker money laundering rules than banks. He later moved a further $389 million to a Singapore account at another Swiss bank held in the name of the "Abu Dhabi Kuwait Malaysia Investment Corp." Despite its multinational moniker, he alone was the beneficiary of the account.

According the DOJ report, Blackstone Asia Real Estate Partners was another major transit node, with around $1.1 billion in 1MDB loot flowing through its accounts. The DOJ called the company "a shell corporation created for the purpose of maintaining a bank account to funnel diverted money."[81] Indeed, it bore many of the classic trademarks of a shell company: it was based in the British Virgin Islands; its accounts lacked evidence of normal business transactions such as payrolls or payments to vendors; it moved money through a money exchange business that was difficult to trace and avoided major banks; and it had a name similar to that of the Blackstone Group, one of the world's largest asset management firms, to help it appear legitimate.

Blackstone Asia did not receive deposits directly from 1MDB. For example, in 2012, the shell company Aabar-BVI sent around $460 million to the bank accounts of two small investment companies located in Curaçao, which then transferred the funds to Blackstone Asia. The DOJ explains how Blackstone Asia then made payments to accounts held by some of the coconspirators: $472 million went to the Luxembourgian account of Al Qubaisi; $66 million went to a German account held by a shell company owned by Al Husseiny; $30 million went to the Malaysian AmBank account of Prime Minister Najib; and $5 million went to a Swiss account held by 1MDB's then general counsel.[82]

The most controversial transaction in the entire 1MDB scandal involved Tanore Finance Corporation, a shell company based in the British Virgin Islands. In 2013, 1MDB sent $1.6 billion into the accounts of three offshore investment funds: one located in the British Virgin Islands, and the two Curaçao funds used the year prior. The three funds next transferred $835 million of this money into a Singaporean bank account held by Tanore. Then, according to the DOJ and other corroborating sources, $681 million left the Tanore account and entered a secret bank account belonging to Prime Minister Najib that Jho Low had set up a couple years earlier.[83] The 2013 transfer was the largest payoff by far to the Malaysian leader from the 1MDB scheme. A few months later, for reasons not entirely known, $620 million were returned from Najib's account to the Tanore account.[84] Perhaps as a sort of consolation prize, Low later spent some of the returned funds on a 22-carat pink diamond pendant and gave it to Malaysia's first lady.

When the $681 million deposit became public, outrage and protests erupted in Malaysia. After a few months of denials and obfuscations, Najib eventually claimed that the money was a gift from the Saudi royal family. The Malaysian attorney general confirmed this story and cleared the prime minister of any wrongdoing. The Saudi foreign minister also backed up this version of events, stating at the time: "it is a genuine donation with nothing expected in return."[85]

Along with Good Star, Blackstone Asia, and Tanore, the DOJ complaint lists over 100 shell companies that were involved one way or another in the 1MDB transactions. The Cayman Islands and the British Virgin Islands appear to be the favorite jurisdictions in this case, but other key shell companies were based in the Abu Dhabi, Hong Kong, Luxembourg, the Seychelles, and several US states, including Delaware, New York, and Nevada. As the DOJ investigation focused only on assets that entered the United States, this is likely a partial list. In each jurisdiction, local laws protecting financial secrecy helped the scheme to work.

The complaint and other investigations also name a slew of banks through whose accounts illicit funds flowed, including banks based in Germany, Hong Kong, Luxembourg, Malaysia, Saudi Arabia, Singapore, Switzerland, and the United States. Most banks are subject to rules designed to prevent money laundering. Several of the banks involved in the 1MDB scandal have been penalized for neglecting those responsibilities. RBS Coutts, the bank that held Good Star's accounts, is one example. RBS sold its Coutts division in 2015. The next year, authorities in Singapore and Switzerland issued millions of dollars in fines against Coutts for their failure to enforce anti-money-laundering standards in the 1MDB affair.[86]

The Singaporean division of the Swiss bank BSI was another favorite of Jho Low and his associates. In 2012, Jho Low even flew a BSI banker to Los Angeles, put him up in a hotel he had bought with stolen 1MDB funds, and discussed how some of the forthcoming transactions would work. Singaporean authorities levied fines and prison sentences against three BSI bankers for their role in abetting the 1MDB corruption, calling it "the worst case of control lapses and gross misconduct that we have seen in the Singapore financial sector."[87] These authorities also ordered BSI and another bank, Falcon, to close their Singapore divisions, sent a former BSI wealth manager to prison, and issued fines against several larger banks, including UBS and Standard Chartered, for ignoring warning signs and approving inappropriate 1MDB transactions.[88]

1MDB's auditors are another set of international actors who could have blown the whistle on the reckless financial behavior. The record suggests that the auditors may not have been as cooperative as the 1MDB bosses would have liked, which is a good sign. Working its way rapidly through the "Big Four" accounting firms, 1MDB fired Ernst & Young as their auditors in 2010, they fired KPMG in 2014, and then Deloitte quit in 2016.[89] The firing of Ernst & Young took place after they asked too many inconvenient questions about the valuation of the PetroSaudi joint venture. Ernst & Young's replacement, KPMG, signed off on the fund's 2010–2012 accounts, relying on information produced by 1MDB that contained lies and on asset valuations from external experts who had been bribed. While KPMG were uncomfortable with what they saw, they moved forward after they received assurances that both governments sanctioned the deal—evidence of which the PetroSaudi bosses and Jho Low managed to summon up.[90]

A couple of years later, KPMG were the ones being fired after 1MDB officials refused to provide them with further information about large assets 1MDB claimed to hold in the Cayman Islands. Deloitte signed on next and, after receiving additional documentation from Aabar, agreed to prepare 1MDB's 2013 and 2014 financial statements. Deloitte quit only after the DOJ issued its complaint, which called out Deloitte by name and criticized its willingness to approve accounts that contained serious warning signs.[91] This is a mixed record: the accounting firms approved the accounts of 1MDB during years when the corruption was widespread but also found practices that they could not overlook.

Part 3: Spend the Money

"Kleptocrats have a strange relationship with the rule of law: contemptuous and corrosive of it at home, they are nevertheless keen on locating their wealth in states with strong property rights and effective laws." J. C. Sharman makes this observation in his 2017 book *The Despot's Guide to Wealth Management*.[92] Indeed, once stolen funds are laundered offshore, they typically are used to buy assets located in stable, well-off countries. This serves a few purposes. Markets like those in North America and Europe are safe places to store money. Unlike many oil-producing countries, they offer stable politics, currencies, and legal regimes. These investments also create safe havens for the elites involved and their families. They can retreat to their palatial overseas homes, send their kids to elite foreign schools, and access top-rate healthcare. The money also buys influence and prestige, especially when plowed into things like legitimate companies, professional sports teams, and university endowments. Finally, the investments help corrupt actors to access the world's political elites or its celebrities, depending on their tastes.

Real estate is perhaps the favorite asset of kleptocrats and their associates, and no place is more popular than London. In 2016, a group of journalists and interested citizens piled aboard a bus for London's first ever Kleptocracy Tour. Sponsored by an anticorruption group, the tour wound through the toniest sections of London as experts pointed out properties of interest. On the banks of the Thames River is Whitehall Court, a building owned by Russia's deputy prime minister that is reportedly worth 100 times his salary.[93] Further along, in Knightsbridge, the tour stopped at 1 Hyde Park, where residents are protected by specially trained guards and bullet-proof glass; their cars are transported on elevators. Sixty-four of the seventy-six sold units belong to anonymous shell companies, including several linked to oil-rich bigwigs.[94] Later editions of the bus tour stopped at properties owned by Nigeria's former petroleum minister, purchased for her by her loyal cronies, as described in chapter 3.

Transparency International used public records to identify London property worth $5.6 billion that politicians and public officials had bought with suspicious wealth. But because anonymous shell companies do most of the buying, this is likely the tip of iceberg. They also identified 44,022 land titles in London owned by overseas companies, 91 percent of which were registered in secrecy havens. Again this is likely far from the actual total.[95] The housing grab has affected property markets to the detriment of the average resident. London property prices skyrocketed during the oil boom, due in part to the influx of buyers from Russia, the Persian Gulf, Nigeria, and Kazakhstan. Reflecting on the new composition of London's superrich since the 2008 financial crisis, one real estate agent commented: "I can't remember the last time I sold a property to a banker. It's been hard for anyone to compete with the Russians, the Kazakhs. They are all in oil, gas—that is what they do."[96]

London is hardly unique. In a 2015 investigation, the *New York Times* uncovered the identities behind shell companies that own units in the Time Warner Center, a landmark tower located across from Central Park. They included at least sixteen foreign buyers who had been the subject of government investigations, including a number for corruption. Others were government officials or their close associates from Russia, Colombia, China, Kazakhstan, and Mexico, as well as our 1MDB friend Jho Low.[97]

Units in properties owned by President Donald Trump were also sold to anonymous shell companies. In the two years prior to his election, only 4 percent of Trump's sales went to shell companies. Upon his nomination, this rate soared to 70 percent, making it difficult to know what domestic or foreign actors are buying into the president's family business.[98]

The French government seized a 101-room Parisian property worth an estimated $180 million from the son of Equatorial Guinea's oil-rich dictator. Other investigations found that the president of Gabon owns thirty-three properties in Paris and holds seventy French bank accounts, while the first family of Congo-Brazzaville enjoys sixteen French properties and 111 bank accounts.[99] Boris and Arkady Rotenberg, two of Putin's favorite oligarchs, introduced in chapter 3, bought up luxury properties in Rome, in Sardinia, and on the French Riviera, though sanctions have recently complicated their ability to enjoy their Mediterranean escapes.[100] Azerbaijan's first family are part owners of a Sofitel hotel and over thirty villas on the exclusive articifial islands of Dubai, another location popular for diverted oil boom wealth.[101]

Jho Low and his 1MDB coconspirators focused their spending spree on the United States. He threw absolutely epic parties. For his thirty-first birthday, he staged one of the most elaborate parties that Las Vegas has ever seen. He flew in many of his 1MDB collaborators from Goldman Sachs, PetroSaudi, and Abu Dhabi. In their book about Jho Low, Wright and Hope describe the festivities in detail. After signing nondisclosure agreements, his guests enjoyed a Ferris wheel, carousel, and cigar lounge and were entertained by Pharrell, Chris Brown, and Psy as well as acrobats, dancers, and around twenty little people dressed as Oompa-Loompas. The party hit its apex when Britney Spears burst out of a cake and sang "Happy Birthday" to Jho Low. A Lamborghini, motorcycles, and a Bugatti were given as gifts. Robin Leach, the former host of *Lifestyles of the Rich and Famous*, attended and called it "the ultimate party."[102]

On another occasion, Jho Low competed in an annual "bottle parade" at a yacht event in Saint-Tropez. As Wright and Hope describe it, Jho Low got into a competition with Winston Fischer, whose family is prominent in New York real estate, over who could spend the most on Cristal champagne. Jho Low won with his $2 million bill; some of that purchase was sprayed with glee by Paris Hilton and the other friends who joined him that night.[103] On other occasions, he would spend millions on a single night of gambling, often with Leonardo DiCaprio and other favorite companions in tow. One year, Jho Low took Jamie Foxx and some other buddies to Australia to ring in the New Year, and then flew to California to do it again a few hours later. Such compulsive spending became the norm for Jho Low. As one friend exclaimed, "he was the biggest spender I've ever met in my life....Nothing was out of reach."[104]

As soon as he scored the PetroSaudi deal, Jho Low had far more money than he could spend on entertainment and elaborate travel. Much of his illicit earnings also went into property.

Remember the shell companies Tanore and Granton, which received 1MDB bond sale proceeds? In 2013, around $218 million traveled from Tanore and Granton's accounts, and through several intermediaries that served no apparent business purpose, and landed in an account held by Jho Low at the prestigious American law firm DLA Piper.[105] The law firm also received $135 million from an investment fund wholly owned by the government of Abu Dhabi to invest in real estate deals alongside Jho Low. Both sets of funds ultimately went toward the purchase of the $654 million Park Lane Hotel from the trust of the infamous New York hotelier and "queen of mean" Leona Helmsley.[106]

The 1MDB crew bought additional properties in New York, California, and London. Funds from the Good Star account bought a $30 million condo in the Time Warner building that Jay-Z and Beyoncé had previously rented for $40,000 a month. Jho Low bought a $44 million hotel, the Viceroy L'Ermitage, in Beverley Hills, a high-end destination with 116 suites and a rooftop pool. Another of their acquisitions was a Beverley Hills mansion that has a 120-foot pool, ten bathrooms, and an indoor gold pyramid surrounded by a reflecting pool.

Jho Low and the others purchased many of their US properties through US-registered limited liability companies (LLCs), a very common practice that allowed them to keep their names from appearing in the sale paperwork. At the time of the 1MDB purchases, US real estate purchases could proceed anonymously as long as no mortgage was involved. No party had an obligation to verify the buyer's or seller's identity or assess the transaction for money laundering risks. Real estate agents, title agents, attorneys, and others therefore had no reason to conduct due diligence on their clients.[107] So agents happily took on the business and charged hefty fees. For example, the brokerage firm Douglas Elliman reaped $1.2 million for arranging the sale of the condo in the Time Warner building.[108]

As in the United Kingdom and other jurisdictions, the illicit funds encountered few obstacles in accessing US property. In 2016, concerned by this state of affairs, the US Treasury Department launched a pilot program to require shell companies buying expensive properties in cash to disclose their identities to authorities. The pilot ran for several months in cities popular with foreign jet-setters, including New York, Los Angeles, Miami, and San Francisco. During this trial period, a full 30 percent of the purchases covered by the new rule involved a purchaser who had been the subject of a "suspicious activity report." This reinforced concerns that drug kingpins, human traffickers, kleptocrats, and other ne'er-do-wells were moving in next door.[109]

Property is not the only way to stash money abroad. During the 1MDB years, Jho Low became a big-time collector of art. His collection included *Dustheads*, a piece by the American graffiti artist Jean-Michel Basquiat. The shell company Tanore purchased it for $49 million at a 2013 auction organized by Christie's and then "gifted it" to Low.[110] From Sotheby's, Jho Low bought Picasso's *Tête de femme* for $39 million in 2013 as well. His prolific art purchases also included two Calders, two Monets, a Rothko, a Van Gogh, a Warhol, a Lichtenstein, and many others. The reported value of his collection topped $350 million at one stage.[111]

Jho Low used several of these masterworks to leverage a $107 million loan from Sotheby's in 2014, part of the wide-ranging toolkit he used to move, hide, and raise money. In the runup to the deal, a Sotheby's representative wrote to update his colleagues on this situation; the content of the message raises questions about Sotheby's internal due diligence systems:

> Just wanted to bring you up to speed on the big loan opportunity.... [The borrower] doesn't want us to use his name in our communications, he wants to be referred to as "the client," and we will refer to this transaction as project Cheetah (referring to the speed at which we are trying to move). Confidentiality is absolutely critical to him. I've been having multiple calls with him and his lawyers on the structure as he will most likely want to use a Cayman/BVI entity as a borrower but keep the ownership and pledge the artwork for the debt of the company plus personally guarantee it.... While he didn't tell me himself, his lawyers indicated he is using the money to buy a yacht.[112]

According to media reports, Sotheby's told investigators that Jho Low had repaid the loan and has stated that it "always cooperates with government investigations."[113]

Jho Low's tastes and his need to move vast quantities of money led him to all corners of the luxury goods market. He bought a $250 million yacht, *Equanimity*, on which he frequently entertained, and a $35 million private jet. The 1MDB funds also procured large diamonds and other jewelry for his mother, his girlfriend, supermodel Miranda Kerr, and the first lady of Malaysia. As with the art market, he took advantage of the ease with which money can be moved through jewelry sales. He bought $200 million of the stuff in just over a year.[114]

Other investments by Jho Low and his associates show how stolen funds can infiltrate otherwise legitimate foreign businesses. The 2013 film *The Wolf of Wall Street* stars Leonardo DiCaprio as a high-flying financier who becomes exorbitantly wealthy through unethical practices and whose life-style overflows with ugly excess. In an ironic episode of life imitating art, the movie was itself bankrolled in part by individuals who became exorbitantly wealthy through unethical practices and whose lifestyles had a lot in common with those depicted on-screen.

In 2012, Aabar-BVI transferred $238 million to Red Granite Capital Limited, a British Virgin Islands entity owned by Riza Aziz, stepson of the Malaysian prime minister and friend of Jho Low. To help justify these transactions, Al Husseiny provided a letter identifying the transfers from Aabar-BVI as nothing but a generous gift to Aziz, indeed a "gratuitous transfer made with detached and disinterested generosity based on our close personal relationship."[115]

From this pot of funds, Aziz transferred $64 million to his US-based film production company, Red Granite Pictures, which received a further $10 million from the Good Star account. From these inflows, Red Granite spent more than $60 million on the production of *The Wolf of Wall Street*. Reflecting all his support, Jho Low received a special thanks in the film's closing credits. Upon winning a Golden Globe for his starring role, DiCaprio called out his collaborators "Riz and Jho" in his acceptance speech.[116] Red Granite Pictures also spent millions from Aabar-BVI to fund the production of *Dumb and Dumber To* and the Mark Walberg and Will Ferrell vehicle *Daddy's Home*. Aziz denies all wrongdoing and denies knowledge of the 1MDB transactions.[117]

At the Cannes Film Festival in 2011, just after Aziz's Red Granite announced that it would produce *The Wolf of Wall Street*, the production company threw a huge party to announce their arrival on the scene. Kanye

West and Jamie Foxx performed, and the guests included Bradley Cooper, Kate Upton, and DiCaprio, who was a regular at 1MDB-funded parties. Red Granite flew over another special guest for the event: Jordan Belfort, the actual disgraced financier on whose memoir the movie was based. After pleading guilty to securities fraud and money laundering, Belfort served twenty-two months in prison—an experience he described as "totally mellow."[118] By 2011, he was out and reinventing himself as a motivational speaker.

Apparently Belfort's background in fraudulently obtained excess left him uniquely qualified to smell the 1MDB rat. When interviewed about the party in 2017, he explained:

> They flew me to Cannes four or five months after they bought the movie and they wanted to announce it in Cannes. It hadn't even gone into production yet, and they threw a launch party. They must have spent $3 million on a launch party. They flew in Kanye West, and I said to Anne [his girlfriend], "this is a fucking scam, anybody who does this has stolen money." You wouldn't spend money you worked for like that. . . . I've learned my lesson. It's all Red Granite. They tried to offer me money and give me things, I never even spoke to these guys. I was like, "I don't need these fucking people." I knew it, it was so obvious.[119]

While Aziz routed stolen money into Hollywood, Jho Low was busy infecting other sectors. He drew $143 million from the Good Star accounts for investment with Electrum, a private equity firm with a focus on minerals, oil, and gas. He routed other Good Star funds through a number of shell companies before investing over $100 million to acquire substantial shares in EMI Music Publishing Group, the world's third largest music publishing company and owner of music by the Beatles and the Beach Boys.[120] Obaid, one of the Saudi coconspirators, invested in Palantir Technologies, a software and data analysis company based in Silicon Valley. All of these companies found themselves tied up in the legal actions related to the 1MDB case.

1MDB contaminated businesses far beyond Malaysia, creating major challenges for those companies and their investors. This reflects a wider trend. Tough questions arose regarding the investments of the billionaire Isabel dos Santos, the daughter of Angola's former dictator, in major telecom and energy companies in Portugal and Spain. Russian oligarchs closely tied to Putin run companies with enormous global operations, for example the oil company Novatek, which is partly owned by Gennady Timchenko. As laid out in chapter 1, President Trump sold his brand to a hotel in Azerbaijan that was bankrolled by one of that country's top political godfathers. The sheer volume of wealth available to many corrupt actors attracts and ensnares businesses worldwide.

Various kinds of facilitators also eagerly received 1MDB funds and either did not see or turned a blind eye to their sketchy provenance. In some cases, like the real estate transactions, sellers and agents faced lenient requirements when it came to checking out the identity of their buyers. They easily sold property to hastily set up LLCs without asking questions about who was behind the sales and how they got their money. The casinos, art dealers, and sellers of yachts, jets, and jewelry behaved in a similar way.

A few US law firms played essential roles in the 1MDB scheme, but they have not been accused of any crimes and are unlikely to face any formal repercussions. Lawyers do not have to conduct the same kind of anti-money-laundering checks as banks, a loophole Jho Low and his associates took full advantage of.[121] As noted, the prominent firm DLA Piper held accounts through which Jho Low moved more than $200 million, and they helped arrange the purchase of several properties, including the Park Lane Hotel.[122] The DOJ file also reveals that the firm Shearman & Sterling held an account that received $368 million from Good Star, and Jho Low would tell the firm whom to pay, including a Vegas casino, his family members, and various luxury vendors. Another top-flight firm, Sullivan & Cromwell, represented entities involved in the purchases of the Los Angeles mansions and other transactions that were made on behalf of Riza Aziz, or "client 37965" in the firm's records.[123] An Oklahoma firm, Crow & Dunleavy, served as escrow agent for Jho Low's purchase of the private jet. Another firm, Costello & Associates, represented a shell company controlled by a top 1MDB official in the purchase of a top-market New York condo using funds from Aabar-BVI.

Helped by this cast of enablers, Jho Low and his associates acquired more than $1.7 billion in foreign assets over just five years—and those are just the investments that the US authorities discovered. Spending at this pace is no easy task. The capacity for a very small group of individuals to move money with such a blistering speed shows just how efficiently the international system helps the superrich move their money, even when the funds have highly suspicious origins.

Corrupt public officials launder their reputations as well as their money. Unlike terrorists or drug traffickers, corrupt political leaders have to maintain a public persona, and they want that persona to be as legitimate and prominent as possible.[124] This is hard work, but the payoffs can be huge. If an embattled leader commands respect in capitals across the globe, he projects an air of credibility and power to domestic audiences. International prestige can also fend off formal and informal sanctions from foreign actors, for example withholding of investments, military assistance, or development aid.

Several scholars working on the offshore behavior of kleptocrats explain that "reputation laundering involves minimizing or obscuring evidence of corruption and authoritarianism in the kleptocrat's home country and rebranding kleptocrats as engaged global citizens."[125] International actors stand ready to help kleptocrats accomplish this aim—especially when oil money can send them home with big paychecks. Public relations firms provide advice to kleptocrats, gather intelligence on their rivals, spiff up their Wikipedia entries, conduct social media campaigns, organize splashy parties, and arrange meetings and photo ops with reputable political or cultural figures.

This work can go wrong in many ways. An official at the UK Foreign Office took unpaid leave, joined a prominent PR firm, and began to handle the firm's Saudi royal family accounts, thereby creating a problematic conflict of interest between his two concurrent positions.[126] The consulting firm of the former UK prime minister Tony Blair took on President Nazarbayev of Kazakhstan as a client and helped him to explain away a 2011 crackdown on oil worker protests that resulted in fourteen deaths.[127] In 2016, a Romanian PR firm hired by Congo-Brazzaville's government created a story that President Sassou-Nguesso would be among the first world leaders to meet with president-elect Donald Trump. A fake photo of the pair together even emerged. It turns out the whole thing was a stunt, and the White House denied that such a meeting had ever been planned.[128]

Despite foibles like this, spending on PR can produce dividends. Equatorial Guinea's government paid millions of dollars to the Washington, DC firm Qorvis/MSLGroup for services, including generating positive press about the economic development gains achieved by the country's president, Teodoro Obiang, who has ruled over this tiny oil-rich country since 1979. United States oil companies also put in a positive word. In 2014 these efforts appeared to pay off. President Barack Obama invited

Obiang to a White House dinner for the US-Africa Leaders' Summit but left out a number of other autocrats.[129]

Along with hiring PR experts, kleptocrats use their money in other ways to win allies and garner respect abroad, often using very subtle (and very legal) techniques. Charitable donations are one tactic. In 2008, the London School of Economics received a $2 million donation from a charity run by Gaddafi's son. When the source of the funds was revealed, a scandal erupted that led to the resignation of the university's top official. Prominent US think tanks, for example the Brookings Institution and the Atlantic Council, accept funds from oil-rich governments, including Bahrain, Kazakhstan, Qatar, Saudi Arabia, and the UAE, and some media reports suggest that these funds impact their programming.[130] UNESCO came under fire for establishing a life sciences research award funded by and named after President Obiang of Equatorial Guinea.

Other international institutions regularly turn a blind eye to kleptocracy, thereby helping to legitimize the regimes. Publicly funded international development institutions, including the World Bank and the European Bank for Reconstruction and Development, continue to lend to governments that routinely engage in large-scale corruption. Foreign governments often make nice with corrupt regimes as well, often for security reasons. The United States, for example, largely ignored the extensive corruption perpetrated by the postconflict governments in Iraq and Afghanistan in order to focus instead on containing extremist groups.[131] The European Bank for Reconstruction and Development provided hundreds of millions of dollars in funding for gas infrastructure projects in Azerbaijan because securing non-Russian supplies of gas is a strategic priority for Europe. Other times, the inaction stems from institutional apathy and a general desire to maintain congenial relations. This could help explain why the International Monetary Fund provided Gabon with a $640 million loan in 2017 or why the international community ignored the staggering and easily observed corruption that took place in Nigeria during the oil boom.[132]

Returning now to our friends from Malaysia, Prime Minister Najib embraced many of these reputation laundering techniques, beginning long before the 1MDB scandal broke open. His government's reputation for corruption and its repressive tactics, including jailing a top political opponent on highly controversial sodomy charges, created the need for a serious image makeover, especially as Malaysia sought to attract foreign tourism, investment, trade deals, and security alliances. Not all of these PR efforts went smoothly.

In 2009, Najib's office hired the global public relations firm APCO to lobby for the government in Washington, DC, and run 1Malaysia, a new media campaign that heralded the Najib government as the harbinger of national unity and efficiency.[133] However, the APCO contract soon attracted controversy when an opposition leader publicly accused APCO of basing the 1Malaysia campaign on a similar effort in Israel, a particularly provocative claim in a Muslim country that does not recognize Israel as a state.[134] The prime minister's office fought back, arguing that the campaign was created by Najib before APCO was even hired.

Following this unpleasant incident, one member of APCO's international team, the PR specialist Paul Stadlen, stuck around Kuala Lumpur to work directly with the prime minister. Contrary to his mission, he and his penchant for spirited nightlife attracted negative press.[135] The prime minister's office has denied that they paid Stadlen for his work, but he continued to perform communications and press duties through 2017, including handling press inquiries around the 1MDB scandal. For instance, he lambasted the *Wall Street Journal* as "a disgrace to journalism" for its extensive reporting on the matter.[136]

APCO and Stadlen weren't the only government PR efforts that actually stirred up negative attention. The Najib administration paid FBC Media, a UK-based communications firm, around $9 million a year for its services in 2010 and 2011. The firm worked for several other heads of state with challenging international images, including Egypt's Hosni Mubarak and Kazakhstan's Nazarbayev.

In 2009, FBC Media made four documentaries about Malaysia that aired in the United Kingdom on the BBC. Presented as informative rather than promotional programs, they addressed sensitive issues, including rainforest preservation and indigenous peoples; one celebrated the growth of the palm oil industry while ignoring the strong environmental opposition to its spread. However, FBC Media never disclosed to the BBC that they worked for the Malaysian government, nor did the documentaries inform viewers of that reality.[137] In 2011, the BBC launched an investigation into the matter and suspended its relationship with FBC Media. The American television channel CNBC also cut its ties with the show *World Business*, produced by FBC, which featured Malaysia on multiple occasions. Najib himself appeared in ten episodes. Questions also arose regarding the impartiality of CNN host John Defterios, who served as president of FBC Media from 2000 to 2011.[138] Defterios interviewed Najib on his CNN show in 2011, just days after the Malaysian government arrested over 1,500 antigovernment protesters. The interview focused on Malaysia's economic prospects. Defterios asked just one question about the protests that the prime minister answered by praising the police for how well they had treated those who were arrested.[139] In response to concerns about the incident, CNN stressed that Defterios had severed his ties with FBC before joining the network and that CNN's editorial standards had not been compromised.[140]

FBC denied any impropriety and said that they maintained separation between their commercial and programming divisions. However, according to an investigation by the UK newspaper the *Independent*, FBC's own promotional materials wooed customers with statement such as "we control blue-chip television editorial time-slots" and can "guarantee controlled messaging from A to Z on the world's leading news channels."[141] The company filed for bankruptcy in 2011, not long after the Malaysia scandal broke.

The taint of kleptocracy spread further still, reaching other foreign media outlets. In 2011, the *Guardian* parted ways with its new conservative commentator Josh Trevino because he had failed to disclose his past ties to the Malaysian government.[142] Trevino had previously published pro-Najib pieces in the *Huffington Post* and the *Washington Times*; both pieces have since been taken down. The Malaysian online investigative group *Sarawak Report*, a frequent critic of Najib, accused FBC of hiring Trevino to write blogs criticizing opposition voices, create fake *Sarawak Report* websites to mislead readers, and manipulate relevant Wikipedia entries.[143] Trevino has denied all the accusations. He did, however, eventually file the paperwork required in the United States for lobbyists working for foreign authorities. The filing said that FBC Media and APCO agreed to pay Trevino $6,200 a month to produce content on several media platforms "casting Malaysia and its governance in a positive light to a general audience."[144]

Presumably the Malaysian government employed more successful public relations efforts too, efforts that silently generated positive press rather than negative headlines. After all, during the years before 1MDB broke open, Najib enjoyed major wins on the global stage. President Obama visited Malaysia twice during his tenure, the first visit by a head of state in five decades. Najib also enjoyed a primo photo op while golfing with Obama in Hawaii over the 2014 Christmas holiday. As noted in Obama's remarks during his 2015 visit to Kuala Lumpur, the United States prioritized the relationship with Malaysia because of the country's participation in the international coalition to fight the Islamic State and because of its role in several measures aimed to counter China's influence in the region, including the Trans-Pacific Partnership trade deal and security in the South China Sea.[145]

While Obama had foreign policy reasons to support the Malaysian government, the spread of 1MDB funds led to uncomfortable questions about whether other motives also helped explain his embrace of Najib. Pras Michel, a member of the 1990s hip-hop group Fugees, was among many celebrities who supported Obama's campaigns. He was also among the many celebrities whom Jho Low befriended. In 2012, according to Wright and Hope, Jho Low transferred $20 million to two companies owned by Michel. The singer then used the money to make a $1.2 million payment to a super PAC, Black Men Vote, which supported Obama's campaign.[146]

Michel also introduced Jho Low to Frank White Jr., a prominent Democratic fundraiser for both Obama and Hillary Clinton. Jho Low invested $10 million in White's renewables energy company, routing the funds through several intermediaries, along with other deals. Media reports allege that White, in return, arranged for Jho Low to attend a White House Christmas party and organized an Oval Office visit for a group associated with *The Wolf of Wall Street*, including Najib's stepson Aziz.[147] According to media reports, United States federal investigators examined the link between the investments and White's efforts to help set up an Oval Office meeting.[148] While the investigation did not lead to charges, it shows how the taint of corruption causes even unwitting government institutions to face controversy.

Najib and Jho Low's public relations needs grew rather more urgent when the 1MDB corruption came to light. Several foreign actors tried to turn the two men's desperation into profits for themselves.

The venture capitalist Elliott Broidy, a prominent Republican fundraiser, sought to help certain Malaysian individuals out of the 1MDB pickle. Broidy served as vice chair of the Trump campaign's joint fund with the Republican Party, which raised over $108 million ahead of the 2016 elections, and then became national deputy finance chair of the Republican National Committee. The *Wall Street Journal* received leaked emails that suggest that Broidy and his wife, the lawyer Robin Rosenzweig, explored a business engagement with Jho Low.[149] One of the emails contained a draft agreement with Jho Low that would have had him pay Rosenzweig's law firm $75 million if the DOJ dropped its 1MDB case within 180 days. A later draft altered the plan to include a fee not tied to DOJ action. Other emails show that Jho Low did not want to pay Rosenzweig directly but sought to route the money through his friend Pras Michel. The emails also indicate that Broidy prepared talking points for Najib on various matters, such as Malaysia's stance toward North Korea.

A few months after the *Wall Street Journal* published its reporting on the leaked Broidy emails, the DOJ moved to seize around $73 million from Pras Michel and George Higginbotham, who worked at the time in a separate division of the DOJ itself.[150] Beginning in 2017, as Jho Low's luck was souring fast, Michel and Higginbotham began setting up shell companies and opening bank accounts to help Jho Low get money into the United States. The two referred to their Malaysian friend Jho Low as "Wu Tang" in their coded emails to each other and met personally with him in Thailand and Macau to discuss how the laundering would work. According to the DOJ, Jho Low needed the two men to help mount "a lobbying campaign" aimed at ending US legal actions against him and other 1MDB parties. Michel and Higginbotham then liaised with two individuals who had the kind of contacts and prominence needed for such a task. While the DOJ charges don't name them, one was a businessman and the other a "business owner, political fundraiser and financier with political connections at high levels of the United States government."[151] A draft agreement revealed the kind of lobbying Jho Low wanted: he would pay one of the individuals a $75 million success fee if the DOJ forfeiture proceedings were resolved in 180 days and a more modest $50 million if the task took a full year.[152]

In 2018, Higginbotham pleaded guilty to conspiracy, admitting that he lied to banks in order to get Jho Low's tainted funds into the country.[153] In 2019, a lawyer working for Michel called for the DOJ complaint to be dismissed, and his client has denied any wrongdoing.[154] Broidy and his wife have also denied wrongdoing and stressed that at no time was Jho Low's case discussed with President Trump, Trump's staff, or anyone at DOJ working on the 1MDB case and that the agreements described in the press were only drafts.[155]

While Jho Low's lobbying efforts ran into some trouble, Trump still ended up providing Prime Minister Najib with an enormous reputational boost. One year *after* the DOJ implicated Najib in the $4.5 billion 1MDB scandal, he received a warm welcome at the White House. He and his retinue also stayed at the nearby Trump International Hotel. Pundits fumed. In a scathing op-ed, former Bush administration official Paul Wolfowitz wrote that Trump "should have found a diplomatic excuse to postpone the embarrassing meeting. Doing so would have sent a strong signal to other lobbyists attempting to sell access to the President."[156] An editorial in the

Washington Post called the meeting "a new low." "Not only is Mr. Najib known for imprisoning peaceful opponents, silencing critical media and reversing Malaysia's progress toward democracy. He is also the subject of the largest foreign kleptocracy investigation ever launched by the US Justice Department."[157] As would become a trend, Trump's decision to meet with Najib flew in the face of conclusions reached by his own Justice Department.

In 2018, after the 1MDB scheme had fallen apart and the charges against him began to multiply, Jho Low disappeared from view. Most say that he fled to China, where he kept a low profile and failed to cooperate with US or Malaysian authorities. From wherever he ended up, he kept reaching out to international enablers, and they kept taking his calls. This time it was specialists in a new but growing subfield of public relations: "litigation communications." He hired two American law firms, Kobre & Kim and Schillings International, to help him manage the cascade of criminal charges, civil actions, and negative publicity he faced.[158]

Among other services, the firms helped him set up a website dedicated to his defense, www.jho-low.com, which contained carefully worded media statements and a flattering bio complete with a very smiley picture of the young financier. British and Australian lawyers hired by Jho Low also worked to protect what was left of his reputation. This included sending letters to UK and Australian bookstores threatening them with libel lawsuits if they carried Wright and Hope's *Billion Dollar Whale*. Despite creative machinations such as this, these international enablers will struggle to rehabilitate Jho Low's standing. By the 2018 holiday season, Malaysians could buy bright red novelty tote bags with a cartoon drawing of Jho Low's boyish face and the slogan "Spending like I stole it."[159]

Complicity and Infiltration

Large-scale graft is not something that happens in faraway locations. An international cast of enablers makes it possible and, in doing so, helps the taint of corruption spread far and wide. In the 1MDB story alone, illicit funds infiltrated otherwise credible business ventures and damaged the reputations of some of the world's most prestigious banks and law firms. The spread of funds called into question the effectiveness of financial regulators in Luxembourg, Singapore, Switzerland, the United Kingdom, and the United States. The money came uncomfortably close to the White House during two successive administrations, with top fundraisers for both Obama and Trump playing bit parts in the scandal. Public relations efforts launched by Najib may have unduly influenced prominent media outlets such as the *Guardian*, the BBC, and CNN.

While significant, the damage to US and other foreign institutions pales in comparison to the cost born by Malaysia. During its short and reckless lifespan, 1MDB accumulated $13 billion in debt that now must be paid off by the Malaysian state. IPIC, the Abu Dhabi sovereign wealth fund, took Malaysia to arbitration over the $6.5 billion in debt the fund claims it is owed. Recovering the stolen money will be extremely difficult for Malaysia, due in large part to the complex international mechanisms used to hide it.

Beyond this heavy financial cost, the 1MDB scheme damaged Malaysia's democracy. From the same account that received the $700 million in 1MDB funds, Najib doled out $140 million to local branches of the ruling party before the 2013 elections.[160] Contractors who benefited from 1MDB deals also supported Najib's political and philanthropic causes during the preelection period.[161] After the scandal broke, and as the 2018 election approached, Najib cracked down on critical voices, purged his cabinet of possible opponents, and reemphasized ethnic and religious tensions in his campaign rhetoric.

But not all is doom and gloom, either in Malaysia or beyond. In 2018, buoyed by widespread outrage at the 1MDB scandal, the opposition candidate, Mahathir Mohamad, dealt Najib a stunning electoral defeat. Three months after the election, Najib was arrested on charges related to his role in the 1MDB case, and his trial began in 2019. He has pleaded not guilty. Whether or not he sees the inside of a jail cell, the Malaysian people used an election to remove a problematic leader from power. This outcome echoes those seen in Nigeria and Brazil, covered in chapter 3, where democracy and the rule of law reined in enormous corruption schemes, eventually.

As for the international enablers, they're not getting off scot-free either. In fact, it was the international aspects of the 1MDB scheme that led to its eventual undoing. The next chapter pays tribute to the international anticorruption champions who, in stories such as this one, play the role of giant-slayer.

CHAPTER 6 | Corruption's Motley Foes

EVERY SINGLE CASE mentioned in this book represents a success for the forces that fight corruption. The company bosses and political bigwigs who engaged in corruption were kept from enjoying their money in peace. Instead, they faced some kind of negative consequence, either reputational, legal, or financial. Overshadowed by the gory details and grim costs of corruption, this tremendous record of success doesn't get the recognition it deserves.

Governments, businesses, civil society, and the media have all helped fight against the oil boom's corruption. The record of any one of these groups is mixed, filled with big wins as well as missteps and missed opportunities. Luckily, their different strengths compensate for each other's weaknesses.

The 1MDB case shows how this complementarity works in practice. Domestic journalists were among the first to publicly raise concerns. In 2013 the Malaysian newspaper *The Edge* launched the first significant investigations into possible wrongdoing at 1MDB. A couple of other media outlets followed. The next year, an opposition politician picked up the matter and wrote a letter to the 1MDB board asking some tough questions. Then, in 2015, the Malaysian authorities opened several inquiries. A special task force headed by the attorney general, a parliamentary group, and the police all began to dig around. They learned enough to make the prime minister nervous, especially when they began to uncover signs of the $681 million that had landed in his personal bank account. So the prime minister shut these investigations down, fired the attorney general, and cracked down on the public outcry that followed.

Thankfully, Malaysian authorities were not the only ones out there fighting corruption. In 2015, the *Wall Street Journal* received some of the files from the thwarted investigation by Malaysian authorities. The Malaysian investigative website *Sarawak Report* received leaked information on the case from a disgruntled employee of PetroSaudi, one of 1MDB's business partners, and from the former employee of a related party in the UAE. Armed with insider information, the media outlets took on the case. They exposed the scheme to the global public, explaining who ran it, what they did with their riches, how funds reached the prime minister, and the role played by various players in Abu Dhabi, Saudi Arabia, Singapore, Switzerland, and the United States.

Journalists can inflict reputational harm and pressure authorities to act. But they cannot formally sanction anyone for getting involved in corruption. International governments can, and they were the next to act.

At a 2016 press conference, US attorney general Loretta Lynch took the podium, flanked by her top DOJ and FBI deputies, and proclaimed: "we are here to announce a significant step in our ongoing work to combat global corruption and to ensure that the United States offers no haven to those who illegally use public funds for private gain. Today, the DOJ filed a civil complaint seeking to forfeit and recover more than $1 billion in assets associated with an international conspiracy to launder funds stolen from 1 Malaysia Development Berhad, or 1MDB, a company wholly owned by the government of Malaysia."[1]

The United States took action under a new program started in 2010, the Kleptocracy Asset Recovery Initiative. Under the program, US authorities use civil rather than criminal proceedings to seize the proceeds of foreign corruption if those funds and assets enter the United States or use the US financial system. The Kleptocracy Initiative is just one of the anticorruption innovations that proved their mettle during the post-oil-boom years.

Along with moving to seize $1.7 billion in assets, the DOJ publicly released a long and detailed account of the 1MDB scheme that identified a number of international companies, banks, and lawyers who played enabling roles.[2] For instance, the DOJ materials detailed a conversation between the CEO of Falcon Bank and Al Husseiny, the Abu Dhabi official who helped run the 1MDB scheme. "Mohammed," the CEO implored, "the rest of the documentation which our friend in Malaysia has delivered is absolutely ridiculous, between you and me....This is...gonna get everybody in trouble. This is done not professionally, unprepared, amateurish at best. The documentation they're sending me is a joke, between you and me, Mohammed, it's a joke!...You're now talking to Jho [Low], and tell him, look, you either, within the next, you know, six hours produce documentation, which my compliance people can live with, or we have a huge problem."[3] Despite these reservations, the DOJ materials indicate that Falcon Bank approved highly suspicious transfers of 1MDB funds.

They may be less apt to ignore such warning signs in the future. Swiss authorities opened a criminal case against the bank, and Singapore revoked its license, part of a suite of legal actions these two countries have taken against players involved in the 1MDB scheme.[4]

As foreign authorities responded to the scandal, Malaysian civil society and opposition groups continued to raise the alarm at home. At great risk of falling victim to Najib's repression, local groups spoke out and organized large protests. Independent media groups continued to cover the scandal as best they could. Their work, combined with global media coverage and the multitude of legal actions taken by the governments of the United States, Luxembourg, Singapore, Switzerland, and beyond, weakened the position of Prime Minister Najib and kept him from brushing the scandal under the carpet. He lost the 2018 elections—an outcome that had once seemed politically impossible.

The story then went full circle. When the new prime minister took power, he directed Malaysian authorities to restart formal investigations into the case, and today its perpetrators, including Najib and Jho Low, face criminal charges from their own government. Aided by top public officials and an army of enablers, the 1MDB crew stole more than $4.5 billion in public funds. However, a diverse collection of anticorruption actors kept them from getting away with it.

The rest of this chapter digs into the anticorruption roles played by domestic governments, foreign governments, businesses, and the media and civil society. For corruption to be thwarted more regularly, the efforts of all these groups are necessary. Each of them is too flawed to make the difference alone.

Cleaning Up at Home

Late one night in 2017, dozens of Saudi Arabia's most powerful businessmen, including eleven members of the royal family, were rounded up from their homes and arrested on corruption charges. Security personnel ushered many of these men to a makeshift "prison" in Riyadh's glittering Ritz Carlton Hotel where, according to some media reports, staff had removed the curtain rods and glass shower doors to guard against suicide attempts. The prisoners lost access to their phones and bank accounts, and some alleged that they endured harsh interrogations, sleep deprivation, and even physical abuse. To secure their release, they agreed to turn over large sums to the state—payments that reportedly topped $100 billion in total.[5]

Soon after the arrests, the Saudi attorney general explained that King Salman and Crown Prince Mohammed bin Salman were "keen to eradicate corruption with utmost force and transparency." The government also defended the legality of the investigations and the treatment of the prisoners, assuring the public that the arrests were "based on specific evidence of criminality and actions that were intended criminal transgressions and resulted in unlawful gains."[6] However, the government released very little information about the charges themselves or the deals the detainees struck in order to regain their freedom.

In 2015, not long before the arrests, the elderly King Salman took over leadership of the oil-rich kingdom following the death of its longtime ruler, King Abdullah. The new king quickly moved to elevate the standing of his son, Prince Mohammed bin Salman, who soon emerged as his heir apparent. With control over a wide portfolio of government functions, the young crown prince moved swiftly to solidify his position and distinguish his approach. MBS, as he is called, announced reforms such as allowing women to drive, an ambitious economic diversification program, and the decision to sell shares in the country's national oil company. These moves earned him some early acclaim in international circles. But this opinion shifted quickly when Saudi operatives murdered the journalist Jamal Khashoggi in Turkey. MBS's aggressive escalation of the conflict in Yemen has also drawn sharp critique. The crackdown on corruption among Saudi elites was another MBS power play.

Saudi Arabia is the world's largest exporter of crude oil, and oil has dominated the kingdom's political and economic affairs since the first barrels left its shores in the 1940s. Throughout this period, the royal family and other political elites have personally benefited from the kingdom's oil wealth—a trend that only accelerated during the recent oil boom. For these privileged individuals, the line between public and private money is imperceptible. The royals adopted famously ostentatious lifestyles, and some used their largesse to build business empires that stretch around the world.

Exact details of how oil money is doled out among Saudi elites remain secret. The system appears to involve a mix of allowances, the allocation of state-owned property and corporations, lucrative government contracts and subsidies, and favorable loans. There is no doubt, however, that these allocations disproportionately benefit a select group of individuals. In such a system, defining what is corruption and what are normal government functions is not easy. Under Transparency International's definition of corruption as "the abuse of entrusted power for private gain," the enrichment of these Saudi elites would certainly qualify. But the rulers of

Saudi Arabia never appeared to share that view before MBS arrived on the scene.

Under MBS's directive, the government charged prominent Saudis with self-dealing and illicitly acquiring public funds, and handed down some heavy penalties for these transgressions. Given how typical these behaviors are in the kingdom, most members of the royal family or business bigwigs could have been hauled in. This includes MBS himself. Less than two weeks after the arrests, amid a push for economic austerity at home, media outlets reported that he spent $450 million for a painting by Leonardo da Vinci—the highest price ever paid at auction for a work of art.[7] In 2015 MBS bought a $300 million estate outside Versailles in France, dubbed by some real estate publications the most expensive home in the world, and picked up a 440-foot yacht from a Russian oligarch for a further $500 million.[8] Given the prince's clear participation in the Saudi system of oil money patronage, what motivated his anticorruption crusade and how did he choose whom to target?

The answer to these questions gets at the mixed, and often quite troubling, record of anticorruption campaigns initiated by strongman leaders. The crackdown did call out elite corruption by name and demanded that the accused return some of the wealth they had acquired by exploiting their positions of power. However, the arrests targeted a number of the crown prince's potential rivals, including the powerful children of King Abdullah, the previous monarch, and the human rights of the accused may well have been violated. The events revealed anew the influence that the royal family exerts over judicial institutions. Meanwhile, the authorities repress the independent media, the political opposition, and other important anticorruption actors, keeping them from doing their jobs. By humiliating the rich and powerful and seizing their assets, MBS's anticorruption crusade sent a clear message that even the most influential Saudis enjoy their privilege at his pleasure.

Anticorruption crusades and political maneuvers also went hand in hand in China. Like the crown prince, President Xi Jinping went after the kind of corruption that had become common among Chinese elites. His campaign targeted several top executives at the country's enormous national oil companies. While Xi's actions helped combat corruption, they also served political ends.

Jiang Jiemin rose up the ranks at CNPC (Chinese National Petroleum Company) thanks to his alliance with Zhou Yongkang, a former CNPC boss and one of President Xi's main political rivals. CNPC is one of China's three giant national oil companies, along with Sinopec and the China National

Offshore Oil Corporation. Charged with expanding China's control over oil and gas resources at home and abroad, the three companies grew to enormous proportions during the early 2000s. By 2013, PetroChina, the publicly listed subsidiary of CNPC, became the fourth largest company in the world. Political and energy security motives drove this expansion more than commercial ones. As a result, CNPC could spend without much concern for their bottom line. Their capital outlays doubled between 2006 and 2012, they spent heavily on politically useful infrastructure projects within China, and they employed a bloated workforce of over 1.5 million. While most oil companies collected record profits during these years, CNPC's profits fell.[9]

When Xi assumed power in 2013, the national oil companies had grown into powerful empires controlled by a "petroleum clique" of top officials. The companies' spending habits had grown unsustainable and included widespread corrupt behavior. At the same time, Xi faced political rivals like Zhou, whose power came in part from his continued influence over the CNPC apparatus. And so, motivated by a mix of political self-interest and a desire to rein in costly elite corruption, Xi took action.

In 2013, the CNPC boss Jiang was fired and then arrested. Two years later he received a sixteen-year prison sentence for "receiving bribes, possessing large amounts of assets of unknown provenance, and abusing power as a state-owned company employee."[10] His patron, Zhou, was jailed for life, and the state seized assets worth over $14 billion from him and his associates.[11] Over 300 of Zhou's relatives and associates faced corruption investigation, including CNPC officials who helped run the company's business in Indonesia, Iran, Kazakhstan, and Turkmenistan.

As in Saudi Arabia, the government released very few details about the corruption charges against CNPC personnel. However, glimpses are out there of what they may have looked like. *Reuters* reported that Jiang used CNPC funds, at Zhou's behest, to help cover up a car crash involving the son of a top party official.[12] China's anticorruption agency criticized CNPC's many nonoil divisions that served patronage purposes, such as its hotel and taxi businesses.[13] Outside China, reports linked CNPC to corruption scandals in Chad, Kazakhstan, and Turkmenistan.[14] Moreover, CNPC officials had a reputation for enjoying huge expense budgets, indulging in elaborate entertaining and luxury gifts, and living large.

So when Xi cracked down on corruption at CNPC and the other national oil companies, he was addressing a real problem, and the crackdown ushered in a period of reform at CNPC and the other state-owned companies. However, his actions served a political purpose too. Like many strongman anticorruption campaigns, the crackdown showcased the flaws of the country's judicial institutions rather than their strengths. Much of the proceedings occurred in secret under the auspices of special courts, and some of the accused reported being tortured. Writing about this record, Human Rights Watch concluded: "in the absence of an independent judiciary, a free media, genuine rule of law, and a criminal justice system that can effectively and fairly investigate and prosecute corruption, it is unlikely that any anti-corruption campaign will succeed."[15]

The anticorruption proceedings launched by Venezuela's president Nicolas Maduro also addressed real corruption problems but likely made matters worse. In 2017, his government fired around seventy national oil company officials on corruption charges, including the company's CEO and the minister of oil. The move came amid a stunning decline in the sector's performance, due largely to bad management.

While corruption at the national oil company was indeed a big problem, the purge was a political move first and foremost. According to Francisco Monaldi, a top analyst of the Venezuelan oil sector, "this purge was widely perceived as politically motivated to achieve multiple objectives: use these executives as scapegoats for the economic collapse, remove Ramirez [a former minister] as a political rival to President Maduro, and open the door for the militarization of the oil industry."[16] A general with little oil sector experience took the reins of the national oil company, , leaving investors even more pessimistic about its ability to reverse its declining fortunes.

In stark contrast to the campaigns launched by the leaders of China, Saudi Arabia, and Venezuela, democratic and oversight institutions have scored some wins in the fight against corruption. They've even proven able to go after corruption that has involved the top leaders themselves.

As recounted in chapter 3, the Brazilian judicial system investigated and prosecuted some of the most powerful politicians and businessmen in the entire country. These authorities faced accusations of political bias, especially as the prosecutions kept former president Lula from running in the 2018 elections. Nonetheless, the success of the Brazilian authorities speaks strongly to how domestic institutions can fight corruption in countries where the rule of law is strong enough. In this regard, Brazil is not alone. A court in Oman sent the former CEO of the national oil company to prison for over twenty years on charges of receiving bribes from a Korean company seeking construction contracts.[17] In Indonesia, the former head of the oil sector regulator got a seven-year sentence for receiving bribes, via his golf coach, from a Singapore-based oil trading company.[18] While not related to oil, heads of state in other countries, for example

Israel and South Korea, faced investigation by their law enforcement authorities for corruption.

In Nigeria and Malaysia, domestic elections served as an anticorruption tool. The contests were just fair enough for voters to send corrupt incumbents home. Again, this dynamic is not limited to oil-rich countries. In recent years, incumbents have lost elections due at least in part to corruption scandals in Argentina, Benin, Costa Rica, Ghana, India, Sierra Leone, and Sri Lanka as well.[19] Government oversight bodies also chip in, sounding the alarm about domestic corruption. In the United States, as described in chapter 3, the inspector general of the Interior Department and the Government Accountability Office revealed conflicts of interest and underperformance at the MMS, the unit in the Interior Department that managed the offshore oil industry.[20]

Despite all this action, the record of domestic anticorruption actors remains spotty at best. Too often, governments manipulate anticorruption actions to make themselves look good. Adopting the rhetoric of anticorruption is easy enough, as is launching (but rarely completing) investigations of a few token officials. At the end of the day, the domestic campaigns often serve political agendas first and anticorruption agendas second. While they may address very real corruption problems and deliver some results, the campaigns are usually partial and flawed. Other anticorruption players can help pick up the slack.

Foreign Governments Bring the Heat, Sometimes

As laid out in the last chapter, the tentacles of corruption reach overseas. While these international linkages make it easier for officials to steal and stash large quantities of money, they also create vulnerabilities. Every time a corruption scheme reaches across borders, it exposes itself to actions by foreign anticorruption actors.

Jason Sharman, an expert on anticorruption movements, has remarked with wonder on how often governments now speak out and act against foreign corruption. This development is surprising, he argues, because fighting corruption abroad does not appeal to domestic voters and often causes trouble for powerful interest groups like the banking sector. Anticorruption actions stand at odds with widely held convictions about sovereignty and can complicate foreign policy and security pursuits.[21] Yet the international movement against corruption and kleptocracy has recorded some big wins.

Foreign governments have a few tools for going after corruption abroad. Let's say the United States wants to help thwart corruption in Nigeria or Malaysia or Azerbaijan. First, the United States can prosecute any entity that paid bribes in the country, as long as that entity has demonstrable ties to the United States. Most often these ties consist of a US headquarters or a listing on a US stock exchange. Second, the United States can move to seize any stolen assets that touch US soil or pass through US banks. Third, the US government can use sanctions and other diplomatic measures to shame corruption officials and make their lives more difficult. Fourth, the United States can enact policies that will make corruption harder to pull off in the future. Finally, it can fund nongovernment actors, such as civil society and media groups, who fight corruption globally or in a specific country. While still uneven, efforts in all five categories are delivering important results.

In its use of the first tool, antibribery prosecutions, the United States has traditionally led the world. The 1977 Foreign Corrupt Practices Act made it illegal for US individuals and companies, or those with strong US ties, to engage in bribery. For a while, authorities failed to do much with the FCPA. But this all changed with a few blockbuster cases in the 2000s in which blue chip companies, including oil giants such as Chevron and BakerHughes, paid major fines for bribery offenses.[22] In a historic action, US authorities saddled Halliburton and its partner KBR with a mammoth $579 million fine for paying bribes in Nigeria during the 1990s, despite the companies' strong political connections.[23] The FCPA was serious business, and oil companies began to pay attention.

More recently, in the wake of the oil boom, antibribery actions accelerated and spread. Without the DOJ and SEC's active enforcement of the FCPA, many of the cases described in this book would have remained undiscovered. Indeed, more FCPA cases have come from the oil and gas industry than any other economic sector. To name just a few: FCPA enforcement led Halliburton to pay a $29 million fine for contracting with a politically connected company in Angola.[24] The DOJ assessed hefty fines against Petrobras and several of the companies who paid bribes to Petrobras, including Odebrecht and SBM Offshore.[25] The enormous US hedge fund Och-Ziff paid a $213 million fine for using bribery to secure oil and mining sector business in Libya, Chad, and the Democratic Republic of the Congo.[26] The United States has opened multiple FCPA investigations of companies that hired the fixer Unaoil to drum up business for them in Iraq and elsewhere. By the end of 2018, a number of businessmen had pleaded guilty to US charges of bribing officials at Venezuela and Ecuador's national oil companies.[27]

The Venezuela cases reveal a promising new tack in the FCPA world. American law enforcement is using money laundering charges to go after the recipients of bribes, after years of focusing mostly on the companies that made the payoffs. In 2018, four officials from Venezuela's national oil company pleaded guilty to US money laundering conspiracy charges related to receiving bribes.[28] In these cases and others, the United States can utilize the expansive role of US correspondent banks and dollar-denominated financial transactions to establish jurisdiction over many transfers of bribe funds. This capability also places US authorities in a strong position to help authorities overseas who are investigating US dollar transactions.

Other countries have become less reluctant to pursue bribery cases. A study by the Organization for Economic Cooperation and Development (OECD) shows how the United States dominated the antibribery landscape in 1999–2014, sanctioning 128 instances of bribery in total. Germany was next in line with twenty-six, then South Korea with eleven. France, Switzerland, the United Kingdom, and the rest of the countries surveyed all had six or fewer.[29]

But these numbers mask some real progress. In the 1990s, in countries such as Australia, France, Germany, the Netherlands, and Switzerland, companies did not face prosecution for bribery. In fact, they could write off bribes as a tax-deductible business expense.[30] Since then, a lot has changed. The OECD passed its Anti-Bribery Convention in 1997 and set about pushing its forty-four member countries to improve their records. In 2012, for example, the OECD publicly chided France for its lame efforts at enforcing antibribery laws, commenting: "we are not impressed by the number of convictions and, further than that, there has not been that much effort.... There have been lots of cases in the past 20 years which got stuck, or were closed, for political reasons."[31]

Since that rebuke, enforcement in France has picked up, and in 2016 the French government passed one of the strictest anticorruption laws in the world. The United Kingdom passed the robust UK Bribery Act in 2010, and Germany strengthened its antibribery legal regime in 2015. Italy passed its own new law in 2012 and launched one of the biggest bribery trials in history with the charges against Shell and Eni in the OPL 245 Nigeria scandal.[32]

Thanks to improvements like these, more governments have gone after oil sector bribery in recent years. They even pursued actions against some of their largest and most influential companies. Swiss police investigated one of the world's largest oil trading companies, Gunvor, for possible corruption in Congo-Brazzaville.[33] Dutch authorities went after the large Amsterdam-based oil services company SBM Offshore for bribing officials in Angola, Brazil, Equatorial Guinea, Kazakhstan, and Iraq, and the company agreed to pay $240 million to settle the charges.[34] The United Kingdom charged Rolls-Royce with bribery in some oil sector deals, and prosecuted several Barclays executives for conspiracy to commit fraud while luring business from gas-rich Qatar, though that trial ended in an acquittal.[35]

The pace of enforcement has also increased. The OECD tracked the total number of antibribery cases pursued to completion by seventeen of the world's richest countries. The number of cases rose from fewer than ten per year prior to 2003 to more than seventy in 2011.[36] Of these cases, 20 percent involved an oil or mining company—the highest rate for any industry.

Governments are finding ways to pursue cases together, too, as is necessary given the cross-border nature of the corruption they aim to fight. The United States and France jointly went after the French bank Société Générale for its bribery of Libyan officials, described in chapter 2.[37] The case ended in a settlement—the first resolution ever coordinated between US and French authorities on a bribery case. Many other antibribery cases have also benefited from joint action, at least among jurisdictions where judicial authorities are allowed to pursue this type of case. United States authorities have heralded their excellent cooperation with Brazilian law enforcement in the Petrobras investigations, for instance.

The United States and a few other countries now go after individual executives for bribery more often, rather than just fining the companies they work for. After all, companies don't engage in bribery; people do. A 2015 DOJ memo encouraged the Department's prosecutors to push this agenda. As a result, 70 percent of the DOJ's 2017 FCPA enforcement actions targeted individuals rather than corporations. A number of these unlucky folks work in the oil industry. Some of them are midlevel players caught making dirty payments. An American lawyer pleaded guilty for covering up bribe payments to Petrobras, as did several Texas businessmen for bribing officials at Venezuela's national oil company.[38] A US court convicted Patrick Ho, a representative of a Chinese oil company, of bribing officials in Chad and Uganda.[39] In Switzerland, Pascal Collard was convicted of bribing Congolese officials when he worked at the oil trading company Gunvor.[40] The Goldman Sachs banker who helped pull off the 1MDB scam has pleaded guilty to US charges of money laundering and FCPA violations.[41]

Companies are often happy to heap blame on employees like these, arguing that the corruption resulted from the action of a few bad eggs rather than a more systemic problem. However, in a smaller set of cases, prosecutors went after the top brass, holding them individually accountable for what had happened on their watch. For example, a US judge sentenced a former CEO of SBM Offshore to thirty-six months in prison due to his company's record of bribery.[42] The DOJ accompanied the verdict with some tough talk: "their sentences should serve as a warning to corporate executives everywhere: if you pay bribes to advance your business interests, we will catch you and we will prosecute you to the fullest extent of the law."[43]

In 2018, after years of delays, an Italian court found a former CEO of the oilfield services company Saipem guilty of bribery and sentenced him to five years in prison. On the CEO's watch, Saipem had paid over $200 million in bribes to Algerian national oil company officials to win over $8 billion in contracts.[44] This former CEO may soon have company. The most powerful oil executives to face legal action to date are the current and former CEOs of Eni and several top Shell executives on trial in Italy for their role in the OPL 245 scandal, described in chapter 2.[45]

Despite all this, proceedings against CEOs and other top company decision-makers don't happen often enough. One US judge, while convicting a midlevel intermediary for his role in arranging bribery for the hedge fund Och-Ziff, observed with frustration how top executives still manage to avoid direct responsibility. Rather than facing consequences, "The rest of the people who participated [in the corruption] were off on some golf course," he remarked in disgust.[46]

Thanks to antibribery prosecutions, oil companies have paid big fines and faced reputational damages with the public and their investors. The uptick in law enforcement activity has also caused most large oil companies to invest heavily in "integrity" systems, including codes of conduct, anticorruption trainings for employees, and divisions dedicated to complying with antibribery laws. Many companies now conduct more thorough due diligence on their contractors and clients, including checks to see if these prospective partners have ties to public officials. While some of these reforms are just window dressing, others represent important behavioral changes by companies who are truly trying to avoid antibribery investigations in the future.

These are admirable and important gains in the fight against corruption. But antibribery laws, even when actively enforced, are far from sufficient. The record suggests that companies go ahead and engage in bribery even if they risk getting caught. In one study, researchers examined the cost-benefit analysis of engaging in bribery. They found that "because of low sanctions in many jurisdictions, companies would still have an interest in investing in the bribery scheme, even if they knew with certainty that they would be caught at the end of the scheme."[47]

The growing popularity of deferred prosecution agreements may further reduce the uncertainty and consequences faced by offending companies. In the United States, as well as Canada, the United Kingdom, and other countries, companies who come forward and cooperate with the authorities can expect to avoid a trial and negotiate their punishment with the authorities. A political scandal erupted when Canada's justice minister accused Prime Minister Justin Trudeau of recommending that a huge Canadian construction company receive such a settlement rather than face trial. The company, which denies wrongdoing, is charged with paying around $48 million in bribes to Libyan officials over a ten-year period.

Along with tolerable fines, companies implicated in bribery face relatively little backlash from investors. Another study compares the performance of two groups of companies listed on the US S & P 500 stock market index, those who were sanctioned for corruption under the FCPA and those who were not. The study concludes, discouragingly: "we find no indication that firms perform worse when under investigation or after being sanctioned for FCPA violations."[48] In his scathing takedown of the DOJ for its failure to punish white-collar crime, the journalist Jesse Eisinger criticizes a recent trend that often applies to oil sector cases: companies agree to admit to guilt, the authorities notch the case as a big win, and the actual punishments inflict negligible harm.[49]

The behavior of some oil companies reinforces this concern. They certainly don't enjoy being caught for corruption. Along with steep fines, they have to endure lots of tough questions from the media, their business partners, and most important, their investors. But they engage in risky behavior anyway. For instance, according to a Global Witness investigation, in 2013 ExxonMobil moved forward with the acquisition of an oil block in Liberia even though they knew the block's owners had ties to public officials.[50] The practices of the Italian oil company Eni have prompted anti-bribery investigations over and over again. In the past decade, the United States, Italian, and other authorities have opened investigations into Eni and their subsidiaries for possible bribery in Algeria, Brazil, Congo-Brazzaville, Iraq, Kazakhstan, Kuwait, Libya, and Nigeria.[51] Some of the investigations have never led to charges, and Eni denies wrongdoing in others, but at a minimum this record indicates that the prospect of investigation has not deterred Eni from engaging in risky business ventures.

In another shortcoming, the FCPA and other laws like it are most useful for going after pretty straightforward acts of bribery. Corruption is often more subtle than quid pro quo bribery, in which a company pays off an official in order to receive a specific advantage. For instance, oil companies may award contracts to politically connected local entities to generally keep up general good relations with the government, even if there is no specific request hanging in the balance. This kind of corruption is much harder to prosecute.

Antibribery cases also typically fail to punish corrupt foreign officials. But here the oil boom years reveal important progress. Through new legal approaches, several governments have reached these actors by seizing their stolen money and all the stuff that it bought.

In 2010, the DOJ debuted the Kleptocracy Asset Recovery Initiative and assembled a team of prosecutors to go after the dirty money that enters the United States. As long as the assets were bought with the proceeds of corruption or other crimes, the DOJ can move to seize US real estate, yachts, jets and other belongings bought in the United States, the profits from US business investments, funds held in US banks, or even funds that have temporarily passed through US banks on their way to other countries. Attorney General Eric Holder offered a lofty explanation for setting up the new initiative: "when kleptocrats loot their nations' treasuries, steal natural resources, and embezzle development aid, they condemn their nations' children to starvation and disease. In the face of this manifest injustice, asset recovery is a global imperative."[52]

An obvious early target for the program was Teodoro Obiang Nguema, the son of the man who has ruled Equatorial Guinea since 1979. Following major discoveries of oil in the 1990s, Equatorial Guinea has become one of the most oil dependent countries in the world. Thanks to its tiny population, its GDP per person topped $30,000 during the oil boom—a figure that exceeds that of its African peers as well as more developed countries, such as Spain and South Korea. Not that the country's citizens ever saw much from this money: the nation's life expectancy and infant mortality rates are worse than the African averages. The oil riches have mostly bankrolled massive state spending on infrastructure, including white elephant projects such as a new capital city in the middle of the jungle.

The ruling family also profited handsomely and began to spend their wealth abroad. Obiang, the president's son, has held several top government posts, including vice-president and minister of agriculture and forestry. Throughout the 2000s, he moved money out of Equatorial Guinea through a number of foreign bank accounts and shell companies, including ones in the United States.

Once his funds entered the global financial system, Obiang used them to outfit his international playboy lifestyle. Clichéd in their excess, his purchases included a fleet of luxury cars, including a Bugatti Veyron and a Koenigsegg One worth around $2 million apiece. He bought real estate in Brazil, France, South Africa, Spain, and the United States, including a $30 million home in Malibu and a Paris mansion worth over $100 million—outfitted with a disco, a spa, a hair salon, a breathtaking view of the Arc de Triomphe, $40 million worth of furniture, a Rodin sculpture, and a dozen Fabergé eggs. He snatched up a Gulfstream jet, an enormous yacht, millions of dollars in jewelry and watches, a world-class wine cellar, paintings by Degas, Renoir, and Matisse, and the crystal-covered white glove Michael Jackson wore on his "Bad" tour. In total, the DOJ estimated that Obiang spent more than $300 million between 2000 and 2011, despite an official salary that never broke six figures.[53]

Unfortunately, there's nothing terribly new or distinct about this behavior, except perhaps the extreme contrast between Obiang's lifestyle and that of the average person living in Equatorial Guinea. A member of the political elite used his position to capture oil wealth; he stashed the money in the global financial system using shell companies, bank accounts, and helpful facilitators; and then he spent it on luxury goods and real estate. Also typical is that Obiang has faced no repercussions for his actions in Equatorial Guinea.

What is new is that foreign governments went after Obiang and his riches. He was one of the first targets of the Kleptocracy Asset Recovery Initiative. The DOJ filed three complaints in 2011–2013 to seize around $70 million in assets from Obiang, including his yacht, the Malibu mansion, and Michael Jackson's white glove. Legally, the DOJ rested its case on two planks: the assets were obtained through actions that were illegal under Equatoguinean law, and the assets then entered the United States. The assistant attorney general chided Obiang: "through relentless embezzlement and extortion, Vice President Nguema Obiang shamelessly looted his government and shook down businesses in his country to support his lavish lifestyle, while many of his fellow citizens lived in extreme poverty. After raking in millions in bribes and kickbacks, Nguema Obiang embarked on a corruption-fueled spending spree in the United States."[54]

French authorities also went after Obiang. In 2007, several French NGOs made a bold and creative move against the foreign politicians who were bringing dirty money into their country. They filed a criminal complaint against the presidents and first family members of three oil-rich African countries: Congo-Brazzaville, Equatorial Guinea, and Gabon. The complaint argued that these individuals held real estate in France that exceeded what they could afford on their official salaries. The president of Gabon and his family, for instance, allegedly owned thirty-nine properties in France, mostly in upscale parts of Paris, seventy French bank accounts, and a $1.5 million fleet of automobiles.[55]

After a few false starts, French authorities eventually opened a judicial investigation into the matter with a specific focus on Obiang, the biggest target among those named in the criminal complaint. A fierce legal battle ensued. French authorities seized Obiang's cars, raided his Paris mansion, and eventually indicted him. Obiang's lawyers and the Equatoguinean government fought back, claiming their client enjoyed immunity from prosecution, turning the mansion into an official government property, and filing objections with the International Court of Justice.[56]

Finally, in 2017, a French court convicted Obiang of embezzling more than $170 million. He received a suspended three-year prison sentence and a suspended fine of $35 million, with the suspension meaning that these penalties will only go into effect if he commits another crime in France. That same year, French authorities charged the daughter and son-in-law of Congo-Brazzaville's president with money laundering and the misuse of public funds, following an investigation of how they had purchased and renovated an expensive home in the Paris suburbs.[57]

"It's a new wind," says William Bourdon, who worked with the NGOs that brought the French complaints. "What was considered absolutely unrealistic 10 or 15 years ago is now considered possible."[58] Indeed, the cases represent a new era in which corrupt officials can face legal consequences if their riches move overseas.

Along with Obiang, several of the characters in this book have also felt the wrath of the DOJ's Kleptocracy Asset Recovery Initiative. The program went after a billion dollars in assets belonging to our friend Jho Low, the chief architect of the 1MDB scheme. They also went after the bribe money received by the former Chadian ambassador to the United States and Canada and his wife from a Canadian oil company, as recounted in chapter 2.[59]

The Nigerian businessman Kola Aluko, introduced in chapter 3, faced similar treatment. Aluko headed Atlantic Energy, the oil company that received hugely profitable contracts during the tenure of Nigeria's former oil minister Diezani Alison-Madueke. All those sweet deals left Aluko with billions of dollars to move, and some of the money entered the United States. In 2017, the DOJ moved to seize Aluko's $50 million New York condo and the $80 million superyacht once rented by Beyoncé and Jay-Z.[60] The DOJ also alleged that Aluko and his associates used shell companies in the British Virgin Islands and the Seychelles to purchase several multimillion-dollar homes in and around London for Alison-Madueke to enjoy.[61]

For Alison-Madueke and many other suspiciously rich public officials, the UK was the destination of choice. When Russian operatives used a nerve agent to poison an ex-spy and his daughter on UK soil, public and political opposition to this trend reached new heights. The UK authorities took a few measures in response, the most interesting of which is a legal tool called Unexplained Wealth Orders. British authorities can issue such an order when politicians and their families hold property that exceeds what they could afford on their official incomes. When the order is issued, the owners must explain how they obtained these properties. While the US and French police had to trace global money flows to prove who owned suspicious properties, the Unexplained Wealth Order places the burden of explanation on the suspect. For this reason, it is a particularly exciting advance.[62]

A few months after the program's launch, the UK authorities issued their first Unexplained Wealth Order against a certain "Mrs. A," who turned out to be the wife of a former official at a state-owned bank in Azerbaijan. She and her husband held properties worth $28 million in the United Kingdom and loved to shop, spending $21 million at Harrods and dropping 150,000 pounds on jewelry in one single-day binge, according to UK authorities. The case documents allege that the couple obtained the properties using funds the husband embezzled while working at the state-run bank; the couple denies wrongdoing.[63]

As with all of these anticorruption tools, the value of the Unexplained Wealth Order will depend on whether British authorities begin to use it more often and in more politically challenging cases. Azerbaijani courts had already convicted the husband of "Mrs. A" on corruption charges, so the UK police did not risk offending the regime in Baku with this first use of their new tool. While the world waits to see what course enforcement will take, foreign officials who spent big money in the United Kingdom are likely feeling nervous. For instance, Transparency International published a list of properties that British authorities should consider looking into, including houses owned by Azerbaijan's first family, a Russian deputy prime minister, a Nigerian senator, and a former Libyan army general.[64]

Even with these new tools, the United Kingdom, the United States, and other governments have their work cut out for them. Seizing assets owned by strings of shell companies based in secretive jurisdictions is no easy business. Investigators also have to prove that the funds are the proceeds of crime in their country of origin, places where politicians often capture funds in ways that are technically legal or where securing the cooperation of local law enforcement is very difficult.[65] For these reasons, relatively few governments are pursuing this kind of case, and the cases take years to reach resolution.

What to do with the seized assets is another challenge. Take the case of Obiang for example. The United States does not want to send the seized funds back to the same government who permitted their theft in the first place. But what other options are there? Some funds have been repatriated, such as a portion of the money stolen by the Nigerian dictator Sani Abacha in the 1990s. In another case, the World Bank set up a special foundation to spend the seized money in Kazakhstan, a mechanism that kept the funds out of the government's coffers. But these arrangements have taken years to develop, and most seized funds remain in a kind of limbo or revert to the authorities who seized them.

Foreign governments have diplomatic tools for punishing corruption as well as legal ones. On the gentler end, they can snub corrupt leaders and their associates. In 2015, President Aliyev rolled out the red carpet to European heads of state for the opening ceremony of the first-ever European Games. The games cost $8 billion of Azerbaijan's oil boom wealth, with the government building elaborate stadiums and footing the bill for all 6,000 athletes.[66] The spending had a clear agenda. As the sports minister proclaimed, "after the European Games in Baku, people across the world will know that Azerbaijan is in Europe."[67]

Leaders from across Europe received invitations to the opening gala and had to decide whether to join Aliyev for the occasion despite his government's reputation for corruption and human rights abuses. Passing up a chance to see Lady Gaga perform, most European Union heads of state stayed home, and only those from Bulgaria, Luxembourg, Monaco, and San Marin were sitting in the stands.[68]

A step up from diplomatic snubs, foreign governments can use sanctions to fight corruption. The notorious Israeli businessman Dan Gertler learned how this worked in 2018. Gertler's companies do big business in the mining sector of the Democratic Republic of the Congo, where he maintains a close friendship with the country's president. Gertler has made billions of dollars from highly favorable mining deals, and a few in the oil sector as well. In 2014, for example, he sold off the rights to a Congolese oil block for 300 times what he paid for it.[69] Operating mostly out of off-shore jurisdictions, Gertler avoided formal repercussions for his activities for many years. Eventually, however, the United States was able to sanction him. In 2017, the US government froze all his US assets and banned US entities from doing business with him and his companies. In the wake of this move, global mining companies hurried to cut ties with Gertler, after having used him for years to remain in good political standing in the Democratic Republic of the Congo.[70]

The United States sanctioned Gertler using another new tool, the Global Magnitsky Act, enacted in 2016 to punish perpetrators of corruption and human rights abuses. The law is named after Sergei Magnitsky, a Russian lawyer who died in prison after he uncovered a large-scale corruption scandal involving Kremlin officials. A few countries, including Canada, Estonia, and Lithuania, have adopted similar measures. The US Magnitsky Act empowered a small group of officials at the Treasury Department to take decisive action against a number of global villains, making tangible gains at a time when the State Department sat in dormant disarray under secretary of state Rex Tillerson.

The Democratic Republic of the Congo is not a big foreign policy priority of the Trump administration, which may help explain why Gertler was sanctioned. For other countries, the use of sanctions has more to do with larger foreign policy or security concerns than with just fighting corruption. The United States and the European Union used aggressive sanctions to target several oil sector oligarchs from Russia, as well as the boss of the country's national oil company, Rosneft, who has helped Putin to assert control over the oil industry. Introduced in 2014, these sanctions sought to punish Russia for its invasion of Crimea, not to address corruption concerns per se. Nevertheless, the measures targeted the oil money flows that benefit Putin and his cronies. Foreign policy motives also explain the recent US sanctions against Venezuela's national oil company, which aim to close an "avenue of corruption" through which officials can enrich themselves.[71]

Finally, along with legal and diplomatic actions, foreign governments can implement policies that make corruption difficult to commit in the first place. Again, there has been progress here. There is now widespread understanding and discussion of what policies could help, and this is the foundation on which actual implementation can be built. One key policy goal is to get rid of anonymous shell companies, the most popular way to obscure dirty money flows. The British government now requires all of its companies to publicly declare their "beneficial owners," that is, the actual people who benefit from the companies, not just the made-up name on the door. In 2018, Parliament took an even more ambitious step by requiring the United Kingdom's overseas territories, including renowned tax havens and secrecy jurisdictions like the British Virgin Islands and Cayman Islands, to do the same in the years ahead. The United States adopted new measures to keep kleptocrats from secretly buying up property. As of 2018, companies must identify their true owners before engaging in all-cash purchases of real estate worth over $300,000 in selected cities. The draft terms of the Trans-Pacific Partnership Agreement and the United States-Mexico-Canada Agreement (the successor to NAFTA) include surprisingly progressive anticorruption measures, such as whistleblower protections and government official asset disclosure requirements, that their signatories would need to adopt.[72] Should any government be at a loss for what policies to adopt, the Financial Action Task Force publishes quite stringent evaluations of how well its thirty-eight member countries are guarding against money laundering, terrorist financing, and other "threats to the integrity of the international financial system."

Thanks to all these measures, governments have never had a better toolkit for going after corruption overseas. Their antibribery laws are stronger and used more often. They can seize stolen assets and enact powerful sanctions against corrupt individuals and companies. If adopted and run well, new policies could make it harder to move money around in secret. But all of these tools have their shortcomings. Worse still, governments use them unevenly. Too often, competing priorities get in the way.

During the boom years, oil sector corruption in Nigeria grew to historic proportions. It was so large that it could not be hidden, and US authorities certainly had enough information to appreciate the scale of the problem. However, they did not take action because they wanted to keep up good relations with the Goodluck Jonathan government. Nigeria was considered an ally in the war on terror, US oil companies wanted smooth relations with local officials, and embassy officials preferred cordiality over fighting corruption.[73] Then, in the 2015 elections, President Buhari defeated Jonathan thanks in large part to his anticorruption credentials. Suddenly members of the international community, including the United States, fell over themselves to help the new leader go after the same corrupt players they had happily glad-handed during the years prior.

As in Nigeria, corruption escalated during the oil boom years in Iraq, during the tenure of the former prime minister Nouri Al-Maliki. The United

States and its international partners looked the other way in hopes of getting some political stability. The approach may have backfired. By the time the threat of the Islamic State emerged, corruption had weakened the military and frustrated many citizens. For instance, an Iraqi parliamentary committee estimated that the military spent $150 billion on arms but received only $20 billion worth of equipment.[74] In Nigeria, security officials were accused of diverting several billion dollars from the fight against Boko Haram to private pockets and Jonathan's 2015 election campaign.[75] In her book *Thieves of State*, the Afghanistan expert Sarah Chayes explains how ignoring corruption likely aided the resurgence of the Taliban and argues that fighting corruption should be a national security priority, rather than something that is deprioritized when national security concerns arise.[76]

While the United States on occasion takes a hard line on corruption, other great powers have been more lenient. Again the 1MDB case provides a useful illustration. The *Wall Street Journal* reported that in 2016, the Chinese government offered to try to help Malaysia out of its 1MDB bind. Specifically, meeting minutes seen by the *Journal* indicated that Chinese officials offered to pressure the United States and other authorities to drop their 1MDB investigations. They also offered to spy on the *Journal* reporters based in Hong Kong who reported on 1MDB. In return, according to the report, Malaysia provided lucrative access to railway and pipeline projects as part of China's enormous international infrastructure initiative, One Belt, One Road.[77]

The Chinese embassy in Malaysia rejected this account of events, calling it "groundless," as did former prime minister Najib.[78] If China did indeed make the offer, such negotiations provide a rather stark example of how economic interests, just like security concerns, can prevent powerful governments from fighting corruption.

Corruption in Malaysia, Nigeria, Iraq, and many other countries received uneven and sometimes even counterproductive responses from governments around the world. While some authorities took decisive action against oil-boom corruption, they just as often sat on their hands.

When Potential Enablers Disrupt Corruption Instead

Wearing a hidden camera, Ralph Kayser (not his real name), an investigator for the anticorruption watchdog group Global Witness, set up meetings at thirteen New York law firms. He told the lawyers that he was an advisor to an African mining minister who wanted to buy a jet, an expensive home, and a yacht in the United States without being detected. The footage from the hidden camera, which aired on the US news program *60 Minutes*, caught twelve of the thirteen lawyers offering suggestions for how to accomplish this task using shell companies.[79]

A couple of the lawyers offered some spot-on advice for anyone seeking to hide illicit funds: you should "set up a little bit of a series of owners in order to protect privacy as much as anything else." Another explained: "so company A is owned by company B which is owned jointly by company C and D and your party owns all or the majority of shares of C and D." They added that the minister would be "probably better off with a smaller bank" and that "there may be other banking systems that are less rigorous on this than the US. . . . We could provide you with a list of countries where the banking systems require less detail on ownership or source of funds."

But one of the lawyers just wasn't having it. The unsuspecting hero, a solo practitioner named Jeffrey M. Herrmann, listened to the scenario while sipping from his Diet Snapple with a straw. "This ain't for me," he responded in an old-school New York accent, furrowing his brow and waving his hands. "My standards are higher." When Kayser asked if he could recommend someone for the job, Herrmann answered, "I don't think so and I would not recommend it either, because those persons would be insulted." And with that, a potential enabler said no to helping with corruption.

The oil sector corruption in every single one of the cases I studied was enabled by some combination of international oil companies, banks, lawyers, and accountants. Foreign enablers make corruption possible. But sometimes potential enablers fight corruption too. The publicly known examples of such actions are few but important to understand if they are to become more common.

Most potential enablers have systems designed to sniff out corruption. They conduct research about prospective partners or clients, digging into whether they have any skeletons in their closets. Most potential enablers also have compliance teams who make sure their companies don't violate the relevant anticorruption laws. As deals advance, these and other systems are quite effective at detecting corruption risks. After all, the stink is usually pretty hard to ignore. The big question is what the potential enabler chooses to do next.

When an accountant or a law firm or a bank suspects that a deal or a prospective client is tainted by corruption, they have a choice to make. They can move forward with the deal, perhaps taking steps to cover their own asses by generating plausible deniability. Or they can reject the deal and walk away. There are plenty of examples that fall in the first category, the expected outcome. Cases from Angola, Azerbaijan, Malaysia, Nigeria, Russia, and beyond show how international banks gave the green light to large, suspicious transactions. Accounting firms signed off on the financial statements of 1MDB and Petrobras during years when corruption racked these institutions. Sometimes the potential enablers reassured each other. When considering whether to undertake some risky Angolan business, a lawyer at the international firm Appleby's wrote in an email: "we would need to understand the source of wealth and source of funds." His colleague replied: "I assume we can also take a certain amount of comfort from the fact that KPMG are advisers to the client and his businesses."[80]

Like Mr. Herrmann, the cases that buck this trend are far more interesting. To be fair to potential enablers, there are probably many cases of good behavior that never come to light. If a company walks away from a stinky deal, the company is unlikely to publicize the decision. Such an announcement might scare off other potential partners in the country, create political blowback, or attract unwanted attention from shareholders, the media, or regulators.

An obscure corporate filing and a leaked letter revealed how Deloitte, one of the "big four" accounting firms, avoided enabling corruption on at least one occasion. In 2016, the firm sent an unusual letter to the management and boards of an oil company, Addax, and its parent company, the enormous state-owned Chinese oil company Sinopec.[81] The letter, obtained and published by a Swiss newspaper, expressed Deloitte's concerns about suspicious payments that they had discovered while auditing Addax's books. The letter also detailed the persistent refusal of Addax and Sinopec to respond to those concerns.

Specifically, in their letter to Addax and Sinopec, Deloitte drew attention to $20 million in payments Addax had made to several Nigerian lawyers and $80 million in payments to an engineering company owned by a prominent Nigerian political figure, both in 2015. Neither set of payments lined up with actual services rendered, according to what Deloitte could see. In addition, the timing was suspicious: Addax made the payments just before it resolved a long-standing dispute with the government over its tax debts, a resolution that benefited the company enormously. The letter also reported how a number of whistleblowers had approached Deloitte auditors as well and had reported fraudulent activities such as the purchase of a $70,000 watch for Nigeria's minister of petroleum, a kickback scheme that benefited Addax executives, and possible corrupt activity in Addax's Gabon business.[82]

In the letter, Deloitte warned that it would need to resign if Addax did not promptly handle the matter by opening its own investigation.[83] Because a small Addax subsidiary was based in the United Kingdom, Deloitte would have to follow British regulations and explain the cause for its resignation in a publicly available statement. And that's exactly what ended up happening. A month after writing the letter, Deloitte resigned and submitted to the United Kingdom's Company House a summary of the suspected fraud that included many of the same scathing details.[84]

At any point prior to writing its letter, Deloitte could have brushed the matter under the carpet, given its seal of approval to the Addax accounts, and received healthy fees for its services. They held firm and escalated the matter instead.

Disgruntled Addax employees made sure that the Swiss media and, in turn, the country's law enforcement agencies became aware of Deloitte's UK regulatory filing. In 2017, Swiss police arrested the CEO and legal director of Addax and charged them and the company with suspected bribery of foreign officials. The case ended with a $32 million fine for Addax and no punishment for the executives.[85] As is often the case, prosecutors proved unable to trace the money from Addax all the way into the hands of Nigerian public officials, and therefore could not prove criminal intent. Following this episode, Sinopec shut down the UK, US, and Switzerland offices of Addax in 2017 and sought to sell off its Nigerian and Gabonese oil businesses.

The Global Witness hidden cameras and the Deloitte letter revealed moments when lawyers and accountants decided not to enable corruption. The oil boom years provide a few other examples, though not many. In 2015, the Venezuelan national oil company contracted a small trucking and trading company, Trenaco, to drill as many as 600 wells in the Orinoco Belt, the world's largest oil reserve. The contract was worth up to $4.5 billion. According to a *Reuters* investigation, Trenaco had no experience operating on such a large scale and started hiring the necessary new staff before the contract had been formally awarded.[86] Had the deal gone through, Trenaco would have worked with the large international oil companies who operate in the Orinoco Belt, including Chevron and Rosneft.

Some of these international companies wrote a protest letter to the national oil company, raising concerns that Trenaco was "not qualified technically or financially" to handle the project. The companies also complained that they might face scrutiny for corruption from their home country governments if they had to partner with Trenaco, especially in light of ongoing US investigations into Venezuelan oil sector corruption. Executives from the companies shared the letters with *Reuters,* providing themselves with extra insurance. The move worked. Instead of going through with the deal, the national oil company split up the tender and awarded its parts to more experienced companies.

Some banks also took steps in the right direction. A Swiss bank alerted authorities to suspicious transfers of funds from accounts held by several of the fixers hired by the oil trading company Gunvor to boost their business in Congo-Brazzaville. Credit Suisse had acquired the small private bank in question, Clariden Leu, and instated tougher anti-money-laundering systems.[87] The bank's report helped prompt the Swiss investigation into bribery by a Gunvor employee, as described in chapter 2. The large UK bank HSBC also filed a "suspicious activity report" when around $500 million entered a privately held account from the Angolan central bank.[88] The son of the former Angolan president faced a corruption investigation related to the transaction, as explained in chapter 4.[89] HSBC publicized this good deed as evidence of its new and improved anticorruption safeguards, put in place following its past money laundering misdeeds, which included helping to launder nearly $1 billion for Mexican drug lords. However, filing a suspicious activity report is not an effective response on its own. The UK National Crime Agency received 463,938 such reports over twelve months in 2017 to 2018, far more than the severely underresourced agency can effectively review.

Discovering examples of potential enablers curbing corruption is challenging. It is even more difficult to parse out the motives behind such actions. Sometimes potential enablers do the right thing because they don't want to get caught. This is especially true if they are subject to strong regulations in their home countries. It's no coincidence that banks are more likely than real estate agents, for example, to report suspicious transactions, as banks are subject to much stronger anti-money-laundering regulations. If legal repercussions are not a problem, a bank may want to avoid reputational blowback if a corruption scandal ever broke open. In other cases, internal anticorruption systems or the moral proclivities of key decision-makers block the scheme.

Even if potential enablers face much stronger rules and begin thwarting corruption more often, the desire to make money will win out sometimes. Like domestic and foreign governments, these companies will continue taking a selective approach to beating back corruption. Their responses will be inadequate and governed by convenience. For this reason, civil society and media are essential.

The Watchdogs

Civil society and the media pick up the slack where government and private sector actors fall short. These players include various types of NGOs, community groups, and journalists who take on corruption in their own countries and abroad. These groups face enormous hurdles. They lack the power, information, and security more official actors enjoy. Yet they are often nimble, highly motivated, and free from political constraints.

Civil society and the media have exposed a number of oil boom corruption cases, from Angola and Azerbaijan to Malaysia and South Sudan.[90] In other instances, these actors have formed the connective tissue in anticorruption actions. As mentioned, journalists became aware of the filing Deloitte made with UK regulators describing the fraud the auditors observed at Addax, and the journalists then brought the matter to the attention of Swiss law enforcement via their reporting. In the 1MDB case, journalists wrote stories based on leaked documents, and then foreign authorities picked up the scent. Journalists and activists also help make sure dirty deals don't get swept under the carpet and pressure the authorities to respond.

Rather than recounting all the stories of this kind, I focus here on three new trends. First, civil society and the media regularly tackle the most difficult kinds of corruption. Of all the types of corruption observed during the oil boom, the hardest to combat was kleptocracy. In kleptocracies, for example in Russia, Azerbaijan, and Angola, those in power use the oil sector to improve their own positions. They siphon off oil revenues into private accounts, award juicy contracts to their allies, and run their political opponents out of business. Anticorruption efforts face an uphill battle in these contexts. Kleptocratic regimes typically don't let the police, courts, elections, and other checks and balances work as they should. Foreign governments and companies also find it difficult to take on kleptocracy. When corruption implicates the head of state, foreign governments and companies often go along with the status quo, especially if they want to maintain goodwill for geopolitical or commercial reasons. Free from these constraints, brave journalists and civil society bear witness to corruption even where its perpetrators enjoy impunity.

"Aliyev Family, Friends Cruise aboard SOCAR Super Yachts," blared a headline released by OCCRP (Organized Crime and Corruption Reporting Project).[91] The story revealed that Socar, Azerbaijan's national oil company, owned two yachts—worth over $20 million apiece—that were regularly enjoyed by political insiders. To build their story, the journalists interviewed former crew members who, despite being hired "for their ability to keep their mouths shut rather than their technical skills," offered accounts of how certain ministers and military officers had spent time aboard the yachts at enticing luxury destinations like Saint-Tropez and Cannes. The reporters dug through documents from Panama, the United States, and Russia to uncover that Socar owned the two glamorous boats. This is just one of dozens of stories from OCCRP that detail how kleptocrats get rich and spend their money at home and abroad.

Journalists and activists who take on kleptocrats face tremendous dangers. Khadija Ismayilova, an Azerbaijani reporter who works with OCCRP, was jailed for eighteen months in 2015 and 2016 on trumped-up charges. In one renowned investigation, she uncovered how companies partly owned by the president's daughters and wife profited from projects funded from the government's oil boom largesse, including the construction of the showpiece stadium for the 2012 Eurovision Song Contest.[92] Upon her release, despite a travel ban and other constraints, Ismayilova resumed her work with vigor, contributing to many recent stories—including the one about Socar's yachts.

Other reporting by OCCRP aims to pick up the work of Daphne Caruana Galizia, a Maltese journalist who paid for her reporting on corruption with her life. In 2017, after years of intrepid reporting, Caruana Galizia was killed by a car bomb. Following her murder, eighteen media organizations from around the world formed the "Daphne Project" to take forward her investigations, including her exposure of the Maltese bank Pilatus, who had helped Azerbaijan's first family launder their riches. Working as part of the project, OCCRP and the *Guardian* uncovered further details about the vast business and real estate holdings of Azerbaijan's political elites, including real estate in Dubai and several French factories owned via offshore companies with accounts at Pilatus.[93]

Regimes often try to paint journalists and activists as enemies of the state. The Angolan journalist Rafael Marques de Morais made a career of courageously exposing how the dos Santos regime and its allies benefited economically from their hold on power, in part through the oil industry. He has faced more than one arrest on charges such as "outrage to a sovereign body" and "insult against a public authority."[94]

The repression often escalates if the activists also pose a political challenge. The Anticorruption Foundation, a Russian nonprofit run by Alexei Navalny, a prominent opposition politician (introduced in chapter 4), published an extensive report about the government's overspending on the Sochi Olympics. The report named which of Putin's favored oligarchs benefited from the various inflated contracts.[95] Since then the outfit has released several slick videos, one of which accuses Prime Minister Dimitry Medvedev of being "crazy about money and real estate."[96] Drone footage shows the elaborate residences allegedly enjoyed by Medvedev. The foundation claimed that the money used to buy the properties flowed through secretive charitable foundations controlled by Medvedev's closest associates.

The Anticorruption Foundation's video winds down with the grim conclusion that "the system is so rotten that there is nothing healthy left. People in this film have been in power for 17 years, and they've built a perfect mechanism to turn Russia's national treasures into palaces and bank accounts for themselves and their children. And this is the main reason why our country on the whole is very rich, but the people who live here are very poor." The tape closes with a plug for Navalny's own 2018 presidential campaign, which was eventually blocked from proceeding by Russian authorities.

The efforts of activists and journalists in kleptocracies seem fruitless at times. But change can come. Few expected any kind of response when, in 2017, journalists exposed some shenanigans at Angola's sovereign wealth fund that involved the son of former president dos Santos.[97] After all, dos Santos had hand-picked his successor. To everyone's surprise, the new president seized on the reporting, fired the son from his role as the fund's director, and opened a criminal investigation.[98] Rather than just bearing witness to intractable trends, the reporting ended up driving dramatic change.

The second trend is how journalists and civil society groups are collaborating transnationally. Just like the corruption they aim to uncover, these actors are crossing borders in innovative and effective ways.

Take OCCRP and its work on Azerbaijan. They published a series of stories about the so-called Azerbaijani Laundromat, the elaborate global structure used by political elites to launder over $2.9 billion over a two-year period. The consortium of groups contributing to the investigation was no less global. It included *Berlingske* (Denmark), the *Guardian* (UK), *Süddeutsche Zeitung* (Germany), *Le Monde* (France), *Tages-Anzeiger* and *Tribune de Genève* (Switzerland), *De Tijd* (Belgium), *Novaya Gazeta*

(Russia), *Dossier* (Austria), *Atlatszo.hu* (Hungary), *Delo* (Slovenia), the RISE Project (Romania), *Bivol* (Bulgaria), *Aripaev* (Estonia), the Czech Center for Investigative Journalism (Czech Republic), and *Barron's* (US).

Another powerful cross-border collaboration kicked off in 2014 when a man referring to himself as John Doe contacted Bastian Obermeyer, a journalist at the German newspaper *Süddeutsche Zeitung,* offering a cache of data that was "more than anything you have ever seen." The ensuing leak, later dubbed the Panama Papers, triggered the most ambitious act of international journalism in history. The US-based International Consortium of Investigative Journalists led the charge. Working with *Süddeutsche Zeitung,* they spent a year organizing and analyzing 11.5 million leaked documents from the Panamanian law firm Mossack Fonseca. The files contained information about over 214,000 offshore companies and named 140 public officials from fifty countries. This analysis included information relevant to oil sector corruption cases in Algeria, Angola, Bahrain, Congo-Brazzaville, Ecuador, Nigeria, Russia, and beyond. To investigate this mammoth trove, the International Consortium of Investigative Journalists helped coordinate journalists from over 100 media outlets in nearly eighty countries. They worked together in secret and dropped the first round of stories in unison, sending a shockwave around the world.

The International Consortium of Investigative Journalists and several other large media outlets had data experts who sorted through the 2.6 terabytes of data. Journalists from specific countries provided the necessary local context. For example, analytical systems set up by the International Consortium flagged several documents linked to public officials at the Ecuadorian national oil company, Petroecuador. They passed the files on to the Ecuadorian newspaper *El Universo,* which then published a story about how a manager at the country's national oil company controlled four suspicious offshore companies in Panama. This revelation helped prompt a Swiss federal prosecutor to freeze the assets held by the manager and his company in Swiss banks and open a broader investigation into possible corruption surrounding the award of over 140 contracts by Petroecuador.[99]

Other global networks push for policy change. The Publish What You Pay coalition joins together over 700 civil society groups across forty countries. In 2002, a few London-based NGOs founded the coalition around a single goal: get oil and mining companies to disclose how much they pay to governments. The rationale is that if such payments are transparent, citizens can spot an unfair deal and hold their governments to account for how the funds are used. Since the coalition's creation, expertise and even protection have flowed through its network. European NGOs rushed to the defense of imprisoned activists in Niger. Members from Myanmar learned from their counterparts in Mongolia ways to engage with foreign mining companies. Ugandan campaigners defended the need for a US oil sector transparency law.

Thanks partly to all this collaboration, journalists and civil society are moving the needle. That's the third big takeaway from observing their anticorruption work in the oil sector. Governments and companies still have more power, but these groups punch way above their weight.

A number of big-time politicians and companies have faced investigation, paid fines, or even ended up in prison because of investigations by NGOs and journalists. In some cases, they have exposed the wrongdoing, and law enforcement has then followed up. In other cases, they have applied pressure, provided background information, or connected the dots in ways that have helped the police and prosecutors build their cases. Media or NGO reporting helped prompt the investigation of Addax and Gunvor in Switzerland, of Cobalt in the United States, and of the 1MDB crew by multiple governments. Media and NGO actions prompted investigations in all the Unaoil cases and the OPL 245 case in Nigeria, along with many others.

Transparency Crusades

Civil society also scored wins on the policy front. In 1999 Global Witness published their report *Crude Awakening*, at a moment when Angola's government was signing huge deals with international oil companies like BP. How would the billions of dollars in anticipated revenues ever benefit the country's poor population if they passed secretly into the hands of a kleptocratic government? At the very least, the report argued, these payments should be transparent.

Global Witness, along with a few other UK and US groups, many with financial support from George Soros's Open Society Foundation, rallied around this idea, and the Publish What You Pay movement was born. BP took notice and started to release more information about their early payments to Angola. But Angolan authorities responded sharply, and BP quickly reversed course. Companies began to complain that the oil-rich governments should be the ones to publish the information first, not them.

In 2002, the UK government announced a new initiative, the Extractive Industries Transparency Initiative (EITI), to address the oil transparency issue. Countries could join the EITI if they agreed to two things: disclose all their oil, gas, and mining revenues, and set up a committee with government, corporate, and civil society members to oversee the process. The initiative has fared well. By 2019, it boasted fifty-two members, including major oil producers like Colombia, Iraq, Mexico, Nigeria, and Norway. In some countries, the EITI's implementation has been deeply flawed. Reports contain old data, civil society participants face harassment, or the payment data sits trapped in 400-page PDF reports no one reads. But elsewhere, the initiative's convening power and disclosures have led to real reform. At the global level, no other actor has done more to legitimize the idea of transparency in the oil sector, a place where secrecy had typically prevailed.

However, the EITI only works in countries that bother to sign up. Major oil producers like Saudi Arabia, Russia, and the UAE never gave it a second glance, not to mention countries like Iran and Venezuela whose fraught relations with the West make participation most unlikely. Some of the more corrupt oil-rich countries have also eschewed the EITI, with Angola, Equatorial Guinea, and Turkmenistan failing to join.

Because the EITI has these major gaps, the Publish What You Pay coalition kept pushing for oil companies to publish their payments. Specifically, it pushed for the governments of the places where oil companies are based, like the United States, the United Kingdom, and the European Union, to pass regulations requiring payment disclosure. The campaign dragged on for years, with a few dogged NGO staff pushing the agenda. Oil companies pushed back hard and argued that the EITI was more than adequate.

Then, in 2010, the activists scored an unexpected victory. Oil prices were soaring at the time, and the specter of the resource curse loomed large in a growing number of developing countries. A few supportive US legislators seized a last-minute opportunity to insert the transparency rule into the Dodd-Frank Wall Street Reform Act. The Act mostly aimed to rein in the excesses that had caused the 2008 financial crisis. But section 1504 focused on the oil and mining industries instead of the financial sector. It required all US-based and US-listed companies to disclose their payments to foreign governments. The companies even had to break down the data by project: detail that would shed light on each individual deal they struck with foreign governments. The Publish What You Pay activists broke out in celebration, popping bottles of budget champagne in Washington and well beyond. Finally, after a decade of work, more light would shine on oil and mining sector deals.

They were right to celebrate. The dam had been broken, but not in the way it first appeared. The SEC, under whose mandate the measure fell, still had to write the detailed regulations to implement section 1504. When the SEC handed down the first draft, the oil industry responded with a lawsuit. The court sided with the oil lobby, ordering the SEC to water down aspects of the regulations. All this took years.

In January 2017, Trump took office just as the SEC was finalizing the revised regulations. In one of his first formal acts in office, he gutted section 1504 in a nod to the oil industry allies. United States oil companies, including ExxonMobil and Chevron, who led the fight against the reporting rule, had won.

The companies enjoyed less success elsewhere. In 2013, the European Union filed new directives requiring its member countries to pass payment disclosure regulations. European leaders had taken note of the US law, and Nicolas Sarkozy emerged as the reform's first EU advocate following a spirited intervention by Bono, the U2 lead singer and antipoverty campaigner. Canada and Norway passed similar rules as well. In 2016, oil companies began publishing their annual payment reports. Some, like Shell, had vociferously opposed the disclosures. But somehow they found it possible to report all their payments, even those made to governments such as China and Qatar, where Shell had previously argued disclosures would be illegal and prompt serious retribution. BP's payments to Angola, the original target of the Publish What You Pay movement, are now reported in detail.

While the United States has remained a laggard, civil society activists succeeded in making hundreds of oil, gas, and mining companies report their payments to governments. This has not been their only victory on the transparency front.

Beneficial ownership disclosure sits at the very top of the anticorruption agenda. Nearly every corruption scheme described in this book used anonymous shell companies in one way or another. There is no better way to receive a bribe, pay off political allies, or launder stolen funds. But what if these companies were not anonymous? Beneficial ownership disclosure requires companies to report the names of the real, flesh-and-blood people who control them and benefit from their activities. No longer can strings of vaguely named companies stretch across jurisdictions, making it nearly impossible for law enforcement—much less the public—to know who owns what.

As they often must do, civil society groups built the case for why beneficial ownership transparency was important, put it in front of policymakers, and then waited for the right political moment to arrive. For several years, NGOs, including Transparency International, Global Financial

Integrity, the Tax Justice Network, and Global Witness promoted the issue. Their first major break came at the 2013 G8 summit when the prime minister of the United Kingdom, David Cameron, pushed beneficial ownership reporting as part of a wider anticorruption agenda. While some G8 members resisted, the United Kingdom began setting up the world's first public registry of beneficial ownership data. In 2016, the EITI adopted beneficial ownership reporting as part of what its fifty-plus member countries must report. The movement to root out anonymous companies had begun.

The 2016 Panama Papers revelations provided the next boost. Partly in response, the European Union passed its own reporting requirements in 2017, though member countries can decide whether or not to make the ownership data available to the public. In 2018, events again interceded, at least in the United Kingdom. As already mentioned, Russian agents launched a nerve agent attack against a former spy and his daughter on UK soil. Pressure mounted on the government to make it more difficult for Russians to secretly launder their money through the United Kingdom. Parliament turned to a demand that civil society had been pressing for years and passed a law requiring UK overseas territories to establish beneficial ownership registries, a potential blow to the secrecy enjoyed by shell companies registered in the British Virgin Islands, among other locations. The UK government has also indicated that it will require foreign companies to disclose their owners before acquiring UK property. While plenty of jurisdictions still allow anonymous companies, the trend toward greater openness has kicked off.

While civil society has helped deliver historic gains, transparency is hardly a silver bullet when it comes to fighting corruption. First off, lots of information still remains secret. Thanks to the influence they enjoy in Washington, US oil companies don't have to report how much they pay in taxes. They have also convinced the United States to drop out of the EITI. In the European Union, progress on beneficial ownership transparency has come up against all kinds of privacy concerns. In developing countries, including many EITI members, governments are struggling to produce data that are thorough and timely. Even in the United Kingdom, the first country to launch a public registry of beneficial ownership data, those data contain all kinds of flaws, and the authorities do little to verify what companies report. For example, an initial dig through the data revealed over 2,000 owners who listed 2016 as their birth year, and a few born in the year 9988.[100]

Even when information is disclosed, it is challenging to observe how and when transparency prevents corruption. In past years, before they started publicly disclosing all their payments to governments, European oil companies made some sketchy outlays. BP and Statoil paid large sums to the Angolan government for a far-fetched research center than never came into existence.[101] Shell and Eni paid the Nigerian government $1.3 billion for the mammoth oil block OPL 245, despite suspecting that the money would then be captured by politicians. Perhaps, now that they are more transparent, European companies avoid making problematic payments like these because their finances are subject to more scrutiny. Unfortunately, as with most nonevents, it is nearly impossible to prove whether this result is happening.

At the same time, the effects of transparency have not been invisible. Following the release of the Panama Papers and the spotlight that information shined on offshore finance, nervous Colombian citizens reported fifteen times more offshore financial holdings to tax authorities, helping to raise the country's tax receipts.[102] In our investigation of Nigeria's corrupt oil trading deals, colleagues and I at the Natural Resource Governance Institute used EITI data extensively, as did Global Witness in their exposé of ExxonMobil's willingness to contract with politically connected companies in Liberia.[103] In one of the world's largest ever money laundering scandals, the Estonian branch of Denmark's Danske Bank allowed over $200 billion in suspicious funds, mostly from Russia, to flow through its accounts. The scandal finally broke open when a midlevel banker did a bit of research using the United Kingdom's registry of companies and found that one company, for example, had moved $480 million in five months, despite having "0.00" listed as its net assets.[104]

Transparency, it appears, works like every other anticorruption force out there. It is a vital ingredient but pretty useless on its own. Just like the efforts of the domestic governments, foreign governments, enablers, and watchdogs profiled in this chapter, sometimes transparency helps to bring down corruption, and sometimes it accomplishes very little.

All these different anticorruption actors flexed their muscles during the aftermath of the oil boom. Dozens of corrupt companies, governments, and individuals felt the effects of their growing strength. The challenge now is how to supercharge their complementary powers.

CHAPTER 7 | We Know How to Fight Corruption

NEW YORKERS USED TO call Queens Boulevard the "Boulevard of Death." At some of its intersections, pedestrians had only thirty-two seconds to dash across twelve lanes of traffic. Some didn't make it. Since 1990, over 130 pedestrians have lost their lives on this one city street. They were not alone. For several years, pedestrian accidents were the top killer of New York City's children. An average of one New Yorker was seriously injured or killed by a vehicle every two hours.[1]

With millions of cars and even more people rushing around in tight quarters, there will always be pedestrian deaths in New York City. But that's no reason to sit back and do nothing. In 2014, the city government launched a campaign to tackle this problem. Officials deployed a mix of tools. They put in place a citywide speed limit, added bike lanes, redesigned busy intersections, and tweaked crossing signals. They ran public safety campaigns, educated younger drivers, and outfitted city vehicles with new safety equipment.

They also targeted the most dangerous streets. If you're trying to reduce pedestrian deaths, the "Boulevard of Death" is probably a good place to start. This suite of efforts appears to be working. In 2017, New York City recorded the lowest number of pedestrian deaths on record.

Like traffic deaths, corruption will never go away entirely in the oil sector or anywhere else people can make a fortune by bending the rules. But that's no excuse for doing nothing. The oil boom's record offers three takeaways about what works. First, rather than trying to address every possible transaction where corruption could appear, focus on the problem areas. Second, anticorruption actors should double down on the remedies that are already working, including targeting corruption's international tentacles. Third, mobilize multiple actors, since none can succeed alone. Observing past corruption cases makes clear both what works and where to start.

Target the Problem Areas

What are the "Boulevards of Death" when it comes to corruption? The oil boom has shown where the casualties run high.

Oilfield services is one obvious problem area. During the oil boom, corruption infiltrated oilfield service deals in Algeria, Angola, Brazil, Colombia, Ecuador, Equatorial Guinea, Iraq, Kazakhstan, Nigeria, Russia, Saudi Arabia, the United Kingdom, and Venezuela.[2] That's a lot of countries, and it's not even a complete list. Of all the oil sector bribery cases pursued by US authorities under the FCPA, well over half target oilfield services companies.

In one prominent case, the Dutch firm SBM Offshore paid $180 million in bribes to national oil company officials in Brazil, Angola, Equatorial Guinea, Kazakhstan, and Iraq in order to gain at least $2.8 billion in business.[3] Service companies also partnered with politically connected companies, helping local elites receive a cut of unearned money. Halliburton, for one, hired an Angolan company with links to government officials and paid the company for doing no real work.[4] Service contracting sat at the center of Brazil's Car Wash scandal, with Petrobras officials receiving several billion dollars in bribes during the boom years and awarding inflated contracts that cost the public dearly.

Despite all these cases, oilfield service companies are usually left out of global efforts to improve oil sector transparency and accountability. Instead, attention has focused on the upstream companies, such as Chevron or Shell, who enter into exploration and production deals with oil-producing governments. Dozens of these upstream companies participate in the EITI, for instance, and several sit on its board. Few service companies have bothered to participate, mostly because no one has pushed them to do so. New regulations that require more oil sector transparency, passed in the European Union and elsewhere, are silent on service companies. Adding to the neglect, national oil company procurement remains an obscure bureaucratic backwater, ignored by domestic and foreign oversight actors until something very big goes wrong.

Many oil trading deals also carried heavy corruption risks during the oil boom. A Brazil petrochemical company, an employee of a giant Swiss oil trader, and executives at a Singapore trading house were among those found guilty of bribing government officials.[5] In Angola, Azerbaijan, Russia, and Ukraine, selected political elites and oligarchs made billions off oil trading deals awarded by national oil companies.[6] Oil trading proved the most vulnerable part of the Nigerian oil sector during the boom years and was milked for billions in illicit profits.[7] These problems and others drew attention to this part of the industry and generated pressure on the large trading houses to open up. In response, a few of the large Swiss trading companies have begun publishing aggregate figures about their dealings with governments. The EITI now also requires its member countries to produce information on oil trading deals. While welcome, these are overdue and overly incremental initial steps. They leave out many of the industry's biggest players, and opportunities for abuse still flourish amid the complexity of oil trading deals.

While the number of service contract and oil trading cases is striking, nothing compares with the ubiquity of national oil companies in oil boom graft. Over and over again, political elites conscripted these mammoth entities into their service. Putin used Rosneft to wrangle the Russian oil sector under his control. Dos Santos used Sonangol as his regime's bank account, keeping large portions of oil revenues out of the central government budget. Petrobras sat at the heart of a corruption scandal that wreaked havoc across Brazil's business and political establishment. NNPC signed deals that sent billions of dollars in public money into private hands. Drawing only from concluded legal cases, it appears that national oil company officials in Algeria, Angola, Brazil, Colombia, Congo-Brazzaville, Ecuador, Equatorial Guinea, Iraq, Kazakhstan, Nigeria, Oman, Russia, and Venezuela solicited or received bribes during the boom years.[8]

Recent research speaks to this trend. Of the 224 bribery cases studied by the OECD, 27 percent involved various kinds of state-owned companies, including national oil companies. Bribes were bigger in these cases: a full 80 percent of the total bribe amounts went to state-owned companies.[9] Another OECD study surveyed 213 state-owned companies in thirty-four countries. Sixty-three percent of respondents from the oil and gas sector said they had observed high risks of corruption or other irregular practices in the last three years. The average across all industries was just 42 percent.[10]

Three other "boulevards" of wrongdoing are less specific to the oil industry. First, officials had an easier time rewarding their friends and allies when they could allocate oil contracts in a secretive and discretionary manner. For instance, when the former Nigerian oil minister Diezani Alison-Madueke steered overly lucrative oil trading contracts toward her favorite companies, she was under no legal obligation to run any kind of competitive tender or to release the basic terms of the deals.[11] Likewise, the president of Chad awarded the rights to oil blocks to the Canadian company Griffiths Energy in a discretionary manner, a transaction that was marred by bribery.[12] Oversight of awards often fell short too. The board of Petrobras did little to rein in its wild overspending. In Russia, Angola, and Azerbaijan, journalists and opposition politicians faced intimidation, prosecution, and other threats when they questioned how their respective presidents steered oil sector business opportunities toward particular oligarchs.

Offshore shell companies appeared in nearly every one of the oil sector corruption cases I examined. Unlike normal companies that deliver a product and have offices, employees, and operating expenses, these secretive entities usually only had a name, an address, and a few bank accounts. Yet they received billions of dollars in bribes, partnered on enormous oil deals, and siphoned illicit wealth offshore. No other tool proved handier in running corruption schemes.

Finally, the use of fixers, agents and intermediaries, appears strikingly prone to corruption. Consider the incentives faced by Unaoil, a company that helped oilfield service companies access business opportunities abroad. As described in chapter 2, if Unaoil succeeded in buttering up the right officials so that their clients won the contracts, it received larger fees in return. For intermediaries like Unaoil, the incentives to engage in bribery become enormously high. The corruption risks are baked into their business model.

There is no need to throw up our hands at the challenge of corruption when such obvious problem areas exist. In the oil sector, oilfield service contracting, oil trading, and national oil companies require urgent attention from anticorruption forces. Corruption's foes should also tackle the discretionary and secretive award of contracts, the abuse of anonymous shell companies, and the practices of agents and intermediaries. This is a tangible to-do list where real progress can be made.

What should be done to tackle these problem areas? One key is to use international strategies, matching the international nature of corruption itself. The other is to rally efforts from all of corruption's disparate foes, given their complementary strengths.

Leverage the International

The international nature of oil sector corruption is its greatest strength and its greatest vulnerability. The 1MDB case from Malaysia shows both sides of this double-edged sword. In his bid to steal over $4.5 billion, Jho Low collaborated with or used a Saudi oil company, a UAE sovereign wealth fund, Goldman Sachs, and banks in Switzerland and Singapore. As chapter 5 laid out, the stolen funds were then routed through offshore companies set up in secrecy havens like the British Virgin Islands and the Cayman Islands. American lawyers, real estate agents, and art dealers then helped Jho Low and his colleagues buy up assets overseas. Meanwhile, American and European public relations firms helped Malaysia's former prime minister and Jho Low brush up their reputations and distract attention away from their misdeeds. As a result of all these tentacles, the taint of the 1MDB corruption case spread to dozens of foreign individuals, neighborhoods, banks, businesses, media outlets, and even the White House under two consecutive US administrations.

An equally global set of anticorruption actors discovered and punished the 1MDB corruption. When Prime Minister Najib shut down domestic investigations into the scheme, foreign journalists picked up the trail. The US government then moved to seize $1.7 billion in assets acquired with stolen 1MDB funds. The DOJ's detailed account of the scheme named many of its enablers, and these players, such as banks from Switzerland and Singapore, began to face legal consequences with their home governments. United States authorities also opened an investigation of Goldman Sachs for their enabling role and charged Jho Low himself.

While the 1MDB case is one of the more eye-popping illustrations of the two-sided global dynamic, it is not unusual. International actors helped pull off the corruption, and international actors caused the perpetrators faced consequences.

My emphasis on international anticorruption actors does not mean that domestic entities matter less. Quite the contrary. Malaysian journalists were the first to uncover the 1MDB scandal, and several Malaysian government bodies dug up crucial evidence before being shut down. A few years later, the country's own electoral system succeeded in showing Prime Minister Najib the door, and he faces trial in Malaysian courts. In Brazil, Nigeria, and the United States, domestic institutions also exposed and punished corruption.

In kleptocracies, however, domestic anticorruption actors face steep uphill battles. Oil-rich autocrats enjoy so many options for shutting them down. However, corrupt officials have less control over the international arena. Kleptocracies rely heavily on foreign parties to function, and these overseas linkages are locations where kleptocrats can be frustrated, shamed, punished, or deterred.

Of course this is easier said than done. Foreign governments regularly collaborate with kleptocrats for security or economic reasons, and foreign companies play along in order to access profits. The Aliyev government in

Azerbaijan has benefited from this dynamic. The publicly funded European Bank of Reconstruction and Development provided loans worth over a billion euros to construct the infrastructure needed to bring Azerbaijani gas to Europe. Washington and its NATO allies leaned on Azerbaijan as a transit point for air cargo needed to support military operations in Afghanistan. BP and other large companies have invested heavily in Azerbaijan's oil and gas fields. Aliyev's regime plays up and sometimes exaggerates his country's geostrategic importance to the West in an effort to drown out criticism of the regime's corruption and human rights abuses.[13]

But even in Azerbaijan, anticorruption actors have latched onto the kleptocracy's overseas tentacles and inflicted harm on the beast. In its investigation of Azerbaijan's national oil company, the British group Global Witness dug into company records from Singapore, Switzerland, and other jurisdictions to shed light on several suspicious transactions. A Berlin-based think tank exposed how the Aliyev regime manipulated the European parliamentarians via the Council of Europe, and Italy's police then investigated the concerns.[14] OCCRP, which connects journalists across thirty-four countries, exposed how the regime launders money overseas, including through British, French, Latvian, and Maltese companies and banks. OCCRP and other global groups have also helped magnify the voices of brave Azerbaijani journalists and activists and publicized their plight when they faced arrest and intimidation.

Taken together, these foreign anticorruption actors created a strong counter-narrative to the one crafted by the Aliyev regime and the public relations firms they hire. By questioning and exposing the conduct of Azerbaijan's political elites, these external actors incrementally chip away at the regime's sense of inevitability. This may, eventually and depending on domestic events, temper the regime's most damaging behaviors or help political sands to shift.

Mobilize Corruption's Motley Foes

For the last couple of years, I've heard the same response from people who asked what this book was about: "Huh. That sounds depressing."

Sometimes it is. Corruption has deprived citizens of billions of dollars that could have paid teachers, repaired roads, and bought medicine for sick kids. When public revenues go missing due to oil sector corruption, lives are lost as a result. And the costs don't stop there. Politicians in Brazil and Nigeria have used stolen oil money to tilt elections in their favor. In Angola, Azerbaijan, and Russia, corruption has strengthened the kind of regimes that turn their allies into billionaires and their enemies into prisoners. The taint of corruption, from Malaysia and elsewhere, has spread overseas and infected foreign property markets, businesses, banks, media outlets, and officials.

But researching this book was encouraging too. Every time a new corruption case broke open, an anticorruption actor had won. No matter how powerful the perpetrators, they didn't get away with it entirely. Politicians, officials, executives, and companies faced prosecution, paid fines, lost revenues, and suffered reputational damage. Some individuals lost their jobs and went to jail. In many cases, the consequences felt too light. But they are not inconsequential. So many corrupt actors were kept from enjoying their loot in peace and were discouraged from running their schemes again.

A motley group of actors fight corruption. Each one has a fatal weakness, as laid out in chapter 6. But thankfully, none of these actors has to fight corruption alone. Their strengths are complementary: when one fails to act, another picks up the slack.

Domestic governments hold great power, as they can take direct legal action against those suspected of corruption. But, especially in authoritarian countries, political leaders too often use anticorruption proceedings to weaken their rivals, as when Crown Prince Mohammad bin Salman locked up dozens of Saudi elites in the Riyadh Ritz-Carlton. Political leaders also repress the freedom of citizens, including journalists and opposition politicians, to scrutinize government behavior and call out problems where they see them. While strongmen readily adopt the rhetoric of anticorruption, they leave behind the attributes of truth and fairness. In contrast, oversight bodies, when allowed to operate independently, tend to have a better record than the strongmen do. As shown in chapter 3, Brazil's judicial system held top political and business elites to account for engaging in corruption, and US government watchdogs called out the oil regulator's coziness with the companies it oversaw.

On a number of occasions, foreign governments have pursued oil boom corruption with great success. They have an impressive toolkit at their disposal. They can prosecute cases of foreign bribery or go after the stolen money that crosses their borders. They can shun corrupt governments on the global stage or whack them with sanctions. They can fund civil society groups that fight corruption at home and abroad and can enact policies that make corruption schemes more difficult to pull off. But foreign governments only deploy this toolkit when it is convenient. Foreign policy, military and energy security agendas, or just complacency and low expectations, often get in the way.

The world needs more of the good stuff. Governments should deploy their anticorruption toolkit with consistency and vigor. Already countries beyond the United States have begun pursuing more big antibribery cases. Better enforcement of antibribery laws will require more resources to investigate the fiendishly complex corruption schemes. Prosecutors then need to push for penalties that actually hurt, even if they continue negotiating settlements with companies rather than going to trial. They must continue going after the executives responsible for corruption schemes as well as the companies they work for. It also helps a great deal when law enforcement publicly disclose detailed information about their cases, as other anticorruption actors can then use this information in their work. These actions have succeeded in exposing and punishing many recent cases of oil sector bribery and should be scaled up.

Foreign governments also used oil industry cases to test out some shiny new tools, including the US Kleptocracy Asset Recovery Initiative and the UK Unexplained Wealth Orders. These tools match the ways corruption actually works in today's global system by tackling offshore financial flows and are a great example of how to go after kleptocracy's international vulnerabilities. The Magnitsky Sanctions adopted by the United States and Canada are another promising new tool that can punish corrupt individuals by limiting their ability to do business abroad. These approaches should be beefed up where they exist and adopted where they do not.

The same goes for policies that make corruption more difficult to pull off. Governments know how to eliminate corruption's favorite mechanisms. At the very top of this list is getting rid of anonymous shell companies. There is no need to wait for more evidence before acting. The United Kingdom requires all its companies to disclose the names of their actual flesh-and-blood owners and will soon require the foreign buyers of property to do the same. While more still needs be done, the government has pushed the UK overseas territories, such as the British Virgin Islands, to clean up their act and has clamped down on so-called golden visas, which have allowed rich investors to enter the country even if their wealth has suspicious origins. These anticorruption policies must spread across a wide set of countries, or dirty money will just seek out the most lenient jurisdiction.

The United Kingdom's record provides a reminder that good policies must be paired with effective enforcement. Their company disclosure policy is great, but the government has allocated too few resources to verifying the ownership data provided by companies. Given the scale of the dirty money estimated to flow through London, the authorities also pursue too few criminal cases and dole out mild reprimands. As the *Economist* argued in 2018,

> the challenge is less to write new laws than to enforce what is on the books—a common malaise in Britain....Devoting greater resources to corruption cases would go a long way towards fixing things. Some of the extra cash should be used to raise investigators' salaries, which are far below those of their American peers. Strengthening oversight of shell companies and the firms that set them up would also help, as would money for the verification of ownership information....Britain's response to the threat posed by illicit financial flows has so far been more thundering rhetoric than meaningful action. It is time to put that right.[15]

While obscured in dry bureaucrat-speak, two intergovernmental review mechanisms lay out a clear and specific agenda for how countries can improve their anticorruption efforts. They get too little attention given their importance. First, the OECD evaluates how well countries are implementing its Anti-Bribery Convention. In the recent evaluation of Switzerland, for instance, the OECD commended the uptick in bribery and money laundering investigations from 24 in 2011 to 137 in 2016 but rebuked the Swiss for their poor protections for whistleblowers and the low penalties they assigned to guilty parties, such as the $0 fine assessed to Odebrecht in the Car Wash case.[16]

Second, the Financial Action Task Force evaluates how well its member governments protect against dirty money flows. In one of its evaluations, the Task Force urged the Seychelles, a popular location for setting up shell companies, to beef up its enforcement activities. Despite the significant flows of dirty money through Seychellois companies, the country has conducted only three money laundering investigations, and all three were related to drug trafficking offenses rather than tax evasion or corruption.[17] The Task Force criticized the United States for failing to address the role lawyers, accountants, and real estate agents play in money laundering.[18] If the existing OECD and Financial Action Task Force monitoring tools can be injected with some real urgency and prominence, there is no need to invent new ones.

In part because the United States and other governments let them off the hook, the professional enablers of corruption rarely become anticorruption heroes. The oil boom provided a few lonely examples of enablers disrupting corruption by refusing to facilitate suspicious deals, though others likely took place without public knowledge. Suspicious activity reports filed by bankers helped prompt the investigation of Gunvor's oil trading deals in Congo-Brazzaville, for example.[19] But many other reports went uninvestigated. Deloitte resigned from auditing Addax's books when they discovered evidence of possible fraud in Addax's Nigerian operations and reported their suspicions in a UK regulatory filing.[20] Employees of several enablers, such as the law firm at the center of the Panama Papers, blew the whistle on corruption when they saw it, helping to expose many of the cases described here. Other companies self-reported fraud and other abuses from within their ranks to authorities, in hopes of receiving more lenient punishments. Corruption was exposed through all these channels, and they need to stay open.

Getting potential enablers to do the right thing more often will require a better mix of carrots and sticks. Through regulation and enforcement actions, governments can take a tougher line on defining what constitutes inappropriate behavior for these players and what penalties they will face when they cross the line. This is happening to some degree already. The United States has investigated Goldman Sachs for arranging the 1MDB bond sales, and one Goldman banker has already pleaded guilty to criminal charges for his role in enabling the scam.[21] The United States has also indicted an American accountant, a German investment advisor, and a Panamanian lawyer connected to Mossack Fonseca, the law firm exposed in the Panama Papers. Potential enablers may avoid suspicious deals more often if they face real sanctions like these. To add some carrots to the sticks, they should also receive greater reputational kudos when they do expose corruption and adopt better safeguards, such as enhanced transparency.

Civil society and the media keep the governments and the potential enablers from shirking their anticorruption responsibilities and help expose corruption as well. But these groups stand on shaky ground. They lack reliable access to information and cannot dole out consequences other than reputational harm. They face daunting legal, professional, and personal risks as a result of their work. Nonetheless, over and over again they've fought corruption and brought about policy changes. They have taken on kleptocrats when no one else would and have forged innovative international partnerships to investigate corruption's global reach.

Activist groups and journalists often work on a shoestring. With more funding, they could hire crack investigators, dive into ever-growing stores of data, collaborate more widely, bring their message to policy-makers in more countries, and retain the lawyers needed to protect themselves from counterattack. Private foundations and donor agencies should increase their support of media and anticorruption groups worldwide, both in oil-producing countries and abroad. Funders should support groups that take on kleptoc-racies, even if this work does not produce the kind of immediately meas-urable results donors like. In many countries, activists and journalists are the only ones offering a counter-narrative to the one spun by the klepto-crats in charge.

All of these anticorruption actors should address the problem areas iden-tified above: oil traders, oilfield service companies, and national oil com-panies; discretionary and secretive awards, anonymous shell companies, and middlemen. Problems in these areas have appeared so consistently that it will hardly be a surprise when they crop up again. Each area would benefit from greater transparency and oversight, better rules that define what behavior is acceptable, the serious enforcement of those rules, more investigations of suspicious behavior, and more severe punishment of behav-ior that breaks the law.

Fighting corruption requires many different actors to take actions, including some that are threatening or inconvenient. Even if this collective action challenge is overcome, the results will not be complete or entirely satisfying. In Brazil, the police broke open the Car Wash scandal, and the courts brought many of those involved to justice. In Nigeria, a president lost his reelection bid in part because he allowed corruption to flourish, and officials who abused their power now face investigation. While these are big wins, they did not eliminate the structural problems that allowed the corruption to grow in the first place, such as economic inequality and money-driven politics. The lack of perfect solutions cannot, however, be allowed to hold back the fight against corruption. Neither should confu-sion over what should be done. Past cases clearly reveal both the problem areas and what remedies are working. To neglect the resulting agenda is to accommodate the corruption of the future.

A Good News Story?

In late 2018, while I was writing this chapter, a headline popped up in my Twitter feed: "World's Biggest Oil Traders Paid Bribes in Brazil Scandal—Prosecutors."[22]

The story announced yet another phase of the enormous Car Wash scandal. Brazilian prosecutors accused three Swiss companies, Glencore, Trafigura, and Vitol, of paying more than $30 million in bribes to officials at the national oil company Petrobras and routing the payments through intermediaries, companies in the British Virgin Islands, and bank accounts in the United States, the United Kingdom, Sweden, Switzerland and Uruguay.[23] According to the prosecutors' investigation, Petrobras then let the trading companies buy and store oil at discounted prices. The scheme reportedly infiltrated 160 separate transactions between 2011 and 2014. Vitol and Glencore said they were cooperating with authorities. Trafigura has denied that its management had any knowledge of the alleged bribery.[24] At the time this book went to press, the investigation was ongoing and none of the companies had been charged.

Is this just more bad news from the oil sector? If the accusations turn out to be true, corruption contaminated an even larger share of Petrobras's business than all the earlier Car Wash proceedings revealed, and even more foreign companies were willing to play along.[25] As is so often the case, the accusations featured foreign banks and intermediaries. Indeed, two NGOs had released an investigation just weeks earlier that criticized the same oil trading companies for working with several middlemen deeply implicated in the Car Wash scandal, including one fellow known as the "Deacon of Bribes."[26]

Or was all this actually good news? Undeterred by the fact that the scheme may implicate politically powerful individuals, Brazilian police and prosecutors dug through reams of seized documents to build their case. Continuing their fruitful collaboration in pursuing Car Wash cases, the US authorities joined their Brazilian counterparts in investigating the matter.[27] The watchdog groups Global Witness in the United Kingdom and its Swiss partner Public Eye also dug into the available information and raised smart and timely questions about the trading companies' Brazilian affairs.[28] In other words, police, prosecutors, and activists took on some of the toughest problem areas identified in this book, including oil trading, national oil companies, intermediaries, and offshore financial flows. A possible cross-border corruption scheme was met with a suitably cross-border response. The companies involved will endure tough questions from their investors and home governments and will face pressure to strengthen their anticorruption controls. Indeed, in 2019, Trafigura and Glencore announced shifts away from using intermediaries to win new deals.[29] If convicted of wrongdoing, the companies and the responsible staff may face steep penalties.

Whatever the outcome of any prosecutions, the scrutiny of these oil deals represents a win in the fight against corruption. Powerful players will meet due process, and the truth looks likely to be exposed. The oil boom revealed how corruption can contaminate the world. However, the cases also showed that we know how to fight corruption. Now it's time to get to work.

APPENDIX | The scale of the oil boom in selected oil-producing countries

	Oil production		Value of oil production	Importance of oil to the national economy
Countries featured in the book	Average barrels per day (2008–2014)	Global rank	Total value of oil produced during oil boom (2008–2014), $ million	Value of oil produced as % of GDP (2008–2014)
Russia	10,482,400	2	$2,567,212	20%
United States	8,599,722	3	$2,129,892	2%
United Arab Emirates	3,238,306	7	$801,455	34%
Iraq	2,790,772	11	$691,001	55%
Nigeria	2,336,443	12	$571,608	21%
Brazil	2,119,712	13	$519,175	3%
Angola	1,751,811	15	$426,749	60%
Libya	1,229,303	19	$288,072	64%
Azerbaijan	934,739	22	$225,856	52%
Equatorial Guinea	313,430	33	$76,156	55%
Congo-Brazzaville	274,667	35	$66,850	74%
Chad	108,676	45	$26,228	32%

SOURCE: Author calculations. Production and price data is from: BP, *Annual Statistical Bulletin*, 2018. GDP data is from: World Bank, *World Development Indicators*, 2018.

NOTES

Chapter 1: The Crisis of Corruption

1. UNICEF Country Data for Nigeria, https://data.unicef.org/country/nga/; UN Population Division, *World Population Prospects 2017*, https://population.un.org/wpp/Download/Standard/Population/; World Poverty Clock, https://worldpoverty.io/.

2. Aaron Sayne, Alexandra Gillies, and Christina Katsouris, *Inside NNPC Oil Sales: A Case for Reform in Nigeria*, Natural Resource Governance Institute, August 2015.

3. US District Court for the Southern District of Texas, *Complaint, United States of America v. The M/Y Galactica Star,* No. 4:17-cv-02166 (S.D. Tex. July 14, 2017), https://www.courtlistener.com/docket/6120284/1/united-states-v-the-my-galactica-star-being-a-65-meter-motor-yacht-built/.

4. Public Prosecution Office at the Ordinary Court of Milan Proc. No. 54772/13 General Criminal Records Registry, Indictment, December 20, 2017, https://shelland-enitrial.org/wp-content/uploads/2018/06/decision-to-open-trial-20.12.2017_English.pdf; Global Witness, *Shell Knew*, Global Witness, April 10, 2017. Shell and Eni deny any wrongdoing. The trial against the two companies was ongoing as this book went to press.

5. Nigeria Economic and Financial Crimes Commission, "Diezani Alison-Madueke: What an Appetite!," August 8, 2017, https://efccnigeria.org/efcc/news/2706-diezani-alison-madueke-what-an-appetite.

6. Julia Payne and Felix Onuah, "Nigeria's Ex–oil minister Alison-Madueke Arrested In London—Sources," *Reuters*, October 2, 2015. Diezani Alison-Madueke denies wrongdoing.

7. Thomas Carothers and Christopher Carothers, "The One Thing Modern Voters Hate Most," *Foreign Policy*, July 24, 2018.

8. International Consortium of Investigative Journalists, *Panama Papers: The Power Players,* ICIJ, January 31, 2017.

9. US District Court for the Southern District of New York, *Petrobras Securities Litigation, Demand for Jury Trial*, Case No. 14-cv-9662 JSR (S.D.N.Y. July 16, 2015), 28–30, http://securities.stanford.edu/filings-documents/1053/PBSP00_01/2015716_r01c_14CV09662.pdf.

10. Edward Robinson, Hugo Miller, and Nariman Gizitdinov, "Was Trump SoHo Used to Hide Part of a Kazakh Bank's Missing Billions?" *Bloomberg,* December 11, 2017; Adam Davidson, "Donald Trump's Worst Deal," *New Yorker*, March 13, 2017.

11. Council of Europe, *Report of the Independent Investigation Body on the Allegations of Corruption within the Parliamentary Assembly*, Council of Europe, April 15, 2018.

12. World Economic Forum, "Corruption Is Costing the Global Economy $3.6 Trillion Dollars Every Year," WEF, December 31, 2018, https://www.weforum.org/agenda/2018/12/the-global-economy-loses-3-6-trillion-to-corruption-each-year-says-u-n/.

13. International Monetary Fund, *Corruption: Costs and Mitigating Strategies*, IMF *Staff Discussion Note*, IMF, 2016.

14. The Sentry, *Fueling Atrocities: Oil and War in South Sudan*, The Sentry, March 2018.

15. " '$2bn Stolen' from Anti–Boko Haram Fight," *BBC News*, November 18, 2015, https://www.bbc.com/news/world-africa-34855695.

16. Sarah Chayes, *Thieves of State* (New York: Norton, 2015).

17. International Monetary Fund, "Corruption: Costs and Mitigating Strategies," *IMF Staff Discussion Note 16/05.* IMF, May, 2016.

18. Extractive Industries Transparency Initiative, Iraq and Republic of Congo country pages, https://eiti.org/countries.

19. Silvana Tordo, *National Oil Companies and Value Creation,* World Bank, 2011.

20. Patrick Heller and David Mihalyi. *Massive and Misunderstood: Data-Driven Insights into National Oil Companies*. Natural Resource Governance Institute, April 2019.

21. Unpublished research by the Natural Resource Governance Institute

22. Simon Clark, Mia Lamar, and Bradley Hope, "The Trouble with Sovereign-Wealth Funds," *Wall Street Journal*, December 23, 2015.

23. Jeffrey Sachs and Michael Warner, "Resource Abundance and Economic Growth," National Bureau of Economic Research Working Paper Series, NBER, 1995.

24. Michael Ross, *The Oil Curse: How Petroleum Wealth Shapes the Development of Nations* (Princeton: Princeton University Press, 2013).

25. Nicholas Shaxson, *Poisoned Wells: The Dirty Politics of African Oil* (London: St. Martin's Griffin, 2008).

26. Independent Inquiry Committee into the United Nations Oil-for-Food Programme, *Manipulation of the Oil-for-Food Programme by the Iraqi Regime*, October 27, 2005, https://www.files.ethz.ch/isn/13894/ManipulationReport.pdf.

27. For more on the concept of legal corruption, see: Daniel Kaufmann and Pedro C. Vicente, "Legal Corruption," *Economics & Politics*, Vol. 23, Issue 2, pp. 195–219, 2011; and, Oguzhan C. Dincer and Michael Johnston, "Measuring Illegal and Legal Corruption in American States," Edmond J. Safra Working Papers, No. 58 (2015).

Chapter 2: "Being a Friend in a Nest of Vipers"

1. Kim Mackrael and Paul Waldie, "Griffiths Remembered as Bay Street Innovator," *Globe and Mail*, July 24, 2011.

2. Ibid.

3. Alexis Flynn, "Glencore Xstrata Buys Caracal Energy," *Wall Street Journal*, April 14, 2014.

4. Court of Queen's Bench of Alberta, *Her Majesty the Queen and Griffiths Energy International, Inc. Agreed Statement of Facts*, January 2013, https://www.millerchevalier.com/sites/default/files/resources/Spring2013_GriffithsAmendedStatmentofFacts.pdf.

5. US District Court for the District of Columbia, *Complaint, US Department of Justice v. Mahamoud Adam Bechir,* Case: 1:14-cv-01178-RJL (D.D.C. July 8, 2014), 5, https://www.justice.gov/sites/default/files/opa/press-releases/attachments/2014/11/07/bechir_complaint.pdf. See also: Court of Queen's Bench of Alberta, *Her Majesty the Queen and Griffiths Energy International, Inc. Agreed Statement of Facts*, January 2013, https://www.millerchevalier.com/sites/default/files/resources/Spring2013_GriffithsAmendedStatmentofFacts.pdf.

6. Court of Queen's Bench of Alberta, January 2013, paras. 20–22, https://www.millerchevalier.com/sites/default/files/resources/Spring2013_GriffithsAmended StatmentofFacts.pdf.

7. US District Court for the District of Columbia, *Complaint, US Department of Justice v. Mahamoud Adam Bechir,* Case: 1:14-cv-01178-RJL (D.D.C. July 8, 2014), 5, https://www.justice.gov/sites/default/files/opa/press-releases/attachments/2014/11/07/bechir_complaint.pdf., 1.

8. UK Serious Fraud Office, "SFO recovers £4.4m from Corrupt Diplomats in 'Chad Oil' Share Deal," press release, March 22, 2018; US District Court for the District of Columbia, *Complaint, US Department of Justice v. Mahamoud Adam Bechir*, Case: 1:14-cv-01178-RJL (D.D.C. July 8, 2014), https://www.justice.gov/sites/default/files/opa/press-releases/attachments/2014/11/07/bechir_complaint.pdf.

9. Flynn, "Glencore Xstrata."

10. Simon Romero and John Holusha, "Exxon Mobil Posts Largest Annual Profit for U.S. Company," *New York Times*, January 30, 2006.

11. "XOM Exxon Mobil Corp Executive Compensation," *Morningstar*, http://insiders.morningstar.com/trading/executive-compensation.action?t=XOM&region=USA&culture=en_US.

12. "Koch Family," in "2016 America's Richest Families Net Worth," *Forbes*, June 29, 2016, https://www.forbes.com/profile/koch/#67fc02aa5a5b. For more, see Jane Mayer, *Dark Money: The Hidden History of the Billionaires behind the Rise of the Radical Right* (New York: Doubleday, 2016).

13. Javier Blas, "Risky Oil Supply Deal Pays Off for Vitol," *Financial Times*, September 5, 2011.

14. US Securities and Exchange Commission, *BHP Billiton Ltd. and BHP Billiton Plc., SEC Order Instituting Cease and Desist Proceedings,* File No. 3–16546, Release No. 74998, May 20, 2015, https://www.sec.gov/litigation/admin/2015/34-74998.pdf.

15. US Securities and Exchange Commission, "SEC Charges BHP Billiton with Violating FCPA at Olympic Games," press release, May 20, 2015, https://www.sec.gov/news/pressrelease/2015-93.html.

16. Miriam Elder, "Jennifer Lopez Sparks Controversy with Show for Turkmenistan President," *Guardian*, June 30, 2013; Brian Spegele and Lukas Alpert, "Jennifer Lopez Turkmenistan Gig Shines Light on Chinese Oil Firm," *Wall Street Journal*, July 1, 2013.

17. US Securities and Exchange Commission, *Bank of New York Mellon Corporation, Respondent, SEC Order Instituting Cease and Desist Proceedings,* File No. 3-16762, Release No. 75720, August 18, 2015, https://www.sec.gov/litigation/admin/2015/34-75720.pdf.

18. Ibid., 4.

19. Simon Clark, Mia Lamar, and Bradley Hope, "The Trouble with Sovereign-Wealth Funds," *Wall Street Journal*, December 23, 2015.

20. Royal Courts of Justice, Judgement Approved in the case of *The Libyan Investment Authority v Goldman Sachs International [2016] EWHC 2530 (Ch)*, October 14, 2016, para.229, http://www.bailii.org/ew/cases/EWHC/Ch/2016/2530.html.

21. Matthew Campbell and Kit Chellel, "How Goldman Sachs Lost $1.2 Billion of Libya's Money," *Bloomberg Businessweek*, September 29, 2016.

22. Royal Courts of Justice, Judgement Approved in the case of *The Libyan Investment Authority v Goldman Sachs International [2016], EWHC 2530 (Ch)*, October 14, 2016, para. 229, http://www.bailii.org/ew/cases/EWHC/Ch/2016/2530.html.

23. Royal Courts of Justice, Judgement Approved in the case of *The Libyan Investment Authority v Goldman Sachs International [2016], EWHC 2530 (Ch)*, October 14, 2016, para. 224e, http://www.bailii.org/ew/cases/EWHC/Ch/2016/2530.html. The UK judge found that the top decision-makers at the LIA did have the capacity to understand the trades offered by Goldman, in contrast with their more junior staff who were the main beneficiaries of the trainings.

24. Jane Croft, "Goldman Sachs Bankers 'Swarmed' around Libya Fund," *Financial Times*, June 16, 2016.

25. Campbell and Chellel, "How Goldman Sachs Lost $1.2 Billion."

26. Royal Courts of Justice, Judgement Approved in the case of *The Libyan Investment Authority v Goldman Sachs International [2016], EWHC 2530 (Ch)*, October 14, 2016, para. 372, http://www.bailii.org/ew/cases/EWHC/Ch/2016/2530.html.

27. Campbell and Chellel, "How Goldman Sachs Lost $1.2 Billion." While some of the wordings vary, this account matches that of two witnesses quoted in the UK Court judgment's description of the "Stormy Meeting" in: Royal Courts of Justice, Judgement Approved in the case of *The Libyan Investment Authority v Goldman Sachs International [2016], EWHC 2530 (Ch)*, October 14, 2016, paras. 126–129, http://www.bailii.org/ew/cases/EWHC/Ch/2016/2530.html.

28. Royal Courts of Justice, Judgement Approved in the case of *The Libyan Investment Authority v Goldman Sachs International [2016], EWHC 2530 (Ch)*, October 14, 2016, http://www.bailii.org/ew/cases/EWHC/Ch/2016/2530.html.

29. Matt Levine, "Goldman's Libya Salesman Was a Little Too Good," *Bloomberg*, September 29, 2016.

30. Croft, "Goldman Sachs Bankers 'Swarmed.'"

31. Royal Courts of Justice, Judgement Approved in the case of *The Libyan Investment Authority v Goldman Sachs International [2016], EWHC 2530 (Ch)*, October 14 2016, paras. 11–12, http://www.bailii.org/ew/cases/EWHC/Ch/2016/2530.html.

32. Royal Courts of Justice, Judgement Approved in the case of *The Libyan Investment Authority v Goldman Sachs International [2016], EWHC 2530 (Ch)*, October 14 2016, paras. 235, 427–428, http://www.bailii.org/ew/cases/EWHC/Ch/2016/2530.html.

33. Jenny Anderson, "Libyan Fund Sues French Bank over $1.5 Billion in Losses on Derivatives," *New York Times DealBook*, March 31, 2014.

34. Margaret Coker, Liz Rappaport, and Noémie Bisserbe, "Libya Fund Accuses Société Générale of Fraud," *Wall Street Journal*, March 30, 2014.

35. Jill Treanor, "Société Générale to Pay £815m to Settle Libyan Lawsuit," *Guardian*, May 5, 2017.

36. US Department of Justice, "Société Générale S.A. Agrees to Pay $860 Million in Criminal Penalties for Bribing Gaddafi-Era Libyan Officials and Manipulating LIBOR

Rate," June 4, 2018, press release, https://www.justice.gov/opa/pr/soci-t-g-n-rale-sa-agrees-pay-860-million-criminal-penalties-bribing-gaddafi-era-libyan.

37. UK Serious Fraud Office, "Unaoil," page as modified on June 27, 2019, https://www.sfo.gov.uk/cases/unaoil/.

38. UK Serious Fraud Office, "Former Unaoil Executive Pleads Guilty to Conspiracy to Give Corrupt Payments," press release, July 19, 2019, https://www.sfo.gov.uk/2019/07/19/former-unaoil-executive-pleads-guilty-to-conspiracy-to-give-corrupt-payments/.

39. US District Court for the Eastern District of New York, *United States v. TechnipFMC plc, Deferred Prosecution Agreement*, Case No. 19-CR-278. (June 25, 2019), A-18, https://www.justice.gov/sites/default/files/criminal-fraud/legacy/2012/11/14/06-28-10-technip-agreement.pdf; In 2017, FMC Technologies merged with Technip to form TechnipFMC. US Department of Justice, "SBM Offshore N.V. and United States-Based Subsidiary Resolve Foreign Corrupt Practices Act Case Involving Bribes in Five Countries," press release, November 29, 2017, https://www.justice.gov/opa/pr/sbm-offshore-nv-and-united-states-based-subsidiary-resolve-foreign-corrupt-practices-act-case.

40. Rebekah Giles, "No Equity When Guilty Verdicts Are Delivered through the Media," *The Australian Business Review,* May 16, 2016.

41. The Unaoil emails quoted here are embedded in the following news stories: Nick McKenzie, Richard Baker, Michael Barchelard, and Daniel Quinlan, "Unaoil: How the West Bought Iraq," *The Age*, March 30, 2016; Jessica Schulberg, Nick Baumann, Nick McKenzie, and Richard Baker, "Unaoil Middleman Paid Millions to Influence Iraqi Officials Had U.S. Ties," *Huffington Post*, May 20, 2016.

42. In 2017, FMC Technologies merged with Technip to form TechnipFMC. US District Court for the Eastern District of New York, *United States v. TechnipFMC plc, Deferred Prosecution Agreement*, Case No. 19-CR-278. (June 25, 2019), A-18, https://www.justice.gov/sites/default/files/criminal-fraud/legacy/2012/11/14/06-28-10-technip-agreement.pdf.

43. McKenzie et al., "Unaoil: How the West Bought Iraq."

44. Ibid.

45. Richard Baker, Michael Bachelard, Daniel Quinlan, and Nick McKenzie, "The Bribe Factory: Unaoil in Africa," *The Age*, March 30, 2016.

46. UK Serious Fraud Office, "Two Charged in SFO's Unaoil Investigation," press release, November 16, 2017, https://www.sfo.gov.uk/2017/11/16/two-charged-sfos-unaoil-investigation/. The case against Unaoil was ongoing at the time this book went to press. US Department of Justice, "SBM Offshore N.V. and United States-Based Subsidiary Resolve Foreign Corrupt Practices Act Case Involving Bribes in Five Countries," press release, November 29, 2017, https://www.justice.gov/opa/pr/sbm-offshore-nv-and-united-states-based-subsidiary-resolve-foreign-corrupt-practices-act-case.

47. UK Serious Fraud Office, "Former Unaoil Executive Pleads Guilty to Conspiracy to Give Corrupt Payments," July 19, 2019, https://www.sfo.gov.uk/2019/07/19/former-unaoil-executive-pleads-guilty-to-conspiracy-to-give-corrupt-payments/.

48. US Department of Justice, "SBM Offshore N.V. and United States–Based Subsidiary Resolve Foreign Corrupt Practices Act Case."

49. US District Court for the Eastern District of New York, *United States v. TechnipFMC plc, Deferred Prosecution Agreement*, Case No. 19-CR-278. (June 25, 2019), https://www.justice.gov/sites/default/files/criminal-fraud/legacy/2012/11/14/06-

28-10-technip-agreement.pdf. In 2017, FMC Technologies merged with Technip to form TechnipFMC.

50. UK Serious Fraud Office, "Former Senior Executive Convicted in Petrofac Investigation," press release, February 7, 2019, https://www.sfo.gov.uk/2019/02/07/former-senior-executive-convicted-in-petrofac-investigation/.

51. Ministère public de la Confédératon de la Suisse, *Act d'Accusation en procedure simplifée Art. 360 CPP En la cause Prévenu: Pascal Collard* [Indictment of Pascal Collard], July 6, 2018. On file with author.

52. Global Witness, *The Riddle of the Sphynx: Where Has Congo's Oil Money Gone?*, Global Witness, December 2005.

53. Marc Guéniat and Agathe Duparc, *Gunvor in Congo*, Public Eye, September 2017; Philippe Engels and Khadija Sharife, *The Unlikely Partnership That Unlocked Congo's Crude,* Organized Crime and Corruption Reporting Project, September 7, 2018.

54. Guéniat and Duparc, *Gunvor in Congo.*

55. Ministère public de la Confédératon de la Suisse, *Act d'Accusation en procedure simplifée Art. 360 CPP En la cause Prévenu: Pascal Collard* [Indictment of Pascal Collard], July 6, 2018; Ministère public de la Confédératon de la Suisse, *Jugement du 28 août 2018 contre A., ressortissant belge*, Numéro du dossier: SK.2018.38. On file with author.

56. Ministère public de la Confédératon de la Suisse, *Act d'Accusation en procedure simplifée Art. 360 CPP En la cause Prévenu: Pascal Collard* [Indictment of Pascal Collard], July 6, 2018. See also Sylvain Besson, "Un ex-trader de Gunvor va être condamné pour corruption au Congo et en Côte d'Ivoire," *Le Temps,* August 15, 2018.

57. Ministère public de la Confédératon de la Suisse, *Jugement du 28 août 2018 contre A., ressortissant belge*, Numéro du dossier: SK.2018.38.

58. Ministère public de la Confédératon de la Suisse, *Act d'Accusation en procedure simplifée Art. 360 CPP En la cause Prévenu: Pascal Collard* [Indictment of Pascal; Collard], July 6, 2018, 6–7; translation from the original French.

59. Guéniat and Duparc, *Gunvor in Congo*, 32.

60. Ministère public de la Confédératon de la Suisse, *Act d'Accusation en procedure simplifée Art. 360 CPP En la cause Prévenu: Pascal Collard* [Indictment of Pascal Collard], July 6, 2018, 15–17.

61. Guéniat and Duparc, *Gunvor in Congo*, 27.

62. As quoted in Guéniat and Duparc, *Gunvor in Congo.*

63. Hugo Miller and Andy Hoffman, "Ex–Gunvor Oil Trader Found Guilty of Bribing African Officials," *Bloomberg*, August 28, 2018.

64. As quoted in Besson, "Un ex-trader de Gunvor va être condamné pour corruption au Congo et en Côte d'Ivoire"; translation from the original French.

65. Julia Payne and Michael Shields, "Swiss Court Approves Gunvor Ex-employee's Congo Bribery Plea Bargain," *Reuters*, August 28, 2018.

66. Tom Burgis, *The Looting Machine: Warlords, Oligarchs, Corporations, Smugglers, and the Theft of Africa's Wealth* (New York: Public Affairs, 2016).

67. "Update 1—Statoil Says Briefed Norwegian Police on Angola Payments," *Reuters*, February 19, 2016, https://www.reuters.com/article/statoil-angola/update-1-statoil-says-briefed-norwegian-police-on-angola-payments-idUSL8N15Y2EB; Tom Burgis, "US Regulator Probes Angolan Deal Involving BP and Cobalt," *Financial Times*, March 16, 2017.

68. Public Eye, *Trafigura's Business in Angola,* Public Eye, February 3, 2013.

69. Burgis, *Looting Machine.*

70. US Securities and Exchange Commission, *Halliburton Company and Jeannot Lorenz, SEC Order Instituting Cease and Desist Proceedings,* File No. 3–18080, Release No. 81222, press release, July 27, 2017, https://www.sec.gov/litigation/admin/2017/34-81222.pdf.

71. Ibid.

72. Ibid.

73. Ibid., 6.

74. Ibid., 7.

75. Ibid., 7.

76. US Securities and Exchange Commission, "Halliburton Paying $29.2 Million to Settle FCPA Violations," press release, July 27, 2017, https://www.sec.gov/news/press-release/2017-133.

77. Sarah Kent and Eric Sylvers, "Inside the Bribery Scandal Sweeping through the Oil Industry," *Wall Street Journal,* February 13, 2018; Global Witness, *Shell Knew,* Global Witness, April 10, 2017.

78. Global Witness, *Shell Knew,* 8.

79. Milan Court, Preliminary Investigations Magistrate Section, Indictment, December 20, 2017, https://shellandenitrial.org/wp-content/uploads/2018/06/decision-to-open-trial-20.12.2017_English.pdf.

80. Milan Court, Preliminary Investigations Magistrate Section, Indictment, December 20, 2017, https://shellandenitrial.org/wp-content/uploads/2018/06/decision-to-open-trial-20.12.2017_English.pdf; Kent and Sylvers, "Inside the Bribery Scandal Sweeping through the Oil Industry."

81. Milan Court, Preliminary Investigations Magistrate Section, Indictment, December 20, 2017, https://shellandenitrial.org/wp-content/uploads/2018/06/decision-to-open-trial-20.12.2017_English.pdf; Federal High Court of Nigeria, *Charges against Aliyu Abubakar et al., Charge No. CR/39/201,* December 16, 2016, https://shellandenitrial.org/wp-content/uploads/2018/08/2-Adoke-etc-Nigeria-charges-scanned-2.pdf; Global Witness, *Shell Knew.*

82. Milan Court, Preliminary Investigations Magistrate Section, Indictment, December 20, 2017, https://shellandenitrial.org/wp-content/uploads/2018/06/decision-to-open-trial-20.12.2017_English.pdf, 9.

83. High Court of Justice of England and Wales Commercial Court, *Case between Federal Republic of Nigeria (Claimant) and (1) Royal Dutch Shell PLC, et al. (Defendants),* April 8, 2019.

84. Adekunle Aliyu, "There Is Nothing New in This Fabricated Bribery Claim, Jonathan Tells FG," *Vanguard,* May 11, 2019; Musikilu Mojeed and Abdulaziz Abdulaziz, "INTERVIEW: Our Roles in the Controversial Malabu OPL 245 Saga—Ex-Minister Adoke," *Premium Times,* June 14, 2019

85. Libby George and Shadia Nasralla, "Don't Neglect to Pay the Middlemen: How Shell and Eni Ended Up on Trial," *Reuters,* May 20, 2018.

86. Federal High Court of Nigeria, *Charges against Aliyu Abubakar et al.,* Charge No. CR/39/201, December 16, 2016, https://shellandenitrial.org/wp-content/uploads/2018/08/2-Adoke-etc-Nigeria-charges-scanned-2.pdf; Federal High Court of Nigeria, *Charges against Shell Nigeria Exploration Production Company Ltd., et al.,* Charge No. CR/124/17, February 28, 2017, https://shellandenitrial.org/wp-content/uploads/2018/08/3-Adoke-etc-Nigeria-charges-scanned-3.pdf.

87. Kent and Sylvers, "Inside the Bribery Scandal Sweeping through the Oil Industry."

88. As quoted in "Safe Sex in Nigeria," *Economist*, June 15, 2013, https://www.economist.com/business/2013/06/15/safe-sex-in-nigeria.

89. All quoted Shell emails are from Global Witness, *Shell Knew*. Most were also published in: James Ball and Claudio Gatti, "Shell Shocks: How one of the world's biggest oil firms secured a $1.3 billion deal mired in corruption allegations," *BuzzFeed News*, April 9, 2017.

90. Ibid.

91. Kent and Sylvers, "Inside the Bribery Scandal Sweeping through the Oil Industry."

92. Global Witness, *Shell Knew*.

93. Ibid.

94. Milan Court, Preliminary Investigations Magistrate Section, Indictment, December 20, 2017, https://shellandenitrial.org/wp-content/uploads/2018/06/decision-to-open-trial-20.12.2017_English.pdf.

95. Brian Grow, Joshua Schneyer, and Jane Roberts, "Special Report: Chesapeake and Rival Plotted to Suppress Land Prices," *Reuters*, June 25, 2012.

96. US Department of Justice, "Former CEO Indicted for Masterminding Conspiracy Not to Compete for Oil and Natural Gas Leases," press release, March 1, 2016, https://www.justice.gov/opa/pr/former-ceo-indicted-masterminding-conspiracy-not-compete-oil-and-natural-gas-leases; Christopher Helman, "The Federal Indictment of Aubrey McClendon," *Forbes*, May 1, 2016.

97. US Department of Justice, "Former CEO Indicted for Masterminding Conspiracy."

98. Bradley Olson, Brent Kendall, and Erin Ailworth, "Ex–Chesapeake Energy CEO Aubrey McClendon Indicted on Antitrust Charges," *Wall Street Journal*, March 1, 2016.

99. Michigan Department of Attorney General, "Schuette, Creagh Announce $25 Million Civil Settlement, Two Criminal No Contest Pleas by Chesapeake Energy Corp. to Resolve Racketeering, Bid-Rigging Allegations," press release, April 24, 2015, https://www.michigan.gov/ag/0,4534,7-359-82916_81983_47203-353198--,00.html.

100. Grow et al., "Special Report."

101. Brian Grow and Joshua Schneyer, "Chesapeake Reaches $25 Million Michigan Settlement over Leasing Charges," *Reuters*, April 24, 2015. Earlier Reuters reporting on the case stated that the average price dropped from $1,413 per acre to $46; Grow et al., "Special Report."

102. Michigan Department of Attorney General, "Schuette Announces $5 Million Civil Settlement, Criminal No Contest Plea by Encana Oil & Gas USA to Resolve Bid-Rigging Allegations," 2014, https://www.michigan.gov/ag/0,4534,7-359-82916_81983_47203-327764--,00.html.

103. Michigan Department of Attorney General, "Schuette, Creagh Announce $25 Million Civil Settlement, Two Criminal No Contest Pleas by Chesapeake Energy Corp. to Resolve Racketeering, Bid-Rigging Allegations," April 24, 2015, https://www.michigan.gov/ag/0,4534,7-359-82916_81983_47203-353198--,00.html.

104. Kevin Helliker, Erin Ailworth, and Ryan Dezember, "Police Probe Finds Nothing to Suggest Aubrey McClendon Committed Suicide," *Wall Street Journal*, June 7, 2016.

105. For more about tax justice concerns, see Nicholas Shaxson, *Treasure Islands: Uncovering the Damage of Offshore Banking and Tax Havens* (London: Palgrave Macmillan, 2011); publications by the Tax Justice Network, https://www.taxjustice.net/; and Gabriel Zucman, Annette Alstadsæter, and Niels Johannesen, "Tax Evasion and Inequality," *American Economic Review,* 2019, 109(6): 2073-2103.

106. "Update 1—Norway Indicts Transocean over Alleged Tax Fraud," *Reuters*, June 22, 2011, https://www.reuters.com/article/transocean-fraud/update-1-norway-indicts-transocean-over-alleged-tax-fraud-idUSN1E75L14B20110622; Norway Public Prosecutors' Office, *Okokrim Indictment Sheet,* Case No. 51/05, June 20, 2011, http://www.internationaltaxreview.com/pdfs/indictment-sheet.pdf.

107. Norway Public Prosecutors' Office, *Okokrim Indictment Sheet*, Case No. 51/05, June 20, 2011, http://www.internationaltaxreview.com/pdfs/indictment-sheet.pdf.

108. Peter Wells, "Chevron Loses Landmark Tax Case on Transfer Pricing," *Financial Times*, April 21, 2017.

109. "Chevron Settles Australian Transfer Pricing Dispute with ATO," NASDAQ.com, August 21, 2017, https://www.nasdaq.com/article/chevron-settles-australian-transfer-pricing-dispute-with-ato-cm834650.

110. Australian Broadcasting Corporation, "Chevron's Taxation Reports—7.30 Report ABC2" (video), ChevronTax.Info, http://www.chevrontax.info/australia/.

111. Publish What You Pay—Norway, *Piping Profits,* Publish What You Pay—Norway, 2015.

112. Deloitte, *Deconstructing the Chevron Transfer Pricing Case,* November 3, 2015, https://www2.deloitte.com/au/en/pages/tax/articles/deconstructing-chevron-case.html.

113. Wells, "Chevron Loses."

114. Oxfam Australia, *The Hidden Billions: How Tax Havens Impact Lives at Home and Abroad*, Oxfam Research Reports, June 2016, https://www.oxfam.org.au/wp-content/uploads/2016/06/OXF003-Tax-Havens-Report-FA-WEB.pdf.

115. Global Witness, *Take the Future—Shell's Scandalous Deal for Nigeria's Oil*, Global Witness, November 2018.

Chapter 3: Corruption and the Competition for Power

1. US District Court for the Southern District of Texas, *Complaint, United States of America v. The M/Y Galactica Star,* No. 4:17-cv-02166 (S.D. Tex. July 14, 2017), https://www.courtlistener.com/docket/6120284/1/united-states-v-the-my-galactica-star-being-a-65-meter-motor-yacht-built/; Crown Court at Southwark, *Restraint Order Prohibiting Disposal of Assets To: (1) Diezanni [sic] Kogbeni Alison Madueke, (2) Benedict Peters, et al.,* September 3, 2016, on file with author.

2. US District Court for the Southern District of Texas, *Complaint, United States of America v. The M/Y Galactica Star,* No. 4:17-cv-02166 (S.D. Tex. July 14, 2017).

3. Ibid.

4. Patrick Heller and David Mihalyi. *Massive and Misunderstood: Data-Driven Insights into National Oil Companies.* Natural Resource Governance Institute, April 2019; Silvana Tordo, *National Oil Companies and Value Creation,* World Bank, 2011.

5. "Jail Term for Nigeria Ex-Governor," *BBC News*, July 26, 2007.

6. Olly Owen and Zainab Usman, "Briefing: Why Goodluck Jonathan Lost the Nigerian Presidential Election of 2015," *African Affairs* 114, no. 456 (July 1, 2015): 455–471.

7. BP, *Statistical Review of World Energy*, June 2018.

8. The calculation includes only leaders who held power for more than three months.

9. Oil and Gas Implementation Committee, *Oil and Gas Sector Reforms Implementation Committee Final Report* (Abuja: Federal Government of Nigeria, 2008).

10. Daniel Adugbo, "Nigeria: 20 Months after Inauguration—NNPC Board Fails to Meet," *Daily Trust*, April 14, 2014, https://allafrica.com/stories/201404141998.html.

11. Bassey Udo, "Exclusive: How Alison-Madueke's Management Style Is Killing Nigeria's Oil Industry," *Premium Times*, August 1, 2014.

12. Ibid.

13. Aaron Sayne, Alexandra Gillies, and Christina Katsouris, *Inside NNPC Oil Sales: A Case for Reform in Nigeria*, Natural Resources Governance Institute, August 2015, 163.

14. PriceWaterhouseCooper, *Investigative Forensic Audit into the Allegations of Unremitted Funds into the Federation Accounts by the NNPC*, February 2015, 16.

15. Sayne, Gillies, and Katsouris, *Inside NNPC Oil Sales*, annex B, 11.

16. Ibid.

17. Aaron Sayne led this project and undertook this groundbreaking analytical work. The findings and much more detail on NNPC's oil sale problems can be found in Sayne, Gillies, and Katsouris, *Inside NNPC Oil Sales*.

18. Ibid., annex B, B46.

19. Prior to receiving the huge oil block in 2014, Aiteo had not participated in exploration and production activities. Margot Gibbs and Musikilu Mojeed, "Exclusive: Another Nigerian Oil Mogul Named in Ex-minister Alison-Madueke's Alleged Corruption, UK Property Frozen," *Premium Times*, August 16, 2017.

20. Onyedimmakachukwu Obiukwu, "Nigeria's Four Newest Billionaires," *Ventures Africa*, November 12, 2014.

21. "Nwosu, Ex-INEC Staff, Convicted over Diezani's Bribe," *Vanguard*, January 24, 2019.

22. Nigeria Economic and Financial Crimes Commission, "Diezani N264.8m Bribe: Two INEC Staff Bag 91 Years Jail Term," EFCC, January 26, 2019, http://efccnigeria.org/efcc/news/3682-diezani-n264-8m-bribe-two-inec-staff-bag-91-years-jail-term.

23. "Wanted: Benedict Peters," Nigeria Economic and Financial Crimes Commission, https://efccnigeria.org/efcc/wanted/2436-benedict-peters; "N23bn Diezani Bribe: EFCC Declares Billionaire Businessman Wanted," *Punch*, August 16, 2016; "EFCC Declares Ex- minister's Ally Wanted over $60m Bribe," *Pulse*, August 16, 2016; Bukola Idowu and Tony Amokeodo, "Diezani: Fidelity Bank MD Returns N40m to EFCC," *Leadership*, April 29, 2016.

24. "Wanted: Benedict Peters," Nigeria Economic and Financial Crimes Commission.

25. "EFCC Removes Benedict Peters' Name from Wanted Persons List," *Vanguard*, November 7, 2018.

26. US District Court for the Southern District of Texas, *Complaint, United States of America v. The M/Y Galactica Star*, No. 4:17-cv-02166 (S.D. Tex. July 14, 2017), 16, https://www.courtlistener.com/docket/6120284/1/united-states-v-the-my-galactica-star-being-a-65-meter-motor-yacht-built/.

27. Ibid., 23–24.

28. Gibbs and Mojeed, "Exclusive: Another Nigerian Oil Mogul Named"; Margot Gibbs, "Exclusive: Noose Tightens around Alison-Madueke in UK, 18 Million Property Uncovered," *Premium Times*, August 27, 2018.

29. Crown Court at Southwark, *Restraint Order Prohibiting Disposal of Assets To: (1) Diezanni [sic] Kogbeni Alison Madueke, (2) Benedict Peters, et al.*, September 3, 2016. On file with author.

30. Alex Enumah, "Court Orders EFCC to Release Seized London Properties of Aiteo Boss," *This Day*, July 7, 2018.

31. Oluseyl Awojulugbe, "Aiteo: We Were Major Players Long before Diezani....It's Ridiculous to Say We Bribed Her," *Cable*, September 12, 2017; "Benedict Peters, Aiteo Executive Vice Chairman, Assembles Legal Team to Address Unfounded Allegations," *Globe Newswire*, October 27, 2017, http://globenewswire.com/news-release/2017/10/27/1159533/0/en/Benedict-Peters-Aiteo-Executive-Vice-Chairman-Assembles-Legal-Team-to-Address-Unfounded-Allegations.html.

32. The oil blocks in question used to be operated by Shell, in a joint venture with NNPC, and were sold by Shell alongside the block that was purchased by Aiteo. After the sale, NNPC asserted its right to take on the operatorship role.

33. Several subsidiaries of Atlantic Energy participated in the various deals, all of which are related and owned by the same two men. I refer to them all as Atlantic. The precise company names can be found in US District Court for the Southern District of Texas, *Complaint, United States of America v. The M/Y Galactica Star*, No. 4:17-cv-02166 (S.D. Tex. July 14, 2017), 10, https://www.courtlistener.com/docket/6120284/1/united-states-v-the-my-galactica-star-being-a-65-meter-motor-yacht-built/.

34. Sayne, Gillies, and Katsouris, *Inside NNPC Oil Sales*, 41; Sanusi Lamido Sanusi, *Memorandum Submitted to the Senate Committee on Finance on the Non-Remittance of the Oil Revenue to the Federation Account*, February 3, 2014, 11. On file with author.; Toyin Akinosho, "Looking beyond the Diezani Tenure," *Africa Oil and Gas Report*, January 29, 2015.

35. US District Court for the Southern District of Texas, *Complaint, United States of America v. The M/Y Galactica Star*, No. 4:17-cv-02166 (S.D. Tex. July 14, 2017), https://www.courtlistener.com/docket/6120284/1/united-states-v-the-my-galactica-star-being-a-65-meter-motor-yacht-built/.

36. Ibid.

37. Ibid.; Federal High Court of Nigeria, *Federal Republic of Nigeria & 2 Ors v. Atlantic Energy Drilling Concepts Nig. Ltd & 3 Ors—Motion for Mareva Orders*, 2016, http://saharareporters.com/sites/default/files/FRN%20V%20ATLANTIC%20ENERGY%20-%20APPLICATION%20FOR%20MAREVA%20ORDER%20(EDITED).pdf.

38. Ibid., 28.

39. US District Court for the Southern District of Texas, *Complaint, United States of America v. The M/Y Galactica Star*, No. 4:17-cv-02166 (S.D. Tex. July 14, 2017), https://www.courtlistener.com/docket/6120284/1/united-states-v-the-my-galactica-star-being-a-65-meter-motor-yacht-built/. This investigation paused in 2018 when the United States filed a motion for a partial stay in order to proceed instead with a criminal investigation into this matter. US District Court for the Southern District of Texas Houston

Division, *US' Motion for Partial Stay under 18 USC 981(g)(1) in USA, Plaintiff, v. The M/Y Galactica Star*, March 9, 2018.

40. US District Court for the Southern District of Texas, *Complaint, United States of America v. The M/Y Galactica Star*; "Beyonce and Jay Z 's $900,000-a-Week Yacht the Galactica Star," *Daily Mail*, October 10, 2016, https://www.dailymail.co.uk/video/tvshowbiz/video-1214889/Beyonce-Jay-Z-s-900-000-week-yacht-Galactica-Star.html.

41. US District Court for the Southern District of Texas, *Complaint, United States of America v. The M/Y Galactica Star*, No. 4:17-cv-02166 (S.D. Tex. July 14, 2017), https://www.courtlistener.com/docket/6120284/1/united-states-v-the-my-galactica-star-being-a-65-meter-motor-yacht-built/.

42. US District Court for the Southern District of Texas, *Complaint, United States of America v. The M/Y Galactica Star*, No. 4:17-cv-02166 (S.D. Tex. July 14, 2017), 25, https://www.courtlistener.com/docket/6120284/1/united-states-v-the-my-galactica-star-being-a-65-meter-motor-yacht-built/.

43. Ibid., 14.

44. Ibid., 28–29.

45. Ibid.

46. Nigeria Economic and Financial Crimes Commission, "Diezani Alison-Madueke: What an Appetite!," EFCC, August 8, 2017, https://efccnigeria.org/efcc/news/2706-diezani-alison-madueke-what-an-appetite.

47. Ben Ezeamalu, "419 Bangles, 315 Rings, 304 Earrings, 189 Wristwatches among 'Diezani Jewellery'Forfeited to Nigerian Govt," *Premium Times*, July 5, 2019.

48. Nigeria Economic and Financial Crimes Commission, "Court Orders Final Forfeiture of Diezani's 56 Houses," EFCC, October 11, 2017, http://efccnigeria.org/efcc/news/2810-court-orders-final-forfeiture-of-diezani-s-56-houses-2.

49. Omokore's lawyers had issued the most elaborated denials of the three, at the time this book went to press. See, for example: Johnbosco Agbakwuru, "Jide Omokore Did Not Steal $3bn—Lawyers," *Vanguard*, May 8, 2018.

50. "Factbox: Nigeria's $6.8 Billion Fuel Subsidy Scam," *Reuters*, May 13, 2012, https://www.reuters.com/article/us-nigeria-subsidy-graft-idUSBRE84C08N20120513.

51. Ibid.

52. Milan Court, Preliminary Investigations Magistrate Section, Indictment, December 20, 2017, https://shellandenitrial.org/milan-trial-documents/; Global Witness, *Shell Knew*, Global Witness, April 10, 2017; ; High Court of Justice of England and Wales Commercial Court, *Case between Federal Republic of Nigeria (Claimant) and (1) Royal Dutch Shell PLC, et al. (Defendants)*, April 8, 2019; Sarah Kent and Eric Sylvers, "Inside the Bribery Scandal Sweeping through the Oil Industry," *Wall Street Journal*, February 13, 2018.

53. For more information on oil theft in Nigeria, see Christina Katsouris and Aaron Sayne, *Nigeria's Criminal Crude: International Options to Combat the Export of Stolen Oil*, Royal Institute for International Affairs, September 19, 2013.

54. Crown Court at Southwark, *Regina v. Rolls-Royce PLC, Statement of Facts (DPA)*, January 17, 2017. https://www.sfo.gov.uk/cases/rolls-royce-plc/.

55. Sylvain Besson, "Addax a écarté ses lanceurs d'alerte avant de sombrer," *Le Temps*, November 21, 2017.

"Addax to Pay 31 Million Swiss Francs to Settle Swiss Bribery Charges," *Reuters*, July 5, 2017; Deloitte LLP, "Statement of Circumstance Relating to the Resignation of Deloitte LLP as Auditors to Addax Petroleum UK Limited," statement to Companies House, December 14, 2016, https://beta.companieshouse.gov.uk/company/08135892/filing-history/MzE2ODc5NjYyNmFkaXF6a2N4/document?format=pdf&download=0.

56. "Addax to Pay 31 Million Swiss Francs to Settle Swiss Bribery Charges," *Reuters*, June 5, 2017, https://uk.reuters.com/article/uk-swiss-addax/addax-to-pay-31-million-swiss-francs-to-settle-swiss-bribery-charges-idUKKBN19Q1OD.

57. Owen and Usman, "Briefing," 455–471.

58. "Six Years of Waste: How Niger Delta Ministry Blew N800b between 2009 and 2015," *SaharaReporters*, August 23, 2016, http://saharareporters.com/2016/08/23/six-years-waste-how-niger-delta-ministry-blew-n800b-between-2009-and-2015.

59. Isiaka Wakili, "'Failed' East-West Road Gulps N300bn," *Daily Trust,* December 14, 2017; Sanit Tukur, "Ex-minister, Godsday Orubebe, Who Almost Derailed 2015 Election, to Face Trial for Corruption," *Premium Times*, October 31, 2015; Fredrick Nwabufo, "Orubebe to Face Corruption Charges over N53.3bn East-West Road," *Cable*, August 4, 2016. Orubebe was charged with diverting public funds, but just before the trial commenced, the prosecution terminated the case. He was found guilty by a Code of Conduct Tribunal of falsely declaring his assets.

60. "Godsday Orubebe Disrupts INEC Result Announcement," *TV 360 Nigeria*, posted to YouTube on March 31, 2015, https://www.youtube.com/watch?v=ha7OXpLUJ6w.

61. Ed Cropley and Tim Cocks, "Exclusive—How Nigeria's 'Smooth' Election Nearly Went Wrong," *Reuters*, April 16, 2015.

62. "INEC Staff Convicted for Receiving Share of N23 Billion Diezani Bribe," *Premium Times*, May 3, 2017, https://www.premiumtimesng.com/news/more-news/230293-inec-staff-convicted-receiving-share-n23-billion-diezani-bribe.html; "Nwosu, Ex–INEC staff, Convicted over Diezani's Bribe."

63. "Petrobras Scandal Revelations Rock Brazilian Elections," *Petroleum World*, October 23, 2014, http://www.petroleumworld.com/storyt14102301.htm.

64. David Segal, "Petrobras Oil Scandal Leaves Brazilians Lamenting a Lost Dream," *New York Times*, August 7, 2015.

65. US District Court of Southern New York, *Petrobras Securities Litigation, Demand for Jury Trial, Consolidated Amended Complaint,* Case No. 14-cv-9662 JSR (S.D.N.Y. July 16, 2015), 21, http://securities.stanford.edu/filings-documents/1053/PBSP00_01/2015716_r01c_14CV09662.pdf. This account aligns with the more general description contained in the nonprosecution agreement between the US government and Petrobras. US Department of Justice, *Non-Prosecution Agreement with Petrobras*, September 26, 2018, https://www.justice.gov/opa/press-release/file/1096706/download.

66. US District Court of Southern New York, *Petrobras Securities Litigation, Demand for Jury Trial, Consolidated Amended Complaint,* Case No. 14-cv-9662 JSR (S.D.N.Y. July 16, 2015), 21, http://securities.stanford.edu/filings-documents/1053/PBSP00_01/2015716_r01c_14CV09662.pdf., 15–16; Simon Romero, "Scandal over Brazilian Oil Company Adds Turmoil to the Presidential Race," *New York Times*, October 19, 2014.

67. Juan Pablo Spinetto and Sabrina Valle, "Brazil Fixated as 'Human Bomb' Revelations Rock Elections," *Bloomberg*, October 20, 2014.

68. Ryan Lloyd and Carlos Oliveira, "How Brazil's Electoral System Led the Country into Political Crisis," *Washington Post*, May 25, 2016.

69. Geert Aalbers and Nick Panes, "Mexico, the Next Brazil?," *Foreign Affairs*, October 7, 2015.

70. Sue Branford, "BNDES Has Long History of Loans to Gigantic Construction Companies," *Mongabay Environmental News*, March 14, 2016.

71. "BNDES: Lender of First Resort for Brazil's Tycoons," *Financial Times*, January 11, 2015, https://www.ft.com/content/c510368e-968e-11e4-922f-00144feabdc0.

72. Eliane Oliveira, Danielle Nogueira, and Ruben Berta, "BNDES: Divulgação de contratos mostra que Odebrecht ficou com 70% do crédito para obras no exterior," *O Globo*, June 3, 2015.

73. Branford, "BNDES Has Long History of Loans."

74. Alex Cuadros, *Brazillionaires: Wealth, Power, Decadence, and Hope in an American Country* (London: Profile Books, 2016), 238.

75. Sue Branford, "Follow the Money," Latin American Bureau, July 1, 2014.

76. Cuadros, *Brazillionaires*, 50.

77. Lise Alves, "Odebrecht Confirms Illegal Donations to Brazil's Rousseff-Temer Campaign," *Rio Times*, March 2, 2017; "Jailed Brazilian Executive to Testify He Oversaw Illegal Donations for Rousseff," *Guardian*, June 21, 2016.

78. Cuadros, *Brazillionaires*, 270.

79. Ibid., 29.

80. There's debate among economists about how much credit Lula deserves for this economic growth. He implemented orthodox fiscal and monetary policies, including controlling public spending. This created a stable platform on which the economy could grow and controlled against the kind of inflation that had plagued Brazil in the past. He and his team skillfully navigated the choppy waters of the global financial crisis, and Brazil was spared its worst effects. But the commodity boom, driven by demand for Brazil's tremendous natural resources from China and beyond, was the boom's engine. For more, see Sergio Fausto, *The Lengthy Brazilian Crisis Is Not Yet Over*, Baker Institute for Public Policy, February 17, 2017.

81. Revenue Watch Institute, *2013 Resource Governance Index,* 2013, https://resourcegovernance.org/sites/default/files/documents/rgi-2013.pdf.

82. US District Court for the Eastern District of New York, *United States v. Odebrecht S.A., Plea Agreement*, No. 16-643 RJD (E.D.N.Y., 2016), B7, https://www.justice.gov/opa/press-release/file/919916/download.

83. Ibid., B10.

84. Ibid., B11.

85. Ibid., B15.

86. Fernando Migliaccio da Silva, "Jailed Odebrecht Executive Key Player in Panama Laundering," *Newsroom Panama*, May 26, 2016; US District Court for the Eastern District of New York, *United States v. Odebrecht S.A Plea Agreement*, No. 16-643 RJD (E.D.N.Y., 2016), B13, https://www.justice.gov/opa/press-release/file/919916/download.

87. US District Court for the Eastern District of New York, *United States v. Odebrecht S.A. Plea Agreement*, No. 16-643 RJD (E.D.N.Y., 2016), B12, https://www.justice.gov/opa/press-release/file/919916/download.

88. US District Court for the Southern District of New York, *Petrobras Securities Litigation, Demand for Jury Trial, Consolidated Amended Complaint,* Case No. 14-cv-9662 JSR (S.D.N.Y. July 16, 2015), 28–30, http://securities.stanford.edu/filings-documents/1053/PBSP00_01/2015716_r01c_14CV09662.pdf, 28–31.

89. US Department of Justice, *Non-prosecution Agreement with Petrobras,* September 26, 2018, A5–A6, https://www.justice.gov/opa/press-release/file/1096706/download.

90. US District Court for the Southern District of New York, Petrobras Securities Litigation, Demand for Jury Trial, *Consolidated Amended Complaint,* Case No. 14-cv-9662 JSR (S.D.N.Y. July 16, 2015), 28–30, http://securities.stanford.edu/filings-documents/1053/PBSP00_01/2015716_r01c_14CV09662.pdf, 28–31.

91. Ibid.

92. US Department of Justice, *Non-prosecution Agreement with Petrobras,* September 26, 2018, A7, https://www.justice.gov/opa/press-release/file/1096706/download.

93. Sergio Fausto, *The Lengthy Brazilian Crisis Is Not Yet Over.*

94. US Department of Justice, *Non-prosecution Agreement with Petrobras,* September 26, 2018, A5–A7, https://www.justice.gov/opa/press-release/file/1096706/download.

95. US District Court for the Eastern District of New York, *USA against Braskem SA, Plea Agreement* (Cr. No. 16-644(RJD)), December 21, 2016, B8–B9, https://www.justice.gov/opa/press-release/file/919906/download.

96. Ibid.

97. US District Court for the Eastern District of New York, *USA against Braskem SA, Plea Agreement* (Cr. No. 16-644(RJD)), December 21, 2016, B16, https://www.justice.gov/opa/press-release/file/919906/download.

98. US District Court for the District of Columbia, *Complaint, Securities and Exchange Commission v. Braskem, S.A.,* No. 1:16-cv-02488 (D.D.C. December 21, 2016), 2–10.

99. US District Court for the Southern District of Texas, *United States v. SBM Offshore N.V., Deferred Prosecution Agreement,* Criminal No. 17–686. (S.D. Tex, November 29, 2017), https://www.justice.gov/opa/press-release/file/1014801/download.

100. US District Court for the Southern District of New York, *Petrobras Securities Litigation, Demand for Jury Trial, Consolidated Amended Complaint.* Case No. 14-cv-9662 JSR (S.D.N.Y. July 16, 2015), 23, http://securities.stanford.edu/filings-documents/1053/PBSP00_01/2015716_r01c_14CV09662.pdf. SBM Offshore and Petrobras have not, that I am aware of, confirmed or denied this version of events.

101. Ibid.

102. US District Court for the Eastern District of New York, *United States v. Odebrecht S.A. Plea Agreement,* No. 16-643 RJD (E.D.N.Y., 2016), B23, https://www.justice.gov/opa/press-release/file/919916/download.

103. Will Connors and Luciana Magalhaes, "How Brazil's 'Nine Horsemen' Cracked a Bribery Scandal," *Wall Street Journal,* April 6, 2015.

104. Ibid.

105. "Eike Batista: Brazilian Ex-billionaire Jailed for Bribery," *BBC News,* July 3, 2018.

106. US Department of Justice, "Petróleo Brasileiro S.A.—Petrobras Agrees to Pay More Than $850 Million for FCPA Violations," press release, September 27, 2018, https://www.justice.gov/opa/pr/petr-leo-brasileiro-sa-petrobras-agrees-pay-more-850-million-fcpa-violations.

107. US Department of Justice, "Odebrecht and Braskem Plead Guilty and Agree to Pay at Least $3.5 Billion in Global Penalties to Resolve Largest Foreign Bribery Case in History," press release, December 21, 2016, https://www.justice.gov/opa/pr/odebrecht-and-braskem-plead-guilty-and-agree-pay-least-35-billion-global-penalties-resolve; Richard Cassin, "DOJ Reduces Odebrecht Penalties, We Revise the Top Ten List," FCPA Blog, April 14, 2017.

108. Gibson Dunn, *2018 Year-End FCPA Update*, January 7, 2019, https://www.gibsondunn.com/2018-year-end-fcpa-update/.

109. "Brazil's President Michel Temer Denies Hush Money Claim," *BBC News*, May 18, 2017.

110. Ibid. The case against Temer was ongoing when this book went to press.

111. Alex Cuadros, "The Most Important Criminal Conviction in Brazil's History," *New Yorker*, July 13, 2017. In 2019, a court extended Lula's sentence.

112. Glenn Greenwald and Victor Pougy, "Exclusive: Brazil's Top Prosecutors Who Indicted Lula Schemed in Secret Messages to Prevent His Party From Winning 2018 Election," *The Intercept*, June 9, 2019.

113. BP, *Statistical Review of World Energy*, June 2018.

114. "Crude Oil Production," Petroleum and Other Liquids, US Energy Information Administration, https://www.eia.gov/dnav/pet/pet_crd_crpdn_adc_mbblpd_a.htm.

115. Eric Lipton, "Energy Firms in Secretive Alliance with Attorney General," *New York Times,* December 6, 2014.

116. Alex Guillén and Esther Whieldon, "Energy Executives, Secretive Nonprofit Raise Money to Back Pruitt," *Politico*, January 6, 2017.

117. Tom DiChristopher, "Scott Pruitt Is Great Pick to Lead EPA, Says Pruitt Ally Harold Hamm," *CNBC*, December 8, 2016.

118. Paul Sahre, "Scott Pruitt's Dirty Politics," *New Yorker*, April 2, 2018.

119. Miranda Green and Timothy Cama, "GAO: EPA Violated Law with Pruitt's Soundproof Booth," *The Hill*, April 16, 2018; Lisa Friedman, "The Investigations That Led to Scott Pruitt's Resignation," *New York Times*, July 13, 2018; Liam Stack, "Scott Pruitt's Wish List: Private Jets, Fancy Furniture, 24-Hour Security," *New York Times*, October 22, 2018.

120. Nick Schwellenbach, *Meet the Oil-Friendly Federal Panel That Could Give Drillers a Sweetheart Deal,* Project on Government Oversight, February 27, 2018; Texans for Public Justice, Public Citizen's Texas Office and the Sierra Club, *Running on Hydrocarbons: Oil and Gas Funding to Every Texas Lawmaker,* Texans for Public Justice, Public Citizen's Texas Office and the Sierra Club, May 2017; http://info.tpj.org/reports/LawmakerHydrocarbons.pdf.

121. Schwellenbach, *Meet the Oil-Friendly Federal Panel.*

122. "Oil & Gas: Long-Term Contribution Trends," OpenSecrets, https://www.opensecrets.org/industries/totals.php?cycle=2016&ind=E01.

123. Jane Mayer, *Dark Money: The Hidden History of the Billionaires behind the Rise of the Radical Right* (New York: Doubleday, 2016), 205.

124. "Lobbying: Oil & Gas Industry Profile: 2015," OpenSecrets, https://www.opensecrets.org/lobby/indusclient.php?id=E01&year=2015.

125. Kimberly Kindy and Dan Eggen, "Three of Every Four Oil and Gas Lobbyists Worked for Federal Government," *Washington Post*, July 22, 2010.

126. Mayer, *Dark Money*, 208–210.

127. Hiroko Tabuchi, "The Oil Industry's Covert Campaign to Rewrite American Car Emissions Rules," *New York Times*, December 13, 2018.

128. Charlie Savage, "Sex, Drug Use and Graft Cited in Interior Department," *New York Times*, September 10, 2008; "Second Interior Official Pleads Guilty in Sex, Drugs and Oil Scandal," *ProPublica*, September 18, 2008, https://www.propublica.org/article/second-interior-official-pleads-guilty-in-sex-drugs-and-oil-scandal-918.

129. US Government Accountability Office, *The Federal System for Collecting Oil and Gas Revenues Needs Comprehensive Reassessment*, Report to Congressional Requesters, September 2008, https://www.gao.gov/new.items/d08691.pdf; US Government Accountability Office, *Mineral Revenues: Data Management Problems and Reliance on Self Reported Data for Compliance Efforts Put MMS Royalty Collections at Risk,* September 12, 2008, https://www.gao.gov/new.items/d08893r.pdf.

130. Adam Rose, "Deepwater Horizon Inspections: MMS Skipped Monthly Inspections on Doomed Rig," *Huffington Post*, May 17, 2010.

131. US Government Accountability Office, *U.S. Environmental Protection Agency—Installation of Soundproof Privacy Booth,* April 16, 2018, https://www.gao.gov/products/B-329603#mt=e-report.

132. US Agency for International Development, *Agency Financial Report*, 2016, 29, https://www.usaid.gov/sites/default/files/documents/1868/USAIDFY2016_AFR_508.pdf.

133. Samantha Pearson, "Brazil, Widening the Hunt for Corruption, Finds It under Every Rock," *Wall Street Journal*, March 7, 2017; Cuadros, *Brazillionaires*, 274.

Chapter 4: The Kleptocracy Kings

1. Christina Vuleta, "The World's Most Powerful Women 2018," *Forbes*, December 4, 2018.

2. Norimitsu Onishi, "Portugal Dominated Angola for Centuries. Now the Roles Are Reversed," *New York Times*, August 22, 2017.

3. "Shareholder Structure," NOS, no date provided, http://www.nos.pt/institucional/EN/investors/bonds-and-shares/Pages/shareholder-structure.aspx.

4. Kerry Dolan, "Daddy's Girl: How an African 'Princess' Banked $3 Billion in a Country Living on $2 a Day," *Forbes*, September 2, 2013.

5. Ibid.

6. "Graft Probe Launched against Dos Santos' Daughter," *eNews Channel Africa*, December 20, 2017, https://www.enca.com/africa/angola-oil-giant-probes-isabel-dos-santos-graft-claims.

7. David Pegg, "Angola Sovereign Wealth Fund's Manager Used Its Cash for His Own Projects," *Guardian*, November 7, 2017; Anna Meisel and David Grossman, "Tycoon Made $41m from 'People's Fund,'" *BBC News*, November 7, 2017.

8. Meisel and Grossman, "Tycoon Made $41m from 'People's Fund.'"

9. Ibid.

10. Stephen Eisenhammer, "Alleged Angolan Fraud Scheme Aimed to Take $1.5 Billion—Finance Ministry," *Reuters*, April 9, 2018.

11. Margot Patrick, Gabriele Steinhauser, and Patricia Kowsmann, "The $500 Million Central Bank Heist—and How It Was Foiled," *Wall Street Journal*, October 3, 2018.

12. Ibid.

13. Ibid.

14. Candido Mendes, "Angola Says it Recovers $3.35 Billion of Assets from Quantum," *Bloomberg*, March 23, 2019; Quantum Global, "Quantum Global Group Announces Closure of Investigation by the Swiss Attorney General," press release, July 4, 2019, http://quantumglobalgroup.com/article/quantum-global-group-announces-closure-investigation-swiss-attorney-general/.

15. Daron Acemoglu, James Robinson, and Thierry Verdier, *Kleptocracy and Divide-and-Rule: A Model of Personal Rule,* NBER working paper no. 10136, National Bureau of Economic Research, December 2013, 1. For more on the meaning of "kleptocracy": Oliver Bullough traces the term's origins in "The Dark Side of Globalization," *Journal of Democracy* 29, no. 1 (2018): 25–38, including its first modern use by Stanislav Andreski in *Parasitism and Subversion: The Case of Latin America* (New York: Pantheon, 1966). Other useful sources include Simon Fan, "Kleptocracy and Corruption," *Journal of Comparative Economics* 34, no. 1 (March 2006): 57–74; Patricia Gloster-Coates and Linda Quest, "Kleptocracy: Curse of Development," *International Social Science Review* 80, nos. 1/2 (2005): 3–19; Anna Grzymala-Busse, "Beyond Clientelism: Incumbent State Capture and State Formation," *Comparative Political Studies* 45, nos. 4–5 (2008): 644; K. J. Holsti, "War, Peace, and the State of the State," *International Political Science Review* 16, no. 4 (October 1995): 319–339; and Tina Søreide, *Drivers of Corruption: A Brief Review* (Washington DC: World Bank, 2014).

16. Michael Ross, *The Oil Curse: How Petroleum Wealth Shapes the Development of Nations* (Princeton: Princeton University Press, 2013); Ricardo Soares de Oliveira, *Oil and Politics in the Gulf of Guinea* (New York: Columbia University Press, 2007); Douglas Yates, *The Rentier State in Africa: Oil Rent Dependency and Neocolonialism in the Republic of Gabon* (Trenton, NJ: Africa World Press, 1996); Terry Karl, *The Paradox of Plenty: Oil Booms and Petro-states* (Berkeley: University of California Press, 1997).

17. Ross, *The Oil Curse*, 75–76.

18. Steffen Hertog, *Rent Distribution, Labour Markets and Development in High Rent Countries,* LSE Kuwait Programme Paper Series 40 (LSE Kuwait Programme, 2016), 12.

19. Steffen Hertog, "Challenges to the Saudi Distributional State in the Age of Austerity," paper presented at *Saudi Arabia: Domestic, Regional and International Challenges*, Middle East Institute, National University of Singapore, December 2016, 9.

20. Angelique Chrisafis, "Son of Equatorial Guinea's President Is Convicted of Corruption in France,'" *Guardian*, October 27, 2017.

21. See, for instance, Soares de Oliveira, *Oil and Politics in the Gulf of Guinea*; Nicholas Shaxson, *Poisoned Wells: The Dirty Politics of African Oil* (London: St. Martin's Griffin, 2008); Brett Carter, "The Rise of Kleptocracy: Autocrats versus Activists in Africa," *Journal of Democracy* 29, 1 (January 2018): 54-68; Alex de Waal,

"When Kleptocracy Becomes Insolvent: Brute Causes of the Civil War in South Sudan," *African Affairs* 113, no. 452 (July 2014): 347–369.

22. "World Bank Open Data," World Bank, https://data.worldbank.org/; "Natural Resource Revenue Dataset," Natural Resource Governance Institute, https://www.re-sourcedata.org/dataset/natural-resource-revenue-dataset.

23. "Russia: Overview," U.S. Energy Information Association, October 31, 2017, https://www.eia.gov/beta/international/analysis.php?iso=RUS.

24. For much more on Putin's inner circle and his rise to power, see Karen Dawisha, *Putin's Kleptocracy: Who Owns Russia?* (New York: Simon and Schuster, 2014).

25. Rosneft 2013 Annual Report, https://www.rosneft.com/upload/site2/document_file/0x6IQABSaM.pdf.

26. "Sechin as Energy Czar: More Powerful, More Vulnerable," WikiLeaks Public Library of U.S. Diplomacy, September 17, 2008, https://wikileaks.org/plusd/cables/08MOSCOW2802_a.html.

27. Stephanie Baker, "BP's Dudley Relives Russian Nightmare alongside Rosneft Boss," *Bloomberg*, December 18, 2014.

28. "Yukos Completes Merger with Smaller Rival Sibneft," *Wall Street Journal*, October 3, 2003; Guy Chazan, "Yukos Trims Oil-Output Forecast as Tax Fight Thwarts Expansion," *Wall Street Journal*, August 24, 2004.

29. Timothy L. O'Brien, "How Russian Oil Tycoon Courted Friends in U.S.," *New York Times*, November 5, 2003.

30. As quoted in Masha Gessen, "The Wrath of Putin," *Vanity Fair*, April 2012.

31. As quoted in Julia Ioffe, "Remote Control: Can an Exiled Oligarch Persuade Russia That Putin Must Go?," *New Yorker*, January 12, 2015.

32. US Senate Committee of Foreign Relations, *Democracy in Retreat in Russia, Hearing* (February 17, 2005), https://www.gpo.gov/fdsys/pkg/CHRG-109shrg22751/html/CHRG-109shrg22751.htm.

33. Erin Arvedlund, "Kremlin Moves to Dismantle Yukos, Setting Auction for Unit," *New York Times*, September 17, 2008.

34. Catherine Belton, "State Steps in for Yukos Unit," *Guardian*, December 22, 2004.

35. Gessen, "The Wrath of Putin"; James Henderson, *Rosneft—On the Road to Global NOC Status?* Oxford Institute for Energy Studies, January 2012, 8.

36. Arvedund, "Kremlin Moves to Dismantle Yukos, Setting Auction for Unit."

37. Gabriele Steinhauser and Gregory White, "Russia Must Compensate Yukos Shareholders, Says European Court," *Wall Street Journal*, July 31, 2014.

38. Mark Milner, "Back Door Yukos Nationalisation Perfectly Normal, Says Putin," *Guardian*, December 23, 2005.

39. "Mechel Bashing—Business in Russia," *Economist*, July 31, 2008.

40. "TNK-BP Update: BP Pulls Staff as Aar Ratchets Up Pressure," WikiLeaks Public Library of U.S. Diplomacy, July 24, 2008, https://wikileaks.org/plusd/cables/08MOSCOW2137_a.html.

41. Baker, "BP's Dudley Relives Russian Nightmare alongside Rosneft Boss."

42. James Herron and Selina Williams, "BP Launches $8 Billion Share Buyback after TNK-BP Sale," *Wall Street Journal*, March 22, 2013.

43. Steve Levine, "The Last Free Oligarch," *Foreign Policy*, July 25, 2012; Leonid Bershidsky, "Not All Russian Billionaires Are Putin Cronies," *Bloomberg,* March 5, 2015.

44. Courtney Weaver, "Cash-Laden Oligarchs Hunt Pastures New," *Financial Times*, April 5, 2013.

45. Baker, "BP's Dudley Relives Russian Nightmare alongside Rosneft Boss."

46. Ibid.

47. Andrey Ostroukh and Olga Razumovskaya, "Russia's Arrest of Sistema Boss Raises Specter of Yukos Case," *Wall Street Journal*, September 17, 2014; Courtney Weaver, "Russian Oligarch Yevtushenkov Placed under House Arrest," *Financial Times*, September 16, 2014.

48. Irina Reznik and Evgenia Pismenaya, "Rosneft CEO Sechin Said to Pitch Putin $16 Billion Sale Deal," *Bloomberg*, August 29, 2016.

49. "Bloomberg: Rosneft CEO Igor Sechin Proposes to Pay $5Bln for Bashneft Controlling Stake," *Moscow Times*, August 29, 2016, http://themoscowtimes.com/news/bloomberg-rosneft-ceo-igor-sechin-proposes-to-pay-5-billion-for-bashneft-controlling-stake-55146.

50. "Russian Minister Charged with $2m Bribe," *BBC News*, November 15, 2016, https://www.bbc.com/news/world-europe-37983744.

51. Alexander Winning, "Exclusive: Arrested Russian Minister Wanted State to Cede Control over Rosneft: Sources," *Reuters*, November 29, 2016, https://in.reuters.com/article/russia-ulyukayev-rosneft-idINKBN13O1L5.

52. Henry Foy, "Sistema Counts $1.7bn Cost of Business in Russia," *Financial Times*, January 3, 2018.

53. James Henderson and Ekaterina Grushevenko, *Russian Oil Production Outlook to 2020*, Oxford Institute for Energy Studies, February 2017, 4.

54. Ricardo Soares de Oliveira, *Magnificent and Beggar Land: Angola since the Civil War* (Oxford: Oxford University Press, 2015), 31.

55. Ibid., 184.

56. Ibid., 36.

57. Steve Levine, *The Oil and the Glory: The Pursuit of Empire and Fortune on the Caspian Sea* (New York: Random House, 2007), 183.

58. Global Witness, *Azerbaijan Anonymous*, Global Witness, December 6, 2013, 12.

59. Socar financial reports.

60. International Monetary Fund, *Angola—Fifth Review under the Stand-by Arrangement, Request for Waiver of Applicability of Performance Criteria, and Request for Modification of Performance Criteria*, IMF, December 2011.

61. US District Court Southern District of Texas Houston Division, *In Re Cobalt International Energy, Inc, Securities Litigation 14-CV-3428, Consolidated Amended Class Action Complaint*, May 1, 2015, http://securities.stanford.edu/filings-documents/1053/CIEI00_01/201551_r01c_14CV03428.pdf.

62. Tom Burgis, *The Looting Machine: Warlords, Oligarchs, Corporations, Smugglers, and the Theft of Africa's Wealth* (New York: Public Affairs, 2016), 18.

63. Cobalt has denied wrongdoing. The DOJ closed its investigation in 2017 without filing charges.

64. I was able to find no further updates on the status of the legal actions against Sam Pa following his arrest. For more on him see Burgis, *Looting Machine*; J. R. Mailey, *The Anatomy of the Resource Curse: Predatory Investment in Africa's Extractive Industries*, Africa Center for Strategic Studies, May 2015.

65. Burgis, *Looting Machine*, 96.

66. Burgis, *Looting Machine*, 96; Mailey, *Anatomy of the Resource Curse*.

67. Burgis, *Looting Machine*, 102.

68. Soares de Oliveira, *Magnificent and Beggar Land*.

69. US District Court for the Southern District of Texas, Houston Division, *United States v. SBM Offshore N.V., Deferred Prosecution Agreement*, Criminal No. 17–686 (S.D. Tex, November 29, 2017), https://www.justice.gov/opa/press-release/file/1014801/download.

70. UK Serious Fraud Office, "F.H. Bertling Lts (Project Jasmine)," December 17, 2018, https://www.sfo.gov.uk/cases/f-h-bertling-ltd-project-jasmine/.

71. Robbie Whelan and Sarah Kent, "BP's Azerbaijan Push Comes at a Cost," *Wall Street Journal*, March 31, 2016.

72. Ibid.

73. US Department of Justice, "Oil Services Companies and a Freight Forwarding Company Agree to Resolve Foreign Bribery Investigations and to Pay More Than $156 Million in Criminal Penalties," November 4, 2010, press release, https://www.justice.gov/opa/pr/oil-services-companies-and-freight-forwarding-company-agree-resolve-foreign-bribery.

74. Joshua Yaffa, "Putin's Shadow Cabinet and the Bridge to Crimea," *New Yorker*, May 29, 2017.

75. Dawisha, *Putin's Kleptocracy*, 92–93.

76. Ibid.

77. Anders Åslund, *Why Gazprom Resembles a Crime Syndicate*, Peterson Institute for International Economics, February 28, 2012.

78. Stephen Grey, Tom Bergin, Sevgil Musaieva, and Roman Anin, "Special Report—Putin's Allies Channelled Billions to Ukraine Oligarch," *Reuters*, November 26, 2014.

79. Ibid.

80. Alexandra Gillies, Marc Guéniat, and Lorenz Kummer, *Big Spenders: Swiss Trading Companies, African Oil and the Risks of Opacity,* Natural Resource Governance Institute, July 20, 2014.

81. Ibid.

82. Global Witness, *Azerbaijan Anonymous*, 18–20.

83. Socar, "Letter to the Advisory Board of Global Witness," February 25, 2015, https://site-media.globalwitness.org/archive/files/20150225%20socar%20letter%20to%20global%20witness.pdf.

84. Anar Alizade, "Interview to 'Business Time' Magazine," May 13, 2014, https://anaralizade.com/post/interview-to-business-time-magazine.

85. "Socar Trading SA," Azerbaijan Anonymous Explained (a Socar Group website), no date given, http://www.azerbaijananonymousexplained.com/eng/azerbaijan-anonymous-explained/socar-trading-sa/.

86. Alizade, "Interview to 'Business Time' Magazine."

87. "Joint Ventures, Tendering and Bidding," Azerbaijan Anonymous Explained (a Socar Group website), no date given,

88. Socar Trading, "Key Statistics," Socar Trading, http://www.socartrading.com/about-us/key-statistics.

89. Rafael Marques de Morais, "Trafigura and the Angolan Presidential Mafia," *Maka Angola*, January 5, 2013; de Morais, "General Dino and the Attorney General's Lies," *Maka Angola*, January 20, 2014; Berne Declaration, *Trafigura's Business in Angola*, Berne Declaration, February 2013, Cochran Group, "Management Team," no date given, Cochan Group, https://www.cochan.com/en/management-team.

90. "Angola: What's behind Trafigura's Ejection from Products Swap?," *Energy Compass*, September 21, 2012.

91. Ibid.

92. "From Petrograd to Petrodollars—Gunvor's Roots," *Economist*, May 5, 2012, https://www.economist.com/international/2012/05/05/from-petrograd-to-petrodollars; Catherine Belton, "Yukos Files Suit against Rosneft," *Financial Times*, September 18, 2009.

93. Ibid.

94. US Treasury Department, "Treasury Sanctions Russian Officials, Members of the Russian Leadership's Inner Circle, and an Entity for Involvement in the Situation in Ukraine," March 20, 2014, https://www.treasury.gov/press-center/press-releases/Pages/jl23331.aspx.

95. Luke Harding, "Russian Billionaire Drops Libel Case against Economist," *Guardian*, July 30, 2009.

96. Dmitry Zhdannikov, "What Does U.S. Know about Putin's Oil Wealth?," *Reuters*, March 21, 2014.

97. Yaffa, "Putin's Shadow Cabinet and the Bridge to Crimea."

98. Ibid.

99. "Azerbaijan: Who Owns What Vol. 2—The Minister of Emergency Situations, Beluga Caviar, and Fruit Juice," WikiLeaks Public Library of U.S. Diplomacy, February 25, 2010, https://wikileaks.org/plusd/cables/10BAKU127_a.html.

100. Juliette Garside and Stephanie Kirchgaessner, "Azeri Ruling Families Linked to Secret Investments via Maltese Bank," *Guardian*, April 23, 2018.

101. Natural Resources Governance Institute, "Dataset: Unlocking EITI Data for MeaningfulReform,"https://resourcegovernance.org/analysis-tools/tools/dataset-unlocking -eiti-data-meaningful-reform.

102. "Azerbaijan: Who Owns What Vol. 2."

103. Ibid.

104. Ibid.

105. Arzu Geybullayeva, "Azerbaijan: Small Bookstore Owner Describes Hostile Takeover by Powerful Minister," *Eurasianet*, February 14, 2018; Facebook post from Nigar Kocharli, February 12, 2018, https://www.facebook.com/nigar.kocharli.1/posts/10156287329849586.

106. Adam Davidson, "Donald Trump's Worst Deal," *New Yorker*, March 13, 2017; Nushabe Fatullayeva, "Mixing Government and Business in Azerbaijan," *Radio Free Europe*, April 4, 2013.

107. Davidson, "Donald Trump's Worst Deal."

108. "Azerbaijan: Who Owns What Vol. 2."

109. Davidson, "Donald Trump's Worst Deal"; Luke Harding, Caelainn Barr, and Dina Nagapetyants, "UK at Centre of Secret $3bn Azerbaijani Money Laundering and Lobbying Scheme," *Guardian*, September 4, 2017.

110. Fatullayeva, "Mixing Government and Business in Azerbaijan."

111. Giorgi Lomsadze, "The Aliyev Daughters: Azerbaijan's First-Family Fashionistas," *Eurasianet*, January 16, 2014.

112. Miranda Patrucic, Eleanor Rose, Irene Velska, and Khadija Ismayilova, "Azerbaijan First Family's London Private Enclave." Organized Crime and Corruption Reporting Project, May 10, 2016; Miranda Patrucic, Juliette Garside, Khadija Ismayilova, and Jean-Baptiste Chastand, "Pilatus, a Private Bank for Azerbaijan's Ruling Elite," Organized Crime and Corruption Reporting Project, April 23, 2018.

113. Khadija Ismayilova, "Eurovision Hall Benefits Azerbaijan's First Family," *Radio Free Europe*, May 9, 2012.

114. Khadija Ismayilova, "Aliyevs Own Some of the Best Hotels in Baku," Organized Crime and Corruption Reporting Project, June 28, 2015.

115. Patrucic, "Pilatus, a Private Bank for Azerbaijan's Ruling Elite"; Garside and Kirchgaessner, "Azeri Ruling Families Linked to Secret Investments via Maltese Bank."

116. Organized Crime and Corruption Reporting Project, "Azerbaijani First Family: Big on Banking," OCCRP, June 11, 2015.

117. Audrey Altstadt, *Frustrated Democracy in Post-Soviet Azerbaijan* (New York: Columbia University Press, 2017); Ismayilova, "Aliyevs Own Some of the Best Hotels in Baku."

118. Nushabe Fatullayeva and Khadija Ismayilova, "Azerbaijani Government Awarded Gold-Field Rights to President's Family," *Radio Free Europe*, May 3, 2012.

119. Ismayilova, "Aliyevs Own Some of the Best Hotels in Baku."

120. Ismayilova, "Eurovision Hall Benefits Azerbaijan's First Family."

121. The architecture of the oil boom could be the topic of its own fascinating book. While Baku received a transformative facelift, it is far from the most dramatic or troubling makeover bought with oil funds. Equatorial Guinea's President Obiang, the world's longest serving leader, built dozens of new government buildings in the tiny country's two largest cities. Then he decided to build a whole new administrative capital called Oyala, deep in the jungle. In a 2012 interview, Obiang said that the new capital would help keep his government safe from possible coup attempts. So far, the cleared patch of rainforest features a flying saucer shaped library for the brand new International University of Central Africa and a 2,000 unit housing complex arranged in a tidy grid. Down the six-lane "Avenue of Justice" will sit a 450-room luxury hotel with an 18-hole golf course. Conveniently, the Obiang family and other political insiders hold business interests in the construction sector. Stephen Sackur, "Equatorial Guinea: Obiang's Future Capital, Oyala," *BBC News*, December 17, 2012, https://www.bbc.com/news/magazine-20731448; Sarah Saadoun, *"Manna from Heaven"? How Health and Education Pay the Price for Self-Dealing in Equatorial Guinea,* Human Rights Watch, June 15, 2017.

122. Heydar Aliyev Foundation Projects, https://heydar-aliyev-foundation.org/en/content/blog/71/Projects.

123. Roxana Jipa, Victor Ilie, and Daniel Bojin, "Building on a Shaky Foundation," Organized Crime and Corruption Reporting Network, December 4, 2015.

124. "Wiki—Who Owns What in Azerbaijan," WikiLeaks the Global Intelligence Files, February 20, 2013, https://wikileaks.org/gifiles/docs/15/1514568_wiki-who-owns-what-in-azerbaijan-.html.

125. Sam Dean, "How Much Does It Cost to Host the Eurovision Song Contest and Is It Worth It?," *Telegraph*, May 13, 2016.

126. Thomas de Waal, "Sochi's Ghost Haunts Baku," *Moscow Times*, June 21, 2015.

127. Michael Weiss, "The Corleones of the Caspian," *Foreign Policy*, June 10, 2014.

128. Davidson, "Donald Trump's Worst Deal."

129. US Treasury Department, "Treasury Sanctions"; Anti-Corruption Foundation, *Sochi 2014: Encyclopedia of Spending,* Anti-Corruption Foundation, 2014.

130. Carl Schreck, "Kremlin Insiders Cashing in on Government Contracts," *Radio Free Europe*, February 29, 2016.

131. Oliver Bullough, *Moneyland: Why Thieves and Crooks Rule the World and How to Take It Back* (London: Profile Books, 2018), 15.

132. Soares de Oliveira, *Magnificent and Beggar Land,* 140.

133. Ibid.

134. Thomas de Waal, "Azerbaijan Doesn't Want to Be Western," *Foreign Affairs*, September 26, 2014; "World Bank Open Data," World Bank, https://data.worldbank.org/.

135. Stephen Grey, Audrey Kuzmin, and Elizabeth Piper, "Putin's Daughter, a Young Billionaire and the President's Friends," *Reuters*, November 10, 2015; Brian Whitmore, "The Heirs of Putinism," *Radio Free Europe*, November 12, 2015.

136. Afgan Mukhtarli, *Personal Debt Crisis Bites in Azerbaijan,* Institute for War and Peace Reporting, March 27, 2015.

137. "Azerbaijani Police Clash with Activists after Baku Rally," *Radio Free Europe*, September 17, 2016, https://www.rferl.org/a/azerbaijan-opposition-rally-baku-aliyev/27997157.html.

138. Aslak Jangård Orre, *Angola from Boom to Bust—to Breaking Point,* Chr. Michelsen Institute, April 8, 2016.

Chapter 5: "An Octopus That Reaches around the Globe"

1. Denmark, Estonia, and the United States have opened criminal investigations into the case that were ongoing at the time this book went to press. Dankse Bank, "Findings of the Investigations Relating to Danske Bank's Branch in Estonia," September 19, 2018, press release, https://danskebank.com/news-and-insights/news-archive/press-releases/2018/pr19092018; Teis Jensen, "Explainer: Danske Bank's 200 Billion Euro Money Laundering Scandal," *Reuters*, November 19, 2018.

2. Oliver Bullough, *Moneyland: Why Thieves and Crooks Rule the World and How to Take It Back* (London: Profile Books, 2018), 21.

3. Alexander Cooley and John Heathershaw, *Dictators without Borders: Power and Money in Central Asia*, 1st ed. (New Haven: Yale University Press, 2017), 29; Ben Judah and Nate Sibley, *The Enablers: How Western Professionals Import Corruption and Strengthen Authoritarianism,* Hudson Institute, September 2018.

4. Oliver Bullough, "The Origins of Modern Kleptocracy," *Power 3.0* (blog), January 9, 2018.

5. Judah, *The Enablers,* 5.

6. Global Witness, *Narco-a-Lago: Money Laudering at the Trump Ocean Club Panama*, Global Witness, 2017.

7. Edward Robinson, Hugo Miller, and Nariman Gizitdinov, "Was Trump SoHo Used to Hide Part of a Kazakh Bank's Missing Billions?," *Bloomberg,* December 11, 2017; Jesse Drucker, "$7 Million Trump Building Condo Tied to Scandal-Scarred Foreign Leader," *New York Times*, April 10, 2019.

8. Other analysts have come up with similar frameworks. In *Moneyland* (2018), Bullough writes about the three stages through which international enablers help corrupt actors to "steal, hide and spend" illicit funds. Judah's framework looks much the same, though he emphasizes how kleptocrats achieve security by enmeshing themselves in the elite life of a Western country: Judah, *The Enablers*, 12. The key difference is my emphasis on the first stage: how kleptocrats grab hold of the wealth in the first place, including from the oil sector.

9. Hannah Ellis-Petersen, "1MDB Scandal: Najib Razak Faces More Charges over $1.6bn Government Coffer," *Guardian*, October 24, 2018. The case against Najib in Malaysia was ongoing at the time this book went to press.

10. Yantoultra Ngui and Tom Wright, "Malaysia Says Saudis Gave Prime Minister Najib Razak a $681 Million 'Donation,'" *Wall Street Journal,* January 26, 2016.

11. Tom Wright and Bradley Hope, *Billion Dollar Whale: The Man Who Fooled Wall Street, Hollywood and the World* (New York: Hatchette Books, 2018); US District Court for the Central District of California, *United States v. Certain Rights to and Interests in the Viceroy Hotel Group, Complaint*, No. CV 17-4438 (C.D. Cal. June 15, 2017), 11, https://www.justice.gov/opa/press-release/file/973671/download.

12. Jho Low, "Statement Regarding the Filing of Charges against Mr. Low—4 December 2018," http://www.jho-low.com/statements-to-media.

13. US District Court for the Southern District of Texas, *Complaint, United States of America v. The M/Y Galactica Star,* No. 4:17-cv-02166 (S.D. Tex. July 14, 2017), 28, https://www.courtlistener.com/docket/6120284/1/united-states-v-the-my-galactica-star-being-a-65-meter-motor-yacht-built/.

14. Ibid.

15. The Sentry, *Fueling Atrocities: Oil and War in South Sudan,* The Sentry, March 2018; Global Witness, *Capture on the Nile: South Sudan's State-Owned Oil Company, Nilepet, Has Been Captured by the Country's Predatory Elite and Security Services*, Global Witness, April 2018.

16. Emilio Parodi, "Italy Court Finds Saipem Guilty in Algeria Graft Case but Acquits Eni," *Reuters*, September 19, 2018; Farid Alilat, "Corruption in Algeria: Farid Bedjaoui, Close to Chakib Khelil, Sentenced to Five Years in Prison," *Jeune Afrique*, September 19, 2018.

17. Alexandra Stevenson and Sharon Tan, "Malaysia Files Criminal Charges against Goldman Sachs over 1MDB Scandal," *New York Times*, December 17, 2018; Anisah Shukry, "Malaysia Fines Deloitte for Failing to Report 1MDB Oddities," *Bloomberg*, January 30, 2019. The case against Goldman Sachs was ongoing at the time this book went to press.

18. Petrobras paid $2.95 billion to settle the suit in 2018. US District Court for the Southern District of New York, *Petrobras Securities Litigation, Demand for Jury Trial, Consolidated Amended Complaint,* Case No. 14-cv-9662 JSR (S.D.N.Y. July 16, 2015), 42–52, http://securities.stanford.edu/filings-documents/1053/PBSP00_01/2015716_r01c_14CV09662.pdf.

19. The United States has investigated all three banks and filed criminal charges against a former Mozambique government official and several former Credit Suisse

bankers, and the case was ongoing at the time this book went to press. Jef Feeley and Zeke Faux, "U.S. Seeks Extradition of Ex–Credit Suisse Bankers Charged in $2 Billion Loan Fraud," *Bloomberg*, January 3, 2019; Matt Wirz, Rebecca Davos O'Brien and Jenny Strasburg, "FBI Investigates European Banks for Allegedly Aiding Corruption in Mozambique," *Wall Street Journal*, November 6, 2017.

20. US District Court for the Central District of California, *United States v. Certain Rights to and Interests in the Viceroy Hotel Group*, No. CV 17-4438 (C.D. Cal. June 15, 2017), 11, https://www.justice.gov/opa/press-release/file/973671/download.

21. Ibid., 23.

22. Ibid., 19.

23. Wright and Hope, *Billion Dollar Whale*, 22–26.

24. Ibid., 40.

25. Ibid., 31.

26. US District Court for the Central District of California, *United States v. Certain Rights to and Interests in the Viceroy Hotel Group*, No. CV 17-4438 (C.D. Cal. June 15, 2017), 8, https://www.justice.gov/opa/press-release/file/973671/download.

27. Ibid., 417–418, 24–28.

28. Ibid., 20–35.

29. Ibid., 35.

30. In 2017, Abu Dhabi merged IPIC with another of its sovereign wealth funds to create the $175 billion Mubadala Investment Co. Stanely Carvalho: "Abu Dhabi Creates $125 Billion Fund by Merging Mubadala, IPIC," *Reuters*, January 21, 2017.

31. Wright and Hope, *Billion Dollar Whale*, 179.

32. US District Court for the Central District of California, *United States v. Certain Rights to and Interests in the Viceroy Hotel Group*, No. CV 17-4438 (C.D. Cal. June 15, 2017), 53–54, 68, https://www.justice.gov/opa/press-release/file/973671/download.

33. Ibid., 56–67.

34. Ibid., 67.

35. Ibid., 89.

36. Ibid., 92–95.

37. Ibid., 112.

38. Ibid., 121.

39. Ibid., 108.

40. Wright and Hope, *Billion Dollar Whale*, 64.

41. Randeep Ramesh, "1MDB: The Inside Story of the World's Biggest Financial Scandal," *Guardian*, July 28, 2016.

42. US District Court for the Central District of California, *United States v. Certain Rights to and Interests in the Viceroy Hotel Group*, No. CV 17-4438 (C.D. Cal. June 15, 2017), 36, 51–52, https://www.justice.gov/opa/press-release/file/973671/download.

43. Ibid., 202–203.

44. Randeep Ramesh, "1MDB"; "Did Tarek Cheat His Prince? Exclusive!," *Sarawak Report*, February 22, 2017, http://www.sarawakreport.org/2017/02/did-tarek-cheat-his-prince-exclusive/. The DOJ complaint also describes these transfers but refers to "Saudi Associate 1" and "Malaysian Official 1" rather than the individuals' names: US District Court for the Central District of California, *United States v. Certain Rights to and Interests in the Viceroy Hotel Group*, No. CV 17-4438 (C.D. Cal. June 15, 2017), 38–43, https://www.justice.gov/opa/press-release/file/973671/download.

45. *Sarawak Report*'s reporting on the 1MDB scandal, including: *"Heist of the Century—How Jho Low Used PetroSaudi as 'A Front' to Siphon Billions out of 1MDB!,"* *Sarawak Report*, February 28, 2015, http://www.sarawakreport.org/2015/02/heist-of-the-century-how-jho-low-used-petrosaudi-as-a-front-to-siphon-billions-out-of-1mdb-world-exclusive/.

46. Justo was released in 2016. "Swiss Man Linked to 1MDB Investigation Released from Thai Prison," *Reuters*, December 20, 2016.

47. Joseph Menn and Katya Golubkova, "Saudi Princes Accused of Bribery, Embezzlement, Money Laundering—Official," *Reuters*, November 5, 2017.

48. "Tarek Joins Jho Low in Court to Contest DOJ's Confiscation of 1MDB Spoils," *Sarawak Report*, October 13, 2017, http://www.sarawakreport.org/2017/10/tarek-joins-jho-low-in-court-to-contest-dojs-confiscation-of-1mdb-spoils/.

49. Michael Peel, David Sheppard, and Anjli Raval, "Saudi Royal Oil Group at Heart of 1MDB Case," *Financial Times*, July 27, 2016.

50. Anatoly Kurmanaev and Bradley Hope, "Venezuela Alleges Fraud in $1.3 Billion Oil-Rig Lease," *Wall Street Journal*, March 15, 2017; Bradley Hope and Anatoly Kurmanaev, "PetroSaudi Used Funds from 1MDB Venture to Finance Venezuela Project," *Wall Street Journal*, March 15, 2017. The outcome of the investigation was unknown at the time this book went to press.

51. US District Court for the Central District of California, *United States v. Certain Rights to and Interests in the Viceroy Hotel Group,* No. CV 17-4438 (C.D. Cal. June 15, 2017), 53, 74–77, https://www.justice.gov/opa/press-release/file/973671/download.

52. Bradley Hope and Tom Wright, "Alleged 1MDB Conspirator Says He Is a Scapegoat for Emiratis," *Wall Street Journal*, January 23, 2019.

53. Bradley Hope and Nicolas Parasie, "Abu Dhabi Sovereign-Wealth Fund Gets Entangled in Global 1MDB Scandal," *Wall Street Journal*, December 1, 2016.

54. Wright and Hope, *Billion Dollar Whale*, 180.

55. US Department of Justice, "Malaysian Financier Low Taek Jho, AKA 'Jho Low,' and Former Banker Ng Chong Hwa, AKA 'Roger Ng,' Indicted for Conspiring to Launder Billions of Dollars in Illegal Proceeds and to Pay Hundreds of Millions of Dollars in Bribes in Connection with 1MDB Fund," November 2018, press release, https://www.justice.gov/usao-edny/pr/malaysian-financier-low-taek-jho-aka-jho-low-and-former-banker-ng-chong-hwa-aka-roger; Wright and Hope, *Billion Dollar Whale,* 220.

56. Wright and Hope, *Billion Dollar Whale*, 55–57, 124.

57. Ibid., 183.

58. Ibid.

59. Justin Baer, Tom Wright, and Bradley Hope, "Goldman Probed over Malaysia Fund 1MDB," *Wall Street Journal*, June 7, 2016.

60. US District Court for the Central District of California, *United States v. Certain Rights to and Interests in the Viceroy Hotel Group,* No. CV 17-4438 (C.D. Cal. June 15, 2017), 90, https://www.justice.gov/opa/press-release/file/973671/download.

61. US Department of Justice, "Malaysian Financier Low Taek Jho, AKA 'Jho Low,' and Former Banker Ng Chong Hwa, AKA 'Roger Ng,' Indicted." Roger Ng has pleaded not guilty and the case against him was ongoing at the time this book went to press.

62. Ramesh, "1MDB."

63. Gabriel Zucman, "Global Wealth Inequality," NBER working paper 25462, National Bureau of Economic Research, January 2019.

64. Thomas Tørsløv, Ludvig Wier, and Gabriel Zucman, "600 Billion and Counting: Why High-Tax Countries Let Tax Havens Flourish," November 2017, https://gabriel-zucman.eu/files/TWZ2017.pdf; Filip Novokmet, Thomas Piketty, and Gabriel Zucman, *From Soviets to Oligarchs: Inequality and Property in Russia, 1905–2016,* National Bureau of Economic Research, August 2017.

65. Annette Alstadsæter, Niels Johannesen, and Gabriel Zucman, "Who Owns the Wealth in Tax Havens? Macro Evidence and Implications for Global Inequality," *Journal of Public Economics* 162 (2018), 89–100.

66. Cooley and Heathershaw, *Dictators without Borders,* 35.

67. Tax Justice Network, "Financial Secrecy Index—2018 Result," https://www.financialsecrecyindex.com/introduction/fsi-2018-results.

68. Michael Findley, Daniel Nielson, and Jason Sharman, *Global Shell Games: Testing Money Launderers' and Terrorist Financiers' Access to Shell Companies*, Centre for Governance and Public Policy, 2012.

69. Von Hannes Munzinger, Bastian Obermayer and Pia Ratzesberger, "Die Aserbaidschan-Connection einer CDU-Abgeordneten," *Suddeutsche Zeitung*, September 19, 2017; "German MP Disciplined for Role in Azerbaijani Laundromat," Organized Crime and Corruption Reporting Project, January 30, 2019.

70. The MP faces charges in Italy in a case that was ongoing at the time this book went to press. He denies all wrongdoing. Council of Europe, *Report of the Independent Investigation Body on the allegations of corruption within the Parliamentary Assembly*, Council of Europe, April 15, 2018; Jennifer Rankin, "Council of Europe Members Suspected of Corruption, Inquiry Reveals," *Guardian*, April 22, 2018; European Stability Initiative, *The European Swamp (Caviar Diplomacy Part 2): Prosecutors, Corruption and the Council of Europe,* ESI Report, December 17, 2016.

71. Council of Europe, *Report of the Independent Investigation Body on the Allegations of Corruption within the Parliamentary Assembly*.

72. Organized Crime and Corruption Reporting Project, "Denmark's Biggest Bank Hosted Azerbaijani Slush Fund," OCCRP, September 5, 2017.

73. Miranda Patrucic, Juliette Garside, Khadija Ismayilova, and Jean-Baptiste Chastand, "Pilatus: A Private Bank for Azerbaijan's Ruling Elite," Organized Crime and Corruption Reporting Project, April 23, 2018.

74. The firm has faced a disciplinary tribunal in a case that was ongoing when this book went to press. Luke Harding, "UK Law Firm Accused of Failings over Azerbaijan's Leader's Daughters' Offshore Assets," *Guardian*, May 16, 2018.

75. The UK solicitors' disciplinary tribunal suspended the lawyer in question in 2007. Juliette Garside et al., "London Law Firm Helped Azerbaijan's First Family Set Up Secret Offshore Firm," *Guardian*, April 5, 2016.

76. US Department of the Treasury, *Notice of Finding That Banca Privada d'Andorra Is a Financial Institution of Primary Money Laundering Concern*, 4810–02, FinCEN, March 6, 2015, https://www.fincen.gov/sites/default/files/shared/BPA_NOF.pdf; José de Córdoba and Juan Forero, "U.S. Investigates Venezuelan Oil Giant," *Wall Street Journal*, October 22, 2015. The Andorran bank's owners denied the accusations and sued the US government but lost the case in court.

77. Córdoba and Forero, "U.S. Investigates Venezuelan Oil Giant."

78. Tax Justice Network, *Financial Secrecy Index 2018: Report on Seychelles,* Tax Justice Network, 2018.

79. US District Court for the Central District of California, *United States v. Certain Rights to and Interests in the Viceroy Hotel Group,* No. CV 17-4438 (C.D. Cal. June 15, 2017), 18, https://www.justice.gov/opa/press-release/file/973671/download.

80. Ibid., 41.

81. Ibid., 71.

82. Ibid., 72–79.

83. Tom Wright and Bradley Hope, "Malaysia Prime Minister's Confidant Had Central Role at Troubled 1MDB Fund," *Wall Street Journal*, April 20, 2016; US District Court for the Central District of California, *United States v. Certain Rights to and Interests in the Viceroy Hotel Group,* No. CV 17-4438 (C.D. Cal. June 15, 2017), 88, https://www.justice.gov/opa/press-release/file/973671/download; Wright and Hope, *Billion Dollar Whale*, 221.

84. US District Court for the Central District of California, *United States v. Certain Rights to and Interests in the Viceroy Hotel Group,* No. CV 17-4438 (C.D. Cal. June 15, 2017), 88, https://www.justice.gov/opa/press-release/file/973671/download.

85. Daniel Victor and Richard C. Paddock, "Path of $681 Million: From Saudi Arabia to Malaysian Premier's Personal Account," *New York Times*, December 21, 2017.

86. "Swiss Financial Watchdog FINMA Sanctions Coutts for 1MDB Breaches," *Reuters*, February 2, 2017.

87. Grace Leong, "1MDB Probe: Former BSI Banker Yeo Jiawei Gets 54 Months' Jail for Money Laundering, Cheating," *Straits Times*, July 12, 2017.

88. Anshuman Daga and Joshua Franklin, "Singapore Shuts Falcon Bank Unit, Fines DBS and UBS over 1MDB," *Reuters*, October 11, 2016; Fatima Ungku, "Singapore Sentences Ex–BSI banker to More Jail Time in 1MDB Linked Case," *Reuters*, July 12, 2017.

89. For fuller discussion, see: Global Witness, *The Real Wolves of Wall Street,* Global Witness, March 2018.

90. Global Witness, *Real Wolves of Wall Street*, 20; Wright and Hope, *Billion Dollar Whale*, 146.

91. US District Court for the Central District of California, *United States v. Certain Rights to and Interests in the Viceroy Hotel Group,* No. CV 17-4438 (C.D. Cal. June 15, 2017), 133, https://www.justice.gov/opa/press-release/file/973671/download. Michael Rapoport, "Deloitte Resigns as 1MDB Auditor," *Wall Street Journal*, July 27, 2016.

92. J. C. Sharman, *The Despot's Guide to Wealth Management* (Ithaca: Cornell University Press, 2017), 6.

93. Linda Kinstler, "London's Latest Tourist Attraction: Russian Oligarchs," *Fortune,* March 26, 2016.

94. Nicholas Shaxson, "A Tale of Two Londons," *Vanity Fair*, April 2013.

95. Transparency International UK, *Faulty Towers: Understanding the impact of Overseas Corruption on the London Property Market*, Transparency International UK, March 2017.

96. Shaxson, "Tale of Two Londons."

97. Louise Story and Stephanie Saul, "Stream of Foreign Wealth Flows to Elite New York Real Estate," *New York Times*, February 7, 2015.

98. Nick Penzenstadler, "Trump's Real Estate: Secretive Sales Continue Unabated," *USA Today*, January 10, 2018.

99. Jarry Emmanuel, "Equatorial Guinea Leader's Son Found Guilty of Embezzlement by French Court," *Reuters*, October 27, 2017; Maïa de la Baume, "For Obiang's Son, High Life in Paris Is Over," *New York Times*, August 23, 2012.

100. Sophie Balay, "How to Hide a Russian Fortune on the French Riviera," Organized Crime and Corruption Reporting Project, February 21, 2018.

101. Garside et al., "London Law Firm."

102. Wright and Hope, *Billion Dollar Whale*, 2–7.

103. Ibid., 134.

104. Ibid., 92.

105. US District Court for the Central District of California, *United States v. Certain Rights to and Interests in the Viceroy Hotel Group,* No. CV 17-4438 (C.D. Cal. June 15, 2017), 162–171, https://www.justice.gov/opa/press-release/file/973671/download.

106. Ibid.

107. Jennifer Calvery and Kevin Bell, "Lifestyles of the Rich and Infamous: Confronting Dirty Money in US Real Estate," *Harvard International Review*, January 9, 2017.

108. Wright and Hope, *Billion Dollar Whale*, 163.

109. Tom Burgis, "US Prime Property Is Magnet for Illicit Wealth, Warns Treasury," *Financial Times*, February 23, 2017.

110. US District Court for the Central District of California, *United States v. Certain Rights to and Interests in the Viceroy Hotel Group,* No. CV 17-4438 (C.D. Cal. June 15, 2017), 194, https://www.justice.gov/opa/press-release/file/973671/download.

111. Kelly Crow and John Letzing, "In the 1MDB Net, an Art-World Whale," *Wall Street Journal*, July 21, 2016.

112. US District Court for the Central District of California, *United States v. Certain Rights to and Interests in the Viceroy Hotel Group,* No. CV 17-4438 (C.D. Cal. June 15, 2017), 195–196, https://www.justice.gov/opa/press-release/file/973671/download.

113. Crow and Letzing, "In the 1MDB Net, an Art-World Whale."

114. Wright and Hope, *Billion Dollar Whale,* 268.

115. US District Court for the Central District of California, *United States v. Certain Rights to and Interests in the Viceroy Hotel Group,* No. CV 17-4438 (C.D. Cal. June 15, 2017), 82, https://www.justice.gov/opa/press-release/file/973671/download.

116. Ibid., 161.

117. "Riza Aziz Contests Seizure of His Beverly Hills Home, Claims Innocence in Money-Laundering Scandal," *Real Deal Los Angeles*, February 17, 2017, https://the-realdeal.com/la/2017/02/17/riza-aziz-contests-seizure-of-his-beverly-hills-home-claims-innocence-in-money-laundering-scandal/.

118. Joanna Robinson, "The Real Wolf of Wall Street, Jordan Belfort, Calls Prison a 'Boys' Club' and 'Totally Mellow,'" *Vanity Fair*, February 27, 2014.

119. Katharina Bart, "Jordan Belfort: I Knew 1MDB Was a Scam," *Finews.com*, January 26, 2017.

120. Global Witness, *Real Wolves of Wall Street*, 5.

121. Ibid., 17.

122. US District Court for the Central District of California, *United States v. Certain Rights to and Interests in the Viceroy Hotel Group*, No. CV 17-4438 (C.D. Cal. June 15, 2017), 162, https://www.justice.gov/opa/press-release/file/973671/download.

123. Ibid., 141.

124. Alexander Cooley, John Heathershaw, and J. C. Sharman, "Laundering Cash, Whitewashing Reputations," *Journal of Democracy* 29, no. 1 (January 2018), 40.

125. Ibid.

126. Abigail Fielding-Smith and Crofton Black, *Foreign Office Diplomat on "Leave" at Saudi Crown Prince's PR Firm,* Bureau of Investigative Journalism, March 6, 2018.

127. Cooley et al., "Laundering Cash, Whitewashing Reputations," 39–53.

128. "The Perils of Lobbying in Africa," *Economist*, July 29, 2017.

129. Erin Quinn, *U.S. Lobbying, PR Firms Give Human Rights Abusers a Friendly Face*, Center for Public Integrity, December 17, 2015.

130. Thor Halvorssen and Alex Gladstein, "The Atlantic Council's Questionable Relationship with Gabon's Leader," *The Hill*, October 26, 2016; Eric Lipton, Brooke Williams, and Nicholas Confessore, "Foreign Powers Buy Influence at Think Tanks," *New York Times*, January 19, 2018.

131. Sarah Chayes, *Thieves of State: Why Corruption Threatens Global Security*, 1st ed. (New York: Norton, 2016).

132. International Monetary Fund, "IMF Executive Board Approves US$642 Million Extended Arrangement under the Extended Fund Facility (EFF) for Gabon," press release, June 20, 2017, https://www.imf.org/en/News/Articles/2017/06/20/imf-executive-board-approves-us642-million-extended-arrangement-under-the-eff-for-gabon; IMF reports glossed over the mounting evidence that billions of dollars in NNPC funds had been diverted, as in this report covering 2013: International Monetary Fund, *Nigeria: Staff Report for the 2014 Article IV Consultation*, IMF, April 2014; some of the missed opportunities by the United States are explained in Matthew Page, *Improving U.S. Anticorruption Policy in Nigeria,* Council on Foreign Relations, July 11, 2016.

133. Richard Pace, "APCO Worldwide PR Firm and a Final Fantasy of Malaysia," *Everything PR*, September 13, 2010.

134. Lee Yuk Peng, "Heated Debates over Apco Issue," *The Star*, April 4, 2010.

135. See, for example: "Too Much Partying by Najib's PR Guru Paul Stadlen?," *Sarawak Report*, February 11, 2015, http://www.sarawakreport.org/2015/02/too-much-partying-by-najibs-pr-guru-paul-stadlen/.

136. Rahmah Ghazali, "Former Apco Malaysia Chief Not Paid by Govt," *The Star*, May 20, 2015; Wright and Hope, *Billion Dollar Whale*, 335. In 2019, Malaysian authorities charged Stadlen with money laundering. He denies wrongdoing, saying the charges are political. Hannah Ellis-Peterson, "British Spin Doctor to Former Malaysian PM Charged with Money Laundering," *Guardian*, Feburary 21, 2019.

137. Ian Burrell and Martin Hickman, "Special Investigation: TV Company Takes Millions from Malaysian Government to Make Documentaries for BBC…about Malaysia," *Independent*, August 17, 2011; "BBC Investigates FBC's Malaysian Links," *BBC News*, August 17, 2011, http://www.bbc.co.uk/ariel/14560249;

138. "FBC Media Scandal—Growing Questions for CNN's John Defterios," *Sarawak Report*, August 5, 2011, http://www.sarawakreport.org/2011/08/fbc-media-scandal-growing-questions-for-cnns-john-defterios-2/; "CNN Faces Questions over Host's Ties," *Politico*, August 8, 2011, https://www.politico.com/blogs/onmedia/0811/CNN_faces_questions_over_hosts_ties.html.

139. "Najib Razak Interviewed about BERSIH 2.0 on CNN—July 2011," YouTube, posted by John Abraham on April 18, 2003 https://www.youtube.com/watch?v=EFTMcLF2RFA.

140. Ibid.

141. Burrell and Hickman, "Special Investigation: TV Company Takes Millions from Malaysian Government"; "BBC Investigates FBC's Malaysian Links"; "FBC Media Scandal."

142. "Joint Statement from the *Guardian* and Joshua Treviño," *Guardian*, August 24, 2012, https://www.theguardian.com/gnm-press-office/10. "Guardian Splits with Conservative Writer over Malaysia Ties," *BuzzFeed News*, August 24, 2012, https://www.buzzfeednews.com/article/buzzfeedpolitics/guardian-splits-conservative-writer-over-malaysia.

143. "Malaysia's Poison Blogger Exposed in the US!," *Sarawak Report*, August 25, 2012, http://www.sarawakreport.org/2012/08/malaysias-poison-blogger-exposed-in-the-us/.

144. US Department of Justice, *Trevino Strategies and Media, Inc., NSD/FARA Registration Statement*, Reg no. 6152 (US DOJ, January 24, 2013), https://www.fara.gov/docs/6152-Exhibit-AB-20130124-1.pdf.

145. "Remarks by President Obama and Prime Minister Najib of Malaysia after Bilateral Meeting," White House, November 20, 2015, press release, https://obamawhitehouse.archives.gov/the-press-office/2015/11/20/remarks-president-obama-and-prime-minister-najib-malaysia-after.

146. Wright and Hope, *Billion Dollar Whale*, 259.

147. Bradley Hope and Colleen Nelson, "Malaysian Fund 1MDB Linked to White House Visit," *Wall Street Journal*, October 13, 2016; Wright and Hope, *Billion Dollar Whale*, 261.

148. Hope and Nelson, "Malaysian Fund 1MDB Linked to White House Visit."

149. Bradley Hope, Tom Wright, and Rebecca Ballhaus, "Trump Ally Was in Talks to Earn Millions in Effort to End 1MDB Probe in U.S.," *Wall Street Journal*, March 1, 2018.

150. US District Court for the District of Columbia, *USA v. $37,564,565.25...*, *Verified Complaint for Forfeiture* in Rem, *Civil Action No. 18-cv-2795*, November 30, 2018, https://www.justice.gov/opa/press-release/file/1116571/download.

151. US District Court for the District of Columbia, *USA v. George Higginbotham*, *Factual Basis for Plea*, November 30, 2018, 2, https://www.justice.gov/opa/press-release/file/1116746/download.

152. US District Court for the District of Columbia, *USA v. $37,564,565.25...*, *Verified Complaint for Forfeiture* in Rem, *Civil Action No. 18-cv-2795*, November 30, 2018, 6, https://www.justice.gov/opa/press-release/file/1116571/download.

153. US District Court for the District of Columbia, *USA v. George Higginbotham*, November 30, 2018, 2, https://www.justice.gov/opa/press-release/file/1116746/download.

154. Eric Tucker, "Ex-Fugees Member Pras Fights US Forfeiture Complaint," Associated Press, January 28, 2019.

155. Hope, Wright, and Ballhaus, "Trump Ally Was in Talks to Earn Millions."

156. Paul Wolfowitz, "Trump's Meeting with Malaysian Crook Najib Reeks of the Swamp," *Newsweek*, September 13, 2017.

157. Editorial Board, "Trump Welcomes an Authoritarian to the White House" (editorial), *Washington Post*, September 11, 2017.

158. Matthew Goldstein and Kenneth P. Vogel, "A Fugitive Financier's Charm Offensive Has P.R. Firms Proceeding with Caution," *New York Times*, November 13, 2018.

159. Euan McKirdy and Sandi Sidhu, "Jho Low: How Man at Center of 1MDB Scandal Is Being Turned into a Figure of Fun," *CNN*, December 18, 2018.

160. Yantoultra Ngui, "1MDB Pays Balance of Missed Debt Installment to Abu Dhabi Fund," *Wall Street Journal*, August 30, 2017.

161. Ken Brown and Tom Wright, "Malaysia's 1MDB Decoded: How Millions Went Missing," *Wall Street Journal*, April 7, 2016.

Chapter 6: Corruption's Motley Foes

1. US Department of Justice, "Attorney General Lynch Announces a Kleptocracy Enforcement Action to Recover More Than $1 Billion Obtained from Corruption Involving Malaysian Sovereign Wealth Fund," press release, July 20, 2016, https://www. justice.gov/opa/video/attorney-general-lynch-announces-kleptocracy-enforcement-action-recover-more-1-billion.

2. US District Court for the Central District of California, *United States v. Certain Rights to and Interests in the Viceroy Hotel Group, Complaint*, No. CV 17-4438 (C.D. Cal. June 15, 2017), https://www.justice.gov/opa/press-release/file/973671/download.

3. Ibid., 98.

4. Anshuman Daga and Joshua Franklin, "Singapore Shuts Falcon Bank Unit, Fines DBS and UBS over 1MDB," *Reuters*, October 10, 2016; Hugo Miller and Anisah Shukry, "Swiss Say 1MDB Used as Ponzi Scheme to Bribe Officials," *Reuters*, July 10, 2018. The Swiss criminal investigation was ongoing when this book went to press.

5. Ben Hubbard, David Kirkpatrick, Kate Kelly, and Mark Mazzetti. "Saudis Said to Use Coercion and Abuse to Seize Billions," *New York Times*, November 1, 2018.

6. Nicholas Kulish and David D. Kirkpatrick, "In Saudi Arabia, Where Family and State Are One, Arrests May Be Selective," *New York Times*, November 7, 2017.

7. The Saudi Embassy to the United States disputed this account. In response, the *New York Times* and *Wall Street Journal* stuck by their reporting that MBS bought the painting via a proxy, citing US intelligence and Arab sources. Embassy of the Kingdom of Saudi Arabia, "Embassy Statement on Art Work Purchase," December 8, 2017, https://www.saudiembassy.net/news/embassy-statement-art-work-purchase. David D. Kirkpatrick, Mark Mazzetti, and Eric Schmitt, "Saudi Crown Prince Was behind Record Bid for a Leonardo," *New York Times*, December 8, 2017. David D. Kirkpatrick and Eric Schmitt, "Saudi Arabia Disputes That Crown Prince Bought 'Salvator Mundi,'" *New York Times,* December 8, 2017. Shane Harris, Kelly Crow, and Summer Said, "Saudi Arabia's Crown Prince Identified as Buyer of Record-Breaking da Vinci," *Wall Street Journal*, December 8, 2017.

8. Nicholas Kulish and Michael Forsythe, "World's Most Expensive Home? Another Bauble for a Saudi Prince," *New York Times*, December 16, 2017.

9. David Lague, Charlie Xhu, and Benjamin Kang Lim, "Special Report: Inside Xi Jinping's Purge of China's Oil Mandarins," *Reuters*, July 25, 2014.

10. "Former Top China Energy Chief Jailed," *BBC News*, October 12, 2015, https://www.bbc.com/news/world-asia-china-34503469.

11. Benjamin Kang Lim and Ben Blanchard, "Exclusive: China Seizes $14.5 Billion Assets from Family, Associates of Ex–Security Chief: Sources," *Reuters*, March 30, 2014; "China Jails for Life Former Top Secret Police Official," *Reuters*, December 27, 2018.

12. Lague et al., "Special Report."

13. Lucy Hornby, "CNPC Forced to Sell Businesses as China's Crackdown Widens," *Financial Times*, September 14, 2015.

14. For more on CNPC and Turkmenistan, see Alexander Cooley and John Heathershaw, *Dictators without Borders: Power and Money in Central Asia*, 1st ed. (New Haven: Yale University Press, 2017); and Juan Pablo Cardenal and Heriberto Araujo, *China's Silent Army: The Pioneers, Traders, Fixers and Workers Who Are Remaking the World in Beijing's Image* (New York: Crown Archetype, 2013), 111. On Kazakhstan: Guy Chazan, "Kazakh Spat Casts Light on China Deals," *Wall Street Journal*, March 26, 2010. On Chad: US District Court for the Southern District of New York, *Complaint, United States v. Chi Ping Patrick Ho, and Cheikh Gadio*,17-mag-8611 (S.D.N.Y., November 20, 2017), https://www.justice.gov/opa/press-release/file/1012531/download.

15. Human Rights Watch, *"Special Measures": Detention and Torture in the Chinese Communist Party's Shuanggui System*, Human Rights Watch, 2016.

16. Francisco Monaldi, *The Collapse of the Venezuelan Oil Industry,* Atlantic Council, March 2018.

17. "Omani CEO Jailed for 23 Years in Graft Case: Court," *Reuters*, February 27, 2014.

18. "Rudy Rubiandini Gets Seven Years for Bribery," *Jakarta Post*, April 29, 2014.

19. Thomas Carothers and Christopher Carothers, "The One Thing Modern Voters Hate Most," *Foreign Policy*, July 24, 2018.

20. Charlie Savage, "Sex, Drug Use and Graft Cited in Interior Department," *New York Times*, September 10, 2008; Sharona Coutts, "Second Interior Official Pleads Guilty in Sex, Drugs and Oil Scandal," *ProPublica*, September 18, 2008; U.S. Government Accountability Office, *The Federal System for Collecting Oil and Gas Revenues Needs Comprehensive Reassessment*, Report to Congressional Requesters (September 2008), https://www.gao.gov/new.items/d08691.pdf; US Government Accountability Office, *Mineral Revenues: Data Management Problems and Reliance on Self-Reported Data for Compliance Efforts Put MMS Royalty Collections at Risk,* September 12, 2008, https://www.gao.gov/new.items/d08893r.pdf; Adam Rose, "Deepwater Horizon Inspections: MMS Skipped Monthly Inspections on Doomed Rig," *Huffington Post*, May 17, 2010.

21. J. C. Shaman, *The Despot's Guide to Wealth Management: On the International Campaign against Grand Corruption* (Ithaca: Cornell University Press, 2017).

22. US Securities and Exchange Commission, "SEC Enforcement Actions: FCPA Cases," https://www.sec.gov/spotlight/fcpa/fcpa-cases.shtml.

23. US Securities and Exchange Commission, "SEC Charges KBR and Halliburton for FCPA Violations," February 11, 2009, https://www.sec.gov/news/press/2009/2009-23.htm.

24. US Securities and Exchange Commission, *Halliburton Company and Jeannot Lorenz, SEC Order Instituting Cease and Desist Proceedings,* File No. 3-18080, Release No. 81222 (July 27, 2017), https://www.sec.gov/litigation/admin/2017/34-81222.pdf.

25. US Department of Justice, "Petróleo Brasileiro S.A.—Petrobras Agrees to Pay More Than $850 Million for FCPA Violations," press release, US Department of Justice, September 27, 2018, https://www.justice.gov/opa/pr/petr-leo-brasileiro-sa-petrobras-agrees-pay-more-850-million-fcpa-violations; US District Court for the Eastern District of New York, *United States v. Odebrecht S.A., Plea Agreement*, No. 16-643 RJD (E.D.N.Y., 2016), https://www.justice.gov/opa/press-release/file/919916/download.

26. US Department of Justice, "Och-Ziff Capital Management Admits to Role in Africa Bribery Conspiracies and Agrees to Pay $213 Million Criminal Fine," US DOJ, September 29, 2016, press release, https://www.justice.gov/opa/pr/och-ziff-capital-management-admits-role-africa-bribery-conspiracies-and-agrees-pay-213.

27. Gibson Dunn, *2018 Year-End FCPA Update*, January 7, 2019, https://www.gibsondunn.com/2018-year-end-fcpa-update/. The Unaoil cases were ongoing at the time of press.

28. Ibid.

29. Organization for Economic Co-operation and Development, *OECD Foreign Bribery Report: An Analysis of the Crime of Bribery of Foreign Public Officials*, OECD, 2014.

30. Martine Milliet-Einbinder, "Writing Off Tax Deductibility," *OECD Observer*, April 2000.

31. Hugh Carney, "OECD Hits Out at France over Bribery," *Financial Times*, October 23, 2012.

32. This case, which is described further in chapter 2, was ongoing at the time this book went to press.

33. See chapter 2 for a full discussion of this case, which was ongoing at the time this book went to press.

34. US Department of Justice, "SBM Offshore N.V. and United States–Based Subsidiary Resolve Foreign Corrupt Practices Act Case Involving Bribes in Five Countries," press release, November 29, 2017, https://www.justice.gov/opa/pr/sbm-offshore-nv-and-united-states-based-subsidiary-resolve-foreign-corrupt-practices-act-case.

35. The Rolls-Royce case ended in a deferred prosecution agreement in which the company agreed to pay over $600 million in fines. The judge in the trial against the Barclays executives discharged the jury in 2019, thereby ending the trial. Crown Court at Southwark. *Regina v. Rolls-Royce PLC, Statement of Facts (DPA)*, January 17, 2017. https://www.sfo.gov.uk/cases/rolls-royce-plc/; Rupert Neate, "Barclays Executive Had Sleepless Nights over Qatar, Court Told," *BBC News*, February 1, 2019.

36. Organization for Economic Co-operation and Development, *OECD Foreign Bribery Report.*

37. US Department of Justice, "Société Générale S.A. Agrees to Pay $860 Million in Criminal Penalties for Bribing Gaddafi-Era Libyan Officials and Manipulating LIBOR Rate," June 4, 2018, press release, https://www.justice.gov/opa/pr/soci-t-g-n-rale-sa-agrees-pay-860-million-criminal-penalties-bribing-gaddafi-era-libyan.

38. Gibson Dunn, *2017 Year-End FCPA Update*, January 2, 2018, https://www.gibsondunn.com/2017-year-end-fcpa-update/.

39. US Department of Justice, "Patrick Ho, Former Head of Organization Backed by Chinese Energy Conglomerate, Convicted of International Bribery, Money Laundering Offenses," press release, December 5, 2018, https://www.justice.gov/usao-sdny/pr/patrick-ho-former-head-organization-backed-chinese-energy-conglomerate-convicted.

40. Hugo Miller and Andy Hoffman, "Ex–Gunvor Oil Trader Found Guilty of Bribing African Officials," *Bloomberg*, August 28, 2018.

41. US Department of Justice, "Malaysian Financier Low Taek Jho, Also Known as "Jho Low," and Former Banker Ng Chong Hwa, Also Known as "Roger Ng," Indicted for Conspiring to Launder Billions of Dollars in Illegal Proceeds and to Pay Hundreds

of Millions of Dollars in Bribes," November 1, 2018, press release, https://www.justice.gov/opa/pr/malaysian-financier-low-taek-jho-also-known-jho-low-and-former-banker-ng-chong-hwa-also-known.

42. US Department of Justice, "Oil Services CEO and Executive Sentenced to Prison for Roles in Foreign Bribery Scheme," September 28, 2018, press release, https://www.justice.gov/opa/pr/oil-services-ceo-and-executive-sentenced-prison-roles-foreign-bribery-scheme.;

43. Ibid.

44. Emilio Parodi, "Italy Court Finds Saipem Guilty in Algeria Graft Case but Acquits Eni," *Reuters*, September 19, 2018.

45. This trial was ongoing at the time this book went to press.

46. Andrew Keshner, "Brooklyn Judge Serves Gabonese National Two-Year Prison Sentence for Being 'Fixer' in Bribery Scheme," *New York Daily News*, May 31, 2017.

47. Organization for Economic Co-operation and Development, "Is Foreign Bribery an Attractive Investment in Some Countries?," in *OECD Business and Finance Outlook 2016* (Paris: OECD, 2016), 207.

48. Knut Are Skjong and Ole Andreas Overland, *The Consequences of Involvement in Foreign Bribery Cases* (Thesis) (Bergen: Norwegian School of Economics, 2018), http://transparency.no/wp-content/uploads/%C3%98verland-og-Skjong-NHH-Master-oppgave.pdf.

49. Jesse Eisinger, *The Chickenshit Club* (New York: Simon and Schuster, 2017), 318.

50. Holly Watt, "ExxonMobil Liberian Oil Deal Went Ahead despite Anti-corruption Concerns," *Guardian*, March 29, 2018.

51. Trace International, "Eni S.p.A.," in *Trace Compendium*, Trace International, https://www.traceinternational.org/TraceCompendium/Detail/411?class=casename_searchresult&type=1. These cases reached various outcomes. In 2018, Italian authorities convicted executives from Saipem, an oilfield service company affiliated with Eni, of bribing Algerian officials. The Brazil, Congo-Brazzaville, and Nigeria investigations appeared to be ongoing at the time this book went to press. Others, such as those pertaining to Kuwait and Kazakhstan, appear to have been abandoned by authorities.

52. US Department of State, *U.S. Asset Recovery Tools & Procedures: A Practical Guide for International Cooperation*, May 2012, https://2009-2017.state.gov/documents/organization/190690.pdf.

53. Angelique Chrisafis, "France Impounds African Autocrats' 'Ill-Gotten Gains,'" *Guardian*, February 6, 2012; US District Court for the Southern District of California, *Amended Complaint, United States v. One White Crystal Covered Bad Tour Glove and Other Michael Jackson Memorabilia*, No. CV 2: 11-3582-GW-SS (S.D. Cal., June 1, 2012), 42–47.

54. The US case ended in a 2014 settlement agreement that required Obiang to sell off belongings worth over $30 million and to give the proceeds to organizations working to further development in Equatorial Guinea. US Department of Justice, "Second Vice President of Equatorial Guinea Agrees to Relinquish More Than $30 Million of Assets Purchased with Corruption Proceeds," press release, October 10, 2014, https://www.justice.gov/opa/pr/second-vice-president-equatorial-guinea-agrees-relinquish-more-30-million-assets-purchased.

55. Transparency International, "'Bien Mal Acquis' Case: French Supreme Court Overrules Court of Appeal's Decision," November 9, 2010, press release, https://www

.transparency.org/news/pressrelease/20101109_biens_mal_acquis_case_french_supreme _court_overrules_court_of_appe.

56. Maud Perdriel-Vaissière, *France's Biens Mal Acquis Affair: Lessons from a Decade of Legal Struggle*, Open Society Foundations, May 2017.

57. "Congo President's Daughter Charged with Corruption in France," *France 24*, June 25, 2017. The case was ongoing at the time this book went to press. As quoted in the piece, the daughter's lawyer stated that the case will be "dismissed through totally legal procedures."

58. Elizabeth Bryant, "French Anti-corruption Group Takes on Powerful Foes," *Deutsch Welle*, December 6, 2017.

59. The DOJ has not issued an update on this case following its initial announce-ment in 2015. The United Kingdom, however, did recover funds related to the case. US Department of Justice, "Department of Justice Seeks Forfeiture of $34 Million in Bribe Payments to the Republic of Chad's Former Ambassador to the U.S. and Canada," June 30, 2015, press release, https://www.justice.gov/opa/pr/department-justice-seeks-forfeiture-34-million-bribe-payments-republic-chad-s-former; UK Serious Fraud Office, "SFO Recovers £4.4m from Corrupt Diplomats in 'Chad Oil' Share Deal," press release, March 22, 2018, https://www.sfo.gov.uk/2018/03/22/sfo-recovers-4-4m-from-corrupt-diplomats-in-chad-oil-share-deal/.

60. US District Court for the Southern District of Texas, *Complaint, United States of America v. The M/Y Galactica Star*, No. 4:17-cv-02166 (S.D. Tex. July 14, 2017), https://www.courtlistener.com/docket/6120284/1/united-states-v-the-my-galactica-star -being-a-65-meter-motor-yacht-built/. At the time this book went to press, the DOJ had suspended the asset seizure case to pursue a criminal investigation into this same matter.

61. Ibid.

62. Barney Thompson and Henry Foy, "Are Unexplained Wealth Orders the Cure for Britain's Reputation as a Haven for Dirty Money?," *Financial Times*, April 30, 2018.

63. Michael Holden and Andrew MacAskill, "Azeri Banker's High-Spending Wife Targeted by New British Anti-graft Powers," *Reuters*, October 10, 2018. The case was ongoing when this book went to press, with the onus on the accused to demonstrate that the asset was obtained by legitimate means.

64. "Unexplained Wealth Orders in Use: Here's at Least 5 Cases the Police Should Consider Today!," Transparency International UK, January 31, 2018, https://www.trans-parency.org.uk/uwo-consider-today/#.W4bPgs5KjIU.

65. For instance, the United Kingdom faced cooperation challenges when pursuing the proceeds of corruption from Ukraine. Oliver Bullough, *Moneyland: Why Thieves and Crooks Rule the World and How to Take It Back* (London: Profile Books, 2018), 190–192.

66. Maeve Shearlaw and Charlie Jones, "From Political Prisoners to Media Bans: Baku's European Games in Numbers," *Guardian*, June 29, 2015.

67. Rayhan Demytrie, "Azerbaijan's Price for Hosting European Games," *BBC News*, June 4, 2015.

68. Max Seddon, "Azerbaijan Pulls Out the Stops for the European Games— Without European Leaders," *BuzzFeed News*, June 12, 2015.

69. Peter Jones, "Israeli Billionaire Sells Congo Oil Rights for 300 Times Purchase Price," *Reuters*, January 22, 2014.

70. US Department of Treasury, "Treasury Sanctions Fourteen Entities Affiliated with Corrupt Businessman Dan Gertler under Global Magnitsky," June 15, 2018, press release, https://home.treasury.gov/news/press-releases/sm0417.

71. Julie Davis, "U.S. Places New Sanctions on Venezuela Day after Election," *New York Times*, May 21, 2018.

72. Collmann Griffin, Richard Mojica, and Marc Alain Bohn, "Takeaways from the Anti-corruption Chapter of the USMCA," *FCPA Blog*, January 9, 2019.

73. Matthew Page, *Improving U.S. Anticorruption Policy in Nigeria: Corruption Brief,* Council on Foreign Relations, July 2016.

74. Ken Silverstein, "The Stolen War," *New Republic,* August 22, 2016. See also Zaid Al-Ali, "How Maliki Ruined Iraq," *Foreign Policy*, June 19, 2014.

75. "Nigeria's Dasuki Arrested over $2bn Arms Fraud," *BBC News*, December 1, 2015, https://www.bbc.com/news/world-africa-34973872.

76. Sarah Chayes, *Thieves of State* (New York: Norton, 2015).

77. Tom Wright and Bradley Hope, "WSJ Investigation: China Offered to Bail Out Troubled Malaysian Fund in Return for Deals," *Wall Street Journal*, January 7, 2019.

78. Tan Xue Ying, "Najib, China Reject 1MDB Bailout Offer Claim," *The Edge Financial Daily*, January 9, 2019.

79. Since these were just preliminary meetings, none of the lawyers actually agreed to take on the minister or his advisor as a client, a process that would likely have involved more thorough vetting. Global Witness, *Undercover in New York: Our Hidden Camera Investigation Reveals How Suspect Money Can Enter the U.S.*, Global Witness, 2016.

80. Will Fitzgibbon, "Angolan Tycoon's Frozen Funds Highlight KPMG's Role in Offshore Secrecy," International Consortium of Investigative Journalists, April 23, 2018.

81. Deloitte, "Re: 2015 Audit of Addax Petroleum Holdings Limited," letter to the boards and management of Sinopec and Addax, November 18, 2016, https://labs.letemps .ch/interactive/2017/pdf/Rapport_Deloitte_complet.pdf. Letter linked from Sylvain Besson, "Addax a écarté ses lanceurs d'alerte avant de sombrer," *Le Temps*, November 21, 2017.

82. Ibid.

83. Ibid.

84. Deloitte LLP, "Statement of Circumstance Relating to the Resignation of Deloitte LLP as Auditors to Addax Petroleum UK Limited," statement to Companies House, December 14, 2016, https://beta.companieshouse.gov.uk/company/08135892/ filing-history/MzE2ODc5NjYyNmFkaXF6a2N4/document?format=pdf&download=0.

85. "Addax to Pay 31 Million Swiss Francs to Settle Swiss Bribery Charges," *Reuters*, July 5, 2017.

86. Alexandra Ulmer and Girish Gupta, "Special Report: In Venezuela's Murky Oil Industry, the Deal That Went Too Far," *Reuters*, July 26, 2016.

87. Public Eye, *Gunvor in Congo*, Public Eye, September 2017.

88. Martin Arnold and Joseph Cotterill, "HSBC Froze Account Linked to Alleged $500m Angolan Fraud," *Financial Times*, March 27, 2018.

89. This case was ongoing at the time this book went to press.

90. Public Eye, *Trafigura's Business in Angola,* Public Eye, February 3, 2013); Global Witness, *Catch Me If You Can: Exxon's Complicity in Liberian Oil Sector Corruption and How Its Washington Lobbyists Fight to Keep Oil Deals Secret,* Global Witness, March 2018; Global Witness, *Capture on the Nile: South Sudan's State-Owned*

Oil Company, Nilepet, Has Been Captured by the Country's Predatory Elite and Security Services, Global Witness, April 2018; The Sentry, *Fueling Atrocities: Oil and War in South Sudan*, The Sentry, March 2018; Global Witness, *Azerbaijan Anonymous,* Global Witness, December 6, 2013.

91. Iggy Ostanin and Lorenzo Di Pietro, *Azerbaijan: Aliyev Family, Friends Cruise aboard SOCAR Super Yachts,* Organized Crime and Corruption Reporting Project, September 1, 2015.

92. Khadija Ismayilova, "Eurovision Hall Benefits Azerbaijan's First Family," *RadioFreeEurope/RadioLiberty*, May 9, 2012.

93. Juliette Garside and Stephanie Kirchgaessner, "Azeri Ruling Families Linked to Secret Investments via Maltese Bank," *Guardian*, April 23, 2018; Miranda Patrucic, Juliette Garside, Khadija Ismayilova, and Jean-Baptiste Chastand, *Pilatus: A Private Bank for Azerbaijan's Ruling Elite,* Organized Crime and Corruption Reporting Project, April 23, 2018.

94. Amnesty International, "Angola: Human Rights Defender and Journalist Charged," June 30, 2017.

95. Anti-Corruption Foundation, *Sochi 2014: Encyclopedia of Spending,* Anti-Corruption Foundation, 2014.

96. "Don't Call Him 'Dimon,'" YouTube video, posted by Alexei Navalny on March 2, 2017, https://www.youtube.com/watch?v=qrwlk7_GF9g.

97. David Pegg, "Angola Sovereign Wealth Fund's Manager Used Its Cash for His Own Projects," *Guardian*, November 7, 2017.

98. This case was ongoing when this book went to press.

99. Will Fitzgibbon and Martha Hamilton, "Passports, Arms Dealers and Frozen Accounts: What Our Partners Found in the New Panama Papers Data," Organized Crime and Corruption Reporting Project, June 28, 2018; "Fiscalía Suiza Congeló Cuentas de Exgerente de Petroecuador," *El Universo*, June 21, 2018, https://www.eluniverso .com/noticias/2018/06/21/nota/6821228/fiscalia-suiza-congelo-cuentas-exgerente -petroecuador.

100. Robert Palmer, "What Does UK Beneficial Ownership Data Show Us?," Global Witness (blog), 2016, https://www.globalwitness.org/ru/blog/what-does-uk-beneficial -ownership-data-show-us/.

101. "Update 1—Statoil Says Briefed Norwegian Police on Angola Payments," *Reuters*, February 19, 2016, https://www.reuters.com/article/statoil-angola/update-1- statoil-says-briefed-norwegian-police-on-angola-payments-idUSL8N15Y2EB; Tom Burgis, "US Regulator Probes Angolan Deal Involving BP and Cobalt," *Financial Times,*March 16, 2017.

102. Will Fitzgibbon, "How the Panama Papers Spooked Colombia's Elite to Own Up about Their Wealth," International Consortium of Investigative Journalists, November 21, 2018.

103. Aaron Sayne, Alexandra Gillies, and Christina Katsouris, *Inside NNPC Oil Sales*, Natural Resource Governance Institute, August 2015; Global Witness, *Catch Me If You Can.*

104. Bradley Hope, Drew Hinshaw, and Patricia Kowsmann, "How One Stubborn Banker Exposed a $200 Billion Russian Money-Laundering Scandal," *Wall Street Journal*, October 23, 2018.

Chapter 7: We Know How to Fight Corruption

1. "Vision Zero," NYC.gov, date not provided, https://www1.nyc.gov/site/visionzero/index.page.

2. The cases involving these countries: Italy v. Saipem (Algeria); UK v. Rolls-Royce (Nigeria, Russia), an executive of Petrofac (Iraq, Saudi Arabia), and F.H. Bertling (Angola, UK); US v. Petrotiger (Colombia), SBM Offshore (Angola, Brazil, Equatorial Guinea, Iraq, Kazakhstan), Technip FMC (Brazil, Iraq), multiple PDVSA officials (Venezuela) and multiple PetroEcuador officials (Ecuador). See chapter 2 for details.

3. US Department of Justice, "SBM Offshore N.V. and United States-Based Subsidiary Resolve Foreign Corrupt Practices Act Case Involving Bribes in Five Countries," press release, November 29, 2017, https://www.justice.gov/opa/pr/sbm-offshore-nv-and-united-states-based-subsidiary-resolve-foreign-corrupt-practices-act-case.

4. US Securities and Exchange Commission, *Halliburton Company and Jeannot Lorenz, SEC Order Instituting Cease and Desist Proceedings,* File No. 3-18080, Release No. 81222, July 27, 2017, https://www.sec.gov/litigation/admin/2017/34-81222.pdf.

5. In Brazil, Braskem admitted to bribing Petrobras officials to receive favorable naptha purchase prices. An employee of the Swiss trading company Gunvor was convicted of bribing Congolese officials. A Singaporean trader employed by the company Kernel was convicted of paying bribes in Indonesia. US District Court for the Eastern District of New York, *USA against Braskem SA, Plea Agreement* (Cr. No. 16-644(RJD)), December 21, 2016, https://www.justice.gov/opa/press-release/file/919906/download; Hugo Miller and Andy Hoffman, "Ex–Gunvor Oil Trader Found Guilty of Bribing African Officials," *Bloomberg*, August 28, 2018. Hans Nicholas Jong, "Kernel Executive Sentenced to Three Years for Bribing Rudi," *Jakarta Post*, December 20, 2013.

6. See chapter 4.

7. See chapter 3.

8. SBM Offshore pleaded guilty to bribing national oil company officials in Angola, Brazil, Equatorial Guinea, Iraq, and Kazakhstan. Swiss courts convicted an employee of Gunvor of bribing officials in Congo-Brazzaville. Various individuals pleaded guilty to FCPA charges of bribing national oil company officials in Colombia, Ecuador, and Venezuela. Saipem was convicted by an Italian court of bribing Algerian officials. Rolls-Royce admitted that intermediaries they hired made payments to Nigerian and Russian national oil company officials. Omani courts convicted the former CEO of Oman's national oil company. See chapters 2 and 6 for more. US District Court for the Southern District of Texas. *United States v. SBM Offshore N.V., Deferred Prosecution Agreement.* Criminal No.17–686 (S.D. Tex. November 29, 2017). https://www.justice.gov/opa/press-release/file/1014801/download; Emilio Parodi, "Italy Court Finds Saipem Guilty in Algeria Graft Case but Acquits Eni," *Reuters*, September 19, 2018; Ministère public de la Conféderaton de la Suisse., *Jugement du 28 août 2018 contre A., ressortissant belge,* Numéro du dossier: SK.2018.38. On file with author; Crown Court at Southwark. *Regina v. Rolls-Royce PLC, Statement of Facts (DPA),* January 17, 2017. https://www.sfo.gov.uk/cases/rolls-royce-plc/; Gibson Dunn. *2017 Year-End FCPA Update.* January 2018, https://www.gibsondunn.com/2018-year-end-fcpa-update/; "Omani CEO Jailed for 23 Years in Graft Case: Court," *Reuters*, February 27, 2014.

9. Organization for Economic Co-operation and Development, *OECD Foreign Bribery Report, An Analysis of the Crime of Bribery of Foreign Public Officials,* OECD, December 2, 2014, 5.

10. Organization for Economic Co-operation and Development, *State-Owned Enterprises and Corruption: What Are the Risks and What Can Be Done?,* OECD, August 27, 2018.

11. See chapter 3.

12. See chapter 2.

13. Joshua Kucera, "Azerbaijan Threatens to Cut Off Military Cooperation with US and NATO," *Eurasianet*, September 11, 2017.

14. Jennifer Rankin, "Council of Europe Members Suspected of Corruption, Inquiry Reveals," *Guardian*, April 22, 2018. European Stability Initiative, *The European Swamp (Caviar Diplomacy Part 2)—Prosecutors, Corruption and the Council of Europe*, ESI Report, December 17, 2016.

15. "London's Financial Flows Are Polluted by Laundered Money: Time to Clean Up," *Economist*, October 11, 2018.

16. Organization for Economic Co-operation and Development, *Implementing the OECD Anti-bribery Convention Phase 4 Report: Switzerland,* OECD Working Group on Bribery, March 15, 2018.

17. Financial Action Task Force, *Anti-money laundering and Counter-terrorist Financing Measures Seychelles Mutual Evaluation Report,* Financial Action Task Force, September 2018.

18. Financial Action Task Force, *Anti-money laundering and Counter-terrorist Financing Measures United States Mutual Evaluation Report,* Financial Action Task Force, December 2016.

19. See chapter 2.

20. Deloitte LLP, "Statement of Circumstance Relating to the Resignation of Deloitte Llp as Auditors to Addax Petroleum UK Limited," Statement to UK Companies House, December 14, 2016, https://beta.companieshouse.gov.uk/company/08135892/filing-history/MzE2ODc5NjYyNmFkaXF6a2N4/document?format=pdf&download=0.

21. Alexandra Stevenson and Sharon Tan, "Malaysia Files Criminal Charges against Goldman Sachs over 1MDB Scandal," *New York Times*, December 17, 2018. The investigation into the bank was ongoing at the time this book went to press. Goldman Sachs denies wrongdoing.

22. Pedro Fonseca and Marcelo Rochabrun, "World's Biggest Oil Traders Paid Bribes in Brazil Scandal—Prosecutors," *Reuters*, December 5, 2018; Ed Davey, *Senior Executives at Top World Oil Companies Implicated in Brazil Bribery Scandal,* Global Witness, December 19, 2018.

23. Pedro Fonseca and Marcelo Rochabrun, "World's Biggest Oil Traders Paid Bribes in Brazil Scandal—Prosecutors," *Reuters*, December 5, 2018.

24. Sabrina Valle, "FBI Joins Brazil's Probe into Alleged Bribery by Top Oil Traders," *Bloomberg*, February 7, 2019.

25. At the time this book went to press, Brazil and the United States were pursuing investigations into the matter, but no wrongdoing had been proven. Petrobras suspended its business with the companies.

26. Global Witness and Public Eye, *Friends in Low Places*, Global Witness, November 2018.

27. Valle, "FBI Joins Brazil's Probe."

28. Global Witness and Public Eye, *Friends in Low Places.*

29. Alexandra Gillies, "Will Extractive Companies Move Away from Corruption-Prone Intermediaries?" *FCPA Blog,* July 29, 2019.

ACKNOWLEDGMENTS

T O WRITE THIS BOOK, I relied on the work of many intrepid individuals who expose and analyze corruption. They do hard work. To uncover the dirty deals struck by powerful politicians and wealthy companies, they must face all manner of personal, professional, and legal risks. They undertake hours of painstaking analysis, untangling dense webs of detail, and then have to communicate all that complexity in a clear way that also catches the public's attention. This book came together only because many individuals took on this challenge and succeeded admirably, and I am in their debt.

I drew heavily on the investigations of Global Witness, a group who punch far above their weight in the fight against oil corruption. The Organized Crime and Corruption Reporting Project, the International Consortium of International Journalists, and Public Eye also produced groundbreaking material about individual cases that I describe. The reporting of journalists from around the world was another crucial source. A few of these journalists, such as Oliver Bullough, Tom Burgis, Alex Cuadros, Bradley Hope, and Tom Wright, turned their reporting into excellent books from which I benefited a great deal, as did the scholars Alex Cooley, Karen Dawisha, John Heathershaw, JC Sharman, and Ricardo Soares de Oliveira—to name a few. Finally, law enforcement officials wrote many of my most cherished sources. Their complaints, statements of facts, and other legal documents provided lucid and on occasion quite lively accounts of the cases they pursued. I am grateful to all them for their work.

The ideas for this book grew out of my work at the Natural Resource Governance Institute, which has been my professional home since 2010. The Institute's leaders, Dani Kaufmann and Suneeta Kaimal, allowed me the space and flexibility to pursue this project. At the Institute, I've worked with remarkably bright and engaging colleagues over the years, too many to name here. Some of them, including Lee Bailey, Max George-Wagner, Marie Lintzer, Sarah Muyonga, Matthieu Salomon, Aaron Sayne, Erica Westenberg, and Joe Williams, worked with me on projects that informed this work. Wise words from Patrick Heller, Karin Lissakers, and Michael Ross helped me stay on course.

Leading the ranks of those who generously read draft chapters is Aaron Sayne, who manages to be optimally brilliant, generous, and acerbic all at the same time. Thank you for all your contributions, and for keeping me company on this journey. Other readers offered thoughtful and expert inputs, from correcting the number of armored cars bought with stolen loot to sniffing out a rotten onion metaphor. They include Will Connors, Galib Efendiev, Marc Guéniat, Patrick Heller, Barnaby Pace, Usha Pitts, Amir Shafaie, and Andrew Walker. Many others generously provided information and answered my questions along the way. Any inaccuracies that remain are my own.

At Oxford University Press, my editor, Angela Chnapko, provided capable and steady guidance as I navigated new publishing waters, and Alexcee Bechthold and Gwen Colvin helped bring this book to fruition. Sharp and strategic feedback from three anonymous reviewers helped raise the quality of the work, as did much-valued contributions from Jeff Miller and Kate Wilson. Thanks to Anna Barnes for her help with the references and to Beth Sutherland for a winning title.

The idea for this book took shape during a month-long sabbatical I mostly spent sitting on the front porch of my parents' home in the lovely speck of a town that is Starks, Maine. That summer, they provided cheerful company and boundless support, as they always do. The book, it turns out, is only the fourth most important thing to come out of that time away. While I can rattle on for hundreds of pages about corruption, I am short on words to explain how grateful I am to have Jeremiah, Emerson, and Jane as my family. They provided the most welcome kinds of distraction from this project. But Jeremiah also made sure that I had the time needed to finish it, and he listened to all the ups and downs along the way. I dedicate this book to them.

SELECTED BIBLIOGRAPHY

Aalbers, Geert, and Nick Panes. "Mexico, the Next Brazil?" *Foreign Affairs*, October 7, 2015.

Abdulmalik, Abdulrahman. "Exclusive: 2015 Polls: How Jonathan Govt. Used Bullion Vans to Cart Away N67.2bn Cash from CBN." *Premium Times*, September 19, 2015.

Acemoglu, Daron, James Robinson, and Thierry Verdier. *Kleptocracy and Divide-and-Rule: A Model of Personal Rule*. NBER working paper no. 10136, National Bureau of Economic Research, December 2013.

Adebayo, Hassan. "How NNPC Dubiously Paid N36.4 Billion Water Projects Money to Ex-NSA Dasuki's Office—Audit Report." *Premium Times*, March 15, 2016.

Adugbo, Daniel. "Nigeria: 20 Months after Inauguration—NNPC Board Fails to Meet." *Daily Trust*, April 14, 2014.

Akinkuotu, Eniola. "N23bn Diezani Bribe: EFCC Declares Billionaire Businessman Wanted." *Punch Newspapers*, August 16, 2016.

Al-Ali, Zaid. "How Maliki Ruined Iraq." *Foreign Policy*, June 19, 2014.

Altstadt, Audrey. *Frustrated Democracy in Post-Soviet Azerbaijan*. New York: Columbia University Press, 2017.

Alstadsæter, Annette, Niels Johannesen, and Gabriel Zucman. *Who Owns the Wealth in Tax Havens? Macro Evidence and Implications for Global Inequality*. National Bureau of Economic Research, September 2017.

Andreski, Stanislav. *The African Predicament: A Study in the Pathology of Modernisation*. London: Joseph, 1968.

Andreski, Stanislav. *Parasitism and Subversion: The Case of Latin America*. New York: Pantheon, 1966.

Anti-Corruption Foundation. *Sochi 2014: Encyclopedia of Spending*. 2014.

Åslund, Anders. *Why Gazprom Resembles a Crime Syndicate*. Peterson Institute for International Economics, February 28, 2012.

Azerbaijan Anonymous Explained (a Socar Group website). http://www.azerbaijananonymousexplained.com/eng/azerbaijan-anonymous-explained/socar-trading-sa/.

"Azerbaijan: Who Owns What Vol. 2—The Minister of Emergency Situations, Beluga Caviar, and Fruit Juice." WikiLeaks Public Library of U.S. Diplomacy. February 25, 2010. https://wikileaks.org/plusd/cables/10BAKU127_a.html.

Babali, Hafiz, and Khadija Ismayilova. "Nowhere to Be Found: Firms with Official Ties Absent from Key Azerbaijani Registry." *Radio Free Europe*, March 24, 2017.

Baker, Richard, Michael Bachelard, Daniel Quinlan, and Nick McKenzie. "The Bribe Factory: Unaoil in Africa." *The Age,* March 30, 2016.

Balay, Sophie. "How to Hide a Russian Fortune on the French Riviera." Organized Crime and Corruption Reporting Initiative, February 21, 2018.

Ball, James, and Claudio Gatti. "Shell Shocks: How One of the World's Biggest Oil Firms Secured a $1.3 Billion Deal Mired in Corruption Allegations," *BuzzFeed News*, April 9, 2017.

Berne Declaration. *Trafigura's Business in Angola.* Berne Declaration, February 3, 2013.

Besson, Sylvain. "Addax a écarté ses lanceurs d'alerte avant de sombrer." *Le Temps*, November 21, 2017.

Besson, Sylvain. "Un ex-trader de Gunvor va être condamné pour corruption au Congo et en Côte d'Ivoire." *Le Temps,* August 15, 2018.

BP. *Statistical Review of World Energy.* June 2018.

Brown, Ken, and Tom Wright. "Malaysia's 1MDB Decoded: How Millions Went Missing." *Wall Street Journal*, April 7, 2016.

Bullough, Oliver. *Moneyland: Why Thieves and Crooks Rule the World and How to Take It Back*. London: Profile Books, 2018.

Bullough, Oliver. "The Dark Side of Globalization." *Journal of Democracy* 29, no. 1 (2018): 25–38.

Bullough, Oliver. "The Origins of Modern Kleptocracy." *Power 3.0* (blog), January 9, 2018.

Bullough, Oliver. *Stage Hands: How Western Enablers Facilitate Kleptocracy*. Hudson Institute, May 2016.

Burgis, Tom. *The Looting Machine: Warlords, Oligarchs, Corporations, Smugglers, and the Theft of Africa's Wealth*. New York: Public Affairs, 2016.

Burgis, Tom. "U.S. Regulator Probes Angolan Deal Involving BP and Cobalt." *Financial Times*, March 16, 2017.

Burrell, Ian, and Martin Hickman. "Special Investigation: TV Company Takes Millions from Malaysian Government to Make Documentaries for BBC...about Malaysia." *Independent*, August 17, 2011.

Calvery, Jennifer, and Kevin Bell. "Lifestyles of the Rich and Infamous: Confronting Dirty Money in US Real Estate." *Harvard International Review*, January 9, 2017.

Campbell, Matthew, and Kit Chellel. "How Goldman Sachs Lost $1.2 Billion of Libya's Money." *Bloomberg Businessweek*, September 29, 2016.

Carothers, Thomas, and Christopher Carothers. "The One Thing Modern Voters Hate Most." *Foreign Policy,* July 24, 2018.

Carter, Brett. "The Rise of Kleptocracy: Autocrats versus Activists in Africa." *Journal of Democracy* 29, 1 (January 2018): 54–68.

Center for Responsive Politics. OpenSecrets.org.

Chayes, Sarah. *Thieves of State: Why Corruption Threatens Global Security*. New York: Norton, 2016.

Chazan, Guy. "Kazakh Spat Casts Light on China Deals." *Wall Street Journal*, March 26, 2010.

Clark, Simon, Mia Lamar, and Bradley Hope. "The Trouble with Sovereign-Wealth Funds." *Wall Street Journal*, December 23, 2015.

Connors, Will, and Luciana Magalhaes. "How Brazil's 'Nine Horsemen' Cracked a Bribery Scandal." *Wall Street Journal*, April 6, 2015.

Cooley, Alexander, and John Heathershaw. *Dictators without Borders: Power and Money in Central Asia*. New Haven: Yale University Press, 2017.

Cooley, Alexander, John Heathershaw, and J. C. Sharman. "Laundering Cash, Whitewashing Reputations." *Journal of Democracy* 29, no. 1 (January 2018): 39–53.

Council of Europe, *Report of the Independent Investigation Body on the Allegations of Corruption within the Parliamentary Assembly*, Council of Europe, April 15, 2018.

Crown Court at Southwark. *Restraint Order Prohibiting Disposal of Assets To: (1) Diezanni [sic] Kogbeni Alison Madueke, (2) Benedict Peters, et al.* September 3, 2016. On file with author.

Crown Court at Southwark. *Regina v. Rolls-Royce PLC, Statement of Facts (DPA)*, January 17, 2017. https://www.sfo.gov.uk/cases/rolls-royce-plc/.

Court of Queen's Bench of Alberta. *Her Majesty the Queen and Griffiths Energy International, Inc. Agreed Statement of Facts*, January 2013. https://www.millerchevalier.com/sites/default/files/resources/Spring2013_GriffithsAmendedStatmentofFacts.pdf.

Cuadros, Alex. *Brazillionaires: Wealth, Power, Decadence, and Hope in an American Country*. London: Profile Books, 2016.

Cuadros, Alex. "The Most Important Criminal Conviction in Brazil's History." *New Yorker*, July 13, 2017.

Davidson, Adam. "Donald Trump's Worst Deal." *New Yorker*, March 13, 2017.

Dawisha, Karen. *Putin's Kleptocracy: Who Owns Russia?* New York: Simon and Schuster, 2014.

De la Baume, Maïa. "For Obiang's Son, High Life in Paris Is Over." *New York Times*, August 23, 2012.

Deloitte. *Deconstructing the Chevron Transfer Pricing Case,* November 3, 2015. https://www2.deloitte.com/au/en/pages/tax/articles/deconstructing-chevron-case.html.

Deloitte. "Re: 2015 Audit of Addax Petroleum Holdings Limited." Letter to the boards and management of Sinopec and Addax. November 18, 2016. https://labs.letemps.ch/interactive/2017/pdf/Rapport_Deloitte_complet.pdf.

Deloitte. "Statement of Circumstance Relating to the Resignation of Deloitte LLP as Auditors to Addax Petroleum UK Limited." Statement to Companies House, December 14, 2016. https://beta.companieshouse.gov.uk/company/08135892/filing-history/MzE2ODc5NjYyNmFkaXF6a2N4/document?format=pdf&download=0.

Economist, "From Petrograd to Petrodollars—Gunvor's Roots," May 5, 2012.

Economist, "Safe Sex in Nigeria," June 15, 2013.

Economist, "The Perils of Lobbying in Africa." July 29, 2017.

Economist, "London's Financial Flows Are Polluted by Laundered Money: Time to Clean Up," October 11, 2018.

Eisinger, Jesse. *The Chickenshit Club*. New York: Simon and Schuster, 2017.

Engels, Philippe, and Khadija Sharife. "The Unlikely Partnership That Unlocked Congo's Crude." Organized Crime and Corruption Reporting Project, September 7, 2018.

European Stability Initiative. *The European Swamp (Caviar Diplomacy Part 2): Prosecutors, Corruption and the Council of Europe*. ESI Report, December 17, 2016.

Fan, Simon. "Kleptocracy and Corruption." *Journal of Comparative Economics* 34, no. 1 (March 2006): 57–74.

Fatullayeva, Nushabe, and Khadija Ismayilova. "Azerbaijani Government Awarded Gold-Field Rights to President's Family." *Radio Free Europe*, May 3, 2012.

Fatullayeva, Nushabe. "Mixing Government and Business in Azerbaijan." *Radio Free Europe*, April 4, 2013.

Fausto, Sergio. *The Lengthy Brazilian Crisis Is Not Yet Over*. Baker Institute for Public Policy, February 17, 2017.

Federal High Court of Nigeria. *Charges against Aliyu Abubakar et al. Charge No. CR/39/201*, December 16, 2016. https://shellandenitrial.org/wp-content/uploads/2018/08/2-Adoke-etc-Nigeria-charges-scanned-2.pdf.

Federal High Court of Nigeria. *Charges against Shell Nigeria Exploration Production Company Ltd., et al. Charge No. CR/124/17*, February 28, 2017. https://shellandenitrial.org/wp-content/uploads/2018/08/3-Adoke-etc-Nigeria-charges-scanned-3.pdf.

Federal High Court of Nigeria. *Federal Republic of Nigeria & 2 Ors v. Atlantic Energy Drilling Concepts Nig. Ltd & 3 Ors—Motion for mareva orders*, 2016. http://saharareporters.com/sites/default/files/FRN%20V%20ATLANTIC%20ENERGY%20-%20APPLICATION%20FOR%20MAREVA%20ORDER%20(EDITED).pdf.

Fielding-Smith, Abigail, and Crofton Black. *Foreign Office Diplomat on "Leave" at Saudi Crown Prince's PR Firm*. Bureau of Investigative Journalism, March 6, 2018.

Financial Action Task Force. *Anti–Money Laundering and Counter-Terrorist Financing Measures United States Mutual Evaluation Report*. Financial Action Task Force, December 2016.

Financial Action Task Force. *Anti–Money Laundering and Counter-Terrorist Financing Measures Seychelles Mutual Evaluation Report*. Financial Action Task Force, September 2018.

"Fiscalía Suiza Congeló Cuentas de Exgerente de Petroecuador." *El Universo*, June 21, 2018. https://www.eluniverso.com/noticias/2018/06/21/nota/6821228/fiscalia-suiza-congelo-cuentas-exgerente-petroecuador.

Fitzgibbon, Will. "Angolan Tycoon's Frozen Funds Highlight KPMG's Role in Offshore Secrecy." International Consortium of Investigative Journalists, April 23, 2018.

Fitzgibbon, Will. "How the Panama Papers Spooked Colombia's Elite to Own Up about Their Wealth." International Consortium of Investigative Journalists, November 21, 2018.

Fitzgibbon, Will. "Secret Offshore Deals Deprive Africa of Billions in Natural Resource Dollars." International Consortium of Investigative Journalists, July 25, 2016.

Fitzgibbon, Will, and Martha Hamilton. "Passports, Arms Dealers and Frozen Accounts: What Our Partners Found in the New Panama Papers Data." International Consortium of Investigative Journalists, June 28, 2018.

Garside, Juliette. "The Azerbaijani President's Children and the Dubai Property Empire." *Guardian*, April 23, 2018.

Garside, Juliette, Luke Harding, David Pegg, and Holly Watt. "London Law Firm Helped Azerbaijan's First Family Set Up Secret Offshore Firm." *Guardian*, April 5, 2016.

Garside, Juliette, and Stephanie Kirchgaessner. "Azeri Ruling Families Linked to Secret Investments via Maltese Bank." *Guardian*, April 23, 2018.

George, Libby, and Shadia Nasralla, "Don't Neglect to Pay the Middlemen: How Shell and Eni Ended Up on Trial." *Reuters*, May 20, 2018.

Gessen, Masha. "The Wrath of Putin." *Vanity Fair*, April 2012.

Geybullayeva, Arzu. "Azerbaijan: Small Bookstore Owner Describes Hostile Takeover by Powerful Minister." *Eurasianet*, February 14, 2018.

Gibbs, Margot, and Musikilu Mojeed. "Exclusive: Another Nigerian Oil Mogul Named in Ex-minister Alison-Madueke's Alleged Corruption, UK Property Frozen." *Premium Times*, August 16, 2017.

Gibson Dunn. *2017 Year-End FCPA Update*. January 2, 2018. https://www.gibsondunn .com/2017-year-end-fcpa-update/.

Gibson Dunn. *2018 Year-End FCPA Update,* January 7, 2019. https://www.gibsondunn .com/2018-year-end-fcpa-update/.

Gillies, Alexandra, Marc Guéniat, and Lorenz Kummer. *Big Spenders: Swiss Trading Companies, African Oil and the Risks of Opacity.* Natural Resource Governance Institute, July 2014.

Global Witness. *Azerbaijan Anonymous*. Global Witness, December 2013.

Global Witness. *Capture on the Nile: South Sudan's State-Owned Oil Company, Nilepet, Has Been Captured by the Country's Predatory Elite and Security Services.* Global Witness, April 2018.

Global Witness. *Catch Me If You Can: Exxon's Complicity in Liberian Oil Sector Corruption and How Its Washington Lobbyists Fight to Keep Oil Deals Secret.* Global Witness, March 2018.

Global Witness. *Congo's Secret Sales*. Global Witness, May 2014.

Global Witness. *The Real Wolves of Wall Street*. Global Witness, March 2018.

Global Witness. *The Riddle of the Sphynx: Where Has Congo's Oil Money Gone?* Global Witness, December 2005.

Global Witness. *Senior Executives at Top World Oil Companies Implicated in Brazil Bribery Scandal.* Global Witness, December 2018.

Global Witness. *Shell Knew*. Global Witness, April 10, 2017.

Global Witness. *Take the Future: Shell's Scandalous Deal for Nigeria's Oil.* Global Witness, November 2018.

Global Witness. *Undercover in New York: Our Hidden Camera Investigation Reveals How Suspect Money Can Enter the U.S.* Global Witness, 2016.

Global Witness and Public Eye. *Friends in Low Places*. Global Witness, November 2018.

Gloster-Coates, Patricia, and Linda Quest. "Kleptocracy: Curse of Development." *International Social Science Review* 80, no. 1/2 (2005).

Grey, Stephen, Tom Bergin, Sevgil Musaieva, and Roman Anin. "Special Report: Putin's Allies Channelled Billions to Ukraine Oligarch." *Reuters*, November 26, 2014.

Grow, Brian, Joshua Schneyer, and Jane Roberts. "Special Report: Chesapeake and Rival Plotted to Suppress Land Prices." *Reuters*, June 25, 2012.

Grzymala-Busse, Anna. "Beyond Clientelism: Incumbent State Capture and State Formation." *Comparative Political Studies* 45, nos. 4–5 (2008): 638–673.

Guéniat, Marc, and Agathe Duparc. *Gunvor in Congo*. Public Eye, September 2017.

Harding, Luke, Caelainn Barr, and Dina Nagapetyants. "UK at Centre of Secret $3bn Azerbaijani Money Laundering and Lobbying Scheme." *Guardian*, September 4, 2017.

Heller, Patrick, and David Mihalyi. *Massive and Misunderstood: Data-Driven Insights into National Oil Companies.* Natural Resource Governance Institute, April 2019.

Henderson, James. *Rosneft—On the Road to Global NOC Status?* Oxford Institute for Energy Studies, January 2012.

Henderson, James, and Ekaterina Grushevenko. *Russian Oil Production Outlook to 2020.* Oxford Institute for Energy Studies, February 2017.

Hertog, Steffen. "Challenges to the Saudi Distributional State in the Age of Austerity." Paper presented at *Saudi Arabia: Domestic, Regional and International Challenges.* Middle East Institute, National University of Singapore, December 2016.

Hertog, Steffen. *A Quest for Significance: Gulf Oil Monarchies' International "Soft Power" Strategies and Their Local Urban Dimensions.* LSE Kuwait Programme Paper Series 42. LSE Kuwait Programme, 2017.

Holsti, K. J. "War, Peace, and the State of the State." *International Political Science Review* 16, no. 4 (October 1995): 319–339.

Hope, Bradley, Drew Hinshaw, and Patricia Kowsmann. "How One Stubborn Banker Exposed a $200 Billion Russian Money-Laundering Scandal." *Wall Street Journal*, October 23, 2018.

Hope, Bradley, and Anatoly Kurmanaev. "PetroSaudi Used Funds from 1MDB Venture to Finance Venezuela Project." *Wall Street Journal*, March 15, 2017.

Hope, Bradley, and Nicolas Parasie. "Abu Dhabi Sovereign-Wealth Fund Gets Entangled in Global 1MDB Scandal." *Wall Street Journal*, December 1, 2016.

Hope, Bradley, and Tom Wright. "U.A.E.'s Ambassador to U.S. Linked to 1MDB Scandal." *Wall Street Journal*, June 30, 2017.

Human Rights Watch. *"Special Measures": Detention and Torture in the Chinese Communist Party's Shuanggui System.* Human Rights Watch, 2016.

International Monetary Fund, *Corruption: Costs and Mitigating Strategies*, *IMF Staff Discussion Note*, IMF, 2016.

Ioffe, Julia. "Remote Control: Can an Exiled Oligarch Persuade Russia That Putin Must Go?" *New Yorker*, January 12, 2015.

Ismayilova, Khadija. "Aliyevs Own Some of the Best Hotels in Baku." Organized Crime and Corruption Reporting Project, June 28, 2015.

Ismayilova, Khadija. "Eurovision Hall Benefits Azerbaijan's First Family." *Radio Free Europe*, May 9, 2012.

Jipa, Roxana, Victor Ilie, and Daniel Bojin. "Building on a Shaky Foundation." Organized Crime and Corruption Reporting Network, December 4, 2015.

Jones, Peter. "Israeli Billionaire Sells Congo Oil Rights for 300 Times Purchase Price." *Reuters*, January 22, 2014.

Judah, Ben, and Nate Sibley. *The Enablers: How Western Professionals Import Corruption and Strengthen Authoritarianism.* Hudson Institute, September 2018.

Karl, Terry. *The Paradox of Plenty: Oil Booms and Petro-States.* Berkeley: University of California Press, 1997.

Katsouris, Christina, and Aaron Sayne. *Nigeria's Criminal Crude: International Options to Combat the Export of Stolen Oil.* Royal Institute for International Affairs, September 2013.

Kent, Sarah, and Eric Sylvers. "Inside the Bribery Scandal Sweeping through the Oil Industry." *Wall Street Journal*, February 13, 2018.

Kulish, Nicholas, and David D. Kirkpatrick. "In Saudi Arabia, Where Family and State Are One, Arrests May Be Selective." *New York Times*, November 7, 2017.

Lague, David, Charlie Xhu, and Benjamin Kang Lim. "Special Report: Inside Xi Jinping's Purge of China's Oil Mandarins." *Reuters*, July 25, 2014.

Le Billon, Phillipe. *Wars of Plunder: Conflicts, Profits and the Politics of Resources.* London: Hurst, 2012.

Levine, Matt. "Goldman's Libya Salesman Was a Little Too Good." *Bloomberg*, September 29, 2016.

Levine, Steve. "The Last Free Oligarch." *Foreign Policy*, July 25, 2012.

Levine, Steve. *The Oil and the Glory: The Pursuit of Empire and Fortune on the Caspian Sea.* New York: Random House, 2007.

Lipton, Eric. "Energy Firms in Secretive Alliance with Attorneys General." *New York Times*, January 19, 2018.

Lipton, Eric, Brooke Williams, and Nicholas Confessore. "Foreign Powers Buy Influence at Think Tanks." *New York Times*, January 19, 2018.

Lloyd, John. "Dons, Donors and the Murky Business of Funding Universities." *Financial Times*, October 27, 2017.

Mailey, J. R. *The Anatomy of the Resource Curse: Predatory Investment in Africa's Extractive Industries.* Africa Center for Strategic Studies, May 2015.

Marques de Morais, Rafael. *The Angolan Presidency: The Epicentre of Corruption. Maka Angola*, August 5, 2010.

Marques de Morais, Rafael. "General Dino and the Attorney General's Lies." *Maka Angola,* January 20, 2014.

Marques de Morais, Rafael. "Trafigura and the Angolan Presidential Mafia." *Maka Angola*, January 5, 2013.

Mayer, Jane. *Dark Money: The Hidden History of the Billionaires behind the Rise of the Radical Right.* New York: Doubleday, 2016.

McKenzie, Nick, Richard Baker, Michael Barchelard, and Daniel Quinlan. "Unaoil: How the West Bought Iraq." *The Age*, March 30, 2016.

Michigan Department of the Attorney General. "Schuette, Creagh Announce $25 Million Civil Settlement, Two Criminal No Contest Pleas by Chesapeake Energy Corp. to Resolve Racketeering, Bid-Rigging Allegations." press release, April 24, 2015, https://www.michigan.gov/ag/0,4534,7-359-82916_81983_47203-353198--,00.html.

Milan Court, Preliminary Investigations Magistrate Section, Indictment, December 20, 2017, https://shellandenitrial.org/wp-content/uploads/2018/06/decision-to-open-trial-20.12.2017_English.pdf.

Ministère public de la Confédératon de la Suisse. *Act d'Accusation en procedure sim-plifée Art. 360 CPP En la cause Prévenu: Pascal Collard* [Indictment of Pascal Collard], July 6, 2018. On file with author.

Ministère public de la Confédératon de la Suisse. *Jugement du 28 août 2018 contre A., ressortissant belge*, Numéro du dossier: SK.2018.38, August 28, 2018. On file with author.

Monaldi, Francisco. *The Collapse of the Venezuelan Oil Industry.* Atlantic Council, March 2018.

Mukhtarli, Afgan. *Personal Debt Crisis Bites in Azerbaijan.* Institute for War and Peace Reporting, March 27, 2015.

Natural Resources Governance Institute. "Dataset: Unlocking EITI Data for Meaningful Reform." https://resourcegovernance.org/analysis-tools/tools/dataset-unlocking-eiti-data-meaningful-reform.

Nigeria Economic and Financial Crimes Commission. "Court Orders Final Forfeiture of Diezani's 56 Houses." Nigeria EFCC, October 11, 2017. http://efccnigeria.org/efcc/news/2810-court-orders-final-forfeiture-of-diezani-s-56-houses-2.

Nigeria Economic and Financial Crimes Commission. "Diezani Alison-Madueke: What an Appetite!" Nigeria EFCC, August 8, 2017. https://efccnigeria.org/efcc/news/2706-diezani-alison-madueke-what-an-appetite.

Norway Public Prosecutors' Office. *Okokrim Indictment Sheet.* Case No. 51/05, June 20, 2011. http://www.internationaltaxreview.com/pdfs/indictment-sheet.pdf.

Novokmet, Filip, Thomas Piketty, and Gabriel Zucman. *From Soviets to Oligarchs: Inequality and Property in Russia, 1905–2016.* National Bureau of Economic Research, August 2017.

Organization for Economic Co-operation and Development. *Implementing the OECD Anti-bribery Convention Phase 4 Report: Switzerland.* OECD Working Group on Bribery, March 15, 2018.

Organization for Economic Co-operation and Development. "Is Foreign Bribery an Attractive Investment in Some Countries?" In *OECD Business and Finance Outlook 2016.* OECD, 2016.

Organization for Economic Co-operation and Development. *OECD Foreign Bribery Report: An Analysis of the Crime of Bribery of Foreign Public Officials.* OECD, 2014.

Organization for Economic Co-operation and Development. *State-Owned Enterprises and Corruption: What Are the Risks and What Can Be Done?* OECD, August 27, 2018.

Olesen, Alexa, and Michael Hudson. "China's Scandal-Torn Oil Industry Embraces Tax Havens." International Consortium of Investigative Journalists, January 22, 2014.

Organized Crime and Corruption Reporting Project. "Denmark's Biggest Bank Hosted Azerbaijani Slush Fund." OCCRP, September 5, 2017.

Organized Crime and Corruption Reporting Project. "German MP Disciplined for Role in Azerbaijani Laundromat." OCCRP, January 30, 2019.

Ostanin, Iggy, and Lorenzo Di Pietro. "Azerbaijan: Aliyev Family, Friends Cruise Aboard SOCAR Super Yachts." Organized Crime and Corruption Reporting Project, September 1, 2015.

Owen, Olly, and Zainab Usman. "Briefing: Why Goodluck Jonathan Lost the Nigerian Presidential Election of 2015." *African Affairs* 114, no. 456 (July 1, 2015): 455–471.

Oxfam Australia. *The Hidden Billions: How Tax Havens Impact Lives at Home and Abroad.* Oxfam Research Reports, June 2016.

Page, Jeremy, Brian Spegele, and Wayne Ma. "Powerful Oil Clique at Center of Chinese Probes." *Wall Street Journal*, September 5, 2013.

Page, Matthew. *Improving U.S. Anticorruption Policy in Nigeria.* Council on Foreign Relations, July 11, 2016.

Palmer, Robert. "What Does UK Beneficial Ownership Data Show Us?" Global Witness, 2016.

Patey, Luke. *The New Kings of Crude: China, India, and the Global Struggle for Oil in Sudan and South Sudan.* London: Hurst, 2014.

Patrick, Margot, Gabriele Steinhauser, and Patricia Kowsmann. "The $500 Million Central Bank Heist—and How It Was Foiled." *Wall Street Journal*, October 3, 2018.

Patrucic, Miranda, Juliette Garside, Khadija Ismayilova, and Jean-Baptiste Chastand. "Pilatus: A Private Bank for Azerbaijan's Ruling Elite." Organized Crime and Corruption Reporting Project, April 23, 2018.

Patrucic, Miranda, Eleanor Rose, Irene Velska, and Khadija Ismayilova. "Azerbaijan First Family's London Private Enclave." Organized Crime and Corruption Reporting Project, May 10, 2016.

Peel, Michael, David Sheppard, and Anjli Raval. "Saudi Royal Oil Group at Heart of 1MDB Case." *Financial Times*, July 27, 2016.

Pegg, David. "Angola Sovereign Wealth Fund's Manager Used Its Cash for His Own Projects." *Guardian*, November 7, 2017.

Penzenstadler, Nick. "Trump's Real Estate: Secretive Sales Continue Unabated." *USA Today*, January 10, 2018.

Perdriel-Vaissière, Maud. *France's Biens Mal Acquis Affair: Lessons from a Decade of Legal Struggle.* Open Society Foundations, May 2017.

Quinn, Erin. *U.S. Lobbying, PR Firms Give Human Rights Abusers a Friendly Face.* Center for Public Integrity, December 17, 2015.

Ramesh, Randeep. "1MDB: The Inside Story of the World's Biggest Financial Scandal." *Guardian*, July 28, 2016.

Ross, Michael. *The Oil Curse: How Petroleum Wealth Shapes the Development of Nations.* Princeton: Princeton University Press, 2013.

Royal Courts of Justice. Judgement Approved in the Case of *The Libyan Investment Authority v Goldman Sachs International [2016] EWHC 2530 (Ch)*. October 14, 2016. http://www.bailii.org/ew/cases/EWHC/Ch/2016/2530.html.

Saadoun, Sarah. *"Manna from Heaven"? How Health and Education Pay the Price for Self-Dealing in Equatorial Guinea.* Human Rights Watch, June 15, 2017.

Sachs, Jeffrey, and Michael Warner. *Resource Abundance and Economic Growth.* National Bureau of Economic Research Working Paper Series. NBER, 1995.

Sahre, Paul. "Scott Pruitt's Dirty Politics." *New Yorker*, April 2, 2018.

Sarawak Report coverage of the 1MDB Scandal, including: "Heist of the Century—How Jho Low Used Petrosaudi as 'A Front' to Siphon Billions Out of 1MDB!" *Sarawak Report*, February 28, 2015.

Sayne, Aaron, Alexandra Gillies, and Christina Katsouris. *Inside NNPC Oil Sales: A Case for Reform in Nigeria.* Natural Resource Governance Institute, August 2015.

Sayne, Aaron, Alexandra Gillies, and Andrew Watkins, *Twelve Red Flags: Corruption Risks in the Award of Extractive Sector Licenses and Contracts.* Natural Resource Governance Institute, 2017.

Schwellenbach, Nick. *Meet the Oil-Friendly Federal Panel That Could Give Drillers a Sweetheart Deal.* Project on Government Oversight, February 27, 2018.

"Sechin as Energy Czar: More Powerful, More Vulnerable." WikiLeaks Public Library of U.S. Diplomacy. September 17, 2008. https://wikileaks.org/plusd/cables/08MOSCOW2802_a.html.

Segal, David. "Deals in Code, Arrests in Raids: The Risky Stakes of Oil Middlemen." *New York Times*, September 23, 2017.

Sharman, J. C. *The Despot's Guide to Wealth Management: On the International Campaign against Grand Corruption.* Ithaca: Cornell University Press, 2017.

Shaxson, Nicholas. *Poisoned Wells: The Dirty Politics of African Oil.* London: St. Martin's Griffin, 2008.

Shaxson, Nicholas. "A Tale of Two Londons." *Vanity Fair*, April 2013.

Shaxson, Nicholas. *Treasure Islands: Uncovering the Damage of Offshore Banking and Tax Havens.* London: Palgrave Macmillan, 2011.

Skjong, Knut Are, and Ole Andreas Overland. *The Consequences of Involvement in Foreign Bribery Cases* (Thesis) (Bergen: Norwegian School of Economics, 2018), http://transparency.no/wp-content/uploads/%C3%98verland-og-Skjong-NHH-Masteroppgave.pdf.

Soares de Oliveira, Ricardo. *Magnificent and Beggar Land: Angola since the Civil War.* Oxford: Oxford University Press, 2015.

Soares de Oliveira, Ricardo. *Oil and Politics in the Gulf of Guinea.* New York: Columbia University Press, 2007.

Søreide, Tina. *Drivers of Corruption: A Brief Review.* World Bank, October 2014.

Story, Louise, and Stephanie Saul. "Stream of Foreign Wealth Flows to Elite New York Real Estate." *New York Times*, February 7, 2015.

Tabuchi, Hiroko. "The Oil Industry's Covert Campaign to Rewrite American Car Emissions Rules." *New York Times*, December 13, 2018.

Tax Justice Network. *Financial Secrecy Index 2018: Report on Seychelles.* Tax Justice Network, 2018.

Tax Justice Network. *Financial Secrecy Index—2018 Results.* Tax Justice Network, 2018.

Texans for Public Justice, Public Citizen's Texas Office, and Sierra Club. *Running on Hydrocarbons: Oil and Gas Funding to Every Texas Lawmaker.* Texans for Public Justice, Public Citizen's Texas Office, and Sierra Club, May 2017.

The Sentry. *Fueling Atrocities: Oil and War in South Sudan.* The Sentry, March 2018.

Thompson, Barney, and Henry Foy. "Are Unexplained Wealth Orders the Cure for Britain's Reputation as a Haven for Dirty Money?" *Financial Times*, April 30, 2018.

Tordo, Silvana. *National Oil Companies and Value Creation.* World Bank, 2011.

Transparency International UK. *Faulty Towers: Understanding the Impact of Overseas Corruption on the London Property Market.* Transparency International UK, March 2017.

Transparency International UK. "Unexplained Wealth Orders in Use: Here's at Least 5 Cases the Police Should Consider Today!" Transparency International UK, January 31, 2018.

Tukur, Sanit. "Ex-Minister, Godsday Orubebe, Who Almost Derailed 2015 Election, to Face Trial for Corruption." *Premium Times*, October 31, 2015.

Udo, Bassey. "Exclusive: How Alison-Madueke's Management Style Is Killing Nigeria's Oil." *Premium Times*, August 1, 2014.

UK Serious Fraud Office. "F. H. Bertling Lts (Project Jasmine)." UK SFO, December 17, 2018. https://www.sfo.gov.uk/cases/f-h-bertling-ltd-project-jasmine/.

UK Serious Fraud Office. "Former Senior Executive Convicted in Petrofac Investigation." UK SFO, February 7, 2019. https://www.sfo.gov.uk/2019/02/07/former-senior-executive-convicted-in-petrofac-investigation/.

UK Serious Fraud Office. "SFO Recovers £4.4m from Corrupt Diplomats in 'Chad Oil' Share Deal." UK SFO, March 22, 2018. https://www.sfo.gov.uk/2018/03/22/sfo-recovers-4-4m-from-corrupt-diplomats-in-chad-oil-share-deal/.

UK Serious Fraud Office. "Two Charged in SFO's Unaoil Investigation." UK SFO, November 16, 2017. https://www.sfo.gov.uk/2017/11/16/two-charged-sfos-unaoil-investigation/.

Ulmer, Alexandra, and Girish Gupta. "Special Report: In Venezuela's Murky Oil Industry, the Deal That Went Too Far." *Reuters*, July 26, 2016.

US Department of Justice. "Former CEO Indicted for Masterminding Conspiracy Not to Compete for Oil and Natural Gas Leases." press release, March 1, 2016, US DOJ. https://www.justice.gov/opa/pr/former-ceo-indicted-masterminding-conspiracy-not-compete-oil-and-natural-gas-leases.

US Department of Justice, *Petrobras Non-Prosecution Agreement and Statement of Facts*, September 26, 2018, https://www.justice.gov/opa/press-release/file/1096706/download.

US Department of State. *US Asset Recovery Tools and Procedures: A Practical Guide for International Cooperation*. US Department of State, May 2012.

US Department of the Treasury. *Notice of Finding That Banca Privada d'Andorra Is a Financial Institution of Primary Money Laundering Concern*. 4810–02. FinCEN, March 6, 2015. https://www.fincen.gov/sites/default/files/shared/BPA_NOF.pdf.

US Department of the Treasury. "Treasury Sanctions Fourteen Entities Affiliated with Corrupt Businessman Dan Gertler under Global Magnitsky." June 15, 2018, press release, US Department of the Treasury. https://home.treasury.gov/news/press-releases/sm0417.

US District Court for the Central District of California. *United States v. Certain Rights to and Interests in the Viceroy Hotel Group, Complaint*. No. CV 17-4438 (C.D. Cal. June 15, 2017). https://www.justice.gov/opa/press-release/file/973671/download.

US District Court for the Central District of California. *United States v. One Michael Jackson Signed Thriller Jacket.... Stipulation and Settlement Agreement*, October 10, 2014. https://www.justice.gov/sites/default/files/press-releases/attachments/2014/10/10/obiang_settlement_agreement.pdf

US District Court for the District of Columbia. *USA v.. George Higginbotham, Factual Basis for Plea*, November 30, 2018. https://www.justice.gov/opa/press-release/file/1116746/download.

US District Court for the District of Columbia. *USA v. $37,564,565.25..., Verified Complaint for Forfeiture* in Rem, *Civil Action No. 18-cv-2795*, November 30, 2018. https://www.justice.gov/opa/press-release/file/1116571/download.

US District Court for the District of Columbia. *Complaint, Securities and Exchange Commission v. Braskem, S.A.* No.1:16-cv-02488 (D.D.C. December 21, 2016). https://www.sec.gov/litigation/complaints/2016/comp-pr2016-271.pdf.

US District Court for the District of Columbia. *Complaint, U.S. Department of Justice v. Mahamoud Adam Bechir, No. 14-01178* (D.D.C. July 8, 2014). https://www.justice.gov/sites/default/files/opa/press-releases/attachments/2014/11/07/bechir_complaint.pdf.

US District Court for the Eastern District of New York. *USA against Braskem SA, Plea Agreement (Cr. No. 16-644(RJD))*, December 21, 2016. https://www.justice.gov/opa/press-release/file/919906/download.

US District Court for the Eastern District of New York. *United States v. Odebrecht S.A., Plea Agreement*, No. 16–643 RJD, December 21, 2016, https://www.justice.gov/opa/press-release/file/919916/download.

US District Court for the Eastern District of New York. *USA v. Societe Generale SA, Deferred Prosecution Agreement*, June 5, 2018. https://www.justice.gov/opa/press-release/file/1068521/download.

US District Court for the Eastern District of New York, *United States v. TechnipFMC plc,, Deferred Prosecution Agreement*, Case No. 19-CR-278. (June 25, 2019), A-18, https://www.justice.gov/sites/default/files/criminal-fraud/legacy/2012/11/14/06-28-10-technip-agreement.pdf.

US District Court for the Southern District of California. *Amended Complaint, United States v. One White Crystal Covered Bad Tour Glove and Other Michael Jackson Memorabilia,* No. CV 2: 11-3582-GW-SS (S.D. Cal., June 1, 2012).

US District Court for the Southern District of New York. *Complaint, United States v. Chi Ping Patrick Ho, and Cheikh Gadio*, 17-mag-8611, November 20, 2017. https://www.justice.gov/opa/press-release/file/1012531/download

US District Court for the Southern District of New York. *Petrobras Securities Litigation, Demand for Jury Trial, Consolidated Amended Complaint.* Case No. 14-cv-9662 JSR (S.D.N.Y. July 16, 2015). http://securities.stanford.edu/filings-documents/1053/PBSP00_01/2015716_r01c_14CV09662.pdf.

US District Court for the Southern District of Texas. *Complaint, United States of America v. The M/Y Galactica Star.* No. 4:17-cv-02166 (S.D. Tex. July 14, 2017). https://www.courtlistener.com/docket/6120284/1/united-states-v-the-my-galactica-star-being-a-65-meter-motor-yacht-built/.

US District Court for the Southern District of Texas. *United States v. SBM Offshore N.V., Deferred Prosecution Agreement.* Criminal No.17-686 (S.D. Tex. November 29, 2017). https://www.justice.gov/opa/press-release/file/1014801/download.

US District Court for the Southern District of Texas Houston Division. *In Re Cobalt International Energy, Inc, Securities Litigation 14-CV-3428, Consolidated Amended Class Action Complaint*, May 1, 2015. http://securities.stanford.edu/filings-documents/1053/CIEI00_01/201551_r01c_14CV03428.pdf.

US Government Accountability Office. *Mineral Revenues: Data Management Problems and Reliance on Self-Reported Data for Compliance Efforts Put MMS Royalty Collections at Risk.* September 12, 2008. https://www.gao.gov/new.items/d08893r.pdf.

US Government Accountability Office. *The Federal System for Collecting Oil and Gas Revenues Needs Comprehensive Reassessment.* Report to Congressional Requesters. September 2008. https://www.gao.gov/new.items/d08691.pdf.

US Government Accountability Office. *U.S. Environmental Protection Agency—Installation of Soundproof Privacy Booth.* April 16, 2018. https://www.gao.gov/products/B-329603#mt=e-report.

US Securities and Exchange Commission. *Bank of New York Mellon Corporation, Respondent, SEC Order Instituting Cease and Desist Proceedings.* File No. 3-16762, Release No. 75720 (August 18, 2015). https://www.sec.gov/litigation/admin/2015/34-75720.pdf.

US Securities and Exchange Commission. *BHP Billiton Ltd. and BHP Billiton Plc., SEC Order Instituting Cease and Desist Proceedings.* File No. 3-16546. Release No. 74998 (May 20, 2015). https://www.sec.gov/litigation/admin/2015/34-74998.pdf.

US Securities and Exchange Commission. *Halliburton Company and Jeannot Lorenz, SEC Order Instituting Cease and Desist Proceedings.* File No. 3-18080, Release No. 81222. July 27, 2017. https://www.sec.gov/litigation/admin/2017/34-81222.pdf.

US Senate Committee of Foreign Relations. *Democracy in Retreat in Russia, Hearing* (February 17, 2005). https://www.gpo.gov/fdsys/pkg/CHRG-109shrg22751/html/CHRG-109shrg22751.htm.

US Treasury Department. "Treasury Sanctions Russian Officials, Members of the Russian Leadership's Inner Circle, and an Entity for Involvement in the Situation in Ukraine."

March 20, 2014. Press release. https://www.treasury.gov/press-center/press-releases/Pages/jl23331.aspx.

Waal, Alex de. "When Kleptocracy Becomes Insolvent: Brute Causes of the Civil War in South Sudan." *African Affairs* 113, no. 452 (July 2014): 347–369.

Waal, Thomas de. "Azerbaijan Doesn't Want to Be Western." *Foreign Affairs*, September 26, 2014.

Watt, Holly. "ExxonMobil Liberian Oil Deal Went Ahead despite Anti-corruption Concerns." *Guardian*, March 29, 2018.

Wedeman, Andrew. *Double Paradox: Rapid Growth and Rising Corruption in China.* Ithaca, NY: Cornell University Press, 2012.

Weiss, Michael. "The Corleones of the Caspian." *Foreign Policy*, June 10, 2014.

Whelan, Robbie, and Sarah Kent. "BP's Azerbaijan Push Comes at a Cost." *Wall Street Journal*, March 31, 2016.

Whitmore, Brian. "The Heirs of Putinism." *Radio Free Europe*, November 12, 2015.

"Wiki—Who Owns What in Azerbaijan." WikiLeaks the Global Intelligence Files. February 20, 2013. https://wikileaks.org/gifiles/docs/15/1514568_wiki-who-owns-what-in-azerbaijan-.html.

Wright, Tom, and Bradley Hope. *Billion Dollar Whale: The Man Who Fooled Wall Street, Hollywood, and the World.* New York: Hachette Books, 2018.

Yaffa, Joshua. "Putin's Shadow Cabinet and the Bridge to Crimea." *New Yorker*, May 29, 2017.

Yates, Douglas. *The Rentier State in Africa: Oil Rent Dependency and Neocolonialism in the Republic of Gabon.* Trenton, NJ: Africa World Press, 1996.

Zucman, Gabriel. "Global Wealth Inequality," NBER working paper 25462, National Bureau of Economic Research, January 2019.

Zucman, Gabriel, Annette Alstadsæter, and Niels Johannesen, "Tax Evasion and Inequality," *American Economic Review,* 2019, 109(6): 2073–2103.

INDEX

For the benefit of digital users, indexed terms that span two pages (e.g., 52–53) may, on occasion, appear on only one of those pages.

Surnames starting with "al" or "al-" are alphabetized by remaining portion of name.

Aabar Investments PJS Limited (Aabar-BVI), 148–150, 152–153, 158, 160, 165, 167
Aabar-Seychelles, 150
Abacha, Sani, 21–22, 49, 193
Abreu e Lima Refinery, 88
accountants, 58, 197–199, 218. See also *specific firms*
Addax, 78, 198–199, 201, 205, 218–219
Adoke, Mohammed Bello, 53
Afghanistan, 15
agents. *See* intermediaries
Aiteo Energy Resources, 70–72, 75–77, 232n18, 233n31
Algeria
  kleptocracy in, 106
  oil production in, 17–18
  protests in, 138
  Saipem deal in, 145
  Unaoil in, 41
Alison-Madueke, Diezani
  patronage machine of, 64–65, 69–78, 98–99, 212–213
  rise of, 66–69
Aliyev, Heydar, 108, 118–119, 133–134
Aliyev, Ilham
  anticorruption efforts against, 214–215

diplomatic snub of, 193
power brokering by, 129–135
Mammadov and, 131
offshore investment and, 156–157
Socar developed by, 118–119
Aliyu, Abubakar, 50–52
Alizade, Anar, 125–127
Aluko, Kola, 73–75, 191–192
Anadarko, 95–96
Angola
  anticorruption efforts in, 215
  China Sonangol in, 121–122
  civil war in, 21–22, 101, 117
  Cobalt in, 120–121
  Halliburton in, 46–48, 59, 184, 211
  investment in Portugal, 12, 102, 117–118
  kleptocracy in, 62, 101–106, 135–138
  Marques de Morais and, 202
  Odebrecht in, 87–88
  oil production in, 17, 46, 101, 107–108, 117
  oil trading in, 125, 127, 211–212
  oligarchs in, 120–121, 123
  poverty in, 135–138
  service contracts in, 47–48, 59–60, 122–123, 144

Anti-Bribery Convention (OECD, 1997), 185, 218
anticorruption and anticorruption actors, 13–14, 176–209. See also *specific countries*
  in Brazil's Car Wash scandal, 90–93, 220–221
  challenges to, 24
  complementarity in, 176, 178, 215–220, 223–227
  domestic actors' role in, 98–100, 178–183
  efficacy of, 60, 176
  "enablers" role in, 197–201
  foreign governments' role in, 183–196
  cross-border cooperation and, 13, 141, 213–215
  mobilization of, 215–220
  new tools for, 15, 22, 193
  in 1MDB scandal, 176–178, 196, 205, 213–214
  as political maneuver, 180, 183, 216
  priorities for, 211–213
  sanctions as, 33, 116–117, 128, 135, 193–194
  transparency initiatives and, 205–209
  uneven enforcement of, 195–196
Anti-corruption Foundation, 203
APCO (public relations firm), 170–171
Appleby, 103, 197–198
art and illicit funds, 164–165, 180, 190, 255n7
asset recovery, 193
Atlantic Energy, 61–62, 73–76, 144–145, 191–192, 233n33
Australia
  anticorruption efforts in, 185
  Chevron's tax avoidance in, 57–58, Unaoil clients from, 144
Azerbaijan
  Aliyev's rise in, 108, 118–119
  anticorruption efforts in, 214–215
  BP in, 118, 123–124, 214–215
  European Bank for Reconstruction and Development in, 169, 214–215, 222
  European Games in, 134, 193

  European parliamentarians and, 12, 156, 215
  kleptocracy in, 62, 105–106, 129–137
  OCCRP reporting on, 203–204
  offshore finance and, 156
  oil production in, 17–18, 107–108, 118–119, 136–137
  oil trading in, 125–127, 211–212
  oligarchy in, 23, 129–132, 134
  service contracts in, 123–124, 130–131
  Trump hotel deal in, 12, 134–135
Azerbaijan Laundromat offshore finance operation, 156–157, 203–204
Aziz, Riza, 165–167, 172

Bahrain, 106, 169
Baku-Tbilisi-Ceyhan pipeline, 119
Bank of New York Mellon, 32–33
banks and banking. *See also* money laundering; *specific banks*
  anticorruption checks in, 154, 159, 196–197, 200
  competing for sovereign wealth fund business, 34, 36
Bashneft, 115–116
Bastos de Morais, Jean-Claude, 102–103
Batista, Eike, 91
Bechir, Mahamoud Adam, 26–27
Bedjaoui, Farid, 145
Belfort, Jordan, 165–166
beneficial ownership disclosure, 207–208, 217–218
Bermuda, 58
BHP Billiton, 23, 31–32
bid rigging, 54–56
Boko Haram, 15, 65, 195–196
Bolsonaro, Jair, 100
bond sales in 1MDB scheme, 148–150, 153–154, 163
Bouteflika, Abdelaziz, 138
BP, 19, 28
  in Angola, 46, 117–118, 209
  in Azerbaijan, 118, 123–124, 214–215
  in Russia, 112–116
  lobbying and, 97
  revenues of, 28–29
  transparency initiatives and, 205–206

Braskem, 89, 91–92, 237n95
Brazil. *See also* Car Wash scandal;
    Petrobras
  anticorruption efforts in, 182–183,
    186, 216, 220–221
  corruption in, 62–63, 80–83, 85, 116
  economic growth and GDP of, 85–86,
    92–93, 237n71
  oil production in, 17
  oligarchs in, 83–85
  political climate of, 83, 89–90
  poverty in, 85–86
  Workers' Party in, 82–84, 89–90, 100
bribery and bribery allegations
  Addax in Nigeria, 199
  Bank of New York Mellon, 32–33
  BHP Billiton and, 31–32
  Car Wash scandal in Brazil, 81, 87–93
  Cobalt deal in Angola, 120–121,
    242n63
  global cost of, 14–15
  Griffiths Energy in Chad, 25–27,
    31, 144
  Gunvor in Congo-Brazzaville,
    44–45
  Halliburton in Nigeria, 184
  intermediaries and, 40–41
  legal definition of, 23, 74, 96
  Lula and, 83
  Nigerian elections and, 72, 78, 80
  Panalpina and, 124
  PDVSA and, 157
  prosecution of, 184–189, 217
  Rolls-Royce and, 43, 81, 95, 192
  Saipem in Algeria, 145
  SBM Offshore and, 211
  SocGen in Libya, 37
  Sonangol and, 123
  Unaoil and, 40–42, 144
  "wooing" vs., 31–38
Brinded, Malcolm, 53
Britain *See* United Kingdom (UK)
British Virgin Islands and shell companies,
    61, 64, 155–159, 194–195, 208, 217
BSI (Swiss bank), 153–154, 159–160
Buhari, Muhammadu, 78–80, 195
Bullough, Oliver, 140–141, 247n8

bunkering, 77
Burgis, Tom, 120–122
Burundi, 31–32

Cabral, Sergio, 91
Camargo Corrêa, 84
Cameroon, 21–22, 26, 67, 106–107
campaign finance, 96–98
Canada
  Corruption of Foreign Public Officials
    Act, 27
  exploration activities in, 30
  oil production in, 17
Car Wash scandal, 11, 80–93
  anticorruption efforts in, 90–93,
    220–221
  Costa's account of, 81–83
  Petrobras and, 82, 88–90, 92, 145–146,
    211–212, 220–221, 224n4
  prosecution of, 90–93, 221
  service contracts in, 211
Caracal Energy, 27
Caruana Galizia, Daphne, 202
Cayman Islands, 57, 155–156, 159,
    194–195
CEOs. *See* executives and CEOs
Chad
  dictatorship in, 59–60
  Griffiths energy and, 25–27, 31, 59,
    212–213
  as low-capacity kleptocracy, 106–107
  Och-Ziff and, 184
  oil dependency in, 17–18
  poverty in, 26
Chesapeake Energy, 54–56, 59, 230n95
Chevron, 19
  bribery fines paid by, 184
  campaign contributions from, 95–96
  executive pay in, 30
  lobbying and, 97
  Nigeria's offshore contracts with,
    68–69
  Sonangol contract with, 117–118
  tax avoidance in Australia and, 57–59
  transparency initiatives resisted by,
    206–207, 211
  Trenaco and, 199–200

China
  anticorruption efforts in, 180–182
  loans to Angola by, 117–118
  national oil companies in, 18–19
  oil demand of, 16
  oil production in, 17
  1MDB and, 196
China Sonangol, 121–122
Chinese National Petroleum Company
    (CNPC), 18–19, 32, 145, 180–181
civil society
  anticorruption role of, 99, 176, 178,
    184, 200–205, 216, 219–220
  repression of, 136
climate change, 11, 15, 96–97
CNPC (Chinese National Petroleum
    Company), 18–19, 32, 145, 180–181
Cobalt International Energy, 46, 120–121,
    205, 242n63
Cochan, 127
Colegate, Guy, 53–54
Collard, Pascal, 44–45, 186
collusion and allegations against
    Chesapeake Energy, 54–56, 59,
    230n101
Colombia, 92, 205–206
Comperj Refinery, 88–89
Congo, Democratic Republic of.
    See Democratic Republic of the
    Congo
Congo-Brazzaville
  corruption in, 43
  French charges against, 191
  Gunvor in, 43–45, 218–219
  as low-capacity kleptocracy, 106–107
  national oil company in, 43
  offshore investments from, 162
  oil production and dependency in,
    17–18, 43
  Russia and, 43–44
  Unaoil in, 41
Copleston, John, 52–53
corruption, 9–15. See also anticorruption
    and anticorruption actors
  controversy in boundaries of, 31–38,
    63, 96, 98–99, 189
  defined, 22–23

international character of, 13–14, 43,
    57–58, 63–64, 139
kleptocracies and, 105, 120
political costs of, 15, 59–60, 215–216
private/public sector blurring and, 63,
    66, 82–83, 179
purpose and method in examining,
    9–11, 22–24
Costa, Paulo Oberto, 81–83, 90
Council of Europe, 12, 14, 156, 214–215
Credit Suisse, 145–146, 200, 222

Danske Bank, 140, 156–157, 209, 246n1
Deby, Idris, 26
Deepwater Horizon explosion, 98,
    113–114, 118
Delaware and financial secrecy, 13, 58,
    155–156, 159
Deloitte, 58, 145–146, 160, 198–199, 201,
    218–219
democracies
  oil corruption in, 62–63, 93–98,
    105–106
  public interest protected by institutions
    of, 78, 80, 91, 98–99
Democratic Republic of the Congo, 11,
    184, 193–194
Department of Justice (DOJ)
  anticorruption role of, 184
  prosecution of individuals for bribery,
    186–187
  Kleptocracy Asset Recovery Initiative,
    177, 189–192
  Malaysian public funds scheme
    (1MDB) and, 13, 139, 143–144,
    149–150, 152, 158–159, 173–174,
    177–178
  McClendon collusion charges by, 54–56
  Atlantic Energy (Nigeria) accusations
    and asset seizure by, 8–9, 72–74,
    233n37
  sovereign wealth fund investigations
    by, 34
Deutsche Bank
  1MDB and, 147–148, 150
  Russian money laundering and, 12
Devon Energy, 93–94

DiCaprio, Leonardo, 139, 162–163, 165–166

dictators and dictatorship. See also *specific countries; specific dictators*
   in African oil-rich nations, 67
   anticorruption efforts against, 140
   oil companies and, 60
   oil revenues and, 21, 26

disclosure regulations, 206–207, 217–218

DLA Piper, 163, 167

Dodd-Frank Wall Street Reform Act, 206

DOJ. *See* Department of Justice

dos Santos, Isabel, 101–103, 137, 166–167

dos Santos, José Eduardo, 46, 101–103, 117, 119–120, 137, 212

dos Santos, José Filomeno, 101–104

Dudley, Bob, 113–114

Dutch disease, 21

economic development. See also *specific countries*
   corruption's impact on, 15, 59, 78
   in kleptocracies, 62

Ecuador, 184, 204

Edge, The (Malaysian newspaper), 176

EITI (Extractive Industries Transparency Initiative), 205–208, 211–212

elites. *See* oligarchs and oligarchy

enablers of corruption, 197–201, 218–219, 247n8

Encana Corp. 55–56

England. *See* United Kingdom

Eni, 19
   bribery controversies of, 188–189
   OPL 245 in Nigeria and, 49–54, 59, 77, 144, 209
   prosecution of executives of, 187, 258n47

Environmental Protection Agency (EPA), 93–95

Equatorial Guinea
   dictatorship in, 21–22, 189–190
   EITI and, 206
   funds misappropriated from, 189–193
   as low-capacity kleptocracy, 106–107

oil dependency in, 17–18, 189

Oyala's construction in, 245n121

poverty in, 190

reputation management and, 169

SBM Offshore and, 213

Ernst & Young, 57, 160

Etete, Dan, 49–54

European Bank for Reconstruction and Development, 169, 214–215

European Games, 134, 193

Eurovision Song Contest, 132, 134, 202

executives and CEOs
   bribery prosecutions of, 187, 199
   pay for, 30
   penalties for corruption of, 31, 48, 50–52, 55, 154, 159–160, 216
   risk-taking among, 30, 46, 48–49

Extractive Industries Transparency Initiative (EITI). See *EITI.*

ExxonMobil, 19
   Arctic deal with Russia, 113–114, 116–117
   campaign contributions from, 96
   Chad pipeline and, 26
   executive pay in, 30
   Iraqi instability and, 30–31
   in Liberia, 188–189
   lobbying and, 97
   Nigeria's offshore contracts with, 68–69
   revenues of, 28–29
   transparency initiatives resisted by, 206–207

FBC Media, 170–171

FCPA. *See* Foreign Corrupt Practices Act

F.H. Bertling, 123

Financial Action Task Force, 194–195, 218

fixers. *See* intermediaries

FMC Technologies (now TechnipFMC), 42, 44

Foreign Corrupt Practices Act (FCPA), 31–32, 42, 47, 184–186, 188–189, 211

fracking, 30, 54, 94, 98

Fragoso do Nascimento, Leopoldino, 46, 127

France
    African dictators in, 12
    anticorruption efforts in, 185–186,
        190–192, 197–198
    foreign real estate purchases in, 162,
        197–198
    SocGen settlement and, 37
Fridman, Mikhail, 114
fuel subsidies, 75–76, 106, 127

Gabon, 106–107, 162, 169, 191
Gaddafi, Muammar, 33–34, 37–38, 138, 169
Galactica Star, 75
Gazprom, 113, 118, 124–125, 127, 135
Germany
    anticorruption efforts in, 185
    Azerbaijani money in, 156
    Financial Secrecy Index on, 155–156
Gertler, Dan, 193–194
Ghana, 183
Glencore, 19, 27–28, 144–145, 220–221
Global Magnitsky Act (2016), 194, 217
global warming, 11, 15, 96–97
Global Witness, 43
    on beneficial ownership disclosure,
        207
    on Car Wash scandal, 221
    on Cobalt's Angola deal, 120–121
    Crude Awakening report and
        transparency initiatives, 205
    EITI data and, 209
    on ExxonMobil in Liberia, 188–189
    law firms investigated by, 199,
        260n81
    on OPL 245 deal, 50–53
    on Socar Trading, 125–126, 215
Goldman Sachs
    Libyan sovereign wealth fund and, 23,
        33–38, 153, 226n22
    in Malaysian public funds scheme
        (1MDB), 13, 145–146, 149–150,
        153–154, 162, 186, 213–214, 219
Good Star, 147–148, 150–151, 157–159,
    163, 165–167
Government Accountability Office,
    98, 183, 189

Granton Property Holdings Limited,
    150, 163
Great Britain. *See* United Kingdom (UK)
Griffiths, Brad, 25–27
Griffiths Energy, 25–28, 30–31, 59,
    212–213
Gunvor
    in Congo-Brazzaville, 43–45,
        218–219
    corruption investigations into,
        185–186, 200, 205
    role of, 19, 28
    in Russia, 127–128

Halliburton, 19
    in Angola, 46–48, 59, 184, 211
    bribery fines paid by, 184
    executive pay in, 30
    revenues of, 28–29
Hamm, Harold, 94–95
Herrmann, Jeffrey M., 197
Heydar Aliyev Foundation, 133–134,
    136–137
Heydarov, Kamaladdin, 129–132, 134
Higginbotham, George, 173
Ho, Patrick, 186
Hope, Bradley, 143–144, 146, 153,
    162–163
hospitality as ethics violation or bribe, 23,
    31–32, 34–37
HSBC, 103–104, 200
Al Husseiny, Mohamed Ahmed Badawy,
    148–150, 152–153, 158, 165, 177

Indonesia, 21–22, 182–183
intermediaries
    in Car Wash scandal, 220–221
    corruption risks among, 60, 213, 220
    difficulty prosecuting, 45
    in OPL 245 deal, 50–52
    role of, 10, 19, 28, 38–39
    SocGen bribery through, 37–38
International Consortium of Investigative
    Journalists, 204
International Monetary Fund, 8, 15, 119,
    169, 253n132

International Petroleum Investment
    Company (IPIC), 148–149, 152–153,
    175, 248n30
internships as ethics violation or bribe,
    32–37
IPIC. *See* International Petroleum
    Investment Company
Iran
    national oil company in, 18
    oil production in, 17
Iraq
    corruption in, 15, 59–60, 169,
        195–196
    ExxonMobil and, 30–31
    national oil company in, 18
    Oil-for-Food program and, 21–22
    oil production in, 17, 39
    oil revenues in, 18, 59
    Unaoil and, 39–42, 59
Ismayilova, Khadija, 132–133, 202
Italy
    anticorruption efforts in, 100, 145, 185
    Azerbaijani money in, 12, 156
    prosecution of OPL 245 deal by,
        50–52, 54, 77
    prosecution of Saipem by, 187

Al Jarah, Basil, 39–42
Jega, Attahiru, 78–79
Jho Low
    asset seizures against, 191
    background of, 146–147
    Malaysian charges against, 143–144
    money laundering methods of,
        157–160
    1MDB scheme and, 147–154
    reputation management and,
        172–174
    spending by, 162–167
Jiang Jiemin, 180–181
Jonathan, Goodluck, 6–7
    2015 election loss of, 78–80, 195–196
    fuel import scheme and, 76
    OPL 245 and, 49–50, 53
    rise of, 64–69
    Sanusi fired by, 70

international community relations
    with, 7–8, 195
journalists and media institutions
    anticorruption role of, 14, 99,
        143–144, 176–178, 201–205,
        219–220
    on exploration and production
        deals, 120
    international collaboration among,
        203–205
    1MDB case and, 176–178, 201
    repression of, 13, 107, 133, 136,
        202–203, 212–213
    reputation laundering and, 168–171
Justo, Xavier, 151–152

Kabbaj, Youssef, 34–37
Kazakhstan
    investment in UK, 12
    kleptocracy in, 106
    offshore investment and, 155,
        161–162
    oil production in, 17–18
    reputation laundering and, 169
    Unaoil in, 41
Keppel Offshore, 91–92
Kerr, Miranda, 139
Khodorkovsky, Mikhail, 109–111
kleptocracies, 12. See also *specific*
    countries
    anticorruption efforts against,
        201–203, 214–215, 219–220
    characteristics of, 62, 104–107
    corruption managed in, 105, 120,
        128–129
    durability of, 136–138
    international infrastructure of,
        140–142
    oil sector in, 12–13, 104–107, 116,
        247n8
    public/private sector blurring in, 100
    "reputation laundering" and, 168–169
    spending wealth of, 160–162
Kleptocracy Asset Recovery Initiative,
    177, 189–192, 217
Kleptocracy Tour of London, 161

Koch, Charles and David, 30, 96
Koch Industries, 96–97
KPMG, 160, 197–198
Kuwait
  as "distributional state," 106
  national oil company in, 18
  oil production in, 17
  sovereign wealth fund of, 34
  Unaoil in, 41

Lava-Jato. *See* Car Wash scandal
law firms and potential enabling roles,
    158, 167, 196–197, 199, 218–219,
    250n74, 260n79. See also *specific
    firms*
Leissner, Tim, 153–154
Libya
  Arab Spring in, 37–38
  dictatorship in, 21–22, 33–34
  Goldman Sachs in, 23, 33–37
  as low-capacity kleptocracy, 106–107
  Och-Ziff and, 184
  oil production in, 17–18, 33–34
  SocGen in, 37–38
  Unaoil in, 41
  Vitol's investment and civil war in,
    30–31
Libyan Investment Authority (LIA),
    33–38, 226n23
lobbyists and lobbying, 94–95, 97–98,
    134, 171, 173
Lorenz, Jeannot, 46–48
Lourenço, João, 101, 103–104, 137–138
Low Taek Jho. *See* Jho Low
Lukoil, 19
Lula da Silva, Luiz Inácio, 83, 86, 92–93,
    100, 236n76, 238n109
Luxembourg, 155–156, 159, 174–175, 178

Maduro, Nicolas, 182
Malabu Oil and Gas, 49–54, 187, 205
Malaysia. *See also* 1Malaysia
    Development Berhad
  anticorruption efforts in, 176, 183
  demographic and economic makeup
    of, 142–143
  Najib charged in, 175, 203

oil production in, 143
  1MDB's damage to, 175
  reputation laundering and, 170–174
Al-Maliki, Nouri, 39, 195–196
Mammadov, Ziya, 130–132, 134–135
Manafort, Paul, 12, 141
Marques de Morais, Rafael, 120–121, 202
MBS. *See* Mohammad bin Salman
McClendon, Aubrey, 54–56
media institutions. *See* journalists and
    media institutions
Medvedev, Dmitri, 137, 203
Mensalão scandal, 83
Mercuria, 19, 28
Mexico
  Car Wash scandal and, 92
  oil production in, 17, 62
  resource curse in, 21
Michel, Pras, 172–173
Michigan and Chesapeake Energy, 55–56,
    59, 230n101
middlemen. *See* intermediaries
Minerals Management Service (MMS),
    97–98, 183
Mohammad bin Salman (MBS), 152,
    179–180, 216, 255n7
money laundering and money laundering
    allegations
  Car Wash scandal and, 81, 87
  Danske Bank and, 145, 162, 215–216
  Deutsche Bank and, 12
  Etete and, 49
  international methods of, 13, 140–142,
    145, 154–157
  law firms and, 158, 167, 218
  Manafort and, 12
  1MDB and, 157–160, 173
  real estate purchases and, 160–164,
    218
Mossack Fonseca, 142, 219
Mozambique, 18, 145–146, 248n19

Najib Razak
  anticorruption investigations resisted
    by, 176, 178
  Jho Low and, 147
  Malaysian charges against, 175, 203

1MDB and, 143, 158–159
reputation management and, 169–173
spending of suspicious funds by, 175
US presidents and, 171–174, 177
national oil companies. See also *specific companies; specific countries*
  boom-time returns of, 18
  bribery and, 212
  corruption risks of, 82–83, 212, 220
  in kleptocracies, 108, 116
  market dominance of, 18–19, 63
  political capture of, 63, 108
Natural Resource Governance Institute, 71, 86, 209
Navalny, Alexei, 137, 203
Nazaki Oil & Gas, 120–121
Nazarbayev, Nursultan, 168, 170
Nevada and financial secrecy, 155–156, 159
Ng, Roger, 249n61
Niam, Nouracham, 26–27
Nigeria 78
  2015 election in, 78–80
  Alison-Madueke's patronage machine in, 70–78, 98–99
  anticorruption efforts in, 183, 195–196
  Boko Haram in, 15, 65, 195–196
  bribery in elections of, 72, 78, 80
  Economic and Financial Crimes Commission, 72, 75
  fuel import scheme in, 75–76
  Jonathan and Alison-Madueke's rise in, 64–69
  oil production in, 6, 17, 65, 67
  oil trading in, 75–76, 211–212
  OPL 245 and, 49–54, 59, 77, 185, 187, 209
  Petroleum Act in, 23
  political climate of, 53, 59–60, 64–69, 78
  poverty in, 6, 8, 10–11
  resource curse in, 21–22
  service contracts in, 70–77, 79, 144
Nigerian National Petroleum Corporation (NNPC)
  Atlantic and, 61, 73
  performance of, 68–70, 73, 75–77, 100, 120

public revenues retained by, 69–70, 212
  Socar compared to, 127
Nigerian Petroleum Development Company (NPDC), 73–74
NNPC. *See* Nigerian National Petroleum Corporation
Norway
  national oil company in, 18–19, 46
  oil production in, 17
  oil revenues in, 20
  sovereign wealth fund of, 34
  Transocean's tax case in, 57
Novatek, 166–167
NPDC (Nigerian Petroleum Development Company), 73–74

OAS, 84, 92–93
Obaid, Tarek, 151–152, 166
Obama, Barack
  environmental regulations and, 94, 98
  Malaysia and, 169, 171–172, 174–175
Obasanjo, Olusegun, 6, 64, 66, 68
Obiang, Teodoro Nguema Mangue (son of president), 168, 252n121
Obiang, Teodoro Nguema Mbasogo (president), 10, 107, 161–162, 189–191
OCCRP, *See* Organized Crime and Corruption Reporting Project
Och-Ziff, 184, 187
Odebrecht, 80–81
  in Angola, 87–88
  Car Wash scandal and, 87–90, 92, 218
  DOJ fines assessed to, 184
  relations between Brazil's government and, 83–85
Odebrecht, Marcelo, 80–81, 91
OECD (Organization for Economic Cooperation and Development), 185, 212, 218
offshore accounts. *See* shell companies and offshore accounts
oil boom, 16–22
  revenues during, 28–30, 63
  risk-taking during, 30–31, 46, 48–50, 59

Oil-for-Food program, 21–22
oil industry. *See also* national oil
    companies; *specific companies*
    actors in, 18–20, 28
    boom-time returns of, 18, 59
    corruption gains vs. costs, 31, 59–60,
        187–189
    as enablers, 144–145
    in kleptocracies, 104–107, 116, 247n8
    lobbyists and, 94–95, 97
    as "point industry," 21
    political influence of, 11, 30, 93–99,
        209
    public relations and, 97
    rents in, 20
    transparency in, 205–209
    undemocratic governance and,
        59–60
oil prices
    boom fluctuations of, 5, 16, 21,
        28, 66
    drop in (2014), 18, 21, 91–92,
        137–138
Oil Prospecting License 245 (OPL 245),
    49–54, 59, 77, 185, 209
oil trading and oil traders
    in Angola, 125, 127, 211–212
    anticorruption efforts and, 60
    in Azerbaijan, 125–127,
        211–212
    in Brazil, 220–221
    in Congo-Brazzaville, 43–45
    corruption risks of, 10, 43, 63,
        211–212, 220
    in Nigeria, 75–76, 211–212
    role of, 19
    in Russia, 127–129, 211–212
oilfield service companies. See also
    specific companies
    boom-time revenues of, 28–29
    corruption risks of, 10, 42, 60, 211,
        213, 220
    role of, 19, 28
    Unaoil and, 39, 42
Oklahoma
    Chesapeake energy collusion charges
        in, 54–56

Department of Interior sued by, 94
    oil production in, 94
oligarchs and oligarchy, 12
    in Angola, 120–121, 123
    in Azerbaijan, 23, 129–132, 134
    in Brazil, 83–85
    oil boom and, 23
    private/public sector blurring and, 63
    in Russia, 23, 108–115, 120, 124–125,
        203
Olympics (2008 Beijing), 23, 31–32, 135
Olympics (2012 Sochi), 135, 203
Olympics (2016 Rio de Janeiro), 84, 91
Oman, 106, 182–183, 262n8
Omokore, Jide, 75, 234n49
1Malaysia Development Berhard
        (1MDB), 142–144. *See also* Jho Low
    anticorruption efforts and, 176–178,
        196, 205, 213–214
    bond sales by, 148–150, 153–154, 163
    consequences for actors in, 151–154,
        175
    funds allegedly stolen from, 143,
        146–151, 178
    journalists' role in revealing, 201
    offshore financial flows and, 157–160
    public relations and, 171–174
    spending funds from, 162–167
    stated purpose of, 143, 146,
        149–150
OPL 245 (Nigeria), *See* Oil Prospecting
    License 245
Organization for Economic Cooperation
    and Development (OECD) 185, 212,
    218
Organized Crime and Corruption
    Reporting Project (OCCRP), 43–44,
    202–204, 215
Orubebe, Godsday, 79–80, 235n59

Pa, Sam, 121–122
Panama Papers, 11
    Deutsche Bank and, 12
    disclosure requirements and, 208
    globalization of kleptocracy and, 142
    journalism and, 204
    Putin and, 128–129

Paradise Papers, 103
PDVSA (Venezuelan national oil company), 18, 157, 182, 186, 199–200, 262n2
Peru, 92
Peters, Benedict, 71–72
Petrobras
  Car Wash scandal and, 82, 88–90, 92, 145–146, 211–212, 220–221, 224n4
  class action suit against, 247n19
  DOJ fines assessed to, 184
  growth of, 85–86
  performance of, 86
  private/public lines blurred by, 85, 88–90
PetroChina, 180–181
Petroecuador, 185, 204
Petrofac, 19, 41–42
PetroSaudi International, 146–148, 150–152, 160, 162–163, 176–177
Pilatus, 156–157
political action committees (PACs), 94, 96, 98, 172
Portugal, 12, 102, 117–118
poverty
  in Angola, 135–138
  in Brazil, 85–86
  in Chad, 26
  in Equatorial Guinea, 190
  in Nigeria, 8, 10–11
  in Russia, 203
PriceWaterhouseCooper, 70, 145–146, 247n19
protests
  in Algeria, 138
  in Angola, 137–138
  in Azerbaijan, 137
  in Brazil, 84, 91–92
  corruption scandals and, 10–11
  fracking and, 30
  in Kazakhstan, 168
  of Keystone and Dakota Access pipelines, 98
  in Malaysia, 159, 170–171, 178
  in Nigeria, 76
  in Russia, 137
Pruitt, Scott, 93–96, 98
Public Eye, 43–45, 221

public relations firms and reputation laundering, 168–169, 174
Publish What You Pay coalition, 204–207
Putin, Vladimir
  relations with oligarchs and, 124–125, 127–129
  oil sector capture and, 108–116, 120, 124, 194, 212
  Panama Papers and, 128–129
  Sochi Olympics spending and, 135
  Trump and, 12

Qatar, 17, 106, 185–186, 187
Al Qubaisi, Khadem, 148–150, 152–153, 158
Queensway Group, 46, 121
quid pro quo, 63, 74, 189

RBS Coutts, 147–148, 157–159
real estate and illicit funds, 160–164, 180, 189–190
Red Granite Pictures, 165–166
refineries
  in Car Wash scandal, 11, 88–89
  NNPC and, 68, 70, 75–77
  Unaoil and, 41
rents and rent-seeking
  in Angola, 46–48, 59
  in Azerbaijan, 131
  defined, 20–21
  in kleptocracies, 120
  oil boom and, 20–23
Republic of Congo. See Congo-Brazzaville
Republican Party (US), 95–96, 98, 172–173
reputation laundering, 168–174
resource curse, 21–22, 26, 206
Robinson, Peter, 52–54
Rolls-Royce, 40, 78, 91–92, 185–186, 257n35
Rosneft
  government bail-out of, 137
  growth and production of, 114–115
  as instrument to control Russia's oil sector, 108–116, 194, 212
  Trenaco and, 199–200

Rotenberg, Arkady and Boris, 124–125,
128–129, 135, 137
Rousseff, Dilma
fall of, 92
Lula and, 83
Odebrecht and, 84–85
Petrobras and, 86, 92
Royal Dutch Shell, 19, 28
Aiteo Energy Resources and,
70–71
Alison-Madueke and, 66, 71
Bribery accusations and,
8–9, 217
lobbying and, 97
Nigeria's offshore contracts with,
68–69, 144
OPL 245 in Nigeria and, 49–54, 59,
77, 209, 233n31
prosecution of executives of, 9, 187
revenues of, 28–29
transparency initiatives and, 19
Russia
Congo-Brazzaville and, 43–44
government consolidation of oil sector
in, 108–116
presence in UK, 12, 192, 207–208
kleptocracy in, 62, 105–106, 111, 113,
135, 137
offshore finances and, 155, 161–162,
208
oil production in, 17, 107–109,
116–117
oligarchy in, 23, 108–115, 120,
124–125, 203
poverty in, 203
service contracts in, 124–125, 144
Sochi Olympics (2012) and, 135

Saipem, 19, 145, 187, 258n44, 262n8
sanctions as anticorruption tool, 33,
116–117, 128, 135, 193–194, 216
Sanusi, Lamido, 69–70
Sarawak Report, 171, 176–177
Sassou Nguesso, Denis, 43–44, 168
Saudi Arabia
anticorruption efforts in, 14, 152,
178–180

as "distributional state," 106
investment in UK, 12
national oil company in, 18–19
offshore accounts and, 155
oil production in, 17, 179
reputation laundering and, 169
resource curse in, 21
sovereign wealth fund of, 34
SBM Offshore, 42, 89–92, 123, 211,
262n8
Schlumberger, 19, 28–30
Sechin, Igor, 108–110, 113–116, 127–128
Securities and Exchange Commission
(SEC)
anticorruption role of, 184
Bank of New York Mellon and, 32–33
BHP Billiton and, 31–32
Halliburton and, 46–48
Publish What You Pay transparency
initiative and, 206–207
self-reporting to, 48
service contracts. See also oilfield service
companies.
Angola and, 47–48, 59–60, 122–123,
144
Azerbaijan and, 123–124, 130–131
corruption risks of, 212–213
national oil companies and, 63, 82–83
Nigeria and, 70–77, 79, 144
Petrobras and, 88
Russia and, 124–125, 144
Unaoil and, 38–43, 213
Seychelles, 61, 155–157, 159, 218
Shah Deniz gas field, 123
Shearman & Sterling LLP, 158, 167
Shell. See Royal Dutch Shell
shell companies and offshore accounts.
See also money laundering; tax
havens
Aliyevs' wealth and, 132, 134–135
Aluko and, 59–60, 191–192
anticorruption efforts against,
194–195, 208, 213, 217, 220
Azerbaijani Laundromat and, 156–157
bribery and, 44
Car Wash scandal and, 82, 88–89
disclosure regulations and, 209

dos Santos and, 103–104
global financial system and, 141–142
law firms and, 196–197
Obiang and, 189–190
Odebrecht and, 87–88
1MDB scheme and, 147, 149–150,
    157–160, 164, 167, 173
Panama Papers and, 11, 204
Peters and, 72
role of, 13, 103, 154–155
subcontracting and, 123
Treasury Department regulation of,
    164
Trump properties sold to, 162
Yukos auction and, 111
Singapore
    banks in, 139
    financial secrecy in, 149, 157–160,
        174–175, 213–214
    1MDB scandal and, 176–178
Sinopec, 18–19, 28, 117–118, 198–199
Sistema, 115–116
SNPC (Societe Nationale des Petroles du
    Congo), 44–45
Socar
    government control over, 108
    growth of, 118–119
    OCCRP reports on, 202
    trading subsidiary of, 125–127
Sochi Olympics, 135, 203
Société Générale (SocGen), 37–38, 186
Société Nationale des Petroles du Congo
    (SNPC), 44–45
Sonangol
    bribery and, 123
    Chevron and, 117–118
    China Sonangol and, 121–123
    Cobalt exploration deal with,
        120–121
    government control over, 108, 118
    DTS Refining and, 127
    Halliburton and, 46–48
    oil production of, 117
    public funds routed through, 119
    performance of, 117–118
    service contracting and, 122–123
Sotheby's, 164–165

South Sudan, 15, 17–18, 106–107,
    145, 201
sovereign wealth funds, 20, 34, 36,
    102–103, 137, 148, 203. See also
    specific countries; specific funds
Stadlen, Paul, 170, 253n135
Statoil, 46
Strategic Alliance Agreements (SAAs),
    73–75
subcontracting and subcontractors.
    See service contracts, oilfield service
    companies and specific companies
subsidies, fuel, 75–76, 106, 127
Sudan, 106–107, 138
Sullivan & Cromwell, 167
super PACS See political action
    committees
swap contracts, 70–71, 127
Switzerland
    African dictators in, 12
    anticorruption efforts in, 185,
        185–186, 186, 218
    financial secrecy in, 155–156,
        174–175
    investigation of Addax by, 198–199
    investigation of Gunvor by, 44–45, 199
    legal action against 1MDB
        actors by, 178

Tanore Finance Corporation, 150,
    158–159, 163
tax havens, 56–57, 87, 103, 155, 194–195
Tax Justice Network, 207–208
taxes and taxation
    evasion/avoidance, 54, 56–59, 103
    in oil-rich nations, 21
    tax havens' impact on, 155, 209
TechnipFMC (previously FMC
    Technologies), 40, 42
Temer, Michel, 92–93
Texas, 93, 95–96
Tillerson, Rex, 30, 194
Timchenko, Gennady, 127–128, 135,
    166–167
TNK-BP, 112–116
Total, 19, 28
Trafigura, 19, 28, 46, 127, 145, 220–221

Trans-Pacific Partnership Agreement, 194–195
Transocean, 19, 29, 57
transparency, 205–209, 211
Transparency International
  on beneficial ownership disclosure, 207–208
  on Congo-Brazzaville, 43
  corruption defined by, 22–23, 179–180
  Corruption Perception Index by, 140
  on suspect UK real estate, 192–193
Treasury Department, 97, 156–157, 164, 194
Trenaco, 199–200
Trudeau, Justin, 187–188
Trump, Donald
  Azerbaijani hotel deal and, 12, 166–167
  Broidy and, 173
  controversial ties of, 15, 141, 162
  Manafort and, 141
  Najib and, 173–174
  oil industry sympathies of, 97
  Pruitt and, 95
  Putin and, 12
  Transparency rule gutted by, 207
Turki bin Abdullah, 151–152
Turkmenistan
  CNPC and Lopez in, 32
  as low-capacity kleptocracy, 106–107
  natural gas dependency in, 17–18

UAE. See United Arab Emirates
UK. See United Kingdom
Ukraine, 12, 211–212, 242n59
Unaoil, 38–42, 59–60, 144, 184, 205, 213
Unexplained Wealth Orders, 192–193, 259n64
United Arab Emirates (UAE)
  as "distributional state," 106
  involvement of UAE sovereign wealth fund in 1MDB scheme, 148–149, 152–153, 175, 248n30
  offshore accounts and, 155
  oil production in, 17
  reputation management and, 169
  sovereign wealth fund of, 34

Unaoil in, 41
United Kingdom (UK)
  anticorruption efforts by, 185–187, 194–195, 205–206, 207–208, 217–218
  Bribery Act in (2010), 185
  LIA suit against Goldman in, 36–37, 226n23
  offshore investment in, 12, 61, 156–157, 161
  Proceeds of Crime Act in, 72
  Unaoil representatives charged by, 38–39, 42
  Unexplained Wealth Orders, 192–193, 259n64
United States. See also Department of Justice; Securities and Exchange Commission; Treasury Department; specific states
  anticorruption efforts in, 183–186, 194–196, 218
  Citizens United decision (2010) in, 96
  Dodd-Frank Wall Street Reform Act (2010), 206
  EITI and, 208
  Financial Secrecy Index on, 155–156
  Foreign Corrupt Practices Act (FCPA) and enforcement, 31–32, 42, 47, 184–186, 188–189, 211
  Global Magnitsky Act (2016), 194, 217
  Kleptocracy Asset Recovery Initiative, 177, 217
  Libyan sanctions, 33
  money laundering and, 13
  oil production in, 17, 93
  oil wealth's influence on politics in, 93–98
  Russian sanctions, 116–117, 128, 135, 194
  SocGen settlement and, 37
  Venezuela sanctions, 194
  wealth distribution in, 155
United States-Mexico-Canada Agreement, 194–195
USAID, 99

Venezuela
 anticorruption efforts in, 182
 Car Wash scandal and, 92
 money laundering accusations in, 157
 national oil company in, 18, 157, 182,
  185–186, 199–200
 Odebrecht in, 87–88
 offshore accounts and, 155
 oil production in, 17
 PetroSaudi and, 152
 resource curse in, 21
Vicente, Manuel, 120–122
Vitol, 19, 28, 30–31, 70, 145, 220–221
Voser, Peter, 53

Weatherford, 19, 41
White, Frank, Jr., 172
wining and dining, 23, 31–32, 34–37

The Wolf of Wall Street (film) funded by
 illicit funds, 165–166, 172
World Bank, 169
 Chadian pipeline and, 26
 Nigeria receiving aid from, 8
 repatriation of seized assets and, 193
Wright, Tom, 143–144, 146, 153,
  162–163

Xi Jinping, 180–182

Yanukovych, Victor, 125, 141
Yar'Adua, Umaru, 64–65
Yevtushenkov, Vladimir, 115–116
Yukos, 109–113, 116, 127–128

Zarti, Mustafa, 34–36
Zhou Yongkang, 180–181